D0282753

HELPING STUDENTS
THINK AND VALUE

HELPING STUDENTS THINK AND VALUE:

Strategies

for Teaching the Social Studies

JACK R. FRAENKEL

Professor of Interdisciplinary Studies in Education
California State University, San Francisco

PRENTICE-HALL, INC.
Englewood Cliffs, New Jersey

Library of Congress Cataloging in Publication Data

FRAENKEL, JACK R.
 Helping students think and value.

 Includes bibliographies.
 1. Social sciences—Study and teaching. 2. Study,
Method of. I. Title.
LB1049.F66   300'.7   72-2457
ISBN 0-13-386557-6

© 1973 by Prentice-Hall, Inc.
Englewood Cliffs, New Jersey

Printed in the United States of America

10 9 8 7 6 5 4 3 2

PRENTICE-HALL INTERNATIONAL, INC., London
PRENTICE-HALL OF AUSTRALIA PTY. LTD., Sydney
PRENTICE-HALL OF CANADA LTD., Toronto
PRENTICE-HALL OF INDIA PRIVATE LIMITED, New Delhi
PRENTICE-HALL OF JAPAN, INC., Tokyo

To Marjorie

CONTENTS

PREFACE

This book has been written for prospective and in-service elementary and secondary school social studies teachers, though teachers-of-teachers, curriculum developers, and anyone else interested in improving social studies (or other) teaching should find it helpful. The book deals with a number of questions that I think are important for teachers to ask if they wish to increase the effectiveness of their instructional efforts. (By "effectiveness," I mean the degree to which students learn as a result of teacher efforts.) These questions are the following:

- What information, skills, attitudes, and values are students to learn or acquire—and why? (Questions having to do with a teacher's purposes and his justification for those purposes.)
- What characteristics do students possess? What have they already learned? How might these prior learnings and characteristics affect further learning? (Questions having to do with pre-instructional diagnosis.)
- What particular information shall students study? Why? How might this information be organized? (Questions having to do with the selection and organization of subject matter.)
- What kinds of learning experiences can help students learn or acquire various types of skills, attitudes, values, and knowledge deemed important? How might these learning experiences be organized? (Questions having to do with the selection and organization of learning activities.)
- What kinds of teacher operations can help students attain various desired objectives? (Questions having to do with the teaching strategies a teacher decides to use.)
- How can the effects of instruction be assessed? (Questions having to do with post-instructional evaluation.)
- How can objectives, subject matter, learning activities, teaching strategies, and evaluative measures be organized and interrelated so as to encourage learning? (Questions having to do with planning.)

It seems logical to assume that the decisions that teachers make with regard to these kinds of questions will affect the degree to which their instructional efforts help rather than hinder student learning. Answers to such questions, however, are not independent of one another, for each of the elements that the questions suggest—objectives, subject matter, learning activities, teaching strategies, and evaluation—influence one another tremendously. For example, objectives influence the selection of subject matter, but subject matter, once selected, often necessitates a reconsideration of objectives. Subject matter may suggest certain kinds of learning activities, but learning activities may also suggest that certain kinds of subject matter are more appropriate than other kinds to develop certain objectives. Learning activities and teaching strategies may suggest that a certain type of evaluation is needed, while evaluation in turn may indicate a need for other kinds of activities or strategies.

The purpose of this book, therefore, is to discuss the nature and use of objectives, subject matter, learning activities, teaching strategies, and evaluation in some detail. It is hypothesized here that regular consideration of these elements and how they affect each other can help teachers, *no matter what grade or type of course they teach*, help students learn. Hopefully, these elements, considered together, suggest a way for teachers to think systematically about planning for instruction. Examples are frequent throughout, and exercises dealing with key points are presented as a form of self-test at the end of every chapter. You will find the answers grouped together at the end of the book.

I have done my best to be consistent in my reasoning, but if you observe logical flaws, or lack of support for an argument, or even if you think there are major errors and mistakes, so much the better. Whether you agree or disagree with what is said is not of utmost importance. If you disagree and can back up your disagreement with ideas or suggestions of your own, I shall be pleased. The book is intended to give you ideas and make you think a bit, and if it does even a bit of that, I shall be rewarded, and the book have served its purpose.

Like all authors, I am indebted to many people: to Morrie Lewenstein, who first turned me on to the possibilities of ideas as an organizing force in social studies teaching; to the late Hilda Taba for her encouragement and support; to my colleagues on the Taba Curriculum Development Project staff at San Francisco State College; to Dave Armstrong, JoAnne Buggey, Peg Carter, Ambrose Clegg, Steve Dobbs, Carole Hahn, Morrie Lewenstein, Sherwood Lingenfelter, Jim Shaver, Nick Sawin, Norm Wallen and Dave Williams, who read parts or all of the early drafts of chapters, thus helping me to make a number of significant changes; to Gene Gilliom and Larry Metcalf who reviewed the manuscript for Prentice-Hall and whose comments helped me make still further changes; to the many teachers whose questions helped me clarify my thinking; to Velma Kingsbury for typing and retyping several drafts; to Helen Harris for her smooth editing; to Art Rittenberg, for his patience and consideration; and to my wife, Marjorie, for her willingness to let me work on the darn thing for so long.

JACK R. FRAENKEL

San Francisco

HELPING STUDENTS
THINK AND VALUE

CHAPTER I

INSTRUCTIONAL

OBJECTIVES

This chapter deals with the nature of instructional objectives. The major thesis of the chapter is that teachers must be clear about what objectives they want to attain in order to plan and assess their instruction effectively.

The first section of the chapter discusses the nature of education as change. Factors which affect changes in students are described, and a distinction made between changes that are possible and changes that are desirable. Sources of desirable changes are then suggested.

The second section discusses the development of instructional objectives. A distinction is made between objectives and goals, and examples of each are presented. Four major categories of social studies objectives are identified. The importance of teachers having a rationale for their instructional objectives is argued, and the possibility of formulating social studies objectives at two levels is suggested.

The third section illustrates and analyzes various ways of stating objectives, stresses that instructional objectives consist of both content and process, and explains the meaning of operational definitions. Examples of such definitions are presented, along with a discussion of how specifically instructional objectives need to be stated. A distinction is made between intent and evidence, and several examples of clearly written instructional objectives presented.

The fourth section involves task description, and illustrates how to use a certain method of task description to insure that descriptions of desired instructional objectives are complete.

The fifth section deals with the value of clear statements of instructional objectives. The relationship of objectives to the tasks of selecting subject matter, learning activities, teaching strategies, and evaluative devices is discussed, and a simple model for planning and instruction is presented.

The sixth section then provides some guidelines that teachers can use to write clear and precise instructional objectives.

When you have finished this chapter, therefore, you should be able to do the following:

- *distinguish* between educational goals and instructional objectives;
- *convert* general statements of educational goals into instructional objectives;
- *classify* social studies objectives as belonging to one of four major categories;
- *explain* the importance of having a rationale for any instructional objectives that are prepared, and *write* such a rationale;
- *describe* the relationship which exists between instructional objectives and evaluative items;
- *write* clear, precise statements of instructional objectives;
- *describe* the relationship which exists among objectives and the tasks of selecting subject matter, learning activities, teaching strategies, and evaluative measures.

EDUCATION AS CHANGE

The overriding accomplishment of education is that it changes people. They acquire knowledge; they develop skills; they acquire attitudes and values; they achieve understandings, insights, and appreciations. Given this fact, a most important task for all teachers is to decide in what ways they want students to change. How will students who have completed a lesson, unit, or course be different from those who have not completed them? In what ways will students be different after they have participated in a course of study than they were before?

The kinds of particular changes a teacher wishes to bring about represent his *instructional objectives.* Once a teacher is clear as to the changes he wants to accomplish, he can select subject matter and plan learning activities to help rather than hinder the attainment of these objectives. He can also select or develop appropriate evaluation devices to determine how well the changes that he desires have been accomplished. And as he interacts with students in the classroom, he can modify, if necessary, his intentions in order to make them more consistent with the nature of the learners with whom he works. The question of intent cannot be avoided. A teacher may not tell students explicitly what he has in mind. But his choice of reading assignments, discussion materials, and learning activities implicitly reveal to students what he intends. It is important for teachers to be clear as to what changes they want to bring about, therefore, so that they may work consciously toward achieving those objectives.

Not all changes, of course, are possible. Some students are most successful with certain types of objectives (e.g., certain kinds of skills). Others can attain objectives at one time in their life that they cannot attain earlier. Age, grade level, ability, previous experience, attitude toward learning, interest, resources available—all are relevant factors here. Whether a given objective can be attained by a particular student or set of students depends on such factors for various reasons. In the first place, these factors influence the kinds of subject matter, learning activities, and teacher operations most likely to encourage student learning. Subject matter, learning activities, and teacher operations effective with one group of learners may be quite ineffective with another. Whether a given class is made up of urban blacks, suburban whites, Mexican-Americans, Puerto Ricans, American Indians, or some combination of these becomes very important when it comes down to planning instructional strategies.

Second, different student ability levels require different emphases. Students who read with difficulty need materials different from those needed by students who read easily; students who are kinesthetically oriented may be motivated by learning activities different from those that motivate the esthetically oriented; students in one geographic location may need different examples to illustrate basic ideas than individuals in other locations.

Third, the attainment of many objectives depends on the attitude toward learning that is established in the classroom. If students believe that learning what the teacher asks them to learn is always beyond their capabilities, they will soon stop trying to achieve these things. If they become convinced that most of what is learned in school is irrelevant, useless, or boring, they will be unwilling to put forth much effort.

Fourth, the nature of the school within which a particular classroom is located—its goals, resources, and administrative arrangements, can affect the attainment of objectives. The degree to which a specific objective can be developed by a particular teacher depends considerably on the degree to which it is supported by other teachers in the school as a whole. Any teacher working independently can attain only a fairly limited set of objectives. Some objectives, of course, can be attained in relation to the specific subject matter studied in a particular course (e.g., in an American History course, knowing the reasons why the American colonists revolted against Great Britain in the 1700s). But many objectives go beyond the boundaries of a particular course (e.g., thinking skill objectives such as hypothesizing, classifying, generalizing, predicting, and explaining data). Teachers can help or hinder the attainment of objectives that other teachers are trying to encourage. Groups of teachers, working cooperatively within a particular school, for example, can mutually support various objectives both across and within several grade levels, courses, and units. This is particularly true of the higher mental processes, attitudes, and values which develop cumulatively over an extended period of time. Many school staffs do not conceptualize the kind of *long-range* changes they desire over a period of years, and thus fail to plan cooperatively and engage students in learning experiences that will bring about those changes in a variety of courses and grades.

Other factors may also affect objectives. The school board of a particular school district may prescribe certain objectives to be accomplished in various grades. This prescription can affect the selection of particular subject matter or the development of certain learning activities. The nature of the community in which the school is located can have an effect. Community pressures on the school, values within the community, and community resources all vary considerably. If a strong anti-war pressure group exists within a community, it may be difficult to help students analyze rationally the effects of war within the classroom. If the community has a poorly developed transportation system, this may minimize the use of field trips as learning activities.

Some individuals would argue that teacher style, personality, ability, and experience are the major determinants of how much and how well a student learns. There is no argument here with the fact that teachers differ markedly in such characteristics. Nevertheless, it is the opinion of the writer, based on considerable experience in teacher-training workshops, that teachers can modify these characteristics sufficiently to help students attain a great variety of objectives previously either not attempted or considered unobtainable. Bloom and others came to a similar conclusion:

> . . . it is our considered judgment that most teachers can learn new ways of teaching students and that most can, if they will make the appropriate effort, help their students attain a great variety of educational objectives. The *teacher* does not, in our thinking, represent the major factor in determining the objectives which are possible. It is the *teaching* which determines the objectives which are possible. If teachers are convinced of the need and are provided with the necessary training and experience, they can become effective in teaching for most of the important objectives in their field.[1]

Each teacher must determine *in his particular situation* which objectives can be attained by his students. Some of the literature in education can be helpful in this respect.[2] But in the main, what objectives are attained in a given classroom will depend on the teacher's philosophy of education (what he considers *worth* learning), the characteristics of the learners involved, and the teacher's skill in interacting with them as he goes about his instruction.

[1]Benjamin S. Bloom, J. Thomas Hastings, and George F. Madaus, *Handbook on Formative and Summative Evaluation of Student Learning* (New York: McGraw-Hill, 1971), p. 11.
[2]The two taxonomies of educational objectives in the Cognitive Domain and the Affective Domain suggest some broad classifications of educational objectives considered attainable by students. See B. S. Bloom *et al., Taxonomy of Educational Objectives: The Classification of Educational Goals, Handbook I: Cognitive Domain* (New York: David McKay, 1956); and D. R. Krathwohl, B. S. Bloom, and B. B. Masia, *Taxonomy of Educational Objectives: The Classification of Educational Goals, Handbook II: Affective Domain* (New York: David McKay, 1964).

Just because a change is possible, however, does not mean that it is *desirable*. Desirability is a question of value that depends in large part upon the teacher's conception of the kind of individual he wants to help students become and the kind of world he wants them to help shape. Bloom and his colleagues speak directly to this point:

> What is desirable for particular students and groups of students is in part dependent on their present characteristics and their goals and aspirations for the future. If we were able to know in advance a person's entire life pattern, there would be little doubt about the desirable educational outcomes. This lacking, *objectives must be selected which are likely to give him maximum flexibility in making a great variety of possible life decisions*. Thus, what is desirable for the individual student may coincide with the greatest range of possibilities available in the light of his ability, previous achievement, and personality.[3]

What may be desirable objectives for particular groups of students at a particular time may be determined partially by analyzing the nature of the society and culture of which they are a part. What are the needs of the United States today? What will be her needs in the future? What problems exist? What changes are occurring? What things do Americans consider important—that is, what values do they hold dear? What about the rest of the world? To what extent do the needs, problems, and values of the United States and those of the remainder of the globe conflict? What knowledge, qualities, and abilities will students need in order to sustain or, when necessary, change the society and culture of which they are or will be a part?

Americans by no means agree upon the answers to these questions. As a result, different answers suggest different objectives, such as developing in students a mind capable of coping with the many problems to be faced in a world that is rapidly changing, or helping them acquire the skills necessary to interact harmoniously with people of widely varying life styles.

As changes occur in American society—changes in government, technology, work habits, family patterns, social structure, living arrangements—the desirability of certain objectives will be increased and others decreased. "It is clear that the nature of careers will be much affected by changes in the society; what implications do these have for desirable educational objectives? It is quite evident that increased leisure will be available to a large segment of the society in the near future; what implications does this have?"[4]

[3]Bloom, Hastings, and Madaus, *Handbook on Formative and Summative Evaluation*, p. 11. (Italics added.)
[4]*Ibid.*, p. 11.

The society and culture within which an educational program is to be developed, however, is but one source to be analyzed in order to determine desirable objectives. A second source lies in what is known about the nature of individuals as human beings, and their needs for self-development and self-fulfillment. What skills and processes seem essential for individual development and fulfillment? What kinds of knowledge do individuals need in order to operate effectively as productive members of society? What qualities can help them to become constructive, contributing human beings?

Once again answers vary. As in the case of societal analysis, different conceptions of the individual suggest different emphases, such as the development of the mental capacities, the promotion of a strong sense of personal identity and worth, or the encouragement of social, intellectual, and emotional maturity.

The subjects to be studied in the school program constitute a third source to consider. Particular sources in this regard for the social studies are the social science disciplines (e.g., anthropology, economics, geography, political science, social psychology, sociology) and history. What do history and these other disciplines suggest as desirable objectives? What insights do they offer into the nature of societies and individuals? What kinds of skills, attitudes, and knowledge can these disciplines help students attain?

The objectives which these sources suggest are by no means mutually exclusive. Objectives related to the development of the individual, for example, may often complement goals related to the improvement of society. The danger lies in assuming that a balanced set of desirable objectives will automatically result from an analysis of the nature of society, the needs of the individual, and the nature of the subjects that make up (or might comprise) the school program.

A central problem facing any educator in the United States is the fact that the members of the society by no means agree on what the chief purpose of education should be. Though most people would probably agree that "education" itself is important, they often have trouble defining exactly what the purpose of education is and how the schools should encourage it. In a culture as complex and pluralistic as that of the United States, this is not surprising. Some individuals, for example, argue that the central purpose of education is an essentially conservative one—to preserve and transmit the cultural heritage and the wisdom of the race as contained in the classics. Others insist that the chief function of education is to encourage students to analyze and evaluate the culture in order to transform and improve it. Still others view education as a means to foster and encourage change, and to manage and control the direction of change in the future. The view (these or others) to which a teacher subscribes can have a marked effect as to the objectives he chooses to implement. Differing conceptions as to the function of education may cause an undue emphasis to be placed upon insights or ideas derived from only one of the sources suggested above to the neglect of the others. Taba illustrated this danger neatly:

> Those who are oriented to social and cultural analysis tend to overstress the social functions of education. Those who derive their concept of the function of education largely from the analysis of the requirements of academic subjects are likely to favor intellectual discipline over some other equally important qualities. Today, with the pressure of national needs uppermost in our minds, there is a danger of allowing the objectives which promise to serve these needs to overbalance the program in comparison to the objectives which are related to the fullest development of the individual as a human being.[5]

The totality of educational objectives for any school program, therefore, may be too narrow or too broad, balanced or unbalanced, depending on the nature of the sources from which the objectives are drawn and the relative emphasis placed upon each. A systematic identification and analysis of the insights from all the sources identified above is essential if a balanced and comprehensive set of educational goals is to result. More and more, teachers will find it essential to keep up to date on the nature of social change and what is known about individual development. They also will need to reflect upon their conception of the good man and the good life —in short, upon the kinds of individuals and the kind of society they want to help develop. This will help them to develop a rationale by which to select or develop objectives that are both possible and desirable.

THE DEVELOPMENT OF INSTRUCTIONAL OBJECTIVES

EDUCATIONAL GOALS

It has become almost a commonplace for writers of texts on education in general and social studies education in particular to cite the importance of educational objectives. Courses of study always include them. Rarely does a workshop in social studies methods or a national or state convention go by without several presentations and sections being devoted to the

[5]Hilda Taba, *Curriculum Development: Theory and Practice* (New York: Harcourt Brace Jovanovich, 1962), p. 195.

topic. Many local, state, and national commissions have prepared extensive lists of such objectives. Rare is the individual teacher who at one time or another has not struggled with their formulation. Yet it cannot be denied that little of this effort has had much effect on the instructional or evaluative practices of teachers. Are objectives really important? "Do they really help improve the education process, or is their formulation merely a rite of passage for the novice and a ritualistic exercise for the more experienced educator?"[6]

Before we answer this question, let us look at some examples of objectives formulated by various groups in different ways. First, a list of goals formulated by the curriculum committee of a national organization. The Committee on Concepts and Values for the National Council for the Social Studies identified the following 14 themes, each of which they designated as a "societal goal" of American democracy.

1. The intelligent uses of the forces of nature.
2. Recognition and understanding of world interdependence.
3. Recognition of the dignity and worth of the individual.
4. Use of intelligence to improve human living.
5. Vitalization of democracy through the intelligent use of our public educational facilities.
6. Intelligent acceptance, by individuals and groups, of responsibility for achieving democratic social action.
7. Increasing effectiveness of the family as a basic social institution.
8. Effective development of moral and spiritual values.
9. Intelligent and responsible sharing of power in order to attain justice.
10. Intelligent utilization of scarce resources to attain the widest general well-being.
11. Achievement of adequate horizons of loyalty.
12. Cooperation in the interest of peace and welfare.
13. Achieving a balance between social stability and social change.
14. Widening and deepening the ability to live more richly.[7]

Second, a statement suggested by the Educational Policies Commission of the National Education Association:

> The purpose which runs through and strengthens all other educational purpose—the common thread of education—is the development of the ability to think. This is the central purpose to which

[6]Bloom, Hastings, and Madaus, *Handbook on Formative and Summative Evaluation*, p. 21.
[7]Committee on Concepts and Values, *A Guide to Content in the Social Studies* (Washington, D.C.: National Council for the Social Studies, 1957), p. 73.

the school must be oriented if it is to accomplish its traditional tasks or those newly accentuated by recent changes in the world. To say that it is central is not to say that it is the sole purpose or in all circumstances the most important purpose, but that it must be a pervasive concern in the work of the school.[8]

Third, an example of social studies goals as suggested by members of a recently completed, federally funded social studies curriculum project:

The major goals of this curriculum call for learning activities which will assist students:
• to develop a number of specified thinking skills, and to use such skills to further understand both themselves and their world;
• to acquire, understand, and use a body of information selected from history and the social sciences and contemporary affairs, through the application of thinking skills or selected content material;
• to form a number of desired attitudes and values, and to examine the attitudes and values which they and others already possess; and (as a contributory goal)
• to develop and use a variety of additional academic and social skills deemed necessary to attain the three prior goals stated above.[9]

Notice that this statement as well as the previous two limits somewhat the conceivable scope of objectives toward which a teacher might strive. Each of these statements identifies one or more long-range objectives in rather general terms.

Statements such as the ones presented in these three lists of objectives are frequently criticized on the basis that they are too general to be of much *specific* help in guiding instruction in social studies classrooms. They are not precise enough to indicate clearly what is to be accomplished from day to day by teachers in the classroom, and accordingly, not of much help to teachers in devising their instructional plans and procedures. Such criticism, however, is unjust. General statements of objectives, like the ones above, are not intended to guide instruction and evaluation in a specific manner. They are intended as policy statements—"to give direction to policy makers at the national, state, and local level. Though lofty, they are still explicit enough to suggest certain types of action to school

[8]Educational Policies Commission, *The Central Purposes of American Education* (Washington, D.C.: Educational Policies Commission of the National Education Association, 1961), pp. 11–12.
[9]During a staff meeting of the Taba Curriculum Development Project at San Francisco State College in October of 1968; see Jack R. Fraenkel, Anthony H. McNaughton, Norman E. Wallen, and Mary C. Durkin, "Improving Elementary School Social Studies: An Idea-Oriented Approach," *The Elementary School Journal*, Dec. 1969, pp. 154–163.

boards and administrators. For example, if a board endorses 'the development of good citizenship' as a statement of purpose for its schools, then it must consider curricula, programs, and activities for its students that will work toward the accomplishment of this intent."[10]

As Bloom and others suggest, perhaps it is better to call such statements and lists "goals" rather than objectives. A goal is broader and more long-range than an objective. It is:

> . . . something presently out of reach; it is something to strive for, to move toward, or to become. It is an aim or purpose so stated that it excites the imagination and gives people something they want to work for, something they don't know how to do, something they can be proud of when they achieve it.[11]

Viewed in this sense, goals are quite important. They establish educational purpose, provide a consistent focus for curriculum planning and development, and suggest the major foci or emphases by which to design an educational program.

INSTRUCTIONAL OBJECTIVES

To be of help to classroom teachers, however, goals must be further broken down into a number of more specific *instructional objectives* so that the particular aspects or components which make up the more general goal become clear. Such instructional objectives should specify as clearly as possible the kinds of *behaviors* desired of students and the *content* they will be expected to learn—that is, indicate as precisely as possible what it is that students will be expected to *understand* and *do* (as defined here, "doing" includes thinking or feeling as well as acting) upon completion of a certain amount of study and instruction.

For example, a teacher might ask, in the first list of social studies goals presented on page 8, "What does a student *do* when he 'uses intelligently the forces of nature'?" or when he " 'cooperates in the interest of peace and welfare'?" How does he feel? How does he think? How does he act? What *content* must he acquire and understand in order to be able to feel, think, or act in this way or these ways? With regard to the second of the two lists of social studies goals, a teacher might inquire: "What do I expect my students to accomplish in the designated categories of knowledge, thinking, attitudes, and skills?" This assumes, of course, that he accepts these goals as important and worthy of implementation.

---

[10]Bloom, Hastings, and Madaus, *Handbook on Formative and Summative Evaluation,* p. 21.

[11]F. R. Kappel, *Vitality in a Business Enterprise* (New York: McGraw-Hill, 1960), quoted in Bloom *et al., Handbook on Formative and Summative Evaluation,* p. 21.

Stating objectives clearly and precisely, however, is not enough. It is also important for teachers to know *why* they expect students to demonstrate certain abilities or perform certain tasks in the first place. When teachers determine why they think something is worth teaching, they clarify its significance for both themselves and their students. (If a social studies teacher comes to the conclusion that what he has selected to emphasize is not conducive to fostering certain long-range educational goals that he endorses, so much the better! He should get on to something that is!) The underlying rationale for every instructional objective, therefore, needs to be made clear.

To illustrate these points more clearly let us take each of the social studies goals presented in the list on page 9 and present an example of a specific instructional objective (together with supporting rationale) in each category:

EXAMPLES OF INSTRUCTIONAL OBJECTIVES[12]

Social Studies Goal: To develop a number of specified thinking skills, and to use such skills to further understand and control both oneself and one's world.

Instructional Objective: Given relevant facts about a society or a personal situation, the student states logically sound, but informally worded, hypotheses (that he had not been previously given) about that society or situation today, in the past, or in the future. Ability to state hypotheses includes but is not limited to, ability to predict future events on the basis of present conditions. Examples of given facts and of hypotheses that students might state are:

KINDS OF FACTS GIVEN	EXAMPLES OF HYPOTHESES
Men lived in other parts of the world long before they lived in North and South America. Oceans and glaciers have not always covered the same parts of the earth's surface. (Students also observe a relief map of the ocean floor.)	It looks as if the very first men to come to the Americas could have come from Asia across what is now the Bering Strait.

[12]The examples of instructional objectives presented here are representative of the kinds prepared, and form used, by the project staff of the Taba Curriculum Development Project at San Francisco State College, San Francisco. For further examples, see Norman E. Wallen, Mary C. Durkin, Jack R. Fraenkel, Anthony H. McNaughton, and Enoch I. Sawin, *Development of a Comprehensive Curriculum Model for Social Studies for Grades One through Eight, Inclusive of Procedures for Implementation and Dissemination*, Final Report, Project No. 5–1314, Grant No. OE–6–10–182 (Washington, D.C.: U.S. Department of Health, Education, and Welfare, Office of Education, Bureau of Research, Oct. 1969).

KINDS OF FACTS GIVEN	EXAMPLES OF HYPOTHESES
A man from Mexico City with low income has moved to another large city in South America and is deciding on where to live.	He probably will decide to live in an area where the language and customs are similar to his and where most of the neighbors have about the same amount of income as he will be getting.
A child lives in an isolated village in Mexico where the language is different from that spoken in most of Mexico.	The child probably would feel that he belonged in the village but most likely would not think of himself as a Mexican.
Warm, moist air blows across many miles of lowlands, then comes to a range of very high mountains. The temperature in the lowlands is above 95° F.	The warm, moist air will be forced to rise until it reaches a height where it is cold enough to cause it to condense.

Rationale: Ability to form hypotheses is part of the general objective of thinking skills and is essential for anyone who hopes to deal constructively with problems in social studies. One of the most important functions of hypotheses is to provide "focus" for thought processes. That is, they make it possible to narrow down the range of concerns so as to increase the likelihood of successfully coping with the problem being considered. One's thinking is likely to be unproductive if the problem is conceived too broadly or if an attempt is made to analyze too many kinds of facts in too many ways all at the same time.

Social Studies Goal: To acquire, understand, and use a body of information selected from history and the social sciences and contemporary affairs, and to do so through the application of thinking skills or selected content material.

Instructional Objective: The student indicates comprehension of the meaning of the concepts of *interdependence* and *power* by such behaviors as giving illustrations, explaining meanings, and other actions involving uses. In making the explanations and descriptions, the student correctly uses factual information about one or more of the peoples of Middle and South America and the environments in which they live. In addition, the student indicates comprehension of other ideas related to these concepts. For example, for the concept *interdependence*, illustrative student statements that indicate comprehension of the concept are:

A man who owns a large ranch could not run it alone even if he wanted to. He has to depend on a number of people for different kinds of help and he needs services such as transportation and processing plants.

People in an industrial country like ours are extremely dependent on others—even on things needed for survival.

The more specialization there is in the jobs in a society the more the people have to rely on what other people produce.

Statements by students suggesting comprehension of the concept *power* are as follows:

Any government must have power. Otherwise they would have no way to regulate what people do.

The natural resources and the skills of the people in a country have a lot to do with how much influence the country has with other nations. What I mean is that they are what makes a country powerful.

If somebody has control over people he has power over them. He can force them to do what he wants.

Rationale: A general objective is the acquisition of a broad base of knowledge of social studies content. Certain generalizations are considered to represent powerful ideas having a general acceptance in the various disciplines dealing with social studies. This knowledge is considered important so that students can understand the world and themselves more adequately. It is necessary to develop thinking skills and attitudes referred to in other objectives.

Social Studies Goal: To form a number of desired attitudes and values and to examine the attitudes and values which they and others already possess.

Instructional Objective: Given a situation in which he is encouraged to express his own thoughts, the student responds to statements of other students and the teacher in ways that the teacher judges to be fair toward the various people involved and that show recognition and acceptance of merits of different ways of living and points of view. He challenges derogatory or belittling statements about people of different cultures or about people who exhibit unusual behavior. Examples of desired statements are:

They've got a right to make different rules.
Maybe he had a reason not to do his work.
We can do it our way, but why not let them do it their way?
The mother works and she takes good care of the children too.

Examples of statements the students will challenge are:

What a funny family!
Susie should be forced to give her brother something for Christmas.
He's just lazy and mean.
It's not right that they should have rules like that in the family.
Whoever heard of anybody doing it that way?

Rationale: The outcome sought here is an attitude of sensitivity to, and acceptance of, personal differences. Sensitivity to, and acceptance of, differences in persons and groups around them represent an important step toward sensitivity to cultural differences. The ultimate goal can perhaps best be conceptualized as the opposite of ethnocentrism.

Social Studies Goal: To develop and use a variety of social and academic skills.

Instructional Objective: Given a globe, an atlas, and certain specified tasks the student responds by locating the place where certain ancient civilizations were located, tracing routes of trade expeditions, identifying boundaries, determining the direction of selected points from other points, estimating distances accurately, determining elevation and landforms, and using the concepts of latitude and longitude to describe locations and to find specified points.

Rationale: These abilities fall within the category of academic skills. Since social studies content deals with features and comparisons of societies in all parts of the world, it is useful for students to be able to make effective use of maps and globes.

The instructional objectives above are but *one example* that can be suggested in each category of these social studies goals. Many other instructional objectives in each category could be proposed. Those that are presented here, however, illustrate what a well-developed and clearly stated instructional objective, together with its supporting rationale, looks like.

The foregoing examples illustrate that educational expectations can be written at more than one level. It seems quite logical to argue, in fact, that the formulation of educational objectives should well be accomplished at several levels. The more general long-range educational goals might be determined by educational philosophers and others qualified to consider the long-range overall purposes of education and schooling, and to examine systematically the sources from which such purposes are derived. The more specific instructional objectives can then be determined at the school level by district curriculum developers and teachers. Taba stated the point clearly:

. . . (I) raise the question whether the formulation of objectives does not involve a twofold task. One is that of determining the main aims of education; this belongs in the hands of persons qualified to consider the whole field of education and to study carefully the sources from which to derive the aims. The other task is the definition and determination of the more specific curricular objectives, including the determination of the specific context in which to achieve the aims and the specific levels of attainment. This formulation should be in the hands of those who develop the local curriculum guides and specific units—the local curriculum groups and the school staffs. A rational and functional platform of objectives emerges, however, *only to the extent that the specific objectives are consistently related to the general aims.*[13]

Sawin[14] makes a similar suggestion. He proposes that instructional objectives, depending on the amount of generability desired and the amount of time available for development, be identified at a *number of levels* ranging from very general to very specific, as in the following example.

Level IV: *Very General:* The student is able to cope with the problems of life. (Lifelong Objective)

Level III: *General:* The student is able to communicate effectively with others. (School Objective)

Level II: *Specific:* The student is able to judge the extent to which certain generalizations about social phenomena are warranted. (Course Objective)

Level I: *Explicit:* Given a number of factual statements and a list of generalizations (only some of which are supported by the factual statements), the student is able to identify which generalizations are supported by which facts, and tell why this is so. (Specific Unit or Lesson Objective)

The decision as to which of many possible specific instructional objectives to implement is essentially an arbitrary one. The responsible teacher, however, will strive for comprehensiveness by developing objectives in each of the major categories (knowledge and understandings; skills; attitudes, feelings and sensitivities; and values) mentioned earlier. He also will check to ensure that the specific instructional objectives formulated or selected are clearly related to one or more of the more general educational goals that he endorses. He will also make it clear (to both himself and his students) why he thinks a particular objective is worthy of being studied. He thus establishes a logically and psychologically sound position for him-

[13]Taba, *Curriculum Development*, p. 210. (Italics added.)
[14]Enoch I. Sawin, *Evaluation and the Work of the Teacher* (Belmont, Calif.: Wadsworth, 1969), p. 59.

self. Others may not agree with his particular estimate of what is significant. That is not, in and of itself, important. What is important is that every teacher *knows and can explain* what he wants to accomplish and why he wants to accomplish certain objectives (Figure 1.1).

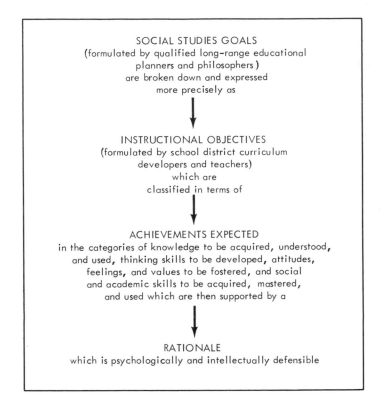

SOCIAL STUDIES GOALS
(formulated by qualified long-range educational
planners and philosophers)
are broken down and expressed
more precisely as

INSTRUCTIONAL OBJECTIVES
(formulated by school district curriculum
developers and teachers)
which are
classified in terms of

ACHIEVEMENTS EXPECTED
in the categories of knowledge to be acquired, understood,
and used, thinking skills to be developed, attitudes,
feelings, and values to be fostered, and social
and academic skills to be acquired, mastered,
and used which are then supported by a

RATIONALE
which is psychologically and intellectually defensible

FIGURE 1.1
(*The Formulation of Objectives*)

MAJOR CLASSIFICATIONS OF SOCIAL STUDIES OBJECTIVES

Objectives may vary considerably in terms of what is desired. Some fall within the general category of knowledge or information to be learned. Others suggest the development and use of one's mental powers. Still others suggest the acquisition of attitudes, feelings, or sensitivities. To ensure comprehensiveness, therefore, social studies (and other) objectives are often classified in terms of general categories. Four rather commonly used categories are the following:

Knowledge—the acquisition and understanding of specific pieces of information and ideas.
Skills—the development of certain abilities in order to use the knowledge that is acquired.
Attitudes—the acquisition, development, and acceptance of certain beliefs, interests, outlooks, and predispositions.
Values—the acquisition of a number of deeply held commitments, supported when necessary, by appropriate action.

Within each of these general categories, a number of more specific behaviors and content can be identified as being particularly germane to social studies education. They include the following:

Knowledge: The major types of information to be studied and learned in the social studies include facts, concepts, generalizations, and theories. These terms will be defined, discussed, and exemplified in detail in Chapter 3.

Skills: The major kinds of social studies skills include thinking skills, academic skills, and social skills.

Thinking Skills include such abilities as describing, defining, classifying, hypothesizing, generalizing, predicting, comparing and contrasting, and offering new ideas.[15] Chapter 5 will discuss the development of such abilities in considerable detail.

Academic Skills include such abilities as reading, viewing, writing, speaking, listening, reading and interpreting maps, outlining, graphing, charting, and note-taking. A particular sub-category of academic skills is often referred to as research skills.

Research Skills include the ability to:

1. Define a problem.
2. Formulate a reasonable hypothesis as to how the problem might be resolved.
3. Locate and gather data dealing with the problem.
4. Analyze this data:
    a. Distinguish relevant from irrelevant data.
    b. Organize the relevant data into categories.
    c. Evaluate the adequacy and accuracy of the data.
    d. Interpret the data as to what it means.
5. Evaluate the hypothesis in light of the data that has been gathered and analyzed.

[15]For a representative list of thinking skills, see P. L. Dressel and Lewis B. Mayhew, *Critical Thinking in Social Science: A Handbook of Suggestions for Evaluation and Teaching* (Dubuque, Iowa: Brown, 1954).

6. Draw a conclusion—accept, reject, or modify the hypothesis as appropriate.[16]

Social Skills include the ability to:

1. Cooperate harmoniously with others on small and large group projects
2. Contribute productively to group tasks and discussions.
3. Supply leadership when, and if, necessary and appropriate.

Both academic and social skills are described in some detail in Chapter 4.

Attitudes: Orlandi[17] has grouped most of the attitudinal objectives of social studies instruction rather neatly into two basic categories. These categories include attitudes for desirable intellectual behavior and attitudes for desirable social behavior. He then further classifies them as follows:

Attitudes for desirable intellectual behavior "lead to the cultivation of an empirical, reasonable, and humane outlook."[18] They include a Scientific approach to human behavior and a Humanitarian outlook on the behavior of others.

A Scientific approach to human behavior includes such attitudes as open-mindedness, objectivity, skepticism, relativity, precision in collecting, analyzing, and interpreting data, a tendency to search for multiple rather than single causes of human behavior, and a belief in natural (as opposed to supernatural) causation of individual and group action.

A Humanitarian outlook on the behavior of others includes attitudes such as empathy and tolerance. Empathy involves the capacity to put oneself in someone else's shoes—to experience things in a manner similar to that of others. Tolerance involves an acceptance of behaviors considered strange or different by one's primary reference group.[19]

Attitudes for desirable social behaviors are divided by Orlandi[20] into three sub-categories—awareness and interest; responsibility, and involvement.

[16]The so-called inquiry method of teaching is actually just another name for helping students develop the skills found in this list. See Barry K. Beyer, *Inquiry in the Social Studies Classroom: A Strategy for Teaching* (Columbus, Ohio: Charles C. Merrill, 1971). A classic and extremely clear treatment of research skills is Harold A. Larrabee, *Reliable Knowledge* (Boston: Houghton Mifflin, 1945, 1964).

[17]Lisanio R. Orlandi, "Evaluation of Learning in Secondary School Social Studies," in Bloom, Hastings, and Madaus, *Handbook on Formative and Summative Evaluation*, pp. 447–498.

[18]*Ibid.*, p. 459.

[19]*Ibid.*, p. 459.

[20]Orlandi, "Evaluation of Learning . . . ," in Bloom *et al., Handbook on Formative and Summative Evaluation.*

Awareness refers to the recognition on the part of students that certain social problems, such as poverty, alienation, and crime, exist, and of the contributions that various members of the society have made to the development of the society as a whole.

Interest reflects the degree of attention students display toward a given social problem. Such interest can be displayed in many ways, as evidenced by reading articles and books about the problem, attending lectures or meetings dealing with the problem, or by frequent efforts to discuss the problem, its causes and effects, with others.

Acceptance of responsibility includes such attitudes as a desire to be well-informed about what goes on in the world, a recognition of the obligation to be well-informed before making a decision about public issues, and a willingness to operate within the limitations of democratic procedures in attempting to further a given cause.

Involvement refers to the extent to which a person is willing to act on the basis of his convictions.[21]

Values: The values to be furthered through social studies instruction are the core values of a democratic society, as found in the basic political documents—the Declaration of Independence and the Constitution—of the nation. These core values include such values as a belief in the worth and dignity of every human being, personal freedom, equality and justice for all, peace and order among men, economic well-being for all, and a sense of responsibility for, and brotherhood with, one's fellows. The core values also include a respect for certain governmental principles, such as rule of law, due process of law, equal rights under the law, and the idea of government by representation and consent. (The development and analysis of values is discussed in Chapter 6.)

It is clear that the categories of objectives presented above are not mutually exclusive. They overlap. This fact has considerable implication for designing learning activities and we shall discuss it further in Chapter 4. The design and implementation of learning activities and teaching strategies that teachers can use to further various objectives in each of these categories will also be discussed in Chapters 4, 5, and 6.

STATING OBJECTIVES

Instructional objectives can be stated in many ways. One possibility is to express objectives in terms of the subject matter to be covered. For example:

[21]*Ibid.,* pp. 459–460.

The underlying causes of the Spanish-American War
The Red Badge of Courage
1763–1776
Cuba under Castro
The election of John F. Kennedy
Capitalism, Socialism, and Communism

The examples given above indicate that certain content is to be dealt with. But in what manner? What are students to do with *The Red Badge of Courage*? Read it? Outline it? Summarize it? Look for examples which refute or qualify the author's theme? What about the "underlying causes of the Spanish-American War"? Are they to be identified? memorized? questioned? analyzed in some manner or another? compared and contrasted with the underlying causes of other wars? If we assume, as suggested earlier, that the purpose of education is to change students in some way, it becomes clear that the mere statement of subject matter by itself, without also describing or illustrating what is to be *done with* that subject matter—in effect, *how* it is to be learned, carries with it very little meaning. As a result, objectives so stated are not of much help to a teacher in planning appropriate lessons or in evaluating the outcomes of instruction.

On the other hand, one sometimes sees objectives listed as follows:

to develop the ability to solve problems
to learn to think
to develop empathy

Such objectives are the reverse of the preceding "content-only" objectives. These objectives indicate certain behaviors to be attained, though in very general terms. They have two weaknesses. First, one wonders what the student is to think about, or develop an empathy for. The subject matter to which the behavior is to be applied is missing. Second, the meaning of the objective is not clear. What does developing "the ability to solve problems" mean? How would one distinguish a student who possesses this ability from one who does not? What evidence would we need in order to know that someone has solved a problem? Teachers often attempt to become more precise by stating objectives such as "to increase one's ability to apply previously learned ideas," or "to learn how to compare and contrast." Notice that these objectives make clear the meaning of the behavior involved, that is, they are less general, but they still ignore the subject matter to which the behavior is to be applied.

Clearly stated objectives, therefore, should indicate what is expected of students in terms of *both* behavior and content (subject matter). As Sawin suggests:

The term behavior refers to the mental or physical behavior that is expected to be manifested as a result of the educational experience. The behaviors include such outcomes as comprehension, ability to interpret data, attitudes, interests, and skills, and ability to make applications.[22]

Two major kinds of subject matter are objects and abstractions.

Examples of objects are works of art, scientific instruments, relief maps and the variety of other concrete objects involved in classroom instruction. Abstractions are probably the most frequently encountered type of content. Examples include number concepts, word meanings, and concepts like democracy and interdependence of peoples. Both objects and abstractions could serve as the content component of an objective. For example, an objective might be stated as follows: The student should comprehend the concept of interdependence of peoples. The behavioral component is comprehend; the content component is the concept of interdependence of peoples.[23]

This twofold conception of what an objective consists of should help eliminate the idea that the essence of education lies only in the acquisition of knowledge. Hopefully it will promote a realization that certain kinds of intellectual skills, attitudes, and values are also hallmarks of an educated person. It also suggests the fact that the same content may be studied in order to achieve several objectives (e.g., reading a certain article to gain insight into the reasons why certain individuals pursued a particular course of action *as well as* to develop an appreciation for the merits of a logical argument).

What *specific* content and behavior will be emphasized as most likely to promote a given goal, however, will vary from teacher to teacher, and will depend upon such additional factors as the characteristics of the learners involved, the materials available, and the philosophy of the school in which the teacher works.

OPERATIONAL DEFINITIONS

You now have some idea of what a clearly stated instructional objective looks like. To further your understanding, we need to consider briefly the meaning of operational definitions. We often can clarify the meaning of a particular term by explaining it with words that refer to observable actions

---

[22]Sawin, *Evaluation and the Work of the Teacher*, p. 61.
[23]*Ibid.*, p. 59.

or things, or by identifying certain operations that individuals can perform. This process is often referred to as *an operational definition*. For example, if we define integrity as "soundness of moral principle," we really aren't much clearer than we were before since the definition "soundness of moral principle" contains words as vague as the term being defined (integrity). On the other hand, if we say that a person who never breaks a verbal promise has integrity, our meaning is clearer. We have given a precise, though limited, explanation of what we mean. In the first instance, the definition of the term consisted of other words, as vague as the term being defined. In the second case, certain operations or behaviors were used to define the term. Bloom and his co-workers illustrate the difference between these two types of definitions, using the concept of "intelligence" as an example:

> "A person received a score of 130 on the California Test of Mental Maturity because *he is intelligent.*" In this non-operational state-ment, the descriptive concept "intelligent," is being used as an ex-planatory word; that is, intelligence is given as the reason for the performance. (Now consider a second statement) "A person is con-sidered intelligent because *he received a score of 130* on the Califor-nia Test of Mental Maturity." In this operational statement, "in-telligence," a descriptive word, is being defined by the person's performance on a given task. While one may disagree, no latitude is left for different interpretations of the term.[24]

Operational definitions are helpful tools. They can help teachers be more clear in communicating their intent. Objectives which ask students "to un-derstand," "to know," "to appreciate," or "to be aware of," are not very clear. It is not clear *how* students are to demonstrate to an impartial ob-server what they know, understand, appreciate, or are aware. The essence of operational definition lies in the type of verb used in these statements.

For example, compare the following two lists of verbs:

List 1	*List 2*
to know	to list
to know thoroughly	to define
to be aware of	to name
to recognize	to write
to comprehend	to ask
to understand	to identify
to really understand	to restate
to grasp the significance of	to locate
to appreciate	to tell why

[24]Bloom, Hastings, and Madaus, *Handbook on Formative and Summative Evalua-tion*, p. 24.

List 1	*List 2*
to enjoy	to illustrate
to believe	to distinguish
to have faith in	to differentiate
to esteem	to discuss
to take satisfaction in	to suggest
to think	to choose
to learn	to rate
to have an interest in	to predict

The verbs in list 2 indicate certain operations which, if performed using various subject matter, can be publicly certified by some means. They can be recognized even by impartial observers. Though they represent somewhat different levels of specificity and preciseness, they clearly indicate what kind of behavior to expect. They indicate the kind of *evidence* to look for. Those in list 1, on the other hand, represent internal states or conditions. They do not indicate clearly what behaviors to expect. Unless examples are given of what these words mean, the teacher would not be able to tell when the actions or processes they imply have been accomplished.

INTENT VS. EVIDENCE

Objectives, therefore, communicate the *intent* of instruction. But *intent* and *evidence* are not the same thing. A teacher should not confuse the communication of intent contained within an objective with a description of the specific evidence that he or his students will accept as indicating that the objective has been attained. The most appropriate evidence, of course, will depend on the nature of the objectives that the teacher and his students wish to attain. In some instances, the most appropriate evidence will consist of certain student *behaviors*, such as describing, interviewing, leading a discussion, or asking certain kinds of questions. In other instances, the most appropriate evidence will consist of certain student *products*, such as essays, models, maps, drawings, diagrams, or outlines. In still other instances, participation by students in certain *experiences*, such as visiting a laboratory, listening to a symphony, holding a kitten, interviewing a public official, or smelling a flower will be more suitable. It is important, therefore, for a teacher to be as clear as possible about the kinds of evidence—behaviors, products, and/or experiences—he wishes to encourage in order to help students attain his and their objectives.

For example, if a teacher wishes to have his students gain some insight into the nature of war, its causes and effects, he needs to ask "What particular subject matter can help provide such insight?" Let us suppose that he and his students decide that an understanding of why the Spanish-American War of 1898 occurred will be particularly illustrative. The teacher must then ask himself, "What student behaviors, products, and/or experiences will most effectively promote such understanding?" Will it be enough for students to see a filmstrip about the war? Should they make a map? Will it suffice if students are able to identify several of the *immediate* causes of the war? Or should they also be able to identify several of the *underlying* causes as well? Perhaps the ability to *identify* causes by itself is not enough to ensure understanding. Perhaps students should also *explain why* these were causes. Perhaps they should *compare* and *contrast* the causes of the Spanish-American War with the immediate and underlying causes of the American Revolutionary War, the American Civil War, and the War in Vietnam. Perhaps the Spanish-American War should be compared with other wars than these.

Consider another example. Suppose a teacher is interested in opening students' eyes to how individuals faced with a choice between two compelling alternatives *feel*, hoping thereby to help them acquire an empathy for individuals in conflict situations. What subject matter is illustrative here? Harry Truman's account of his agonizing decision to drop the atomic bomb on Hiroshima and Nagasaki? John F. Kennedy's *Profiles in Courage?* Richard Wright's *Black Boy?* Perhaps *The Autobiography of Malcolm X?* Whatever his choice (or the class's), he must again determine what behaviors, products, or experiences might promote the insight he desires. Will it suffice if students simply *read* or *see a film* about the actions of such individuals (e.g., Richard Wright in *Black Boy*)? Should they *make inferences,* based on a character's actions, about his feelings? Perhaps they should *discuss* the character's feelings? Perhaps they should *act out* the character's feelings through role-playing? Perhaps they should be asked to imagine themselves in a similar situation and then to write an essay or *discuss* what they think their *own feelings* might be. Perhaps none of these. But if none of these, what instead?

The point being made here is that the teacher must be clear as to what skills, understandings, and attitudes he wants students to acquire. He then can determine what kinds of specific evidence will indicate that his objectives have been (or are being) attained. In some cases this evidence will consist of certain student *behaviors*, such as describing, discussing, or explaining. In other cases, the most appropriate evidence will consist of certain student *products*, such as essays, reports, maps, or models. In still other instances, participation by students in certain *experiences,* such as interviewing their parents, attending a ballet, going to a museum, or helping another person solve a problem will be most appropriate. Regardless of which kind of evidence (behavior, product, or experience) is most appropriate for a given objective, the necessity for considering both subject matter and behavior—both content and process—is apparent.

How specifically should an objective be stated? There is no absolute answer to this question. It depends in part on the generalizability of the behaviors desired and in part on what can be accomplished in a given period of time. Thus, a highly specific statement, such as expecting students to describe the major events between 1763 and 1776 that led up to the American Declaration of Independence may be perfectly appropriate for one particular lesson. A more generally expressed objective, such as expecting students to be able to apply social science generalizations to new data may be more appropriate for a semester (or longer) course. Thus, the specificity of the content and behavior identified in an objective can vary.

When is an objective clear? When it has been operationalized sufficiently so that different impartial observers agree as to what it means (though not necessarily *with* what it means, however)—i.e., they agree that certain student performances, products, or experiences, if completed, will indicate *in this instance* (though not necessarily another) that the objective has been attained.

The following are all clearly stated examples of instructional objectives: Students can:

- describe several (more than three) of the causes of poverty in the United States, and explain why they are causes;
- apply previously learned ideas about the effect of the discovery of metal on men's lives by suggesting what might happen if a new metal, harder yet more malleable than any yet known, were to be discovered;
- write an original poem;
- ask a number of questions of a guest speaker, all of which require the speaker to give his impressions as to the worth of a given object, event, or idea;
- restate a speaker's argument in their own words;
- locate and present evidence to support or refute a particular argument;
- distinguish between fact and opinion by offering examples of each;
- organize previously unrelated data into groups, tables, or charts;
- identify similarities and differences among the underlying causes of the American, French, Russian, and Cuban Revolutions;
- choose a public official and interview him as to his views on the effectiveness of mass transit systems for use in cities of 100,000 population or over;
- attend a concert of their own choosing;
- help another individual solve a problem or complete a task;
- design a mural to illustrate a concept they consider important.

TASK DESCRIPTION

A task description is just what its name implies—a complete description of a task that a teacher wishes his students to accomplish. Such descriptions should meet the following criteria:

• They should be as complete as a teacher can make them (i.e., they should indicate as much as possible about what it is that the teacher expects his students to accomplish);
• they should be unambiguous (i.e., there should be no confusion over the meanings of the words used);
• they should be internally consistent (i.e., one set of requirements should not conflict with another);
• they should be reliable (i.e., two readers should agree on the basic performance expected of the learner).[25]

Mager has devised a method of task description which suggests the characteristics that he argues instructional objectives must possess if they are to meet the preceding criteria. According to Mager, meaningfully stated instructional objectives are those which:

• specify the kind of behavior that will be accepted as evidence that the learner has achieved the objective (terminal performance desired).
• describe the important conditions under which the behavior will be expected to occur.
• describe how well the learner must perform to be considered acceptable.[26]

Let us look at one example of a task description:

Given a set of events, one of which is to be explained, students give a logically sound and plausible explanation of the chain of cause and effect connections which resulted in the occurrence of the event.

Let us apply Mager's three requirements to this example. Has the terminal performance expected of the learner been identified? (What will students be expected to do?)

Yes, it has. Students will be expected to "give an explanation of the chain of cause and effect connections which resulted in the occurrence of an event."

[25]Robert F. Mager, *Preparing Instructional Objectives* (Palo Alto, Calif.: Fearon Publishers, 1961), p. 11; reprinted by permission of Fearon Publishers, 6 Davis Drive, Belmont CA 94002, from their publication *Preparing Instructional Objectives*; $2.00.
[26]*Ibid.*, p. 12.

Have the important conditions under which the terminal performance will be expected to occur been described?

Yes, they have. The conditions under which behavior is to occur is "given a set of events, one of which is to be explained."

Has the level of acceptable performance been described? (How *well* will students be expected to perform?)

Yes, it has. Students will be expected to "give a *logically sound and plausible explanation* . . ."

Take a look once again at the objectives listed on page 25. Do these objectives possess Mager's three characteristics? If not, try to provide one or more possibilities for those characteristics that are missing.

With regard to the third requirement of Mager's, notice that the *particular* levels or standards of achievement expected will vary from teacher to teacher. The level of achievement (*how well* a student performs or the *quality* of the product(s) expected of him) depends on the difficulty of the material being studied, personal capabilities of the students involved, and the learning conditions that exist. The level of achievement expected, therefore, is essentially an arbitrary matter, but the responsible teacher will continually weigh what he expects against the kind of materials, students, and situations with and in which he is working.

Low- vs. High-Level Objectives

It is essential that teachers not ignore those objectives that are difficult to define explicitly. Low-level objectives like "Knowing several causes of the American Revolution" are fairly easy to define in explicit terms. Those who prepare lists of objectives, in fact, often have a tendency to concentrate on writing objectives at this level because they can be so easily defined. The development of more complex objectives suffers as a result. As Gronlund points out:

> Objectives pertaining to thinking skills, attitudes, and appreciation should not be slighted because of the difficulty of clearly defining them. It would seem better to list the specific types of behavior that can be identified before instruction begins and then to revise and improve that list as relevant examples of student reaction become apparent.[27]

He goes on to illustrate how one teacher compiled the following tentative list of types of behavior for the objective "appreciates good literature."

[27]Norman E. Gronlund, *Stating Behavioral Objectives for Classroom Instruction* (New York: The Macmillan Company, 1970), p. 16.

Appreciates good literature.
1. Describes the differences between good and poor literature.
2. Distinguishes between selections of good and poor literature.
3. Gives critical reasons for classifying a selection as good or poor.
4. Selects and reads good literature during free reading periods.
5. Explains why he likes the particular selections of good literature that he reads.[28]

Though this list is far from complete, the teacher involved had a fairly good idea of what he meant by the abstract concept *appreciation*. (Notice that he and his class must also be clear as to what constitutes "good" literature in the first place. Otherwise, the specific instructional objectives would make no sense.) His list provides some fairly specific guidelines that can be used for instructional planning, but that also can be revised and/or expanded as future teaching and testing deem necessary.[29]

It is to be reiterated at this point that *just because an objective is clear does not mean it is significant.* There are many things that are important to a student's growth and development that are difficult to name or even identify in a precise way. "Appreciation" of the same story by different students may be illustrated by a vigorous verbal rebuttal, by stunned silence, by tears, by laughter, by the recounting of a similar personal experience in real life, or by none of these. It is for this reason that teachers need to think about (and encourage students to suggest) a variety of *different* kinds of behaviors, products, or experiences that might serve as indications that an objective is being or has been attained.

THE VALUE OF CLEARLY STATED INSTRUCTIONAL OBJECTIVES

Why are clearly stated instructional objectives so important? The most persuasive arguments are the following:

1. Clearly stated instructional objectives make it easier to plan instructional procedures. They clarify and suggest what steps a teacher needs to take in order to help students accomplish certain goals of instruction. A fable written by Mager illustrates this advantage rather nicely.

> Once upon a time a Sea Horse gathered up his seven pieces of eight and cantered out to find his fortune. Before he traveled very far he met an Eel, who said,
>
> "Psst. Hey, bud. Where 'ya goin'?"
>
> "I'm going out to find my fortune," replied the Sea Horse, proudly.

[28]Gronlund, *Stating Behavioral Objectives*, p. 16.
[29]*Ibid.*

"You're in luck," said the Eel, "for four pieces of eight you can have this speedy flipper, and then you'll be able to get there a lot faster."

"Gee, that's swell," said the Sea Horse, and paid the money and put on the flipper and slithered off at twice the speed. Soon he came upon a Sponge, who said,

"Psst. Hey, bud. Where 'ya goin'?"

"I'm going to find my fortune" replied the Sea Horse.

"You're in luck," said the Sponge. "For a small fee I will let you have this jet-propelled scooter so that you will be able to travel a lot faster."

So the Sea Horse bought the scooter with his remaining money and went zooming through the sea five times as fast. Soon he came upon a Shark, who said,

"Psst. Hey, bud. Where 'ya goin'?"

"I'm going out to find my fortune," replied the Sea Horse.

"You're in luck. If you take this shortcut," said the Shark, pointing to his open mouth, "you'll save yourself a lot of time."

"Gee, thanks," said the Sea Horse, and zoomed off into the interior of the Shark, there to be devoured.[30]

The moral of the fable, according to Mager, is that if you are not sure where you are going, you very well may end up somewhere else. As Abraham Lincoln stated in his "House Divided Against Itself" speech, "if we could first know where we are and whither we are tending, we could better judge what we do and how to do it." One way to avoid the possibility of both teacher and students not knowing where they are going is for teacher and students to decide *jointly* where they want to go (i.e., what they want to learn or experience) and then determine what knowledge, skills, or feelings they must master or experience if certain desired learnings are to take place. It is impossible for teachers and students to determine all the intermediate steps they must take to accomplish a given objective unless both teacher and students are clear about what it is the students are to learn, and what behavior, products, and/or experiences will illustrate that such learning has occurred. Thus an extremely important reason for stating instructional objectives as clearly and precisely as possible is the considerable assistance they can provide teachers and students in planning their instructional procedures—what content to select for study and what learning activities to stress.

2. Clear and precise statements of instructional objectives can help teachers to differentiate that which is significant and important from that

[30]Mager, *Preparing Instructional Objectives*, p. ix.

which is merely incidental. There are many levels of performance which can be required of students. Bloom and his associates developed a system for classifying instructional objectives in their *Taxonomy of Educational Objectives*.[31] They defined a number of categories by which to classify many objectives in education. This taxonomy is divided into three domains —cognitive, affective, and psychomotor, with each domain including several classes of behavior that suggest how information might be used. Here is a list of these categories in the cognitive domain, along with a definition of the thought processes involved in each.

2–1: *Knowledge:* Knowledge simply involves the recalling of specific items of information.

2–2: *Comprehension:* Comprehension involves more than knowledge. For example, a person who comprehends something can not only recall it, but can paraphrase it, review it, define it, or discuss it to some extent.

2–3: *Application:* The person who can use this thought process can do everything in categories (1) and (2) above. He can also demonstrate his ability to take information of an abstract nature and use it in concrete situations. It is this ability to apply information to new problems that makes the process unique.

2–4: *Analysis:* The essential ingredients of analysis include the breaking down of a communication into its constituent parts, and revealing the relationships of those parts.

2–5: *Synthesis:* Synthesis is a word used to describe the process of pulling together many disorganized elements or parts so as to form a whole. It is the arranging, combining, and relating parts that makes this process unique.

2–6: *Evaluation:* Judgments about the value of materials or methods are evaluative judgments. This thought process requires many of the abilities of categories 1 through 5, as well as some abilities unique to category 6.[32]

The Oregon State Board of Education[33] has prepared a list of verbs as a guide for teachers trying to prepare clearer and more explicit statements of instructional objectives that involve higher level thought processes. Here are a few of the verbs they list under each category:

[31]Benjamin S. Bloom (ed.), *Taxonomy of Educational Objectives: The Classification of Educational Goals, Handbook I: Cognitive Domain* (New York: McKay, 1956); D. R. Krathwohl (ed.), *Taxonomy of Educational Objectives: The Classification of Educational Goals, Handbook II: Affective Domain* (New York: McKay, 1964).

[32]Bloom, ed., *Taxonomy of Educational Objectives.*

[33]*The Development of Higher Level Thought Processes*, Oregon Small Schools Program (Salem, Oregon: State Department of Education, n.d.).

Knowledge	Comprehension	Application
define	restate	translate
repeat	describe	interpret
list	recognize	use
name	identify	demonstrate
state	locate	dramatize
	report	illustrate
	review	operate
	tell	schedule
		sketch

Analysis	Synthesis	Evaluation
distinguish	compose	judge
analyze	plan	appraise
differentiate	propose	evaluate
calculate	design	rate
experiment	formulate	value
test	arrange	revise
compare	assemble	score
contrast	collect	choose
diagram	construct	estimate
inspect	create	measure
debate	set up	criticize
inventory	organize	
question	prepare	
relate	summarize	

Gronlund[34] performed a similar task for the affective and psychomotor domains. He presented a brief description of the various categories in all three domains, along with examples of general instructional objectives and illustrative behavioral terms that could be used for stating specific learning outcomes for each category. These are reproduced on the following pages in Tables 1.1, 1.2, and 1.3.

The three domains are not mutually exclusive, however. Gronlund describes clearly how they overlap:

> Instructional objectives in the psychomotor domain typically include concomitant cognitive and affective elements, but the demonstration of a motor skill is the dominant characteristic of the student's response. This overlapping of behavior from the different domains is, of course, not limited to performance skills. Learning outcomes in the cognitive area have some affective elements, and outcomes in the affective area have some cognitive components. The three domains of the taxonomy provide a useful classification system, but they simply represent particular emphases in stating objectives and not mutually exclusive divisions.

[34]Gronlund, *Stating Behavioral Objectives for Classroom Instruction* (New York: The Macmillan Company, 1970).

TABLE 1.1*

MAJOR CATEGORIES IN THE COGNITIVE DOMAIN OF THE TAXONOMY OF EDUCATIONAL
OBJECTIVES (BLOOM, 1956) EXAMPLES OF GENERAL INSTRUCTIONAL
OBJECTIVES AND BEHAVIORAL TERMS FOR THE COGNITIVE DOMAIN OF THE TAXONOMY

Descriptions of the Major Categories in the Cognitive Domain	Illustrative General Instructional Objectives	Illustrative Behavioral Terms for Stating Specific Learning Outcomes
1. Knowledge. Knowledge is defined as the remembering of previously learned material. This may involve the recall of a wide range of material, from specific facts to complete theories, but all that is required is the bringing to mind of the appropriate information. Knowledge represents the lowest level of learning outcomes in the cognitive domain.	Knows common terms Knows specific facts Knows methods and procedures Knows basic concepts Knows principles	Defines, describes, identifies, labels, lists, matches, names, outlines, reproduces, selects, states
2. Comprehension. Comprehension is defined as the ability to grasp the meaning of material. This may be shown by translating material from one form to another (words to numbers), by interpreting material (explaining or summarizing), and by estimating future trends (predicting consequences or effects). These learning outcomes go one step beyond the simple remembering of material, and represent the lowest level of understanding.	Understands facts and principles Interprets verbal material Interprets charts and graphs Translates verbal material to mathematical formulas Estimates future consequences implied in data Justifies methods and procedures	Converts, defends, distinguishes, estimates, explains, extends, generalizes, gives examples, infers, paraphrases, predicts, rewrites, summarizes
3. Application. Application refers to the ability to use learned material in new and concrete situations. This may include the application of such things as rules, methods, concepts, principles, laws, and theories. Learning outcomes in this area require a higher level of understanding than those under comprehension.	Applies concepts and principles to new situations Applies laws and theories to practical situations Solves mathematical problems Constructs charts and graphs Demonstrates correct usage of a method or procedure	Changes, computes, demonstrates, discovers, manipulates, modifies, operates, predicts, prepares, produces, relates, shows, solves, uses

Descriptive statements	Illustrative behavioral terms for stating specific learning outcomes	Illustrative verbs
4. **Analysis.** Analysis refers to the ability to break down material into its component parts so that its organizational structure may be understood. This may include the identification of the parts, analysis of the relationships between parts, and recognition of the organizational principles involved. Learning outcomes here represent a higher intellectual level than comprehension and application because they require an understanding of both the content and the structural form of the material.	Recognizes unstated assumptions Recognizes logical fallacies in reasoning Distinguishes between facts and inferences Evaluates the relevancy of data Analyzes the organizational structure of a work (art, music, writing)	Breaks down, diagrams, differentiates, discriminates, distinguishes, identifies, illustrates, infers, outlines, points out, relates, selects, separates, subdivides.
5. **Synthesis.** Synthesis refers to the ability to put parts together to form a new whole. This may involve the production of a unique communication (theme or speech), a plan of operations (research proposal), or a set of abstract relations (scheme for classifying information). Learning outcomes in this area stress creative behaviors, with major emphasis on the formulation of *new* patterns or structures.	Writes a well organized theme Gives a well organized speech Writes a creative short story (or poem, or music) Proposes a plan for an experiment Integrates learning from different areas into a plan for solving a problem Formulates a new scheme for classifying objects (or events, or ideas)	Categorizes, combines, compiles, composes, creates, devises, designs, explains, generates, modifies, organizes, plans, rearranges, reconstructs, relates, reorganizes, revises, rewrites, summarizes, tells, writes
6. **Evaluation.** Evaluation is concerned with the ability to judge the value of material (statement, novel, poem, research report) for a given purpose. The judgments are to be based on definite criteria. These may be internal criteria (organization) or external criteria (relevance to the purpose) and the student may determine the criteria or be given them. Learning outcomes in this area are highest in the cognitive hierarchy because they contain elements of all of the other categories, plus conscious value judgments based on clearly defined criteria.	Judges the logical consistency of written material Judges the adequacy with which conclusions are supported by data Judges the value of a work (art, music, writing) by use of internal criteria Judges the value of a work (art, music, writing) by use of external standards of excellence	Appraises, compares, concludes, contrasts, criticizes, describes, discriminates, explains, justifies, interprets, relates, summarizes, supports

*Reprinted with permission of The Macmillan Company from *Stating Behavioral Objectives for Classroom Instruction* by Norman E. Gronlund. Copyright © 1970 by Norman E. Gronlund.

TABLE 1.2*

MAJOR CATEGORIES IN THE AFFECTIVE DOMAIN OF THE TAXONOMY OF EDUCATIONAL
OBJECTIVES (KRATHWOHL, 1964) EXAMPLES OF GENERAL INSTRUCTIONAL
OBJECTIVES AND BEHAVIORAL TERMS FOR THE AFFECTIVE DOMAIN OF THE TAXONOMY

Descriptions of the Major Categories in the Affective Domain	Illustrative General Instructional Objectives	Illustrative Behavioral Terms for Stating Specific Learning Outcomes
1. Receiving. Receiving refers to the student's willingness to attend to particular phenomena or stimuli (classroom activities, textbook, music, etc.). From a teaching standpoint, it is concerned with getting, holding, and directing the student's attention. Learning outcomes in this area range from the simple awareness that a thing exists to selective attention on the part of the learner. Receiving represents the lowest level of learning outcomes in the affective domain.	Listens attentively Shows awareness of the importance of learning Shows sensitivity to human needs and social problems Accepts differences of race and culture Attends closely to the classroom activities	Asks, chooses, describes, follows, gives, holds, identifies, locates, names, points to, selects, sits erect, replies, uses
2. Responding. Responding refers to active participation on the part of the student. At this level he not only attends to a particular phenomenon but also reacts to it in some way. Learning outcomes in this area may emphasize acquiescence in responding (reads assigned material), willingness to respond (voluntarily reads beyond assignment), or satisfaction in responding (reads for pleasure or enjoyment). The higher levels of this category include those instructional objectives that are commonly classified under "interests"; that is, those that stress the seeking out and enjoyment of particular activities.	Completes assigned homework Obeys school rules Participates in class discussion Completes laboratory work Volunteers for special tasks Shows interest in subject Enjoys helping others	Answers, assists, complies, conforms, discusses, greets, helps, labels, performs, practices, presents, reads, recites, reports, selects, tells, writes
3. Valuing. Valuing is concerned with the worth or value a student attaches to a particular object, phenomenon, or behavior. This ranges in degree from the more simple acceptance of a value (desires to improve group skills) to the more complex level of commitment (assumes responsibility for the effective	Demonstrates belief in the democratic process Appreciates good literature (art or music) Appreciates the role of science (or other subjects) in everyday life	Completes, describes, differentiates, explains, follows, forms, initiates, invites, joins, justifies, proposes, reads, reports, selects, shares, studies, works

Taxonomy Categories and Definitions	Illustrative General Instructional Objectives	Illustrative Behavioral Terms
functioning of the group). Valuing is based on the internalization of a set of specified values, but clues to these values are expressed in the student's overt behavior. Learning outcomes in this area are concerned with behavior that is consistent and stable enough to make the value clearly identifiable. Instructional objectives that are commonly classified under "attitudes" and "appreciation" would fall into this category.	Shows concern for the welfare of others Demonstrates problem-solving attitude Demonstrates commitment to social improvement	
4. Organization. Organization is concerned with bringing together different values, resolving conflicts between them, and beginning the building of an internally consistent value system. Thus the emphasis is on comparing, relating, and synthesizing values. Learning outcomes may be concerned with the conceptualization of a value (recognizes the responsibility of each individual for improving human relations) or with the organization of a value system (develops a vocational plan that satisfies his need for both economic security and social service). Instructional objectives relating to the development of a philosophy of life would fall into this category.	Recognizes the need for balance between freedom and responsibility in a democracy Recognizes the role of systematic planning in solving problems Accepts responsibility for his own behavior Understands and accepts his own strengths and limitations Formulates a life plan in harmony with his abilities, interests, and beliefs	Adheres, alters, arranges, combines, compares, completes, defends, explains, generalizes, identifies, integrates, modifies, orders, organizes, prepares, relates, synthesizes
5. Characterization by a Value or Value Complex. At this level of the affective domain, the individual has a value system that has controlled his behavior for a sufficiently long time for him to have developed a characteristic "life style." Thus the behavior is pervasive, consistent, and predictable. Learning outcomes at this level cover a broad range of activities, but the major emphasis is on the fact that the behavior is typical or characteristic of the student. Instructional objectives that are concerned with the student's general patterns of adjustment (personal, social, emotional) would be appropriate here.	Displays safety consciousness Demonstrates self-reliance in working independently Practices cooperation in group activities Uses objective approach in problem solving Demonstrates industry, punctuality and self-discipline Maintains good health habits	Acts, discriminates, displays, influences, listens, modifies, performs, practices, proposes, qualifies, questions, revises, serves, solves, uses, verifies

*Reprinted with permission of The Macmillan Company from *Stating Behavioral Objectives for Classroom Instruction* by Norman E. Gronlund. Copyright © 1970 by Norman E. Gronlund.

TABLE 1.3*

*EXAMPLES OF GENERAL INSTRUCTIONAL OBJECTIVES AND
BEHAVIORAL TERMS FOR THE PSYCHOMOTOR DOMAIN
OF THE TAXONOMY*

Taxonomy Categories	Illustrative General Instructional Objectives	Illustrative Behavioral Terms for Stating Specific Learning Outcomes
(Development of categories in this domain is still under-way)	Writes smoothly and legibly Draws accurate reproduction of a picture (or map, biology specimen, etc.) Sets up laboratory equipment quickly and correctly Types with speed and accuracy Operates a sewing machine skill-fully Operates a power saw safely and skillfully Performs skillfully on the violin Performs a dance step correctly Demonstrates correct form in swimming Demonstrates skill in driving an automobile Repairs an electric motor quickly and effectively Creates new ways of performing (creative dance, etc.)	Assembles, builds, calibrates, changes, cleans, composes, connects, constructs, corrects, creates, designs, dismantles, drills, fastens, fixes, follows, grinds, grips, hammers, heats, hooks, identifies, locates, makes, manipulates, mends, mixes, nails, paints, sands, saws, sharpens, sets, sews, sketches, starts, stirs, uses, weighs, wraps

*Reprinted with permission of The Macmillan Company from *Stating Behavioral Objectives for Classroom Instruction* by Norman E. Gronlund. Copyright © 1970 by Norman E. Gronlund.

In summary, the *Taxonomy of Educational Objectives* provides a three-domain scheme (cognitive, affective, and psychomotor) for classifying all possible instructional objectives. Each domain is sub-divided into a series·of categories that are arranged in hierarchical order—from simple to complex. A review of these categories and the illustrative objectives and behavioral terms accompanying them (Tables 1.1 to 1.3) should aid in (1) identifying objectives for a particular instructional unit, (2) stating objectives at the proper level of generality, (3) defining objectives in the most relevant behavioral terms, (4) checking on the comprehensiveness of a list of objectives, and (5) communicating with others concerning the nature and level of learning outcomes included in a list of objectives.[35]

By identifying clearly and precisely those tasks which they wish students to perform, those products that they desire them to create, those behaviors

[35]Gronlund, *Stating Behavioral Objectives*, p. 24.

that they desire them to demonstrate, or those experiences in which they wish them to engage, in order to achieve objectives they consider important, teachers can determine the degree to which they are helping students to learn important relationships and concepts rather than simply to exercise their memories. For example, if a teacher wishes students to understand why the American colonists revolted against Great Britain, to *list* from memory three immediate causes of the American Revolution doesn't require very much in the way of abstract reasoning and doesn't appear likely to bring about the understanding the teacher wishes to encourage. On the other hand, asking them to *tell why* the three were immediate causes requires them to explain the reasons behind their choice and appears more likely to promote understanding. A category system, such as the one just described, which includes a list of verbs in each category that lend themselves to clearer and more explicitly stated instructional objectives, can serve as a checklist against which to determine and balance the different kinds of tasks, mental and otherwise, that teachers require of students.

3. Clear and precise statements of instructional objectives enable teachers to evaluate whether or not the desired outcomes of instruction have been attained by students. This assumes, of course, that teachers want their students to be able to do something after a certain amount of instruction is completed that they could not do before instruction began. To determine whether instructional efforts have been successful or not in this regard, therefore, teachers must determine the degree to which students have changed after instruction has occurred. If they have not changed as the teacher had hoped (that is, if they cannot perform as anticipated), then further instruction is required. (Modification of existing instructional procedures may also be necessary.) But teachers cannot determine whether students can or cannot perform a given task or produce a particular product unless they can evaluate them in some way or another. And it is very difficult to construct or select test items to measure vague, unclear statements of instructional objectives. It is very difficult to prepare test items for instructional objectives which contain verbs like "to appreciate" or "to grasp the significance of" unless the evaluator has some idea of what "appreciation" or "significance" means. As Taba remarked, "the often-referred-to intangibility of some objectives is nothing but a smoke screen for lack of clarity."[36] Once again it is important to emphasize that adequately stated instructional objectives indicate clearly *both* the content to be learned and the process to be engaged in. For example, here is an explicitly stated instructional objective, together with one of many test items which might be designed to measure that objective:

[36]Taba, *Curriculum Development*, p. 199.

Instructional Objective: Given examples of inductive and deductive reasoning students identify which are examples of deductive reasoning and which are examples of inductive reasoning, and then explain why they are examples.

Test Item: "For every action, there is an opposite and equal reaction." This is Newton's Third Law of Thermodynamics. If he arrived at this conclusion after reading Aristotle, without any experimentation, this would represent an example of:

a. inductive reasoning
b. deductive reasoning
c. both inductive and deductive reasoning
d. neither inductive nor deductive reasoning

Explain why you selected the answer you did.

Here is a second example:

Instructional Objective: Given reading material containing the views of Alexander Hamilton and Thomas Jefferson with respect to the powers of the national government, students compare and contrast in writing their points of view on the issue and then explain what importance and implications, if any, the issue has today.

Test Item: The first paragraph below is quoted from an Inaugural address by Thomas Jefferson; the second paragraph is taken from one of the essays in *The Federalist*, written by Alexander Hamilton. Read these quotations for the purpose of identifying the major controversial issue inherent in them. Then write a brief essay in which you compare and contrast the views of each on this issue, and then indicate the current importance and implications of this issue.

"About to enter, fellow-citizens, on the exercise of duties which comprehend everything dear and valuable to you, it is proper you should understand what I deem the essential principles of our Government, and consequently those which ought to shape its Administration. I will compress them within the narrowest compass they will bear, stating the general principle, but not all its limitations. Equal and exact justice to all men, of whatever state or persuasion, religious or political; peace, commerce, and honest friendship with all nations, entangling alliances with none; the support of the State governments in all their rights, as the most competent administrations for our domestic concerns and the surest bulwarks against anti-republican tendencies; the preservation of the General Government in its whole constitutional vigor, as the sheet anchor of our peace at home and safety abroad; a jealous care of the right of election by the people—a mild and safe corrective of abuses which are lopped by the sword of revolution where peaceable remedies are unprovided; absolute acquiescence in the decisions of the majority, the vital principle of republics, from which is no appeal but to force, the vital principle and immediate parent of despotism; a well-disciplined militia, our best reliance in peace and for the first moments of war, till regulars may relieve them; the supremacy of the civil over the military authority; economy in the public expense, that labor may be lightly burthened; the honest payment of our debts and sacred preservation of the public faith; encouragement of agriculture, and of commerce as its handmaid; the diffusion of information and arraignment of all abuses at the bar of the public reason; freedom of the press; the freedom of person under the protection of the *habeas corpus*, and trial by juries impartially selected. These principles form the bright constellation which has gone before us and guided our steps through an age of revolution and reformation."

"The result of these observations to an intelligent mind must be clearly this, that if it be possible at any rate to construct a federal government capable of regulating the common concerns, and preserving the general tranquility, it must be founded, as to the objects committed to its care, upon the reverse of the principle contended for by the opponents of the proposed constitution. It must carry its agency to the persons of the citizens. It must stand in need of no intermediate legislations; but must itself be empowered to employ the arm of the ordinary magistrate to execute its own resolutions. The majesty of the national authority must be manifested through the medium of the courts of justice. The government of the union, like that of each state, must be able to address itself immediately to the hopes and fears of individuals; and to attract to its support those passions which have the strongest influence upon the human heart. It must, in short, possess all the means, and have a right to resort to all the methods, of executing the powers with which it is entrusted, that are possessed and exercised by the governments of the particular states."[37]

Clear and precise statements of instructional objectives, therefore, suggest certain kinds of test items, such as the examples presented above. By correctly identifying the one statement as an example of deductive reasoning and being able to explain why it is such, students can demonstrate their achievement of the first instructional objective—their accomplishment of the desired performance. When they are able to write an essay comparing and contrasting Hamilton's and Jefferson's viewpoints on the powers of the national government, they fulfill the task desired in the second objective. Thus valid test items are intimately related to clear and explicit statements of instructional objectives.

4. Clear and precise statements of instructional objectives are a con-

[37]B. S. Bloom (ed.), *Taxonomy of Educational Objectives, Handbook I: Cognitive Domain* (New York: McKay, 1956), pp. 115–116. Used by permission of David McKay Company, Inc.

siderable help to students. By defining as precisely as they can what behaviors they expect students to demonstrate, what products they want them
to produce, or what kinds of experiences they want them to have, teachers
can help students focus their attention on those tasks, performances, or experiences that will help them learn most effectively. When students are
clear as to where they are going, they are often better able to determine
which actions of their own are appropriate to the task at hand.

A MODEL
FOR PLANNING AND INSTRUCTION

It is difficult to set down instructional objectives without also considering subject matter, learning activities, teaching strategies, and evaluative
measures. This is due to the interactive relationship that exists among each
of these elements. As we have seen, clearly stated instructional objectives
consist of both subject matter and process. Hence a teacher must of necessity think about the *particular* subject matter he wants students to study,
the *particular* learning activities in which they'll be engaged, the *particular*
teaching strategies he will use to so engage them, and the *particular* evaluative devices of various types he will use to determine how well and to what
extent the objectives have been or are being attained. The actual preparation of teaching plans, therefore, is a continual back and forth affair.

The process, however, is difficult to describe. A teacher may, through
reading, discussion, suggestions from students, or other learning, have
some particular ideas in mind that he believes are important for students
to learn. Further reading and discussion may substantiate his belief. He
might draw up an outline of content which he could use to develop these
ideas. Then a tentative list of instructional objectives might be prepared.
He then might begin to write up his plans in unit or lesson form. (Planning will be discussed in detail in Chapter 8.) With his content outline and
objectives in front of him, he may then discover that he does not have sufficient materials, time, space, etc., to be able to accomplish certain of his
objectives. Hence, he revises his list of objectives. This in turn, causes him
to change his content outline. Discussion with and suggestions from students may indicate a need for further revision.

The important point to understand is that there is, of necessity, an interaction between the formulation of objectives and the selection of subject
matter, learning activities, teaching strategies, and evaluative measures
needed to implement and assess the attainment of these objectives.

Let us illustrate this inter-relationship by discussing a bit further the
connection between objectives and learning activities. We have seen that
social studies objectives are often classified in terms of knowledge, attitu-

dinal, value, and skill objectives to ensure balance and comprehensiveness. A social studies teacher who desires to be comprehensive must ask himself what he wants to accomplish in each of these categories. What knowledge does he want students to acquire and understand? What kinds of skills does he want them to master? What kinds of attitudes and values does he want them to develop?

Notice, however, that objectives in each of these various categories cannot be attained without considering the learning activities in which students are to be engaged.

Students cannot deal with a particular subject or amount of data without engaging in some mental or physical process at the same time. One cannot learn something about economics, for example, unless one learns it *in some way*. One cannot learn to think unless one thinks about *something*. One does not become skilled in working with other people unless one works with them on *some task*.

Teachers need to concern themselves, therefore, not only with *what* they expect students to learn, but also *how* they expect them to learn it.

Knowledge alone, whether it be knowledge *of* (e.g., the reasons why people revolt), or knowledge *how* (e.g., to play a musical instrument) does not in and of itself, encourage students to think; does not change attitudes and predispositions; does not build certain kinds of skills. These objectives are achieved primarily by engaging students with content—by having them *do something* with the knowledge they acquire. In short, objectives represent the *ends* of instruction—the knowledge a teacher hopes his students will acquire and understand, the attitudes they will develop, the skills they will master. The *means* by which he helps them attain these objectives, however, can vary tremendously. Reading books, magazines, and newspapers, interviewing people, listening to lectures or records, and watching films, filmstrips, and slides are all possibilities. So are such activities as diagramming, outlining, library research, reporting, discussing, role-playing, drawing, mapping, hypothesizing, analyzing or generalizing. The possibilities are varied and numerous. (The importance of this means-ends relationship will be discussed further in Chapter 4.)

Any teacher concerned with effective instruction, therefore, must do more than just identify his objectives, no matter how clearly he states them. He must also perform a number of additional tasks, all of which are basic to effective planning and instruction in social studies and other subjects. As mentioned,

1. He must decide on the objectives he hopes to attain by the end of each course that he teaches, and of particular units within each of those courses. But also,
2. He must select or prepare appropriate diagnostic evaluation devices in order

to determine the kinds of understandings, attitudes, and skills students already possess that may help or hinder the attainment of the objectives;

3. He must select appropriate subject matter that will help students acquire the understandings he considers important;
4. He must select or design appropriate learning activities in which to engage students to help them attain certain desired attitudes, skills, and values;
5. He must select or design appropriate teaching strategies by which to help students engage in these learning activities;
6. He must select or prepare appropriate evaluation devices to determine how well and to what extent his objectives have been attained by his students.

The overall sequence of these tasks is shown in the simple model presented in Figure 1.2. The remaining chapters of this book discuss each of these tasks in considerable detail.

Guidelines to the Writing of Instructional Objectives

As a guide to formulating instructional objectives, the following criteria are suggested, many of which are explained more fully by Sawin.[38]

- Instructional objectives should provide for the student's continual development in the areas of knowledge, values, attitudes, and skills.
- Instructional objectives should indicate clearly what is expected of students in terms of both behavior and content. Too often instructional objectives are written so that they only suggest the content to be covered without at the same time indicating what is to be done *with* this content. Sometimes, however, the reverse happens. Only a generalized description of behavior is given (e.g., developing an ability to analyze data) without indicating to what specific content the behavior is to apply:
- Instructional objectives should be both intellectually and emotionally attainable by students.
- Instructional objectives should be general enough to indicate the full scope of that which a teacher wants a student to achieve yet also be as precise as possible so that the specific kinds of changes desired in students are clear.
- Instructional objectives should be worded as simply and clearly as possible.
- Instructional objectives should be precise enough to indicate the kinds of learning experiences in which students need to be involved in order to attain different behaviors. Learning activities designed to help students acquire information, for example, may not be suitable for developing attitudes. A realization of this fact should help teachers to plan the kinds of learning experiences that will at the same time allow them to learn new facts, under-

[38]Enoch I. Sawin, *Evaluation and the Work of the Teacher* (Belmont, Calif.: Wadsworth, 1969), pp. 59–63.

FIGURE 1.2
A Model for Planning and Instruction

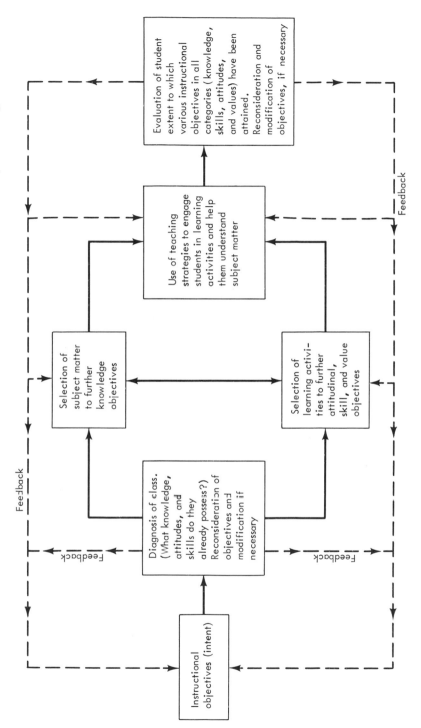

stand new concepts, improve their thinking skills, and affect their attitudes and values.

- Instructional objectives should be so formulated that it is possible to conceive of a way by which to evaluate whether they have been attained. However, not everything that is worth trying to teach can at present be adequately evaluated (e.g., concern for the rights of others). It would be less than desirable to argue that evaluation devices must be available before attempting to develop objectives in various areas.

- Related objectives should be combined whenever possible in order to avoid duplicate (and overlong) lists of instructional objectives.

- Lastly, objectives should indicate the direction in which changes in students are desired. As Sawin indicates, however, they need not suggest "*complete* attainment, since relatively few educational objectives can be attained in an absolutely complete sense. There is almost always more than can be learned."[39] Hence, once again, the argument that objectives may need to be written at varying levels of specificity, depending on purposes, time available for attainment, and audience.

SUMMARY

This chapter dealt with the nature of instructional objectives. Its major thesis was that teachers must be clear about the objectives they wish to attain if they are to plan and assess their instruction effectively.

Two basic assumptions of the author were set forth—that education changes people and that teaching, if carefully planned and executed, can produce significant changes in learners. A distinction was made between possible and desirable changes, with some sources from which desirable changes can be determined being suggested. It was pointed out that the changes in students that a teacher desires and tries to bring about constitute his instructional objectives.

A distinction was made between instructional objectives and educational goals. Several categories of social studies goals and objectives were described, and examples in each of these categories, along with a supporting rationale for each example, were presented. The importance of a rationale was argued.

Various ways of stating instructional objectives were illustrated and the degree of specificity needed in statements of instructional objectives discussed. Several examples of clearly written, yet significant, objectives were presented. The value of clearly stated instructional objectives was argued and the relationship of objectives to subject matter, learning activities, teaching strategies, and evaluative measures suggested and diagrammed.

[39]*Ibid.*, p. 63.

Lastly, guidelines that teachers can use to write clear and precise statements of instructional objectives were suggested. In general, the relationship between clear and precise statements of instructional objectives and decisions on instructional procedures was emphasized, and *clarity* was stressed.

EXERCISES*

I. Do the following objectives indicate an act the learner is to perform, or a product he is to produce, in order to demonstrate that he has achieved (at least to some degree) the objective?

	YES	NO
a. To understand three causes of the Spanish-American War.	____	____
b. To know the reasons why President Harry S. Truman sent American troops, under United Nations auspices, to Korea.	____	____
c. To *really* understand why the League of Nations failed to keep the peace.	____	____
d. To participate as a member of a panel in a discussion of the causes of alienation in the United States today.	____	____
e. To encourage other students, verbally or by gestures, to offer their opinions during class discussions.	____	____
f. To appreciate the contributions of minority groups.	____	____
g. To think critically.	____	____
h. To suggest several (more than four) reasons why some people in the United States are opposed to busing as a means of bringing about school desegregation.	____	____
i. To visit a factory and report on one's impressions.	____	____

*The answers to many of these end-of-chapter Exercises can be found on pages 397–98.

II. Following are several statements of instructional objectives. Place an X in the space provided after each of the objectives that indicate *clearly* what students will be expected to *do* (i.e., think, feel, or act) in order to provide at least some evidence that they have achieved the objective to some degree. Write the verb which indicates what students are to do on the third line following each objective.

	CLEAR	NOT CLEAR	WRITE VERB HERE
a. Given a list of reasons offered by the Joint Chiefs of Staff for U.S. involvement in Vietnam, students evaluate each reason. (EXAMPLE)		X	Evaluate
b. Students develop logical approaches to the solving of personal problems within three class periods of 50 minutes.			
c. Given two or more lists of information, students indicate correctly which items in the first list are associated with the various items in the second list, with no more than one error occurring.			
d. Given a set of events (one of which is identified as the event to be explained), students give a plausible and logically sound explanation of the chains of cause-and-effect relationships that resulted in the occurrence of the event.			

e. Given a situation in which he is encouraged to express his own thoughts, the student responds to statements of other students and the teacher in ways that the teacher judges to be fair toward the people involved and that show recognition and acceptance of the merits of different ways of life and points of view. The student challenges any derogatory or belittling

	NOT	WRITE
CLEAR	CLEAR	VERB HERE

statements about people of different cultures or about people who exhibit unusual behavior. ____ ____ _____

f. Students know *well* the names and dates of office of at least 14 Presidents of the United States. ____ ____ _____

g. When discussing various countries of the world, students ask questions pertaining to people and how they live more often than about impersonal matters like the size, population, or physical features of the countries. ____ ____ _____

III. Listed below are a number of instructional objectives. Place an X after those which you believe require the student to do something more complex than just recall or recognize information. Assume that the students have previously studied or been exposed to the material to which the objective refers.

	Requires students to do more than recall or recognize	
		WRITE
YES	NO	VERB HERE

a. Locate on a map of the U.S. seven towns previously identified as being important during the colonial period of American history. ____ ____ _____

b. Explain why, in your opinion, the towns located on the map in (a) above were important. (These reasons not previously discussed by teacher or text.) ____ ____ _____

c. Describe at least five things a Hopi Indian boy might do on a January day, after reading a description of Hopi activities. ____ ____ _____

d. Ask three questions of a guest speaker which will require him to defend a position he has previously expressed. ____ ____ _____

Requires students to do more than recall or recognize

	YES	NO	WRITE VERB HERE
e. Tell the meaning of the first sentence in the Preamble to the U.S. Constitution in your own words.	____	____	_____
f. Judge which of two diagrams more accurately explains the concept "division-of-labor."	____	____	_____
g. Choose the one of four dates which does not belong in a given group, and tell why you think it does not.	____	____	_____
h. Hypothesize what might have happened if the United States had not become involved in Vietnam.	____	____	_____
i. Compare the types of architecture developed in Greece and Rome by identifying several (at least six) similarities you notice in pictures of Greek and Roman temples.	____	____	_____
j. Define the concept of "values" as given in a standard dictionary.	____	____	_____
k. Describe the conditions under which many slaves were brought to the United States from Africa during the seventeenth and eighteenth centuries after reading a description of these conditions in the text.	____	____	_____
l. Name in order all the vice-presidents of the Federal Republic of West Germany.	____	____	_____
m. List five of the chief exports of Chile.	____	____	_____

Requires students to do more than recall or recognize

	YES	NO	WRITE VERB HERE

n. Design a poster illustrating the dangers involved in cigarette smoking.

o. Plan and implement a two-week campaign to clean up the school grounds.

p. Apply previously learned ideas about the discovery of water in uninhabited areas by suggesting what might happen if water were discovered in parts of the Sahara Desert where none exists at present.

IV. Listed below are several different types of instructional objectives. Place the letter of the correct category from Column A in front of the objective or objectives in Column B that the category *primarily* describes. If you feel that a given objective might logically fall within *more* than one category, place the *letters* of the appropriate categories in the space provided.

A

B

The acquisition of knowledge (K)

The development of thinking skills (T)

The development of research skills (R)

The development of social skills (S)

The development of attitudes (A)

The development of values (V)

T **a.** Given two or more different samples of information, students correctly state differences and similarities. (EXAMPLE)

_____ **b.** Given two or more lists of information, students indicate correctly which items in the first list are associated with various items in the second list.

_____ **c.** Given a filmstrip on the people of Thailand, students make correct statements that represent accurate information that can be obtained from it that pertains to the Thai people.

_____ **d.** Given a situation that encourages free expression, students make statements that describe their own values.

_____ **e.** Students indicate comprehension of the meaning of the concept *cooperation*.

_____ **f.** Given a situation in which they are encouraged to express their own thoughts, students respond to statements of other students and the teacher in ways that the teacher judges to be fair toward the people involved and that show recognition and acceptance of the merits of different ways of life and points of view.

_____ **g.** Given a detailed set of facts, students state valid generalizations that they have not been given previously, and, when asked, provide the sources and limitations of the generalizations.

_____ **h.** Students indicate an interest in the causes and effects of poverty in the United States by checking out of the school library a number of articles and books on poverty.

_____ **i.** Students plan, research, and present a group report.

_____ **j.** Students locate information correctly in a card catalog.

_____ **k.** Students apply information in one situation to another new and different situation.

V. Which of the test questions below would give us evidence that students had attained, to some degree, the desired objective?
Objective: Given a list of recent Supreme Court decisions, students can explain in their own words what the decisions mean, can identify situations in which the decisions would apply, and can hypothesize as to what effect(s) the decisions might have on at least three different minority groups within the continental United States.

Test Questions	Appropriate	Not Appropriate
a. Write the name of each of the justices of the Supreme Court.	_____	_____
b. Tell which of the following Supreme Court decisions would apply if a minority individual is refused admission to a crowded restaurant.	_____	_____

Test Questions	*Appropriate*	*Not Appropriate*

c. Summarize in your own words what each of the following Supreme Court decisions mean, identify which (if any) would apply should a particular school district in a given state refuse to integrate its schools, tell why you think they would apply, and then make a statement in which you predict what may happen to the students and officials involved.   _____   _____

d. List the steps a court case must go through before the Supreme Court will consider it.   _____   _____

VI. Try to write some statements of objectives of your own, using the guidelines suggested in this chapter. Prepare two or three examples in the categories of knowledge, thinking skills, research skills, attitudes, and values. Compare your statements with those of your classmates. Which ones are most clear? Be prepared to defend the *significance* of your objectives.

VII. Prepare one or two possible test questions for each of your objectives. What difficulties do you encounter?

VIII. Now try to write one or more learning experiences (I.e., some activity for students to engage in, experience to have, or product to produce) that you think would help students attain one of the objectives you prepared in VI. Have one or more of your classmates look *only* at the activity and then tell you what *kind* of objective it seems to be directed toward.

IX. Look at a number of commercially available textbooks (you may have to look at the accompanying teacher's manual) for use at a particular grade level in which you are interested. What objectives does the author specify for students? What categories does he appear to emphasize? Underemphasize? Omit? If he does not state his objectives, what do you surmise are his purposes? Would you use any of the books you've reviewed? Why or why not?

DIAGNOSTIC EVALUATION

This chapter deals with the nature and use of informal diagnostic tools. Once the instructional objectives for a given course, unit, or lesson have been set forth, teachers need to determine what knowledge, skills, or attitudes students possess that may facilitate or hinder (or perhaps make unnecessary) the attaining of these objectives. To gain this information, assessment prior to and during instruction is necessary.

The first section of this chapter defines what is meant by the term "diagnosis," discusses briefly how diagnostic data can be used, explains what is meant by diagnostic, formative, and summative evaluation, and distinguishes between antecedent, transaction, and outcome conditions.

The second section of the chapter discusses some of the diagnostic tools that teachers can use to gain insight into the kinds of information, skills, and attitudes that students possess.

The third section briefly considers the major limitations of informal diagnostic devices, and summarizes why it is important for teachers to be aware of and use a variety of informal diagnostic tools before and during classroom instruction.

When you have finished reading this chapter, therefore, you should be able to do the following:

- *explain* what the terms "diagnostic evaluation" and "diagnostic device" mean;
- *distinguish* in a general sense between diagnostic, formative, and summative evaluation;
- *suggest* several (at least five) ways in which diagnostic data might be used;
- *describe* how you would use (orally or in writing) at least five different kinds of informal devices for purposes of diagnostic evaluation in your classroom and *use* those devices;

- *describe* the major limitations of informal diagnostic devices, and how to counter these limitations;
- *give* at least three reasons why the use of informal diagnostic tools before and during instruction is important.

Clear and significant objectives are just a starting point. Effective teaching also involves determining as far as possible what *already existing* attitudes, interests, perceptions, beliefs, knowledge, and experience students possess that will help or hinder them in attaining the desired objectives, or make the attainment of these objectives via instruction unnecessary. This kind of information is usually referred to as *diagnostic data*, and the process of obtaining it as *diagnostic evaluation*.

Many of us forget that the nature of the classroom environment is a powerful factor in determining the success or failure of instruction. Effective classroom instruction involves more than just a teacher presenting information, no matter how significant and interesting that information may be. Learning does not occur merely because a teacher talks and students listen (or even if he inquires, questions, and discusses). Too many other forces are at work in the classroom. Student attitudes, beliefs, interests, and past experiences, group values, the teacher's personality, teaching style, teacher-student and student-teacher relationships and perceptions, all can have a marked effect on the effectiveness of any teacher's efforts. All individuals have certain personality characteristics which may affect their success or failure in certain endeavors, and thus their motivation to continue these endeavors. This is especially true in school. All students bring to the classroom a variety of feelings, values, and concepts about school, books, teachers, and themselves. Some students are warm and engaging; others hostile, rebellious or withdrawn. Some harbor positive feelings toward teachers and schools; others the reverse. Some are independent in nature; others more dependent. Some are outgoing, others withdrawn. Some make friends easily; others have difficulty in relating to their peers. Any classroom represents a complex network of many social interactions, which can encourage or discourage a student's motivation to learn.

The more a teacher knows about his own and his students' perceptions, attitudes, feelings, beliefs, values, abilities, and past experiences, the more he will be able to use this knowledge to modify his instructional efforts and design learning experiences to help all students make the most of their abilities. Others have made a similar point:

> If the schools are to help our children maximize their abilities and become effective citizens, teachers must know more about their pupils than their current IQ's and their achievement levels in various academic areas. Although the teacher may not be able fully to

control all the attitudes and relations that influence his pupils and the classroom climate, he should be able to identify and understand them. Also, if he is to create and maintain a classroom environment that supports learning, he should plan and execute ways of modifying them.[1]

In order to identify and understand some of the attitudes and relations which influence students and affect the climate of the classroom in which they work, teachers must obtain as much data as they can about students so that reasonable inferences can be made as to what their attitudes and relations are. In order to determine student attitudes, interests, and abilities, their feelings, thoughts, and actions must be assessed at frequent intervals. Different kinds of evaluation, therefore, become necessary.

KINDS OF EVALUATION

Evaluation of student attitude, progress, and achievement can, and should, occur at many places, depending on what kinds of information a teacher wants to obtain. Evaluation which takes place prior to beginning a unit of instruction is called *diagnostic evaluation* or often simply *diagnosis*. Such pre-instructional evaluation can help teachers obtain information as to what kinds of attitudes, skills, and knowledge students *already possess* that will encourage, limit, or prevent teacher and student efforts to achieve desired objectives. For example, a teacher may find that many students *lack* certain prerequisites necessary to understand or perform certain things he has planned for them to learn. Students differ widely in knowledge, ability, and attitude toward learning. Goodlad and Anderson,[2] for example, found that some second graders read at a fourth-grade level. Balow[3] illustrated that some fifth graders could read on a ninth-grade level while others could only handle second-grade material. Teachers may find that many students lack certain prerequisites of knowledge or skill necessary to understand certain things, or to perform certain operations. For example, if a student does not understand the meaning of the concepts of "revolution," "cause," and "effect," he will not be able to analyze the causes and effects of a particular revolution. If another student does not know the meaning of the terms "latitude" and "longitude," he will have difficulty finding the

[1] Robert Fox, Margaret Barron Lusyki, and Richard Schmuck, *Diagnosing Classroom Learning Environments* (Chicago: Science Research Associates, 1966), pp. 1–2.

[2] J. I. Goodlad and R. H. Anderson, *The Non-Graded Elementary School* (New York: Harcourt Brace Jovanovich, 1959).

[3] I. H. Balow, "Does Homogeneous Grouping Give Homogeneous Groups?" *Elementary School Journal*, Jan. 1962, pp. 28–32.

location of various places on a map. If a student lacks the ability to synthesize data into some kind of organized form, he will have trouble preparing a research report on a given topic. If a student doesn't know the difference between verifiable and unverifiable data, he will be unable to distinguish rationally between facts and opinions.

Teachers might also discover that some students hold certain attitudes which, unless dealt with directly, make them unable to consider particular issues rationally, or work at particular tasks. If a student is not accepted by his classmates, he may be unwilling to work on a group research project; if another holds certain prejudices, he may refuse to cooperate with specific others; if a third perceives certain classroom activities as boring and irrelevant to his needs, he may refuse to take part in them.

Diagnostic evaluation can help a teacher discover instances like or similar to the above. If certain prerequisites necessary to learning a given task have not been acquired, the teacher can reorganize his instructional sequence in order to help students learn these prerequisites. If certain attitudes inimical to learning are discovered, the teacher can attempt, if possible, to remedy the causes of these attitudes. If such remedy is beyond the teacher's capabilities or qualifications, further assistance can be sought from appropriate psychological or medical sources.

To the contrary, a teacher might discover that some students have *already* acquired certain of the skills, knowledge, or attitudes that he planned to develop, making further instruction in these areas unnecessary. Some students, for example, may already understand why the American Revolution occurred. Others may be able to explain more clearly than the teacher how to use longitude and latitude to locate places on a globe. These students, perhaps, can pursue more advanced work, or different material, or topics of special interest or need.

Many students have acquired and understand far more than many teachers seem willing to recognize. The point to stress is that unless teachers are aware of prior student knowledge, skills, and attitudes, much of the effort they expend in their day-to-day classroom activities may be ineffective, unnecessary, or both. What bores one student may challenge a second; what one accomplishes with ease may cause another considerable difficulty. It is unrealistic, not to mention unwise, for teachers to assume that all the students in a particular class are at the same level of ability or point of departure, either mentally, emotionally, or physically.

Diagnostic evaluation can also occur *during* a unit of instruction. The use of diagnostic tools during instruction can help teachers determine the degree to which certain *non-instructional factors*, such as attitudes toward the teacher, personal habits, relationships with parents, or peer rivalry are affecting student progress toward attaining desired objectives. For example, a student may have no place where he can study at home and thus be unable to complete assigned homework. The teacher may unconsciously be using certain words or gestures that are offensive to some students. Certain students may come to school without adequate sleep, making it difficult for them to attend to lessons. Perception of assigned work as continually beyond their capabilities may cause others to quit trying. Fear of failure may cause still others not to try at all.

Diagnostic evaluation in this sense should be distinguished from formative evaluation. *Formative evaluation*[4] is evaluation that also is conducted during (rather than before or after) a unit of instruction, but with a different purpose in mind. The purpose of formative evaluation is to help teachers determine how well students are progressing toward attaining desired objectives, and provide teachers and learners with *specific* feedback as to the degree to which students have mastered certain skills or knowledge studied or presented up to this point, and if they are not understanding the material, to pinpoint exactly where in a unit they are having difficulty.

For example, suppose that a teacher and class planned a unit of study on the American Revolution to last approximately four weeks. The unit includes material dealing with the nature of the leaders of the Revolution, the underlying and immediate causes of the event, effects of the Revolution, and speculation by various scholars as to whether or not it could have been avoided. The class has been engaged with the material for about eight days, reading about and discussing the underlying and immediate causes of the event. Several students, however, are having trouble understanding some of the underlying causes, particularly the concept of "mercantilism." The teacher, therefore, prepares a set of questions, *all* of which have to do *only* with the underlying causes of the Revolution. He thus hopes to pinpoint exactly what it is in the material that is causing the students' difficulty. Once he identifies what it is that is causing the trouble, he can take action accordingly. Various learning experiences and/or instructional procedures can be modified, deleted, or continued as seems appropriate. Previously studied subject matter, if necessary, can be repeated or developed in a different way in order to clear up student misconceptions or lack of understanding. Materials, procedures, or activities that are too easy or too difficult can be identified and corrections made.

Diagnostic evaluation is most helpful in obtaining insight into rather general skills, attitudes, and characteristics of students, such as how students feel about activities which occur in the classroom, or inter-student perceptions and power relationships. Formative evaluation, on the other hand, is designed specifically for a *particular* unit of instruction and is in-

---

[4]Michael Scriven, *The Methodology of Evaluation*, AERA Monograph Series on Curriculum Evaluation, No. 1, 1967, pp. 39–83.

tended to locate *exactly* where in the unit the student is experiencing difficulty.

Lastly, evaluation can occur at the *end* of a unit of instruction in order to determine how much and how well students have learned and to what extent desired objectives have been attained. This kind of evaluation is referred to as *summative evaluation*. It will be discussed in considerable detail in Chapter 7.

A common assumption, as noted by several recent observers,[5] of many teachers is that any assessment of student learning is performed only upon completion of a unit (or other prescribed amount) of instruction using some variation of a pencil-and-paper test. This asssumption is erroneous, not to mention terribly limiting in its view of the possible range and purposes of evaluation in the social studies. Assessment of student attitude, progress, and achievement needs to occur before, during, and after instruction, using a variety of evaluative devices and procedures.

Stake[6] has presented a model which summarizes this three-part conception of evaluation. For teachers to make rational decisions concerning variations in instructional procedures, changes in subject matter, modification of learning activities and teaching strategies, or provision for remedial or advanced work, they require evaluation information concerning "Antecedent," "Transaction," and "Outcome" conditions.

Antecedent conditions refer to "all the responses that are carried to the educational situation by the student and teacher participants and which may have an effect on the outcomes."[7] Examples of interest here would include the attitudes of students towards social studies as a subject, and the feelings of students towards teacher and peers (especially toward members of minority groups and people of other cultures).

Transaction conditions refer to feelings, attitudes, and values associated with ". . . planned interactions among persons in the educational setting for the purpose of achieving educational outcomes."[8] Examples of such transaction conditions would include the social climate of the classroom and the emotional involvement of teachers and pupils in classroom activities.

---

[5]See Robert F. Stake, "The Countenance of Educational Evaluation," *Teachers College Record*, April 1967, pp. 523–540; Roland F. Payette and C. Benjamin Cox, "New Dimensions in Evaluation of Social Studies Programs," in Dorothy M. Fraser (ed.), *Social Studies Curriculum Development: Prospects and Problems*, Thirty-ninth Yearbook of the National Council for the Social Studies (Washington, D.C.: NCSS, 1969), pp. 206–228.

[6]R. E. Stake, "The Countenance of Educational Evaluation," *Teachers College Record*.

[7]R. F. Payette and C. B. Cox, "New Dimensions in Evaluation of Social Studies Programs," in D. M. Fraser (ed.), *Social Studies Curriculum Development*, p. 209.

[8]*Ibid.*, p. 216.

Outcome conditions refer to "any modification in the response of participants that can be linked empirically or logically to the educational process."[9] Outcomes in the social studies include changes in teacher and student attitudes, feelings, and values, the improvement of acquired skills, and the acquisition of new knowledge and skills.

If education in the social studies is to be regarded as a deliberate, conscious, and planned enterprise rather than a more or less haphazard occurrence, then social studies teachers must attempt to evaluate not only the intended (and unintended) outcomes of instruction, but also the antecedent and transactional conditions influencing these outcomes.

It is worth repeating, therefore, that assessment of student achievement needs to occur before, during, and after instruction, using a variety of evaluative tools. Pre-instructional assessment (Diagnostic Evaluation) can help teachers determine the most appropriate starting point for individual instruction (or, in some cases, suggest more advanced or remedial study), and identify noneducational causes that are handicapping student learning. Assessment during instruction (Formative Evaluation) can pinpoint specific difficulties that students are having, and suggest, where necessary, appropriate remedial measures or modifications in learning activities engaged in, teaching strategies used, or subject matter selected. Assessment at the end of instruction (Summative Evaluation) can indicate the degree to which instruction has succeeded and learning has taken place in terms of specific objectives attained.

Such assessment, be it diagnostic, formative, or summative, can be done in a variety of ways, using a variety of devices. To illustrate this, the remainder of this chapter will concentrate on identifying and discussing various methods of diagnostic evaluation, leaving further discussion of formative and summative evaluation to Chapter 7.

INFORMAL DIAGNOSTIC TOOLS FOR USE IN SOCIAL STUDIES

It has already been pointed out that evaluation has frequently been conceived as the pencil-and-paper assessment of student achievement. However, evaluation may be "formal or informal, objective or subjective, verbal or non-verbal, written or oral, or performed in some other manner."[10] A variety of evaluation procedures are especially necessary if a teacher desires

[9]*Ibid.*, p. 210.
[10]*Ibid.*, p. 82.

FIGURE 2.1

*Gordon's Model of Sources of Evidence Concerning the "Self"**

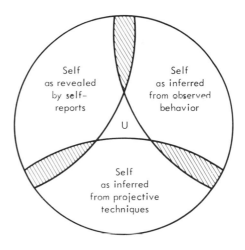

*From Ira J. Gordon, STUDYING THE CHILD IN SCHOOL. Copyright © 1966 by John Wiley & Sons, Inc. Reprinted by permission of John Wiley & Sons, Inc.

to obtain evidence as to the genuine feelings, attitudes, and values of students.

Gordon[11] has suggested a model which identifies three kinds of evidence that might be obtained by teachers in order to gain some insight into student thoughts, attitudes, feelings, and values. (See Figure 2.1.) The entire circle shown in Figure 2.1 represents the total "self" of an individual or, as Williams[12] has suggested, the total status of a particular attitude that an individual may hold at a given time. Each of the three sources of evidence (self-reports, observed behavior, and projective techniques) may be considered as partially overlapping "portions of the self." The "U" indicates that some portion of every individual self remains uniquely private and unavailable to detection by any technique of external observation. Williams has suggested that one implication of this model is that more facets of a particular self or of an attitude will be revealed by multiple techniques of

[11]Ira J. Gordon, *Studying the Child in School* (New York: John Wiley, 1966), p. 53.
[12]David M. Williams, "Problems in the Evaluation of Affect in Social Studies Education" (Unpublished paper, University of British Columbia, 1971), p. 10.

evaluation than by use of a single approach, a point essentially the same as the one being argued in this chapter.[13]

> *Self-Reports* are devices by which students reveal orally or in writing what they know or how they feel. Examples include checklists, inventories, essay tests, and sociograms.
>
> *Projective Techniques* involve the use of unstructured or "open-ended" stimulus situations or objects in order to elicit from students various remarks that will give us clues as to some of their feelings, thoughts, or beliefs. Examples include such devices as the famous Rorschach inkblot test, open-ended sentences to fill in, and unfinished stories to complete.
>
> *Observed Behavior Devices* include various rating or category systems by which teachers can record observed instances of certain actions or behaviors. Such instruments are particularly useful for analyzing *transactional* conditions, such as classroom interaction. Examples include flow charts, tally sheets, anecdotal records, and time-and-motion studies.

We shall now discuss examples in each of these categories.

SELF-REPORT DEVICES

PRIOR ORAL OR WRITTEN DISCUSSION OF UNIT MATERIAL

One of the most helpful things that a teacher can do is to take a sounding on what students already know about a subject or topic before instruction begins. This technique, often called a "pre-test," can be oral or written, used with an entire class or individuals. It consists of asking students questions to determine to what extent they understand and how they feel about various aspects of the material to be studied. Examples include:

* What do policemen do?
* What does the term "civil rights" mean to you?
* How should dissenters be dealt with—or should they?
* What would you like to know about the people of India?
* What comes to mind when I say "communication"?

Student answers to such questions can provide considerable insight into their backgrounds and previous learnings and form a basis for deciding what material, if necessary, to review before developing a new unit of in-

[13]*Ibid.*, p. 10.

struction. A more appropriate beginning level of instruction is thus insured. For example, if an eleventh-grade class has decided to investigate the nature of revolutions and in so doing, to focus particularly on the nature, causes, and effects of selected revolutions (e.g., American, French, Russian, Cuban), it would be profitable for the teacher to spend some time (prior to starting the unit) discussing with the class their understanding of the concept "revolution," and its related dimensions. Such a discussion would not only point out individual differences in understanding among class members, but also suggest at what level or levels to begin, as well as areas and topics for investigation as the unit progresses.

There are several variations of this "pre-development" discussion that teachers can employ. Various key concepts related to the material can be discussed, a number of key terms can be written on the board and the class asked to define them, or a short quiz can be given on significant points. Another possibility is to have the class ask questions about various aspects of the material to be studied that they would like to know more about. Taba, for example, tells of a fourth-grade teacher who in redesigning her world geography unit to bring about a greater emphasis on people, asked her students to propose questions suggesting what they wanted to know about various regions that they wanted to study.[14] This helped the teacher to diagnose their level of understanding and to identify misconceptions they possessed which needed correcting. Thus, she discovered that her students wanted to know how Baffin Islanders kept clean. Since the students viewed bathtubs as the only way of keeping clean, they wondered how the Islanders, who had no bathtubs, managed. Here was an interesting misconception which diagnostic questioning revealed.

A further possibility is to construct a simple attitude scale consisting of a set of questions designed to provide some idea of how *intense* are student feelings for or against a given topic. This kind of question asks students to indicate whether they strongly agree (SA), agree (A), are undecided (U), disagree (D), or strongly disagree (SD) with each statement given. Here are some examples, part of a larger set of statements designed to gain insight into students' general attitude toward the study of history:

SA A U D SD	History is a fascinating story.
SA A U D SD	You can learn a lot about events today by studying what happened in similar events in the past.
SA A U D SD	History is of no use to anybody today.
SA A U D SD	My friends think that studying history is a waste of time.
SA A U D SD	I frequently discuss things learned in my history class with my friends.

[14]Hilda Taba, *Curriculum Development: Theory and Practice*, pp. 245–246.

Items like these could be used at different times and with different aspects of a subject to ascertain changes in students' attitudes toward a subject or parts of it.

O'Hara[15] describes a simple method that teachers can use to measure the degree to which a student perceives himself as being interested in a particular subject, skill, or procedure. This procedure involves presenting students with a definition of a given skill, procedure, or concept and then asking each student to rate himself with regard to the skill or trait along a nine-point scale. Here is an example:

• PARTICIPATION IN CLASS DISCUSSIONS—Participating in class discussions means talking with other students and the teacher about various ideas, events, or actions that are studied in the course.

1	2	3	4	5
My interest ranks with the lowest group of people who might be interested in this.	I have very much less interest than most people.	I have much less interest than most people.	I have less interest than most people.	I have the same amount of interest as most people.

6	7	8	9
I have a little more interest than most people.	I have much more interest than most people.	I have very much more interest than most people.	My interest ranks with the highest group of people who might be interested in this.

Another technique that teachers can use is the semantic differential devised by Osgood, Suci, and Tannenbaum[16] to measure the general attitude of students toward a particular concept. Students are presented with a particular concept of interest to the teacher and then asked to rate it along a continuum in terms of several pairs of adjectives such as "good-bad," "beautiful-ugly," "valuable-worthless," and "pleasant-unpleasant." The student checks the scale value along the continuum that indicates his attitude toward the concept in question. The Social Studies Evaluation Program of the Education Development Center in Cambridge, Massachusetts, that developed "Man: A Course of Study," used this technique to evaluate student attitudes toward certain concepts contained in their social studies

[15]R. P. O'Hara, "A Cross-Sectional Study of Growth in the Relationship of Self-Ratings and Test Scores" (Doctoral dissertation, Harvard University, 1958). Cited in Bloom, Hastings, and Madaus, *Handbook on Formative and Summative Evaluation*, p. 241.

[16]Charles Osgood, G. Suci, and P. Tannenbaum, *The Measurement of Meaning* (Urbana, Ill.: University of Illinois Press, 1967).

unit on the Netsilik Eskimos.[17] Here is one example that they designed to gain insight into student attitudes toward the concept "arctic."

ARCTIC
(The Arctic is the area near the North Pole.)

ugly	:_:_:_:_:_:_:	beautiful
changing	:_:_:_:_:_:_:	changeless
windy	:_:_:_:_:_:_:	calm
strange	:_:_:_:_:_:_:	familiar
explored	:_:_:_:_:_:_:	unexplored
tame	:_:_:_:_:_:_:	wild
good	:_:_:_:_:_:_:	bad
deserted	:_:_:_:_:_:_:	inhabited
fierce	:_:_:_:_:_:_:	gentle
livable	:_:_:_:_:_:_:	not livable[18]

Almost any concept could be studied in this way. Teachers could explore student attitudes toward a particular region, group, or topic studied, certain class activities or specific teaching procedures.

Pre-tests, such as these or others, can help teachers in a number of ways. They can indicate missing or weak skills that need to be developed. For example, if a pre-test requiring students to read and analyze a particular passage in a text reveals that many are poor readers, additional activities to improve their reading skills might be planned for and included within the original unit. Pre-tests can provide some idea of the level of abstraction of which students are capable, language patterns, vocabulary strengths and weaknesses, interpretive and analytic abilities, and discussion skills.

To obtain information about a specific skill or process, however, teachers need to ask students to perform the skill or engage in the process. Thus insight into students' ability to identify relationships can be gained by asking them to compare and contrast two passages in a text or other piece of written material. Student ability to make logical inferences can be determined by asking them to read a given passage containing a number of assumptions and then indicate what conclusions might logically be drawn from these assumptions. Student ability to use maps, charts, and graphs can be assessed by giving them a problem, the solution to which depends on the use of maps or charts. Their ability to detect bias in an argument

[17]The Social Studies Evaluation Program, Netsilik Unit Test (Cambridge, Mass.: Education Development Corporation, Spring 1969). Cited in B. S. Bloom, J. T. Hastings, and G. F. Madaus, *Handbook*, p. 243.

[18]From a test developed by the Social Studies Program of Education Development Center, Inc., for the experimental edition of *Man: A Course of Study*. Reprinted by permission of Education Development Center, Inc.

can be diagnosed by having them analyze campaign speeches or product endorsements. Ability to organize data can be diagnosed by having them take notes and outline a short talk given by a guest speaker. Ability to apply information learned in one situation to another new and different situation can be assessed by asking students to build logical chains of an "if-then" or cause-and-effect nature. Even young children can hypothesize about "What might happen if——?" "If a family were to move to a new neighborhood, what might happen?" "If the Democrats were to gain control of the Senate, what might happen?" "If a nation willingly decides to intervene in the affairs of another country smaller and weaker than itself, what might happen?"

MULTIPLE CHOICE ENDINGS

Multiple-choice endings constitute a direct type of diagnostic measurement. Students are asked to choose one of four multiple-choice endings for an incomplete sentence or one of several multiple-choice answers to a direct question. Here are two examples to illustrate the use of multiple-choice endings:

> When I'm in this class, I
> ——— a. usually feel wide awake and very interested
> ——— b. am pretty interested, kind of bored part of the time
> ——— c. am not very interested, bored quite a lot of the time
> ——— d. don't like it, feel bored and not with it

Or:

> How often do the students in this class cooperate and work together on class assignments?
> ——— a. Always
> ——— b. Most of the time
> ——— c. Sometimes
> ——— d. Hardly ever[19]

Questions such as these ask students to respond directly in written form to various aspects of their environment. For purposes of diagnosis, they can be used to gather information about how the class *feels* about classroom climate, learning activities, subject matter, teacher actions, interpersonal relations (both teacher-student and student-student) or anything else that goes on in the classroom.

A variation of this technique for the primary grades (as low as Kinder-

[19]Fox, Lusyki, and Schmuck, *Diagnosing Classroom Learning Environments*, pp. 11–12.

garten) is the use of simply drawn faces, as suggested by Fox and his asso-ciates.[20] When working with very young children, the teacher, using simply worded statements and few words, asks students to place an "X" under the face, such as one of those in Figure 2.2, that illustrates how he feels.

FIGURE 2.2

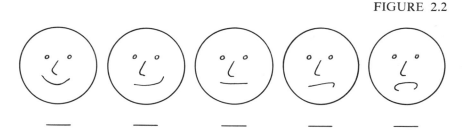

Many teachers raise the question of whether or not student anonymity should be maintained in order to insure the utmost frankness and honesty in giving responses. Fox and his co-workers suggest the use of a committee of respected student leaders to collect, tabulate, and report the overall class response. "Particularly where criticism of the teacher is involved, pupils are more free to express their feelings to their peers than to the teacher. Such anonymity, however, results in the loss of valuable data, and the pre-ferred procedure is for teachers to try to allay fears of reprisal for frank replies. By showing that they will be objective about the results and genuinely interested in doing something about them, many teachers have encouraged their pupils to be frank and to use this opportunity construc-tively."[21]

SOCIOGRAMS

Another element to diagnose is the climate and structure of interpersonal relations that exist within the classroom. The structure of interpersonal relationships which exists in a particular class "affects the atmosphere of the classroom, controls the energy available for learning, determines the range of roles individuals can play and also, therefore, their access to op-portunities to learn, determines the communication lines, and influences the frequency of discipline problems."[22]

A useful device for obtaining this information is the *sociogram*. A socio-gram is a visual representation, usually by means of arrows, of the choices

[20]*Ibid.*
[21]*Ibid.*, p. 10.
[22]H. Taba, *Curriculum Development*, p. 252.

various students make with regard to other students that are in their class. Each student is usually represented by a circle (if female) or a triangle (if male) and arrows are then drawn to indicate different student choices in response to a particular question. Students may be asked to list three persons they like most, like least, believe are most cooperative, are most able to get other students to do things, would most want to work on a committee with, sit next to, participate in a research project, have as a debate partner, or otherwise do something that can be done in a small group. The chief criterion here again is realism—that the teacher is asking for information that will be actually used to make a decision affecting the members of the class (such as changing committee assignments). Student responses are then used to construct the sociogram. Figure 2.3 is an illustration of a sociogram.

A disguised variation of this technique is suggested by McDonald.[23] Instead of asking students to choose someone to be on a committee with, etc., ask them to assign various members of the class to different roles. Called the "guess-who" technique,[24] it involves asking students to guess who is the most helpful, the most trusted, the best-liked, and so on. A further variation is to ask students to assign certain class members to parts in a play (see Figure 2.4).

Sociograms are quite valuable. They can provide a teacher with insights into the nature of the power structure in the class, who the leaders are, the isolates, the rejected, the sub-groups. Caution must be exercised in interpreting sociograms, however. A student who is chosen by several other students in response to one question may not be chosen at all in response to another kind of question. For example, class members may choose the best athlete when asked with whom they would most like to be on a team, but the best scholar when asked with whom they'd most like to work with on a research project. Data collected at different times or with different groups may produce strikingly different results. Furthermore, students' responses must always be interpreted cautiously. They may be hesitant to reveal their true feelings. As Sawin points out,[25] this suggests the necessity of preparing several sociograms, at different times and with different questions, rather than relying on a single set of results. As mentioned earlier, the more accurate data we can obtain on students, the more reliable any interpretations and judgments based on such data will be.

[23]Frederick J. McDonald, *Educational Psychology*, 2nd ed. (Belmont, Calif.: Wadsworth, 1965), p. 633.
[24]See H. Hartshorne and M. A. May, *Studies in Service and Self-Control* (New York: Macmillan, 1929) for examples of the use of this technique in studying child behavior.
[25]Enoch I. Sawin, *Evaluation and the Work of the Teacher*, p. 182.

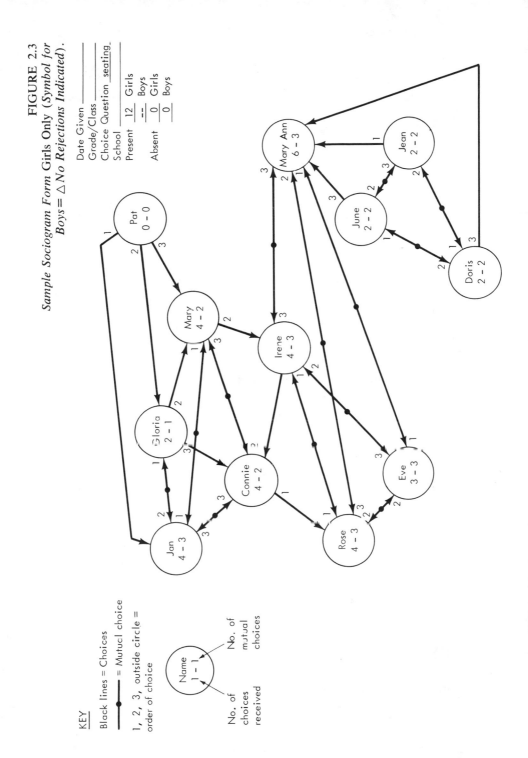

FIGURE 2.3

Sample Sociogram Form Girls Only (Symbol for Boys = △ No Rejections Indicated).

Date Given _____
Grade/Class _____
Choice Question seating
School _____

	Present	Absent
Girls	12	0
Boys	--	0

KEY

Black lines = Choices

●——— = Mutual choice

1, 2, 3, outside circle = order of choice

No. of choices received → Name 1 - 1 ← No. of mutual choices

67

FIGURE 2.4
ASSIGNING PARTS IN A PLAY*

Name _____ School _____ Grade _____

THE CLASS PLAY

Just imagine your class is going to put on a play and you are selected to direct it. Below you will see the kinds of parts that will be needed for this play. As director of the play, you have the responsibility of selecting any boy or girl in your class for any of the parts. Since many of the parts are very small, you may, if you wish, select the same boy or girl for more than one part.

In order to make this play successful, you will need to choose boys and girls who you think would be *most natural* for the part, that is, who are most like the part in real life. Make your choices carefully, and, if you have any questions about the meaning of a word or anything else, be sure to ask your teacher.

THESE ARE THE PARTS

Part 1—The Hero—someone who is good in sports and in school work   _____

Part 2—Someone who is often mean and gets into fights a great deal (boy or girl)   _____

Part 3—The Heroine—someone who gets along well with other boys and girls and with the teacher.   _____

Part 4—Someone who is always getting angry about little things.   _____

Part 5—Someone who could be the hero's friend—a kind, helpful boy or girl.   _____

Part 6—Someone who could play the part of a bully—picks on boys and girls smaller or weaker than himself.   _____

Part 7—Someone who has a good sense of humor but is always careful not to disturb the teacher or the class.   _____

Part 8—Someone who could play the part of a person who doesn't ever say anything.   _____

*Prepared by California State Dept. of Education. Reprinted in McDonald, *op. cit.*, p. 636.

Part 9—Someone who is never mean and always friendly.

          _____

Part 10—Someone who could act like the la-
ziest person in the world—never
does anything.

          _____

Part 11—A boy or girl you would choose to
be in charge when the teacher left
the room.

          _____

Part 12—This person knows all the answers
and usually works alone.

          _____

Section II

A. Which part or parts would you like to play best (Write
number(s) here)   _____

B. Which part or parts do you think you could play?   _____

C. Which part or parts do you think the teacher might
ask you to play?   _____

D. Which part or parts do you think most of the other
kids would ask you to play?   _____

CHECKLISTS

Checklists can be used by students to diagnose their *own* performance. A class can jointly prepare a checklist to assess their accomplishment of certain objectives and then each student can use it individually. An example of such a self-checklist that one teacher developed with his class is shown in Figure 2.5.

FIGURE 2.5
SELF-CHECKLIST

Date _____   Name _____

    1 = Outstanding   **3** = Satisfactory

    2 = Above Average   **4** = Needs Improvement

	1st Week	2nd Week	3rd Week	4th Week
1. I participated in class discussions.				
2. I listened attentively.				

	1st Week	2nd Week	3rd Week	4th Week
3. I encouraged others to offer their opinions.				
4. I completed work that I assigned myself.				
5. I helped others when asked.				
6. I used several different source materials.				
7. I asked questions when I was unsure or didn't know.				
8. I defined my terms when asked.				
9. I thought about why I preferred certain ways of proceeding or acting rather than others.				
10. I considered the suggestions of others.				

INTEREST INVENTORIES OR QUESTIONNAIRES

Student interests are a further source of information that teachers can utilize to plan effective instruction. If teachers are to capitalize on student interests, they must, of course, know what these interests are. One way to gain some idea of what students are interested in is through the use of an interest inventory. Interest inventories may take a variety of forms, but all essentially involve asking students to respond in one form or another to a series of questions regarding their likes and dislikes. An example of a student interest inventory is shown in Figure 2.6:

FIGURE 2.6
STUDENT INTEREST INVENTORY

Student Interest Inventory

1. What subjects do you like best in school? ⎯⎯⎯⎯⎯⎯⎯⎯

2. What subjects do you like least in school? ⎯⎯⎯⎯⎯⎯⎯⎯

3. Of the subjects that you like best, what is it about each of them that causes you to like them so? ⎯⎯⎯⎯⎯⎯⎯⎯

4. What subjects that are not presently included would you like to see included in your school program? _____

5. What magazines do you read at home? _____

6. What are the names of some of the books that you've read that you especially liked? _____

7. Circle the answer that best indicates how often you read the newspaper:

Every day   Every week   Every two weeks   Once in a while   Never

8. Circle the parts of the paper that you read most frequently:

Sports   Weather   Comics   Editorials   Local News

Domestic News   Foreign News   Advertisements   Fashion

Society   Theatre   Radio and Television   Financial Page   Travel

9. Circle the answer that best indicates how often you listen to the radio:

Never   Occasionally   Once a week   Once a day   More than once a day

10. What are the names of some of the radio programs that you like best?

_____

11. Circle the answer that best indicates how often you watch television:

Never   Occasionally   An hour or less a day   One to three hours a day

More than three hours a day

12. What are the names of some of the television programs that you like best? _____

13. Circle the answer that best indicates how often you go to the movies:

Never   Occasionally   Once a week   Twice a week   More that twice a week

14. What are the names of some movies that you have seen that really impressed you? _____

15. What things do you like to do best in your spare time? _____

_____

16. What places in the state have you visited alone or with your family?

_____

17. What other states in the United States have you visited? ―――――――

―――――――――――――――――――――――――――――――――――

18. What other countries have you visited outside the United States? ―――

―――――――――――――――――――――――――――――――――――

19. To what clubs or organizations do you belong? ――――――――――

―――――――――――――――――――――――――――――――――――

Sometimes a teacher may wish to gain some idea about the extent of a *particular* interest, such as the degree to which students involve themselves in current social or political problems. The following example indicates how students can be asked to respond to a number of statements that suggest activities related to a particular interest:

> *Directions:* For each of the following activities mark:
>   A if you perform the activity occasionally or frequently.
>   N if you never perform the activity.
>   13. Attend public meetings to protest against something which you regard as unfair.
>   63. Write about political or social issues, problems, or events, such as bills passed by Congress, revolutions, etc.
> 188. Study the history of present political and social problems to find out what causes them and what has been done about such problems in the past.[26]

PROJECTIVE TECHNIQUES

OPEN-ENDED TITLES

This device is not only effective, but simple to use. It consists of asking students indirectly to write, discuss or act out a question, theme, or topic that is open-ended in nature in order to gain some insight into their underlying feelings, conception, or understandings about same. Examples of such open-ended questions or themes include the following:

What I like most about myself
What makes me happy (or unhappy)

―――――――――――――――――――――――――――――――――――

[26]*Test: Adapted from Interest Index: Test 8.2a* (Chicago: Evaluation in the Eight-Year Study, Progressive Education Association, 1939). Cited in: D. R. Krathwohl, B.S. Bloom, and B. B. Masia, *Taxonomy of Educational Objectives, Handbook II: Affective Domain*, p. 152.

What I'd like to change about the United States
The kind of people I like best
What I think about capital punishment
How I feel about dissent

A variation is to ask students to respond, in writing, to open-ended sentences such as: "When I think about this class, I_____," "The best thing about this class is _____," "If I were asked to participate in a panel discussion on international affairs, I'd feel _____," which the student completes according to his own volition. The concept development strategy described in Chapter 5 is another example of how the use of open-ended questions can serve a diagnostic function (see pp. 190-198).

Questions or themes such as these are particularly helpful in revealing how students *feel* about what goes on in the classroom. Many students are unable or unwilling to discuss their feelings about classroom activities and atmosphere openly. The use of open-ended titles allows and encourages them to react in writing. Open-ended titles and questions can be used to assess student reactions to classroom atmosphere in general, specific learning experiences, the sequence of instruction, materials, or teacher personality and technique. Such questions can offer insight into student perceptions of their own strengths and weaknesses, likes and dislikes, achievement, motivation, or involvement in the learning activities. As Fox and his associates point out, when students complete open-ended sentences such as "Some of the best things about this class are _____," and, "Some of the worst things about this class are _____," they can provide very incisive comments, both positive and negative, on classroom life.[27]

Thus, if a teacher were interested in determining how well a particular kind of learning activity, such as a panel discussion, was received by students, he might ask them to respond to an open-ended question such as, "What kinds of things happen on a good day in our class?" and see how many students write down "the use of panel discussions" in their replies. Replies to a question like "What really turns me off in this class?" can identify unmotivated students, as well as suggest a variety of reasons for their lack of motivation.

It is essential that such themes (or questions) be sufficiently open-ended so as not to suggest to students (or "cue" them) that certain responses are expected (e.g., "How we should behave when Mr. Jones leaves the room"). What is important is that spontaneous rather than planned reactions come forth, else the diagnostic value of the exercise is limited. The responses

[27]R. Fox, M. B. Lusyki, and R. S. Schmuck, *Diagnosing Classroom Learning Environments*, p. 15.

which students give to such questions can help teachers considerably in planning further learning activities (e.g., if a number of students seem emotionally committed to capital punishment, the teacher may wish to engage them in experiences, such as role-playing, which will enable them to *feel* similarly to those who favor its abolition), and content (e.g., if an open-ended question reveals a strong, but unexamined pro-war sentiment, the teacher may wish to help students to examine logically the arguments for and against this position).

Students need to be prepared for this kind of writing—a teacher cannot take such for granted. Many teachers have found it helpful to tell students about their own lives first, and to discuss certain of their own feelings, or to let them discuss characters in literature or in films. A simple hierarchy to consider in this regard is shown in Figure 2.7, the lowest level being the easiest for many students to deal with, with each succeeding level becoming more difficult.

FIGURE 2.7
Levels of Discussion

Discussing or Writing about Themselves
↑
Discussing or Writing about (Anonymous) People They Know
↑
Discussing or Writing about Characters in a Role-Playing Incident
↑
Discussing or Writing about Characters in a Story
↑
Discussing or Writing about Characters in a Movie

UNFINISHED STORIES

A variation of the open-ended question, discussion of unfinished stories (in written, film, or role-played form) can also serve a diagnostic function. The most common means of using this technique is to have the class read (view, act out, read to the class, etc.) a story whose ending is incomplete—i.e., unfinished, and then to discuss, using a carefully planned questioning sequence, how the story might end. As various students give their predictions, and the reasons behind these predictions, insight into feelings, perceptions, sensitivities, and values may be gained. Two examples of such stories, the first designed for third graders, and the second for high school students, follow:

How Did Anatouck Feel?

It was Anatouck's first day at school in a strange land. Anatouck was an Eskimo and he had just come to California for the first time. He was eight years old and he had never been to school in "the States" (as the main part of the United States is known to Alaskans). It was all like a dream—the sun and grass, the cities, the traffic. All were so strange.

Anatouck came from a land where it was cold and snow-covered all year round. He had spent part of the first five years of his life in an igloo. Then his mother and father had died in an accident. A short time later he was sent by missionaries to the Mission School in a nearby small village. Here he met Mr. and Mrs. Barnaby, two teachers from California who were working as teachers in the Mission School. He grew to love them and they loved him. They arranged to adopt him. Then when Anatouck finished the second grade, Mrs. Barnaby told him that the family (his family now) would be going home to California. Anatouck would start third grade in a California school!

Anatouck had heard many wonderful things about California. He thought a lot about going to school there. He wondered what it would be like. He soon found out. Some of the kids in the neighborhood his family moved to laughed at him. They called him names such as "flat nose" and "slanty eyes." He didn't like that much at all. Why did they call him such names? A few kids asked him to play Football, but he didn't know how. He wanted to learn, though.

And so today Anatouck wondered—it was his first day in the new California school. Would the children in the class laugh at him? Would they call him names? Would they play with him? What would school be like? He'd just have to wait and see.

. . .

An Idealist Loses His Ideals[28]

A young businessman in the used-car business in Chicago describes the process by which he was inducted into crime.

When I graduated from college I had plenty of ideals of honesty, fair play, and cooperation which I had acquired at home, in school, and from literature. My first job after graduation was selling typewriters. During the first day I learned that these machines were not sold at a uniform price but that a person who haggled and waited could get a machine at about half the list price. The other salesmen laughed at me and could not understand my silly attitude. They told me to forget the things I had learned in school, and that you

[28]From White Collar Crime by Edwin H. Sutherland. Copyright, 1949, by Holt, Rinehart and Winston, Inc. Reprinted by permission of Holt, Rinehart and Winston, Inc.

couldn't earn a pile of money by being strictly honest. When I replied that money wasn't everything they mocked me: "Oh! No?
Well, it helps." I resigned.

My next job was selling sewing machines. I was informed that
one machine, which cost the company $18, was to be sold for $40
and another machine, which cost the company $19, was to be sold
for $70, and that I was to sell the deluxe model whenever possible
in preference to the cheaper model, and was given a list of the
reasons why it was a better buy. When I told the sales manager that
the business was dishonest and that I was quitting right then, he
looked at me as if he thought I was crazy and said angrily: "There's
not a cleaner business in the country."

It was quite a time before I could find another job. During this
time I occasionally met some of my classmates and they related
experiences similar to mine. They said they would starve if they
were rigidly honest. All of them had girls and were looking for-
ward to marriage and a comfortable standard of living, and they
said they did not see how they could afford to be rigidly honest . . . .

Then I had an opportunity in the used-car business. I learned that
this business had more tricks . . . than either of those I had tried
previously. Cars with cracked cylinders, with half the teeth missing
from the fly wheel, with everything wrong, were sold as "guaranteed." When the customer returned and demanded his guarantee,
he had to sue to get it and very few went to that trouble and expense: the boss said you could depend on human nature. If hot cars
could be taken in and sold safely, the boss did not hesitate. When I
learned these things I did not quit as I had previously. I sometimes
. . . wanted to quit, but I argued that I did not have much chance
to find a legitimate firm. I knew that the game was rotten but it
had to be played—the law of the jungle and that sort of thing . . . .
The thing that struck me as strange was that all these people were
proud of their ability to fleece customers. They boasted of their
crookedness and were admired by their friends and enemies in proportion to their ability to get away with a crooked deal: it was
called shrewdness. Another thing was that these people were unan-
imous in their denunciation of gangsters, robbers, burglars, and
petty thieves. They never regarded themselves as in the same class
and were bitterly indignant if accused of dishonesty: it was just
good business.

. . . If you had accused me of dishonesty I would have denied
the charge, but with slightly less vehemence than my fellow businessmen, for after all I had learned a different code of behavior.

The important thing to remember in using this technique is to ensure
that the stories involve real people, involved in real-life situations and
dealing with real problems. Equally important, the stories must not only be
truly open-ended, but also care must be taken once again to ensure that no
cues are given in the story as to how the character(s) in the story feels. For
example, it would be inappropriate to start out the first story above with

the statement, "Anatouck was worried," for this would be putting an idea in the students' heads rather than allowing them to (possibly) infer this from the material as written. Unfinished stories should be descriptive rather than analytical in nature. The students who read them must do the analyzing if they are to serve their intended diagnostic purpose and provide information about student perceptions, sensitivities, values, and attitudes.

To probe student understanding of, and reaction to, such stories, question sequences can be planned to get at various dimensions. One possible sequence follows:

1) What happened in this story (What is the story about)?
2) Why did these things happen?
3) How did _____ (the person(s) to whom things happened) feel?
4) Has anything like this ever happened to you?
5) How did you feel?
6) What could be done to make this situation come out better?[29]

Question 1 establishes the facts of the case, helps the class get off on a common footing, and indicates the level of perception and understanding possessed by various members of the class.

Question 2 asks for reasons, thus providing some insight into the level of explanation of which the class is capable. What do they perceive as causes for the incident occurring the way it did?

Question 3 asks for empathy or identification at the feeling level. Students are asked to infer how the central character(s) felt in this situation. Their answers should provide some insight into how well they are able to place themselves in another's shoes, and to some degree the range of feelings they can imagine.

Question 4 shifts the emphasis from the characters in the story to the students themselves by asking them to recall a similar occurrence in their own lives. As Taba has suggested,[30] the kinds of responses students give to this question indicate the level of abstraction of which they are capable. Some will suggest specific instances at a given place in time, highly similar to the incident in the story. Others may offer responses of a more abstract nature, such as reacting in a similar manner, but in a different situation, or vice versa.

Question 5 enables the student to express his own feelings. Student responses to this question are often truly revealing of inner thoughts and feelings. This sharing of feelings can also be most rewarding. The teacher must take care at this point, however, to make no evaluative comments

[29]H. Taba, *Curriculum Development*, p. 247.
[30]*Ibid.*

about a student's response, but to accept noncommittally (by saying "I see" or "Hmm") all reactions as given. Judgment is not required; acceptance and empathy is. Student replies will indicate the degree to which various class members can express their feelings.

Question 6 encourages students to think about and suggest alternative outcomes. One hypothesis here is that through such continual thinking about better ways to do things, students may think about their own actions and perhaps act more positively when faced with situations in which they must interact with others.

OBSERVING STUDENT BEHAVIOR

ANALYSIS OF CLASS DISCUSSIONS

The actual statements that students make in class, and the manner in which they make them, if looked at systematically, are still another source of information about students' needs and development. Two possibilities suggest themselves. The *number* and *direction* of student remarks can be diagrammed in order to gain some idea of the *quantity* and focus of student participation. The *kind* of statements that students make can be charted to determine the nature and *quality* of student remarks.

One of the easiest methods to use in charting individual student participation, suggested by Sawin,[31] is to prepare a seating chart on which a box is drawn for each student in the class. A tally mark is then placed in the box of a particular student each time he contributes to the discussion and makes a comment to the class as a whole. To dictate the direction of particular student comments, arrows can be drawn from the box of a student who initiates a comment to the box of the student(s) toward whom the comment is directed. Figure 2.8 illustrates how such a participation flow chart might look for a hypothetical discussion involving 12 persons.

This chart would suggest that the discussion was dominated by Tom, Jack, and Rachel, with Alice and Joan contributing. Phyllis and Yolanda said nothing. As with any other diagnostic device, caution is in order. Care should be taken not to rely very heavily on the results of charting any *one* particular discussion. Subsequent discussions may reveal quite different patterns, as would discussions involving different groups or topics. Furthermore, relying on the results of even several diagnostic devices at any one time is prone to error. The more data that can be obtained using a variety of diagnostic tools over a period of time, the more likely any interpretation can be viewed as reliable. One way of increasing reliability while at the same time providing a learning experience for students is to assign two

---

[31]E. I. Sawin, *Evaluation and the Work of the Teacher*, pp. 178–179.

FIGURE 2.8

*A Participation Flow Chart Showing Direction
and Quantity of Comments**

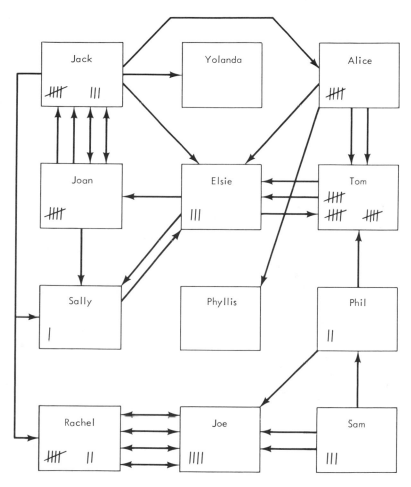

*Adapted from Enoch I. Sawin, Evaluation and the Work of the Teacher (Belmont, Calif.: Wadsworth, 1969), p. 179.

students as observers (rotating the assignment among students continually). The observers are charged with recording the flow of comments rather than participating in the discussion. This opportunity to serve as an observer should be rotated frequently and the results of the observations by pairs of students compared.

Tallying the number of times a student contributes to a discussion and diagramming by means of arrows the direction of his comments only provides information about the *quantity* of student remarks. To gain insight into the *quality* of these remarks—that is, the different kinds of comments that students make—some type of discussion analysis sheet needs to be used. The technique involved is to tally student remarks during specified time intervals (e.g., every 3 minutes for a 12-minute period) into previously determined categories, such as asks questions, summarizes, gives example, asks for information, etc. The possible category systems that might be devised are probably endless, but one example of a list of categories designed to identify student questioning patterns is shown in Table 2.1.

TABLE 2.1
DISCUSSION ANALYSIS TALLY SHEET
STUDENT QUESTIONING PATTERNS

Questions 1. Answer to question asked requires factual information. Only one correct answer possible (e.g., "Who is the Lieutenant Governor of California?")	Related to lesson	
	Not related to lesson	
2. Answer to question asked requires descriptive information. Only one correct answer possible, though it may have many parts to it (e.g., "Under what kinds of conditions did the enlisted men on nineteenth-century British sailing ships live, and how did these living conditions differ from those of their officers?")	Related to lesson	
	Not related to lesson	
3. Answer to question asked requires explanation. Several correct answers are possible (e.g., "What makes a people want to revolt against the established government?")	Related to lesson	
	Not related to lesson	
4. Answer to question asked requires speculation, since there is no correct answer to the question. Divergent rather than convergent thinking is necessary (e.g., "What might happen if a new metal, harder yet more malleable than any yet known, were to be discovered today?")	Related to lesson	
	Not related to lesson	
Other Student Responses 5. Any replies to the teacher that are not a question	Related to lesson	
	Not related to lesson	·
6. Silence		
7. Confusion—random noise		

It is important to remember that flow charts such as the one shown in Figure 2.8 indicate only *one* kind of participation—the quantity of student comments. In the hypothetical class referred to, Phyllis and Yolanda, though saying nothing, may be participating in other ways, such as listening and thinking. This suggests once again the need for teachers to use a *variety* of diagnostic devices in order to obtain as much and as varied data on students as possible in order to make realistic and reliable inferences about their attitudes and abilities.

RECORDS OF CLASS PERFORMANCE

Not only student statements, but also student *actions* can be systematically observed in order to make logical inferences about the reasons for certain aspects of their behavior. "If one wants to see what skills a committee chairman has in working with a group, one can watch him in action. . . . To discover how adequate or inadequate the work habits of students are, one can observe them taking notes, browsing in books, or planning dimensions of a topic to study."[32] Systematic observation of students as they read, work with maps and charts, give reports, write, ask and answer questions, recite, work in small groups of two or more, plan together, lead or participate in discussions, or roleplay, may identify particular actions that prevent them from utilizing their time and talents as productively as they might.

One effective means of recording student behavior is the *anecdotal record*. Anecdotal records are just what their name implies—records of observed classroom behavior written down in the form of anecdotes. Like other diagnostic devices, however, anecdotal records can mislead as well as inform. To be most useful and informative, anecdotal records should describe student behavior in specific factual terms. Evaluative, interpretative, or generalized descriptions should be avoided. Thus, the American Council on Education, in describing the four kinds of anecdotal records listed below, states that only the fourth is the type desired. Can you see why?

1. Anecdotes that evaluate or judge the behavior of the child as good or bad, desirable or undesirable, acceptable or unacceptable . . . evaluative statements.
2. Anecdotes that account for or explain the child's behavior, usually on the basis of a single fact or thesis . . . interpretive statements.
3. Anecdotes that describe certain behavior in general terms, as happening frequently, or as characterizing the child . . . generalized descriptive statements.
4. Anecdotes that tell exactly what the child did or said, that de-

[32]H. Taba, *Curriculum Development*, p. 250.

scribe concretely the situation in which the action or comment occurred, and that tell clearly what other persons also did or said . . . specific or concrete descriptive statements.[33]

An example of each of the four types of anecdote follows:

An evaluative statement:

Julius talked loud and much during poetry; wanted to do and say just what he wanted and didn't consider the right working out of things. Had to ask him to sit by me. Showed a bad attitude about it.

An interpretive statement:

For the last week Sammy has been a perfect wiggle-tail. He is growing so fast he cannot be settled . . . Of course the inward change that is taking place causes the restlessness.

A generalized description:

Sammy is awfully restless these days. He is whispering most of the time he is not kept busy. In the circle, during various discussions, even though he is interested, his arms are moving or he is punching the one sitting next to him. He smiles when I speak to him.

A specific description (the type desired):

The weather was so bitterly cold that we did not go on the playground today. The children played games in the room during the regular recess period. Andrew and Larry chose sides for a game which is known as stealing the bacon. I was talking to a group of children in the front of the room while the choosing was in process and in a moment I heard a loud altercation. Larry said that all the children wanted to be on Andrew's side rather than on his. Andrew . . . remarked, "I can't help it if they all want to be on my side."[34]

A useful list of rules for preparing anecdotal records is the following:

1. Focus on the behavior and the situation of the subject.
2. Observe and report as fully as possible the situation of the subject and the specific stimuli to which he is reacting.
3. Never make interpretations carry the burden of descriptions.

[33]American Council on Education, *Helping Teachers Understand Children* (Washington, D.C.: American Council on Education, 1945), pp. 32–33. As quoted in E. I. Sawin, *Evaluation and the Work of the Teacher*, p. 83.
[34]American Council on Education, *Helping Teachers Understand Children*, p. 33.

4. Give the "how" of everything the subject does.
5. Give the "how" of everything done by any person who interacts with the subject.
6. Report in order in the final version all the main steps through the course of every action by the subject.
7. Whenever possible, state descriptions of behavior positively.
8. Describe in some detail the scene as it is when each period of observation begins.[35]

At times a more intensive and detailed observation of a class's work habits may be needed. If a more detailed analysis is desired, a time-and-motion study can be performed. A *time-and-motion study* is the observation and detailed recording over a given period of time (e.g., a 30-minute study session) of the activities of one or more students. The observer tries to record, as objectively as possible and at brief regular intervals (e.g., every three minutes) everything a student does during the period. Taba[36] cites the example of a fourth-grade teacher who believed that her class's considerable slowness was due to the fact that they were extremely meticulous in their work. To check this out, a detailed time-and-motion study of one fairly typical student was made. The results of the study indicated that the students rather than being overly meticulous as a casual observer might think, actually seemed unable to focus their attention on a single task for any concerted period of time. Table 2.2 illustrates the observers' record.

A third means of recording student performance is through the use of a *checklist*, to which you were introduced earlier. Desired objectives can be listed horizontally on a sheet of paper and student names placed vertically down the side. Student performance in a given activity can then be observed on a regular basis, and comments can be recorded in the space available as to how well (or if) students are meeting each of these objectives. An example of such a checklist is shown in Figure 2.9.

UNOBTRUSIVE MEASURES

Several authors[37] have emphasized the value of unobtrusive measures in providing information about student abilities and perceptions, especially in the area of attitudes. Unobtrusive measures refer to those obtained without the individual involved being aware that he is being evaluated. When

[35]Roger G. Barker and Herbert F. Wright, *Midwest and Its Children: The Psychological Ecology of an American Town* (New York: Harper & Row, 1954), pp. 216–218. As quoted in E. I. Sawin, *Evaluation and the Work of the Teacher*, p. 84.
[36]H. Taba, *Curriculum Development*, p. 250.
[37]See Sawin, *Evaluation and the Work of the Teacher;* Taba, *Curriculum Development;* and E. J. Webb et al., *Unobtrusive Measures* (Skokie, Ill.: Rand McNally, 1966).

TABLE 2.2

TIME-AND-MOTION OBSERVATION*

Time	Activity	Time	Activity
11:32	Stacked paper	11:48	(*Continued*)
	Picked up pencil		Watched me
	Wrote name		Watched L.
	Moved paper closer		Laughed at her
	Continued with heading		Erased
	Rubbed nose		Hand up
	Read problem—lips moving		Made faces at girls
	Looked at Art's paper		Laughed. Watched D.
	Started to work . . .		Got help.
11:45	Worked and watched	11:50	Looked at Lorrie
	Made funny faces		Tapped fingers on desk.
	Giggled. Looked at		Wrote
	Lorrie and smiled.		Slid down in desk
	Borrowed Art's paper		Hand to head, listened to D.
	Erased		helping Lorrie.
	Stacked paper		Blew breath out hard
	Read		Fidgeted with paper
	Slid paper around		Looked at other group
	Worked briefly		Held chin
	Picked up paper and read		Watched Charles
	Thumb in mouth, watched		Read—hands holding head
	Miss D.		Erased
11:48	Worked and watched		Watched other group, chin on
	Made funny face		hand
	Giggled. Looked and smiled		Made faces—yawned—fidgeted
	at Lorrie		Held head
	Paper up—read		Read, pointing to words
	Picked eye		Wrote
	Studied bulletin board		Put head on arm on desk
	Paper down—read again		Held chin
	Fidgeted with paper		Read
	Played with pencil and fingers		Rubbed eye
		11:55	Wrote

*From Hilda Taba, "Problem Identification," in *Research for Curriculum Improvement*, 1957 Yearbook of the Association for Supervisors and Curriculum Directors (Washington, D.C.: ASCD, 1957), Chapter 3, pp. 60–61.

looked at systematically for example, collections of student reading and writing can be illustrative as to the nature, scope, variety, quantity, quality, maturity, and depth of student interests and habits. Cumulative folders containing student examples of reading (e.g., book reports, bibliographies, library check-outs, paperback purchases, requests for information about books) and writing (e.g., essays, themes, term papers, poems, exams, reports, summaries) can be maintained and analyzed systematically from time to time for evidence of growth (or lack thereof) in originality, organization, style, attitudes, values, and patterns of thinking. A number of other

FIGURE 2.9
A Checklist for Assessing Student Performance in Working in Small Groups

Class ________

Date ________

Performance Being Diagnosed Ability to work in small groups

OBJECTIVES →	Works steadily at assigned or selected tasks	Works harmoni-ously with other students in group	Suggests relevant ideas and ways of proceeding	Encourages other students to offer their ideas	Accepts ideas of others	Completes tasks assigned or selected	Helps others complete their tasks
GROUP I	X	X	X	X	X	X	X
Susan							
Phil							
Tom							
Robert							
Jane							
John							
GROUP II	X	X	X	X	X	X	X
Betty							
Sally							
Mary							
Willie							
Bruce							
Angela							
GROUP III	X	X	X	X	X	X	X
Oscar							
Agnes							
Carmen							
Lew							
Jack							
Sam							
TOTALS							

unobtrusive measures, some of which are explored more fully by Sawin[38] and Webb[39] to consider are:

1. Observing the amount of wear and tear on library books, magazines, and phonograph records to gain some idea of their use and accordingly students' interests and concerns.

2. Checking local police records for evidence of a rise or fall in juvenile arrest records as some indication of the effect of instruction on social relations or community problems.

3. Checking for number and kind of library books checked out or paperback books purchased as evidence of changing or developing student interest.

4. Observing student willingness over time to participate in various social or political affairs (e.g., election campaigns), to participate in student government, sign a petition, conduct a survey, answer a questionnaire, or otherwise volunteer to engage in some activity as evidence of interest in a certain area.

5. Tape recording classroom discussions or free-time periods to gain some idea of development in English usage or skill in interpersonal relations. Sawin suggests that to make this procedure truly unobtrusive, the recording could be made at a time when the teacher is not present.[40]

6. Noting the kinds of records, movies, TV shows, and radio programs that students frequently talk about in the halls, lunchroom, and during free discussion periods.

7. Observing changes in student dress, slang, associations, or mannerisms as evidence of developing or changing interests.

8. Noting the kinds of things, events, objects, individuals, behavior, or ideas that students ask questions about as evidence of underlying concerns.

9. Noting the kinds of topics or actions that make students especially angry, sad, or happy.

10. Noting the remarks that other teachers, administrators, or students make about students as evidence of reactions to activities and assignments in a particular class.

11. Noticing student *un*willingness to talk about certain matters.

LIMITATIONS OF INFORMAL DEVICES

You are now aware of a variety of informal diagnostic devices that teachers can use to assess to some degree the attitudes, interests, beliefs, feelings, knowledge, and experiences that students possess. It is important to repeat at this point, however, that the major limitation of these devices is their lack of established reliability and validity. (The nature of reliabil-

[38]E. I. Sawin, *Evaluation and the Work of the Teacher*, pp. 182–184.
[39]E. J. Webb et al., *Unobtrusive Measures.*
[40]E. I. Sawin, *Evaluation and the Work of the Teacher*, p. 184.

ity and validity will be discussed in Chapter 7. If you are not sure to what these terms refer, see pp. 280-284.) It is for this reason that it is so important to gather as much data on students as possible, using many different kinds of devices and procedures over a fairly long period of time, and cross-checking findings with personal observations, scores on more formal evaluative measures, reports of other teachers, counselors, and administrators, parents, and peers. Inferences about student attitudes, feelings, perceptions, interests, or beliefs, that are based on results obtained from applying a single device, or even several devices on a single occasion, are prone to serious error.

This is not to say, however, that teachers should not use these informal diagnostic devices. Diagnostic devices such as the ones described in this chapter are extremely useful in gathering data in a systematic way for large groups of students. Until reliable and valid tests for measuring complex behavior changes are more readily available, teachers must rely on procedures and tools such as those described herein. But any inferences drawn should be based on the results obtained from applying several such devices, and these inferences should be frequently cross-checked with other findings and reports and then reviewed and reconsidered.

SUMMARY

This chapter discussed the nature and use of informal diagnostic devices. The main thesis of the chapter was that teachers need to assess continually the knowledge, skills, and attitudes their students possess if they are to help them attain various objectives.

The terms "diagnosis" and "diagnostic evaluation" were defined. A distinction was made among diagnostic, formative, and summative evaluation, as well as among antecedent, transaction, and outcome conditions. The value of diagnosis before, during, and after instruction was discussed.

Several informal diagnostic tools that teachers can use to obtain data about the learning environment that exists in their classroom were then presented. A final note of caution about the use of informal diagnostic tools was made.

In sum, diagnostic data is important to acquire for several reasons:

- To keep a teacher's instructional objectives and efforts in tune with the needs and interests of students. Diagnostic evaluation can reveal what many of these needs and interests are, as well as changes in them that occur over a period of time.

- To identify certain non-instructional factors that may be limiting student progress. Diagnosis of a class can reveal to what extent such factors (e.g., diet) are affecting student learning and thus hindering their movement toward the attainment of desired objectives. If such factors seem to pervade, hypotheses can be suggested and investigated by checking with school counselors and nurse, the administration, parents, medical officials, and the like.
- To suggest possible causes of student strengths and weaknesses in attaining objectives. Diagnostic and formative evaluation can reveal the possession or lack of certain attitudes, skills, or understandings, information about cultural backgrounds, motivational patterns, and previous learnings that may be contributing to or detracting from student achievement.
- To suggest appropriate points at which to begin a unit of instruction. Diagnosis can reveal the lack of certain prerequisites necessary to understand further instruction.
- To accommodate different kinds of learners. Diagnosis can reveal differences in student ability, understanding, attitude, and interest. The level of attainment (upper levels of expectation) for various students can then be gauged and reasonable standards of performance expected can be established. As Taba[11] put it, "benchmarks" for evaluation of growth can be determined. Appropriate content, materials, learning activities, and procedures can then be planned.

EXERCISES*

I. Place an X in front of those statements listed below that might be given as a reason why evaluation during or before instruction is important.

1._____ To determine to what extent a particular objective has been achieved.

2._____ To obtain information prior to beginning instruction as to what kinds of attitudes, skills, and/or knowledge students already possess.

3._____ To determine to what extent non-educational factors are hindering students from making progress toward achieving previously determined objectives.

4._____ To identify materials that are too easy or too hard for students.

[11]H. Taba, *Curriculum Development*, p. 234.
*The author's suggestions are on page 398.

5._____ To suggest areas or points of instruction that may need to be repeated or approached in a different manner.

6._____ To identify particular strengths or weaknesses that students have.

7._____ To suggest possible causes of student strengths or weaknesses.

8._____ To reveal differences in student ability.

9._____ To point up teacher misconceptions of student ability.

10._____ To assist in determining reasonable standards of performance expected of students.

II. Column B lists different kinds of information about students that teachers often would like to know. Column A contains a number of informal diagnostic devices that teachers might use to obtain such information. Which device or devices from Column A might be used to obtain each of the kinds of information listed in Column B? Explain your reasoning.

A	B
a. Oral or Written Pre-tests	**1.** The *kind* of statements that students make in class.
b. Open-Ended Titles	
c. Unfinished Stories	**2.** The *number* and *direction* of remarks that students make in class.
d. Sociograms	
e. Anecdotal Records	**3.** A detailed recording of the activities of one or more students over a class period.
f. Checklists	
g. Participation Flow Charts	**4.** Student impressions of a particular learning activity in which they participated.
h. Discussion Analysis Sheets	
i. Unobtrusive Measures	**5.** Suggestions from students as to peoples or areas of the world they would be interested in studying.
j. Time-and-Motion Studies	
k. Attitude Scales	**6.** How students feel about individuals in other cultures.
	7. The student power structure or "pecking order" that exists in the classroom.
	8. How well various students perform in the role of discussion leader.
	9. Student reading interests.

III. Is there any time when a teacher might *not* want to obtain diagnostic information about a class? Discuss.

IV. Make up a list of various antecedent, transaction, and outcome conditions that you would be interested in obtaining about any students that you might teach. Compare your list with ones made up by your classmates or colleagues. What differences do you notice? Similarities? How would you explain these similarities and differences?

V. Try out some of the diagnostic techniques described in this chapter. What difficulties do you encounter? Can you improve on them in any way?

VI. How long should a teacher keep information of a diagnostic nature? Explain your reasoning.

VII. Are there any techniques described in this chapter that you would not use? If so, why not? Which ones seem most feasible to use? Least feasible? Why?

VIII. See if you can't work out some sort of category system of your own to observe student behavior in the classroom similar to what was done in Table 2.1. What behavior would you think especially important to observe in detail? Why? (Take a look at this point in Richard L. Ober, Ernest L. Bentley, and Edith Miller, *Systematic Observation of Teaching* (Englewood Cliffs, N.J.: Prentice-Hall, Inc., 1971) and Edmund Amielon and Elizabeth Hunter, *Improving Teaching: The Analysis of Classroom Verbal Interaction* (New York: Holt, Rinehart & Winston, Inc., 1967) for some ideas in this regard.)

THE SELECTION AND ORGANIZATION OF SUBJECT MATTER

This chapter deals with the problem of selecting and organizing subject matter in social studies courses. Once a teacher has determined his educational goals, and diagnosed his class, he still faces further problems of selection and organization. One of these problems involves the matter of selecting (or of helping his students select) subject matter for students to learn.

The first section of the chapter, therefore, discusses the nature and importance of statements of fact, concept, generalization, and theory, and presents examples of each. Criteria by which powerful concepts, generalizations and theories can be formulated or identified are suggested.

The second section presents several examples of powerful generalizations selected from five social science disciplines, and then illustrates how such generalizations can be used as an organizing focus around which to build teaching/learning units.

The third section illustrates how powerful concepts can serve as guidelines for selecting or formulating key questions to ask of data, and also how such concepts can be used as organizing threads to be developed throughout several grades.

The last section then emphasizes that choice is inevitable in selecting social studies content, and suggests a variety of criteria that teachers can use to help them choose such content.

When you have finished reading this chapter, therefore, you should be able to do the following:

- *distinguish* among facts, concepts, generalizations, and theories, and *demonstrate* what these terms mean by identifying or offering examples of each;
- *specify* (orally or in writing) at least six criteria that you could use to distinguish more powerful ideas and concepts from less powerful ideas

and concepts, and *use* these criteria to select or formulate such powerful ideas and concepts;

- *name* several (five or more) ideas that certain scholars in the disciplines of anthropology, geography, economics, political science, and
sociology have suggested as fundamental ideas of their disciplines;

- *explain* how generalizations might be used as a focal point around
which to develop teaching/learning units;

- *explain* how powerful concepts can be used as guidelines in preparing
key questions to ask of data;

- *explain* how powerful concepts can be used as organizing threads in
planning, and in selecting social studies content for various grades;

- *state* (orally or in writing) at least six criteria that you could use as
guidelines for selecting content for inclusion in social studies courses.

THE PROBLEM OF CONTENT SELECTION

One of the major problems facing any social studies teacher is that he
has at his disposal an extremely vast amount of data from which to choose.
For the most part, the content of the social studies is drawn from the disciplines of history and the social sciences—traditionally geography, political science, and economics; more recently anthropology, sociology, and
social psychology.[1] But that is not all—certainly art, literature, music,
ethics, education, current events, occasionally the natural sciences—indeed
all of life itself—might be considered as a data bank for the social studies.

It becomes quickly obvious, therefore, that scholarly knowledge has
reached such immense proportions today that no person can possibly learn
(or teach) it all. It has become almost a cliché to state that man's stockpile
of information now *doubles* every ten years. More and more data is added
to the social studies curriculum every year. Of necessity, a teacher must
choose only certain bits of knowledge with which to work. "But that is no
problem," say some. "Have students learn the facts." Unfortunately this
suggestion does not help very much, since there are far too many "facts"
for any of us to learn in our lifetime, let alone for students to learn in
school. Since the curriculum is already overcrowded, any attempt to
"cover" what amounts to an ever-increasing range and amount of factual
data creates considerable distress (to both teachers and students alike).
More than ever before, teachers need to possess a viable method of sorting
information so that the information which they ask students to learn will
have maximum educational value.

---

[1]Whether it should be so drawn, at least exclusively, is a subject of considerable
debate. See Fred M. Newmann, "Questioning the Place of Social Science Disciplines
in Education," *Social Education*, Nov. 1967, pp. 593–596; and James P. Shaver,
"Social Studies: The Need for Redefinition," in *Ibid.*, pp. 588–592.

What might such a method be? To answer this question, we must first consider the nature of different levels of knowledge—in particular, statements of fact, concept, generalization, and theory. Each of these is discussed in turn below.

FACTS

Facts are what logicians refer to as contingent statements or testable propositions. Their proof is contingent upon the presence or absence of empirical evidence with which any disinterested or nonpartial observer would agree. They represent things which actually exist or which have happened in the past. The activities of individuals, the dates of events, the locations of places, the size of objects, specific rules of procedure—all are facts. Statements of fact provide us with information and can be verified as being true or false, such as the "fact" that the United States of America landed men on the moon in the year 1969. The following are all examples of facts:

Henry Thoreau was the author of *Walden*.

The State of Virginia set up a land office in Kentucky in 1780.

Babe Ruth hit a total of 714 home runs—60 in 1927 alone—during his career in baseball.

Some four million Japanese soldiers and sailors were demobilized during the American occupation of Japan after World War II.

Notice that each of these statements refers to a particular occurrence, incident, event, or individual. Each states that a specific and unique phenomenon occurred in a particular time and place. They all say something about the world. If these statements are supported by evidence, we consider them to be true facts, though they are true in one instance rather than being generally applicable over many instances. They refer to particulars rather than universals. And social studies textbooks are full of them.

Teachers frequently insist that students learn facts like the above. In many cases, however, they are not clear in their own minds as to just why they are doing so. As a result, they often emphasize information of only minor import. Fantini and Weinstein put it well:

> Considering that so many of the largest problems facing the world and the United States today are predominantly a matter of inadequate human relations and lack of cooperation among different peoples, one wonders why we spend so much time trying to get our young children to memorize such facts as the order of American Presidents, the precise dates on which this or that event occurred,

the area in square miles of this or that state (or nation or continent), and the locations of natural resources in the world. We do not deny the importance of knowledge in these areas but we become concerned when schools emphasize these areas to the exclusion of others.

How many of us can remember these facts now, name even two products of Chile? Can you right off the top of your head, so to speak, list all the Presidents from Washington through Johnson in perfect order? Can you remember the year in which Texas was admitted to the Union? . . .[2]

This is not to say that facts are unimportant. The context in which facts are used, of course, determines to a considerable degree which facts are important to learn. Knowing the products of Chile, for example, might be of considerable import to a Chilean businessman. Furthermore, if we consider the situations or settings in which most people operate, it seems evident that some facts are more important than other facts. Thus, it probably is more important to know one's basic rights as guaranteed under the United States Constitution than to be able to name the dates that each amendment to the Constitution was passed; probably more important to know how Presidents are elected than to be able to name them all in perfect order; probably more important to know the reasons why various wars occurred than the names of all the battles fought in them.

Students need to acquire as much factual information as their individual capabilities permit, since facts are the building blocks of knowledge. It is impossible to make sense out of the world without facts, since they tell us something, as illustrated earlier, about occurrences, incidents, events, or individuals which exist today, or have existed in the past. But students must also learn how to tie together the facts they acquire into meaningful *relationships* of various sorts that will help them understand and explain more fully some part of their personal or social existence. Thus, if teachers wish to help students understand themselves and their world more completely, they must do more than merely help students to learn facts. They must help them acquire more theoretical knowledge such as concepts and generalizations.

CONCEPTS

Unlike facts, concepts are definitional in nature. They represent those characteristics that are common to a group of experiences. Whereas facts

[2]Mario D. Fantini and Gerald Weinstein, *The Disadvantaged: Challenge to Education* (New York: Harper & Row, 1968), pp. 139–140.

refer to a single object, event, or individual, concepts represent something common to several events, objects, or individuals. "The term 'religion' usually functions as a concept because there is no single object called religion; rather there are many events that are characterized by a reference to God and church and a commitment to moral principles."[3]

Concepts do not "exist" in reality, but represent our attempts to give order to reality—to order that information from our environment which we receive through our senses. We attempt to bring order to this sensory imput by attaching symbols (word-labels) to certain similarities we perceive in our experience.

> We observe that certain features of our experience keep cropping up, that certain experiences are recurrent. If the same experience recurs often enough to make it worth our while, we invent a word or sign to use on any occasion when we wish to communicate the experience. We see that pillar-boxes, poppies, and stop-lights are similar in one respect; and so we use the word "red" to express this similarity. We perceive that certain things are similar in many respects: say, they are all small, circular, and hard; and we invent a noun for the occasions when we wish to speak of any of these things, the noun "penny." We observe the penny doing something on various occasions, which we afterwards call "rolling." We see it rolling in certain recurrent ways, which we call "quickly" or "slowly."[4]

Notice, however, that concepts are invented rather than discovered. "Science and common-sense inquiry alike do not discover the ways in which events are grouped in the world; they invent ways of grouping. . . . Do such categories as tomatoes, lions, snobs, atoms, and mammalia exist? Insofar as they have been invented and found applicable to instances of nature, they do. They exist as inventions, not discoveries."[5]

Concepts thus are mental constructions invented by man to describe the characteristics that are common to a number of experiences. They enable us to relate a wide variety of individual and separate pieces of information into categories we devise, including in these categories those items which belong (that is, which have physical or psychological characteristics in common) and excluding those which do not. For example, "the concept of 'climate' . . . involves a combination of a number of specific facts, including the temperature, air pressure, moisture, and angle of the

[3]Jerome Kagan, *Understanding Children: Behavior, Motives and Thought* (New York: Harcourt Brace Jovanovich, 1971), p. 86.

[4]John Wilson, *Language and the Pursuit of Truth* (Cambridge: University Press, 1967), pp. 20–21.

[5]Jerome S. Bruner, Jacqueline J. Goodnow, and George A. Austin, *A Study of Thinking* (New York: John Wiley, 1956), p. 7.

sun to be found in a specific geographic area (over a period of time). None of these bits of data has much significance when standing alone, but when related together under the general concept of climate, they all have meaning and consequences for a wide variety of human activities."[6] The point to be noted here is that concepts facilitate understanding, for they make communication easier. It would be very difficult to communicate with others if we could not conceptualize that similar objects have a common identity. Thus we are saved ordinarily from having to describe in detail the specifics of poodles, cocker spaniels, and beagles, but can simply refer to them all as dogs.

Concepts, however, are not always indicated verbally. Kagan illustrates this clearly with the following example:

> A ten-year-old whose father frequently gave him orders may have experienced feelings of resentment toward him. As a result, whenever the boy encounters an older, authoritarian male, he feels anger and resentment. The dimensions (characteristics) "old," "male," and "give orders" lead him to experience a particular emotion that, although unnamed, is a *concept*. As the child grows older, he may begin to wonder why he has this emotional reaction and may even give it a name. He may say to himself, "Authority bugs me." The boy has now tied the verbal concept "authority" to the dimensions "old," "male," "give orders" and has made the concept more accessible to consciousness."[7]

KINDS OF CONCEPTS

Concepts can be classified in several ways. One useful way is to distinguish between concepts as classifications and concepts as connotations. *Classificatory* concepts represent ideas that refer to certain sets of characteristics that different objects, events, or individuals have in common. Often these characteristics can be experienced directly. Bruner and others[8] distinguish between two kinds of classificatory concepts. A *conjunctive* concept is defined by the presence of two or more attributes, all of which must be present. Thus, the concept of "tourist" is conjunctive in nature for the idea that it represents includes the characteristics "travel," "for pleasure," and "permanent home elsewhere." For an individual to qualify as a tourist, he must possess all three of the characteristics. A *disjunctive* concept, on

[6]Morris R. Lewenstein, *Teaching Social Studies in Junior and Senior High Schools: An Ends and Means Approach* (Skokie, Ill.: Rand McNally, 1963), p. 84.
[7]J. Kagan, *Understanding Children*, p. 87.
[8]J. S. Bruner *et al.*, *A Study of Thinking*.

the other hand, involves an either-or decision. Thus, the concept of "extra point" in football is based on the characteristic of kicking the ball through the goal posts (after a touchdown has been scored without a penalty being called), *or* running the ball over the goal line, *or* throwing a completed pass over the goal line. If *any one* of these events takes place, we say that an extra point has been scored.

Many concepts, however, are not classificatory, but connotative in nature. Highly complex concepts like causality, dignity, honor, nationalism, and interdependence are examples. The characteristics of such concepts cannot be pointed to or experienced directly. Their attributes are other concepts. They are usually relational in nature.

A *relational* concept represents a specific relationship between or among attributes, and is expressed numerically as a ratio or a product. For example, the concept of "population density" is usually defined as the number of people living in a square mile. The concept, usually expressed in numerical terms, indicates that a relationship exists between a certain number of people and the amount of land on which they live.

Thus the concept of "income tax bracket" (after deductions) is defined as the relationship between number of dependents and level of income.[9] The concept of "speed" is expressed as a ratio between the distance a person travels and the amount of time it takes him to travel the distance.[10] Notice that the concept is not the numerical ratio or product itself, but the *insight* into the relationship that exists between or among the attributes.[11]

We can increase the clarity of connotative concepts by expressing the ideas they represent in words that refer to observable actions or things, or by illustrating their meaning by performing (or having students perform or engage in) certain actions. This represents, as was described and illustrated in Chapter 1, an *operational* definition of a concept. An operational definition, you will recall, illustrates how doing things in a certain way will lead to a particular result. For example, the characteristics which define the concept of "causality" are not observable. If we define causality as "the relation of cause and effect," we understand very little, since the definition includes words no clearer than the word "causality" itself. We clarify the meaning of causality by defining it operationally.

For example, we might illustrate what we mean in a simple manner by lifting one edge of a table with our hand and then pointing out that the upward pressure of our hand against the bottom-side of the table's edge made the table move upward. We say that this is what we mean by cause—our

---

[9]J. S. Bruner *et al., A Study of Thinking,* p. 43.
[10]Harry S. Broudy, B. Othanel Smith, and Joe R. Burnett, *Democracy and Excellence in American Secondary Education* (Skokie, Ill.: Rand McNally, 1964), p. 123.
[11]*Ibid.*

hand "caused" the table to move upward. The fact that the table moved is what we mean by effect—the movement of the table resulted from the upward pressure of our hand. We then might illustrate that hitting one ball with another will usually make the second ball move (as in the game of pool); that yelling at someone unawares will usually make them jump; or that smiling at someone will usually make them smile back. In each case we say that the first event "caused" the second event to occur. The occurrence of the second event is a result or "effect" of the first event. We then point out that this relationship between cause and effect—that certain actions may produce other actions—is what we mean by "causality." Operational definitions "may also refer to various forms of order, such that we can say of a given attribute that a is greater, less than, or equal to b with respect to it. For instance, " 'harder than' may be defined as 'x scratches y, but y does not scratch x.' "[12] To illustrate this concept, we might bring in a number of metals and see which ones could be scratched.

SPECIAL CONSIDERATIONS

Broudy and others[13] have pointed out that some concepts cannot even be formulated beyond a common-sense level of understanding. The concept of "importance" is such an example. Yet the idea has meaning. If someone says "This is an important message," we know we are supposed to pay it particular heed.[14]

Some concepts are unclear because the attributes used to define the concept are themselves unclear. For example, if we define "patriotism" as "devotion to one's country," we would have difficulty getting a number of observers to agree as to whether or not various acts were examples of patriotism. The distinguishing characteristic in this case—"devotion to one's country"—is unclear. Defining "paternal" as "being characteristic of or befitting a father" is another case in point.

Furthermore, some concepts such as "democracy" cannot be completely defined because it is impossible to specify all of their attributes. They are "open-ended" in the sense that it is easy to keep on adding attributes that throw into question whether a given instance truly is an example of the concept. Broudy and his colleagues use the concept of murder as an example.

> From the standpoint of a court of law, murder is not an act committed by an individual. To kill someone is an act. To class a killing

[12]H. S. Broudy, B. O. Smith, and J. R. Burnett, *Democracy and Excellence*, p. 123.
[13]H. S. Broudy, B. O. Smith, and J. R. Burnett, *Democracy and Excellence*.
[14]*Ibid.*, p. 128.

is to make a judgment of the act. If we try to specify the criteria by which the act of killing would be decided to be a case of murder it is found that the list is theoretically interminable. We now know, for example, that if X kills Y, it is murder provided X was not insane at the time of the act, or he did not commit it in self-defense, or it was not done accidentally or incidentally to the performance of some duty, to mention only a few of the criteria by which a court may rule the act of killing out of the category of murder. Even were we to extend the list to include all criteria previously used, theoretically the list would still be incomplete. It is possible that some astute attorney would come forth with an argument giving rise to some new criterion.[15]

It is important for teachers to realize how concepts may differ if they wish to help students understand the meaning of various concepts. The type of concept determines the kind of strategy most effective for a teacher to use. We shall illustrate how to teach various kinds of concepts in Chapter 5.

THE ATTRIBUTES OF CONCEPTS

Kagan[16] suggests that there are four important qualities that can be applied to all concepts, regardless of the meaning of the common characteristics that the concept represents. These qualities are degree of abstraction, complexity, differentiation, and centrality of dimensions.

1. *Degree of Abstraction.* Concepts vary in terms of the nature of their characteristics. Concepts whose characteristics can be pointed to or experienced directly—such as flowers, dogs, and factories—are often referred to as "low-level" abstractions, and sometimes referred to as concrete. Concepts whose characteristics cannot be pointed to or experienced directly—such as freedom, honor, or intelligence—are said to be "higher-level" abstractions. The attributes of concrete concepts can usually be identified by the senses. They can be tasted, touched, heard, seen, or felt. The characteristics of the more abstract, or "higher-level" concepts are often other concepts. Writes Kagan: "The concept of intelligence, for example, rests on the dimensions of language proficiency, alertness, adaptability, and learning ability. Each of these four dimensions is itself an abstract concept resting on its own set of dimensions."[17]

2. *Complexity.* Concepts also differ in the *number* of attributes needed to define them. The more attributes needed, the more complex the concept

[15]H. S. Broudy, B. O. Smith, and J. R. Burnett, *Democracy and Excellence*, p. 130.
[16]J. Kagan, *Understanding Children.*
[17]*Ibid.*, p. 87.

is considered to be. The concept of cat, for example, is fairly simple, for it rests on only a few dimensions (four-legged, furry, purrs, meows, retractable claws, elongated pupils, rough tongue, whiskers, and pointed ears). The concept of culture, on the other hand, is quite complex, since it is defined by a host of attributes that include, among others, such concepts as ideas, customs, laws, traditions, institutions, and patterns of behavior, with each of these concepts being defined by a number of further attributes of their own. The more complex a concept is, the greater its capacity to organize and synthesize large numbers of simpler concepts and specific facts. The more complex a concept is, however, the more difficult it becomes for students to understand. Students vary widely in the degree to which they understand complex concepts. (No one probably understands any concept totally, since individual understanding is always based on individual experience which can never be total.) This represents a major problem for social studies teachers since much social content includes such complex concepts. (For example, urbanization, democracy, institution, fair play, nationalism, leadership, culture, and cooperation.)

It is important to remember, however, that concepts are formed through experience. The kinds of experiences a person has enable him to develop concepts of differing levels of abstraction. Thus concrete experiences that directly involve the senses (i.e., the actual touching, tasting, hearing, smelling or seeing of concrete objects), as is the case with particular colors, sounds, or shapes, enable us to formulate such concepts as "house" or "blue." Experiences which involve varying combinations of concrete objects over a period of time enable us to formulate concepts which are somewhat more complex such as "home" or "blueness" or highly complex as in those cases when we experience what we later refer to as examples of "patriotism," "democracy," or "justice." This developmental process is a gradual one, dependent on age as well as experience. Thus "from 'things I can drive this tent stake with' we move to the concept 'hammer' and from there to 'mechanical force,' each step being freer of definition by specific use than the former."[18] It is for this reason that *many different kinds* of experiences, both direct (the actual touching, viewing, etc. of things) and indirect (the use of words and symbols), are important if students are not only to acquire an adequate repertoire of concepts in general, but also to understand the meaning of complex concepts in particular.

3. *Differentiation.* Concepts also differ in the degree to which the basic set of common characteristics that they stand for can assume varied but related forms to express slightly different versions of the idea that the concept represents. Thus a concept like "screwdriver" is not very finely differ-

[18]J. S. Bruner *et al., A Study of Thinking*, p. 6.

entiated, since it can only take one form and there are no other words in our language which describe different kinds of screwdrivers. A concept like "fruit," however, is highly differentiated, for it can take many forms, from banana to peach to cherry. Kagan suggests that the concepts that are most central to a particular culture are those that are most highly differentiated. Thus, in our society, "the concept of property is captured by many related ideas, including land, money, furniture, stocks, bonds, cattle, and rights to an invention. The concept of inheritance, which is of considerably less significance to our society, has relatively few terms that distinguish among its forms."[19]

4. *Centrality of Dimensions.* The meaning of some concepts is derived from one or two key or critical attributes which point to the central features of the idea that the concept represents. The meaning of other concepts can only be understood by considering a number of attributes, each of which is equally important in defining the concept. Thus the meaning of the concept of "tourist," for example, rests on the key attributes of "travel," "for pleasure," and "permanent home elsewhere," ignoring more peripheral characteristics such as type of clothes worn by individuals or the color of their skin. The meaning of the "concept 'living animal' by contrast rests equally on the dimensions: capacity to reproduce, to exchange oxygen, and to ingest food and egest waste. Each of these dimensions is of approximately equal significance in defining the concept."[20] (The teaching of concepts will be discussed and exemplified in Chapter 5.)

THE IMPORTANCE OF CONCEPTS

Concepts are useful or affect us in many ways. DeCecco[21] suggests that several of these ways are as follows:

1. Concepts help us to deal with the tremendous complexity of our environment and to reduce it to manageable proportions. This is especially important in education since the amount of information available increases daily at an almost astronomical rate. Concepts involve classes of objects, events, individuals, or ideas. If we had to respond anew to each and every stimulus that we meet, our environment would overwhelm us. Through concepts, we simplify and order the varying perceptions that we receive through our senses. Bruner and his associates point this out with regard to color:

[19]J. Kagan, *Understanding Children*, p. 88.
[20]*Ibid.*, p. 89.
[21]John P. DeCecco, *The Psychology of Learning and Instruction* (Englewood Cliffs, N.J.: Prentice-Hall, 1968).

Consider only the task of acquiring a vocabulary fully adequate to cope with the world of color differences. . . . (This) is achieved by man's capacity to categorize. To categorize is to render discriminably different things equivalent, to group the objects and events and people around us into classes, and to respond to them in terms of their class membership rather than their uniqueness. . . . In place of a color lexicon of 7 million items, people in our society get along with a dozen or so commonly used color names. It suffices to note that the book on the desk has a "blue" cover. If the task calls for finer discrimination, we may narrow the category and note that it is in the class of things called "medium blue."[22]

2. Concepts help us to identify and make sense out of the various objects we find around us. When an individual identifies an object, he places it into a class. Thus a particular "thing" takes on meaning for us as we realize that it is one of many similar "tables," "books," or "exciting ideas." To make sense out of one's world, an individual must identify the objects, individuals, or sensations that are a part of it. And for any kind of identification to be something more than just perception, classification is essential.

3. Concepts reduce the necessity for continual re-learning. Once an individual has learned what a "dog" is, for example, he can apply the concept to a large number of examples (e.g., wire-haired terriers, basset hounds, collies, etc.) without having to re-learn it.

4. Concepts help us in solving problems. By placing items in the correct class, for example, we often can gain some insight into how to proceed to deal with a problem that is before us. As Thomson suggests, "once an object is classified not as an edible mushroom but as a poisonous fungus, we desist from eating it and prevent others from tasting it."[23] One reason that we often have difficulty dealing with particular situations is because the individuals involved are difficult to sort into categories that enable us to establish a meaningful way to proceed in our dealings with them. Whether an approaching individual is conceptualized as "friend" or "enemy" affects considerably how we react to him.

5. Concepts make more complicated instruction and explanation possible. As we proceed through the grades, much that we learn is based on what we have presumably learned before. Much instruction in the social studies, for example, is verbal in nature and is based on the assumption that students have learned earlier the concepts necessary to understand that which is now being presented. Concepts bring to mind information (other concepts, ideas, principles, laws, etc.) that have been learned pre-

[22]J. S. Bruner, J. J. Goodnow, and G. A. Austin, *A Study of Thinking*, pp. 1–2.
[23]Robert Thomson, *The Psychology of Thinking* (Baltimore: Penguin Books, 1959), p. 65.

viously and thus prevent us from having to go over the same ground again and again. The important thing for teachers to realize, however, is that concepts (or concept-words) are shorthand labels which we use to put together in our minds the characteristics in common which otherwise quite different items possess. If students have not previously come in contact with, or otherwise experienced (actually or vicariously) examples of a particular concept, any use by the teacher of the concept may draw only stares of incomprehension. Thus the continual necessity for any teacher to relate the concepts he is using to specific concrete examples that exist in the student's environment.

6. Concepts as stereotypes. Hunt and Metcalf[24] define a stereotype as a category that implies several characteristics, but the characteristics do not imply the category. Thus the stereotype which many people have for Negroes is that Negroes are lazy, stupid, and untrustworthy. If an individual accepts this stereotype he would reason that all Negroes have these characteristics. They would not argue the reverse, however, that anyone who is lazy, stupid, and trustworthy is a Negro. The point here is that stupidity, laziness, and unreliability are not defining attributes of the category, Negro. *Some* Negroes probably are lazy, stupid, and untrustworthy. But so are *some* Caucasians and Orientals. The key attributes by which a Negro is differentiated from other individuals are the physical traits which Negroes possess in common, but which Caucasians and Orientals lack.[25]

Stereotypes are inadequate classifications. They are danger signals, therefore, and suggest that students misunderstand a concept. They are not clear about what the essential characteristics are which *all* members of the category possess. It is the teacher's job at this point to help the student form a more adequate concept. He does this by providing additional experiences for students so that they can perceive a wider variety of examples and nonexamples of the concept than they have experienced heretofore, and then to encourage them *to discuss* their perceptions. (This approach is discussed further in Chapter 5.)

7. Finally, concepts represent our picture of "reality" and thus describe our world for us. We cannot think or really even perceive without them. We could not communicate, create a society, or carry out anything but the simplest and most animalistic behavior without them. The ability to conceptualize distinguishes man from all other forms of life. Since the categories into which children will sort out and place items reflects heavily,

---

[24]Maurice P. Hunt and Lawrence E. Metcalf, *Teaching High School Social Studies,* 2nd ed. (New York: Harper & Row, 1968).
[25]*Ibid.*, p. 95.

however, the culture into which they were born, and thus the kind of world to which they have been exposed, there is strong reason for every teacher to provide as many varied and different experiences (i.e., exposure to and discussion of a wide variety of different people, situations, beliefs, values, customs, cultural settings, etc.) as he or she possibly can in order to avoid the forming of inadequate concepts or stereotypes.

GENERALIZATIONS

Generalizations are statements that express relationships among concepts. Like facts, they can be supported or refuted by recourse to observable evidence of various kinds. Like concepts, they are important to develop in the social studies since they help students make sense out of their world. As long ago as 1916 John Dewey urged an emphasis upon the "main ideas" of a discipline as a means to help students make greater sense out of their experience.[26] Alfred North Whitehead made the same point when he said:

> We enunciate two educational commandments, "Do not teach too many subjects," and again, "What you teach, teach thoroughly."
> The result of teaching small parts of a large number of subjects is the passive reception of disconnected ideas, not illumined with any spark of vitality. Let the main ideas which are introduced into a child's education be few and important, and let them be thrown into every combination possible. The child should make them his own, and should understand their application here and now in the circumstances of his actual life. From the very beginning of his education, the child should experience the joy of discovery. The discovery which he has to make is that general ideas give an understanding of that stream of events which pours through his life, which is his life.[27]

Such ideas (or generalizations) suggest relationships which appear to exist in the world, and offer insights into the way the world "works." Their validity is attested to by the amount of factual data in existence which supports the relationship they suggest. The following are all examples of generalizations:

The daily activities of a people reflect their values.
The ways in which people see themselves and their problems affects the ways in which they try to deal with those problems.

[26]J. Dewey, *Democracy and Education* (New York: Macmillan, 1916).
[27]A. N. Whitehead, *The Aims of Education and Other Essays* (New York: Macmillan, 1929, Free Press paperback edition), p. 2.

Political change results from dissatisfaction with the status quo. Change reflects an attempt to deal with the causes of the dissatisfaction.

Generalizations are aids to thinking and understanding. They not only describe data but also give structure to this data. Whereas facts refer to *unique* events, individuals, or situations, the relationships which generalizations suggest refer to *more* than one example. Thus, as illustrations of the generalization that "man's ways of living are affected by the physical and social environment in which he lives," factual examples from ancient Egypt, France during the days of Louis XIV, or contemporary San Francisco could be selected.

Some ideas are obviously more powerful than others, and students must be exposed to the most powerful ideas of which we are capable. Thus criteria need to be identified that we can use as a basis for distinguishing more powerful ideas from less powerful ideas. But what criteria? The following questions may be suggested:

1. To how many varied areas, events, people, ideas, objects, etc., does the generalization apply? (Applicability)
2. How likely is it that the relationship which the generalization suggests does indeed exist in actuality? (Accuracy)
3. To what degree does the generalization, as stated, lead on to other insights? (Depth)
4. To what extent does (do) the relationship(s) which the generalization suggests describe important aspects of human behavior and explain important segments of today's world? (Significance)
5. How much information does it encompass? (Breadth)
6. How many powerful (complex) concepts does it include? (Conceptual strength)

Consider the two generalizations listed below:

Blondes have more fun.
How quickly any change comes about depends not only on the nature of the change itself, but also on the pressures for and against that change.

Which is the more powerful? If we apply the criteria listed above, it becomes obvious that the second example exceeds the first in power, since the second example is more widely applicable, is more representative of the world as we really find it, gives us more information about why people behave as they do, suggests other insights, can encompass a greater amount of information, and includes a greater number of powerful (i.e., complex) concepts. If we were asked to choose which of these two ideas would be most helpful to students in understanding their world, example two would stand us in better stead than example one.

THEORIES

Generalizations can be combined into theories. A *theory* is a set of interrelated propositions which indicate relationships among several generalizations. The power of a theory lies in its capability to explain and predict phenomena. Skager and Weinberg[28] point out that the more youthful a field of inquiry is, the more likely it is that its theories will rely on propositions of *fact*. They go on to point out as an example that in Physical Education many relationships are suggested about the relationship of a particular body characteristic, for instance, to the performance of a given physical act. Though objective (i.e., easily observable), these propositions are highly specific—that is they lack the generalizability characteristic of propositions which suggest relationship among concepts. Propositions which suggest relationships among facts, therefore, constitute a lower order of theorizing than propositions which suggest relationships among concepts, while relationships among concepts constitute a lower order of theorizing than propositions which suggest relationships among generalizations. Thus, in education, "a proposition of fact might state a relationship between a particular type of achievement and a certain behavior on the part of the teacher, such as saying 'good' when students give a correct answer to a question. A higher order theory would relate the more general construct (concept) of reinforcement, covering many types of teacher behavior, to a variety of aspects of student achievement."[29]

Theories in the social sciences, like generalizations, can be ranked in terms of their power. To perform such rankings, of course, we again need certain criteria. Drawing on the criteria listed previously on page 105, the following are suggested:

1. How *many* propositions are interrelated? (Breadth)
2. How *complex* are the propositions that are interrelated? (Complexity)
3. To how many *varied* areas, events, people, ideas, or objects does the theory apply? (Applicability)
4. To what extent do the relationships suggested by the interrelated propositions contained within the theory *describe* and *explain* important elements of human behavior and explain important segments of today's world? (Explanatory power)
5. To what extent does the theory lead on to other *insights*? (Depth)
6. How many *powerful* (i.e., complex) concepts as opposed to facts does the theory include? (Conceptual strength)
7. How *testable* are the hypotheses that can be derived from the propositions interrelated within the theory? (Testability)

[28]Rodney W. Skager and Carl Weinberg, *Fundamentals of Educational Research: An Introductory Approach* (Glenview, Ill.: Scott, Foresman, 1971).
[29]*Ibid.*, p. 75.

Table 3.1 illustrates several propositions ordered on the basis of the above criteria, with Level VI representing the most and Level I the least powerful.

The proposition at Level V suggests a limited set of relationships among the concepts anxiety, social class, and student ability to solve problems. The propositions at Level VI suggest a more extensive relationship among social class, anxiety, family activity, and student achievement.[30] Using the criteria listed just above, we would rank the proposition at Level VI as the most powerful, since it contains a greater number of complex propositions, is more widely applicable than the previous propositions, explains an important part of human behavior, leads on to other insights, includes a number of complex concepts, and suggests a number of testable hypotheses. As defined here, propositions I–IV would not represent theories, but

TABLE 3.1

*LEVELS OF PROPOSITIONS**

Proposition	*Example*
I. Abstract Definition	Man is an anxious being.
II. Proposition relating a fact to a fact	Boys bite their fingernails more than do girls.
III. Proposition relating a fact to a concept	Men are more prone to anxiety than are women.
IV. Proposition relating a concept to a concept	Anxiety interferes with problem-solving ability.
V. A limited set of interrelated propositions	Anxiety differs according to social class. Anxiety interferes with problem-solving ability.
VI. An extensive set of interrelated propositions	Academic progress is related to social-class background. Middle-class students are more anxious than lower-class students. Anxiety which is produced in the home takes its outlet in academic striving. Actual neurosis appearing in academic settings is a function of the academic striving, exaggerated by anxiety, which is frustrated by lack of ability.

*FUNDAMENTALS OF EDUCATIONAL RESEARCH: AN INTRODUCTORY APPROACH, by Rodney W. Skager and Carl Weinberg (Glenview, Ill.: Scott Foresman & Co., 1971), Copyright © by Scott Foresman & Co. Reprinted by permission.

[30]R. W. Skager and C. Weinberg, *Fundamentals of Educational Research*, p. 76.

rather statements of fact (II), concept (I), and generalization (III and IV). Only the sets of *interrelated* propositions at levels V and VI represent theories, and Level VI is more powerful than Level V.

SUMMARY:

FACTS, CONCEPTS, GENERALIZATIONS

In sum, facts refer to a single object, event, or individual, concepts represent something common to several events, objects, or individuals, while generalizations represent relationships that exist among a number of concepts (see Table 3.2). Theories represent sets of interrelated generalizations. Facts, generalizations, and theories, however, differ significantly from concepts in one very important respect. Concepts are *definitions*. Facts, generalizations, and theories represent propositions. As a result we verify them differently. Theories, generalizations, and facts all represent examples of statements that can be supported or refuted by recourse to publicly observable evidence. The truth or falsity of a fact lies in the existence or absence of such evidence to show that it does or did occur. The degree to which a generalization or theory is warranted lies in the amount of facts there are to support the relationship which it suggests. The more facts to be found that support the relationship, the more warranted we consider the generalization or theory to be.

It is impossible to verify the existence of a concept in the same way that facts and generalizations are verified. Concepts cannot be tested in experience, for they do not "exist" in experience. They exist in the minds of men. They represent the meanings which men give to experience. They cannot be tested experientially for no conceivable test for them exists. Their meaning can only be understood through the use of examples which illustrate the set of common physical or psychological characteristics to which the concept refers.

THE SELECTION OF GENERALIZATIONS

There is still the problem of selecting generalizations for teaching and learning. Where can generalizations be found? There are numerous lists of social science generalizations already in existence from which a teacher might choose,[31] using the criteria identified on page 105. Textbooks are

---

[31]California State Department of Education, *Social Studies Framework for the Public Schools of California*, Part III, prepared by the State Curriculum Commission (Sacramento, Calif.: State Dept. of Education, June 1962), pp. 89–109.

TABLE 3.2

LEVELS OF KNOWLEDGE

History and the Social Science Disciplines	Ideas (Generalizations)	Complex Concepts	Specific Concepts	Specific Judgments of Fact
ANTHROPOLOGY	The life style of a culture is shaped by the contributions of groups that make up that culture.	CULTURE	digging stick	Orthodox Hindus do not eat beef.
ECONOMICS	Every society faces a conflict between unlimited wants and limited resources.	SCARCITY	factory	The per capita income of the United States in 1965 was roughly twice that of Great Britain and four times that of India.
GEOGRAPHY	Every geographic area is affected by physical, biotic, and societal forces.	CLIMATE	seaport	Latosolic soils develop in the humid low latitudes where temperatures are high and rainfall heavy.
HISTORY	Historical events can rarely, if ever, be explained in terms of a single cause.	CAUSALITY	historical document	The Quebec Act was passed in 1774.
POLITICAL SCIENCE	All societies establish authoritative institutions that can make decisions that are binding on the members of the society.	POLITICAL SYSTEM	citizen	The Federal Government of the United States has three main branches.
PSYCHOLOGY	The social groups to which an individual belongs helps to shape his behavior.	PERSONALITY	person	The higher an animal is in the ontogenetic scale, the more complex is the organization of its nervous system.
SOCIOLOGY	All social systems are important and meaningful to those individuals who are their members.	SOCIAL SYSTEM	family	Some Pakistani families make their living by raising sheep on the plains of central Asia.

full of generalizations, as is the daily press and other media. Or a teacher might have a go at formulating his own. Through reading, discussing, thinking about the world and its problems, it may appear that certain relationships exist. If further reading and discussion appears to substantiate one or more of the ideas, an attempt might then be made to develop a teaching-learning unit[32] with one of these generalizations (selected or created) as the focus.

The social science disciplines, however, are the most profitable source, since they represent at the present time, the largest amount of theoretical knowledge available in organized form.[33]

Each of these disciplines (anthropology, geography, economics, political science, sociology, and psychology) suggest a number of fundamental insights about the way the world works. They include not only gigantic stockpiles of facts, but also concepts, generalizations, and theories which give *order* and *power* to the factual content in their stockpiles. For example, various social scientists have diagrammed what they believe to be the fundamental ideas of their disciplines. Five of these schematics, together with a list of statements which these scholars believe to be the fundamental ideas of their discipline, are presented on the following pages.

Fundamental Ideas in Anthropology.   Certain fundamental ideas of anthropology have been suggested by Professor Paul Bohannan of Northwestern University. Figure 3.1 shows the following idea relationships.

1. Man may be looked upon as a
   a. mammalian animal,
   b. social animal, and
   c. cultural animal.
2. Man, in these three capacities, has needs.
3. Man's needs are satisfied within a social structure.

[32]A teaching-learning unit is a certain amount of content and learning activities selected and organized so as to help students achieve certain desired and pre-determined objectives. Such units will be discussed and exemplified in Chapter 8.

[33]It is not the purpose of this book to describe and discuss the nature of the social science disciplines. There are, however, a number of other sources to which teachers can turn. See the volume produced by the American Council of Learned Societies in collaboration with the National Council for the Social Studies, *The Social Studies and the Social Sciences* (New York: Harcourt Brace Jovanovich, 1962): Also, Erling Hunt (ed.), *High School Social Studies Perspectives* (Boston: Houghton Mifflin, 1962); William T. Lowe, *Structure and the Social Studies* (Ithaca, New York: Cornell University Press, 1969); John U. Michaelis and A. Montgomery Johnston, *The Social Sciences—Foundations of the Social Studies* (Boston: Allyn and Bacon, 1965); Irving Morrissett (ed.), *Concepts and Structure in the New Social Science* (New York: Holt, Rinehart & Winston, 1967); Irving Morrissett and W. W. Stevens, Jr., (eds.), *Social Science—The Search for Rationale* (New York: Holt, Rinehart & Winston, 1971); Raymond H. Muessig and Vincent R. Rogers (eds.), *Social Science Seminar Series* (6 volumes) (Columbus, Ohio: Charles E. Merrill, 1965).

FIGURE 3.1

Fundamental Ideas of Anthropology*

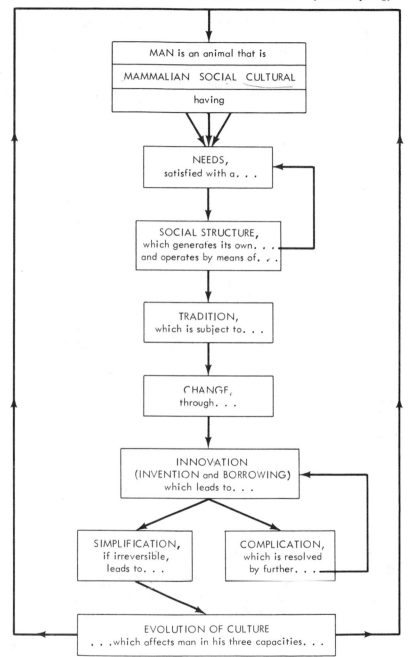

4. Social structure itself has needs (called "requisites") which must be satisfied if it is to persist.
5. Needs are satisfied within a particular set of patterned behavior: tradition.
6. All traditions leave some wants unsatisfied.
7. Dissatisfaction leads to changes in traditions.
8. Changes take the form of invention and borrowing: innovation.
9. Innovation leads to complication and simplification.
10. Complication leads to social dislocations. Problems caused by dislocations may be resolved through further innovation.
11. If simplification is of such a magnitude that it forms an irreversible base for man's behavior (for example, the use of fire), it leads to evolution of culture.
12. The evolution of culture affects man in his three capacities as a mammalian, social, and cultural animal.[34]

Fundamental Ideas in Geography.   Fundamental ideas in geography, as worked out by Professor Peter Greco of Syracuse University, are shown in Figure 3.2, and described below.

1. Every geographic area is affected by physical, biotic, and societal forces.
2. The impact of these forces on a geographic area creates similarities among areas. These similar areas are called uniform regions. They are static in character.
3. The similarities among different areas have been brought about through different combinations of physical, biotic, and societal forces.
4. An area may be kept together through a pattern of circulation binding the area to a central place. This area is called a nodal region, held together by functional relationships. The nodal region is dynamic in character.
5. Uniform and nodal regions are often related to each other through gravitation to the same central place.[35]

Fundamental Ideas in Political Science.   Important idea relationships in political science have been suggested by Professor David Easton of the University of Chicago. Figure 3.3 contains the following ideas:

1. Members of society have many wants which they hope to satisfy.
2. Some of these wants will be satisfied through the economic system, family system, educational system, and religious system. Wants that cannot be satisfied by any of these systems are channeled to the political system.
3. As the people's wants enter the political system for satisfaction, they become demands. These demands are screened.

[34]Lawrence Senesh, "Organizing a Curriculum Around Social Science Concepts," in Irving Morrissett (ed.), *Concepts and Structure in the New Social Science Curricula* (New York: Holt, Rinehart & Winston, 1967), pp. 32–35.
[35]*Ibid.*, pp. 35–37.

FIGURE 3.2

*Fundamental Ideas of Geography**

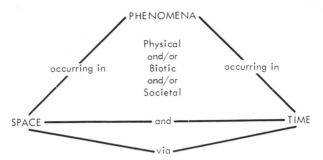

PHENOMENA

Physical
and/or
Biotic
and/or
Societal

occurring in   occurring in

SPACE ——————— and ——————— TIME

— via —

First and Second-Hand knowledge

fieldwork   mapping   expository reports

photo-interpretation

statistical techniques

constitute

GEOGRAPHIC FACTS

which on a certain

SCALE

constitute

GEOGRAPHIC DISTRIBUTION

which on a certain

SCALE

— via —

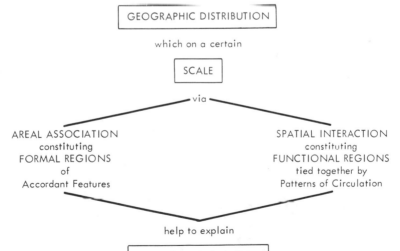

AREAL ASSOCIATION   SPATIAL INTERACTION
constituting   constituting
FORMAL REGIONS   FUNCTIONAL REGIONS
of   tied together by
Accordant Features   Patterns of Circulation

help to explain

AREAL DIFFERENTIATION

*From Concepts and Structure in the New Social Science Curricula edited
by Irving Morrissett. Copyright © 1967 by Holt, Rinehart and Winston, Inc. Reprinted by permission of Holt, Rinehart and Winston, Inc.

FIGURE 3.3
*Systems Analysis of Political Life**

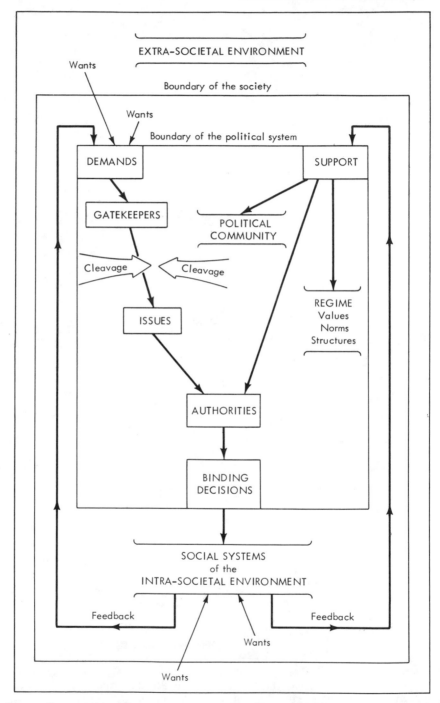

4. The screening process operates through formal or informal organizations. These organizations act as gate keepers. Some of the demands vanish. Others become issues debated in the political community (a group who share a desire to work together as a unit in the political solution of problems).

5. The issues are molded by cleavages in the political community and by the authorities which translate these demands into binding decisions.

6. The binding decisions affect the social systems and the participants in them, generating positive or negative support.

7. The support may be directed toward the political community, toward the regime (a political system which incorporates a particular set of values and norms, and a particular structure of authority), and/or toward the authorities (the particular persons who occupy positions of political power within the structure of authority).

8. The binding decisions generate new wants which appear again at the gate of the political system asking for recognition.

9. The source of the support for the political community, regime, and authorities may originate from the social systems in the form of education, patriotism, and other mechanisms.[36]

Fundamental Ideas in Sociology.   Professor Robert Perrucci of Purdue University has suggested a fundamental structure of sociology whose core idea is that of values and norms. The system is illustrated in Figure 3.4.

1. Values and norms are the main sources of energy to individuals and society.

2. Societies' values and norms shape social institutions, which are embodied in organizations and groups, where people occupy positions and roles.

3. People's positions and roles affect their attitudes toward society's values and norms, and result either in support of the existing values and norms, or in demands for modification of them, and the circle starts again.[37]

Fundamental Ideas in Economics.   The following ideas have been suggested as fundamental to economics by Professor Lawrence Senesh of the University of Colorado. The same ideas and relationships are shown in chart form in Figure 3.5.

1. The central idea of economics is the scarcity concept, namely, that every society faces a conflict between unlimited wants and limited means.

2. Out of the scarcity concept a family of ideas emerge. Because of scarcity, man has tried to develop methods to produce more in less time, or more with less material, and in shorter time. Various types of specialization were discovered in order to overcome the conflict between unlimited wants and limited resources. We specialize geographically, occupationally, and technologically. The third family of ideas grows out of specialization.

[36]*Ibid.*, pp. 28–30.
[37]*Ibid.*, pp. 30–32.

FIGURE 3.4
*Fundamental Ideas of Sociology**

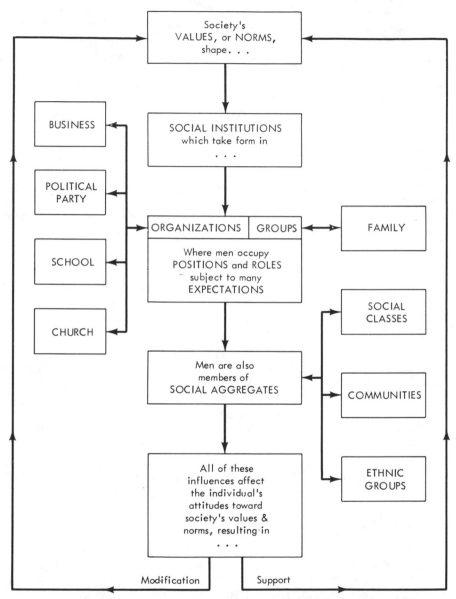

FIGURE 3.5
*Fundamental Ideas of Economics**

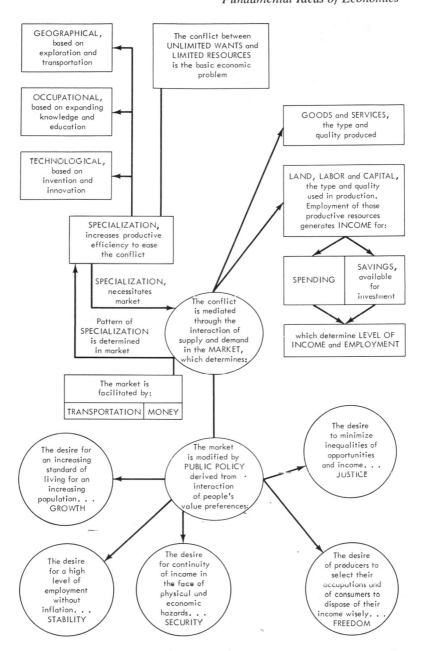

3. Because of specialization, we are interdependent; interdependence necessitates a monetary system and a transportation system. The fourth idea emerges from the first, scarcity, and from interdependence.
4. Men had to discover an allocating mechanism and this is the market, where through the interaction of buyers and sellers price changes occur. Prices determine the pattern of production, the method of production, income distribution and the level of spending and saving, which, in turn, decide the level of total economic activity. The fifth family of ideas grows out of the fact that the economic system is a part of political society.
5. The market decision is modified by public policies, carried out by the government, to assure welfare objectives. These welfare objectives are determined in the United States through the political interaction of 200 million people which generates thousands of welfare objectives which I have reduced to five: our attempts to accelerate growth, to promote stability, to assure economic security, to promote economic freedom, and to promote economic justice.[38]

Each of these statements and schematics (in anthropology, geography, political science, economics, and sociology) represent how one scholar views the fundamental ideas of his particular discipline, though there are certainly other ideas which might be suggested. These ideas, at least at present, represent some of the most powerful insights currently available about the ways of man and his world. They offer considerable potential for teachers to use as organizers around which to build teaching-learning units in social studies courses in all the grades. But how? How can teachers use generalizations to help guide not only the selection, but also the organization of content?

THE USE OF CONCEPTS AND GENERALIZATIONS IN SELECTING AND ORGANIZING SOCIAL STUDIES CONTENT

GENERALIZATIONS AS ORGANIZERS

Suppose an eleventh-grade teacher of American history believes that students can gain considerable insight into reasons for, and reactions to, present-day governmental activities through studying about and investigating the "New Deal" programs inaugurated under President Franklin D. Roosevelt in the 1930s, their causes, and their subsequent effects. One way to proceed might be for the teacher to select one or more social science (or other) generalizations he believes particularly insightful that are illustrated to some degree by individuals who existed or by events which

[38]*Ibid.*, pp. 24–28.

took place during the years 1932–1939, and then to use these ideas as organizing foci around which to build teaching-learning units. For example, the following generalization illustrates an idea, selected from the discipline of anthropology, that might be used:

> The culture in which men live largely shapes how they feel, behave, and perceive as they adapt to the world.

The selection of subject matter (content) for study is now somewhat simplified. The teacher, along with his students, can select for study those facts which they think may help them investigate (and at a later date, support, refute, or modify) the degree to which the above idea is warranted. Table 3.3 illustrates how one teacher outlined this idea, together with certain supporting content samples, as a guideline for investigation.

Learning activities (see Chapter 4) can now be designed to engage students in experiences that will further their investigation. Through the use of stories, vivid readings, guest speakers, films, pictures, recordings, filmstrips, and the like, presented as clearly and simply as possible, students could be helped, as mentioned above, to see the variety of problems which existed during this period and the attempted efforts made by FDR and the Congress to deal with them. Individuals, events, actions, arguments, etc., which existed or occurred during the period of the New Deal could be investigated to determine whether the organizing idea (generalization) should be supported, refuted, or modified. (An example of a complete teaching-learning unit organized around generalizations is presented in Chapter 7.)

Ideas of similar power can be used as organizing foci for units in other subjects and at other grade levels, from K through 12, though of course the content samples would differ in complexity depending on grade level. This organization should not be considered a "lesson plan" however. (See Chapter 8.) It is primarily a way of organizing material to promote student investigation and understanding of the relationships suggested by powerful generalizations. How many "lessons" will be necessary to present, think about, discuss, and understand this material will depend on the nature of the students and the skill of the teacher involved. Nevertheless, it is argued here that through such organization teachers will be able to work more effectively toward the general goal of promoting not only understanding of the world in which we live, but also the more specific objective of having students investigate the relationships suggested by powerful ideas.

Caution is in order, however. There is considerable temptation among teachers to present generalizations as truth and to teach them as truth. But

TABLE 3.3

AN OUTLINE FOR A UNIT ON THE NEW DEAL, ORGANIZED AROUND A POWERFUL GENERALIZATION TOGETHER WITH POSSIBLE SUPPORTING CONTENT SAMPLES

Objectives	Organizing Idea	Outline of Factual Content Samples
Given appropriate reading material and other sources, students should be able to:	The culture in which men live largely shapes how they feel, behave, and perceive as they adapt to the world.	
I. *State* several (five or more) examples of ways in which the conditions under which people live can affect their actions.		I. Nature of the Depression A. Problems facing the New Administration in 1933. B. Effects of the Depression on people's lives.

II. *State* several (at least three) examples of ways in which people might react to a crisis in their lives, *give* at least three different ways in which nations reacted to the Great Depression of the 1930s, and *explain*, in each case, why the nation reacted as it did.		II. Totalitarian Models.
		A. Fascist Italy and the idea of the corporate state.
		B. Germany—the program of Adolf Hitler.
		C. The Soviet Union—a planned economy.
		D. Appeals in the U.S.
		  1. Socialists
		  2. Townsend Plan
		  3. EPIC—Upton Sinclair
		  4. Share the Wealth—Huey Long
		  5. The Radio Priest, Father Coughlin

III. *Name* several (at least four) examples of legislation initiated under FDR's leadership to deal with the domestic problems facing the United States in the 1930s, *explain* how each was intended to alleviate a certain problem, and *describe* at least two of the ways in which various people reacted to these pieces of legislation.		III. Dealing with the Depression in the U.S.
		A. Prevailing philosophy of government prior to 1932.
		B. Legislation
		  1. Emergency Relief
		  2. Recovery
		  3. Reform
		C. Reactions to FDR's program

IV. *Summarize* at least two conflicting evaluations that		IV. Evaluation of the New Deal

Objectives	Organizing Idea	Outline of Factual Content Samples
have been made of the New Deal, *give* an estimate as to why the individual concerned rated the New Deal as he did, and then *evaluate* the effectiveness of the New Deal by discussing, in writing, the question: "Did the New Deal solve the basic problems facing the United States that emerged during the 1920s?"		A. Did it solve the basic problems which emerged in the 1920s? Conflicting viewpoints: 1. Hoover 2. FDR himself 3. Freidel (*New Deal in Historical Perspective*, Bulletin Serv. Cent. Teachers History) 4. Perkins (*New Age of FDR*) 5. Burns (*Lion and the Fox*) 6. Zinn (*History and Politics*)

generalizations are of value only when an individual understands the relationship which the generalization represents and realizes why (or if) it is warranted. "Generalizing results from finding relationships among specific bits of information. *Without those recallable understandings and pieces of information, generalizations are virtually meaningless and will be remembered only when memorized.* In addition, they are soon forgotten."[39]

It is to be emphasized, therefore, that generalizations are not to be presented to students as "givens" but rather as statements to be investigated. Both teachers and students may propose such statements. But students also need to be helped to generalize for themselves. (See Chapter 5). Thus teachers need to devote considerable energy and time to helping students discover relationships among data rather than giving them relationships which they (teachers) have chosen or worked out ahead of time. "Since generalizations themselves tend to be abstract, unspecific, and relevant *only* when they illustrate particular conditions—in a sense the antithesis of childhood experiencing and learning—it may readily be seen that generalizations cannot be presented full-blown, ready to be unquestionably accepted by eager minds."[40] Teachers must find ways by which children may discover generalizations as a consequence of their own thinking, and then encourage them to look continually for exceptions to all generalizations they propose or are given, and to modify them, if necessary, as seems appropriate.

[39]Malcolm P. Douglass, *Social Studies from Theory to Practice in Elementary Education* (Philadelphia: Lippincott, 1967), p. 93. Italics added.
[40]*Ibid.*, p. 94.

It does students little good for the teacher to give them various generalizations to accept as truth. Generalizations are testable propositions—they can be supported, modified, or refuted with evidence. But it is the student who must be helped to do the testing. This is where facts come into the picture, and frequent assertions to the contrary, why they are important to acquire. They are important because they serve as evidence to test generalizations and theories. The more facts there are to support an idea, the more warranted is the relationship that the idea suggests. Hence the need to ask students continually: What facts exist with regard to this idea? Do they support the idea? refute it? qualify it? What additional facts do we need? How might we determine if such facts exist? locate them?

No one can study all the facts, however. Several different factual samples can be used by students to investigate the same generalization. Which facts are selected for investigation depend on such factors as the materials that are available, the kinds of students involved, what problems or concerns teachers and students are interested in, and the contrasts the different factual samples provide.

As was mentioned previously, therefore, facts should be sampled in order to help students develop important ideas rather than being covered for their own sake. Understanding and testing of the insights suggested by powerful generalizations can be accomplished best through an in-depth study of a few samplings of contrasting data rather than a limited study of several samples. For example, in studying American History, a generalization which could be investigated might be "that the way of life in the colonies was influenced by two factors:

1. Who the people were and what they brought with them (ideas, beliefs, skills, tastes, etc.) and
2. Whether or not the characteristics of their landing place (people, climate, soil, etc.) were hospitable."

It is possible that students can consider this aspect of colonial life more effectively by a detailed study of two contrasting colonies than by a rapid and superficial study of all 13 colonies. This does not imply that the other 11 colonies would not be mentioned, but rather that some important ideas about colonization could best be considered through limited depth studies.

Notice that building teaching-learning units around generalizations simplifies revisions. A teacher does not have to take everything apart every so often in order to remain up to date. Ideas can be eliminated, developed in greater depth or combined as further scholarship and investigation suggest. Current factual data can be substituted for that which is obsolete. Units can be expanded or condensed as needed. Any one generalization can be developed in several ways and with a variety of different facts, making it possible for teachers to adjust particular units to differing interests and motivational patterns.

In short, generalizations can be of value in a number of ways. They can provide a focal point for the building of teaching-learning units throughout the grades and in all subject areas, help determine what is important to emphasize, select, or ignore, encourage cross-disciplinary study (and thus the integration of knowledge), suggest content and learning activities which will help students think about important relationships and issues of concern, and clarify goals to work toward. In sum, they help keep teaching and learning focused on primary rather than secondary matters.

CONCEPTS AS ORGANIZERS

We have seen that powerful generalizations can serve as organizing ideas around which to build teaching-learning units. Scholars in the social science disciplines, however, have also identified certain *basic concepts* as being particularly germane to their discipline—that is, as being particularly useful in suggesting key questions to ask as they go about their investigations. Schultz, for example, identified the following concepts (among others) as basic to political scientists:

1. Political Leadership: the group of people who make, interpret, and enforce the rules by which a political system operates.
2. Political Decision-Making: the process by which these rules are made, interpreted, and enforced.
3. Political Institutions: accepted organizations for or ways of handling political decision-making.
4. Political Ideology: the body of beliefs, attitudes, values, and goals underlying political decisions.
5. Citizenship: the role played by the individual in the system.[41]

She then went on to suggest that each of these concepts is useful as a guide to analytical questions that can be asked about any political system in order to gain insight into the ways in which the system operates. In analyzing the political system of a World War II prisoner-of-war camp, therefore, she suggests that there are many questions that might be asked. "How did the 150 American prisoners in the camp decide who their leaders would be? How did the prisoners make decisions? What governmental institutions did they set up? What ideology influenced them? What was the role of the

[41]Mindella Schultz, *Comparative Political Systems: An Inquiry Approach* (New York: Holt, Rinehart & Winston, 1967), pp. 2–3.

individual citizen?"[42] The relationship between the basic concepts and these questions is obvious.

Similar concepts exist in other disciplines. Pelto[43] discusses clearly the power of the concept of *culture* as the most basic concept used by anthropologists. Broek[44] suggests that the discipline of geography represents a way of looking at the earth through the use of, among others, such basic concepts as *region, areal association, spatial interaction, localization,* and *scale.* Rose[45] identifies such concepts as *socialization, role, primary group* and *secondary group, communication,* and *conflict* as basic to the discipline of sociology. Economists use concepts like *scarcity, goods, services, market, investment,* and *capital.* Psychologists work with terms such as *personality, behavior, motivation, need, goal, role,* and *value.*

Such complex concepts can suggest organizing generalizations which can serve as a focus around which teaching-learning units in various grades can be developed. The concept of "societal control," for example, suggests the idea: "In order to preserve their culture, the elders of many societies try to inculcate the young into the established ways of life." Basic concepts, as we have seen, also suggest key questions for students to ask about such generalizations. These key questions, in turn, can help to identify the dimensions of a generalization which might be investigated, and to suggest facts to use as examples to illustrate such generalizations.

The essential point being made here is that the basic concepts of a discipline can be used to good advantage by teachers as guidelines to preparing a set of key questions for students to ask about the data they are studying. Thus, teachers who teach courses in government can use the basic concepts of political science; those who teach courses in geography, the basic concepts of geography, and so on. This would hold true for courses relating to any of the other social sciences as well.[46]

Furthermore, concepts from a *variety* of disciplines can be used to enhance the study of history. For example, Engle has suggested the following concepts for use in studying about selected societies throughout history:

[42]*Ibid.,* p. 3.

[43]Pertti J. Pelto, *The Study of Anthropology* (Columbus, Ohio: Charles E. Merrill, 1965), pp. 67–80.

[44]Jan O. M. Broek, *Geography: Its Scope and Spirit* (Columbus, Ohio: Charles E. Merrill, 1965), pp. 72–76.

[45]Caroline B. Rose, *Sociology: The Study of Man in Society* (Columbus, Ohio: Charles E. Merrill, 1965), pp. 44–58.

[46]There are a number of sources to which teachers can turn for lists of social science concepts. See Verna S. Fancett *et al., Social Science Concepts and the Classroom* (Syracuse, New York: Social Studies Curriculum Center, 1968); Roy Price *et al., Major Concepts for the Social Studies* (Syracuse, New York: Social Studies Curriculum Center, 1965); or any of the sources listed at the bottom of page 110.

a. The concept of culture, including the way in which a culture is preserved and/or changed.

b. The concept of man in a culture interacting with the forces of nature, including both man's dependence on nature and his increasing control over nature.

c. The concept of social group, including the relation of the group to the development of the individual.

d. The concept of economic organization, including the relation of economic organization to human goals and to developing technology; division of labor and corporate production; growth through economic planning; capital saving and investment.

e. The concept of political organization, including the nature of political rights and responsibilities and means of political control.

f. The concept of freedom in relationship to personal security and social control.

g. The concept of growing interdependence between individuals and groups.

h. The concept of science and the scientific approach to knowing.

i. The concept of the suprarational, including religion, aesthetics, and philosophy.[47]

Teachers must take care, however, to insure that the list of key questions they give students is comprehensive—that it will help them to gain as total a picture as possible of a given society and its problems. To assist teachers in this regard the concept of the "cultural pyramid" as suggested by Lewenstein and others[48] is helpful. The concept of the cultural pyramid, as diagrammed in Figure 3.6, represents a frame of reference that teachers might use in preparing lists of basic study questions for students to use.

This concept of the cultural pyramid can help teachers think about the kinds of questions they need to ask in order to help students gain a holistic view of the societies they study. Students can be encouraged, for example, to focus on the conditions of the natural environment in which a society originated, the state of technological development which existed or exists, the means of economic production employed and the kinds of goods and services produced, the political, economic, and social institutions which the people have organized, the values and ideas which were or are deemed important, and the effects of all these factors on the daily and long-term

[47]Shirley H. Engle, "Model Building: The Function of World History," in Shirley H. Engle, ed., *New Perspectives in World History*, Thirty-fourth Yearbook of the National Council for the Social Studies (Washington, D.C.: National Council for the Social Studies, 1964), p. 566.

[48]M. R. Lewenstein, *Teaching Social Studies in Junior and Senior High School*, p. 88. See also Leon Marshall and Rachel Goetz, *Curriculum Making in the Social Studies: A Social Process Approach* (New York: Scribner's, 1936), and Earl S. Johnson, *Theory and Practice of the Social Studies* (New York: Macmillan, 1956), Chap. 5.

FIGURE 3.6
*The Cultural Pyramid**

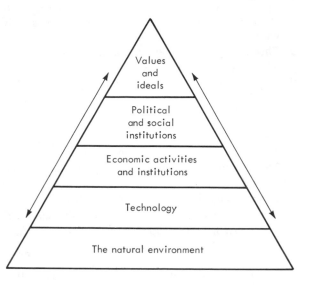

*From TEACHING SOCIAL STUDIES IN JUNIOR AND SENIOR HIGH SCHOOLS by Morris R. Lewenstein, © 1963 by Rand McNally & Company, Chicago, figure on p. 89.

activities of the people involved. It should be emphasized, however, that the direction of influence on each of the layers of the pyramid, as indicated by the arrows in the diagram, moves both up and down. Thus the geographical environment affects what values and ideals people in a society hold, but these values and ideals may also markedly affect the nature of the physical environment.

Lewenstein suggests that the cultural pyramid can be of value to teachers in helping students to understand more completely the totality of their world. For example, imagine that there is a picture in a secondary social studies textbook which shows a number of slaves being brought to the United States from Africa during the eighteenth century. Let us assume that a teacher considers it important for students to learn about slavery as an institution and its effects upon slave and master alike. He must now decide what questions he needs to have students ask in order to understand the concept. It can be argued that these questions should not ask for the date the first slaves appeared in the "New World," the size of the ships that brought them, or the price for which they were bought and sold, since these facts by themselves are of rather trivial import—they do not help students to understand and evaluate the nature of slavery as an institution.

The concept of "slavery" and the diverse evaluations which exist of it as an institution will have more meaning for students if they ask questions to help them understand how slavery started in the first place, what purposes it served, how it affected men's lives and why men supported or opposed its existence. The cultural pyramid "suggests" the kinds of questions that teachers need to ask in order to help students obtain such understanding. The need for slaves grew in part out of a particular kind of economic system which flourished at the time. The use of slaves was particularly affected by the geographical conditions existing in a certain geographical area. The state of technological development must have reached a certain level for certain types of ships to be built. The pressure necessary to acquire slaves came from individuals who stood to profit financially from their acquisition and sale. Slavery changed not only the physical environment, but also the economic and social activities of people in the area to which they came. And slaves affected and were affected by the values and ideals of the men who owned them. Slavery could not have existed at all had not a certain set of beliefs and values prevailed in many parts of the United States and elsewhere during the nineteenth century and before.

The following questions, based on the concepts suggested by Engle and the cultural pyramid, are therefore proposed as a basic set to be asked about any society being studied. Other questions, of course, may be necessary, depending on the nature of the topic under investigation.

a. Who were the _____ (people being studied)?
b. When did they live (i.e., time period)?
c. Where did they live (i.e., location)?
d. What things did they leave behind (i.e., artifacts, writings, etc.) that tell us something about them?
e. What kinds of work did they do, and where did they do it (i.e., jobs and occupations and kinds of places where these are located)?
f. What objects or things did they produce or create (i.e., products?)
g. What did they do for recreation (i.e., how did they entertain or amuse themselves)?
h. What kinds of family patterns did they develop?
community structure?
i. How did they educate their young (i.e., practices for inculcating the young into the established culture)?
j. How did they govern and control (i.e., type of government)?
k. What customs and beliefs did they hold (i.e., traditions, religious views, etc.)?
l. What events, individuals, or ideas are they particularly known for? How did these events, individuals, or ideas affect their lives?
m. What problems did they have (i.e., conflicts, difficulties, changes, etc.)?

n. How did they attempt to deal with these problems (i.e., ways they went about trying to eliminate or ease the problem)?

Notice that these are all factual questions, and can be answered by obtaining information directly. Once this information is collected, however, we may want to ask a different *kind* of question *about* this information, such as "What do they consider important (i.e., their values)?" This is an inferential question—i.e., the answers are inferred from the factual information earlier obtained.

Through the use of the cultural pyramid, therefore, teachers are not only more likely to be comprehensive in their questioning, but also more likely to help students develop a greater understanding of the total world in which they live.

CONCEPTS AS CONNECTING LINKS

It has been suggested that the basic concepts of the social science disciplines can be used as guidelines for preparing sets of key questions for students to ask about the data they acquire in studying about societies and their problems. But concepts can also be used to link units and courses together, both within and throughout the grades. A more careful analysis of the basic concepts used by scholars in various disciplines should reveal many which have relevance to many different disciplines (e.g., culture, conflict, values, cooperation, interdependence, causality) and which permit illustration and development through a variety of experiences (e.g., music, drama, reading, role-playing, question-asking).

The most powerful concepts (in the sense of being able to organize and synthesize large numbers of specific facts and ideas) should be selected. Because of their power, such concepts (the complex concepts referred to earlier) can be developed in an increasingly more abstract manner throughout the social studies. For example, Table 3.4 illustrates how the concept of "change" might be developed throughout a hypothetical set of courses in grades 7–12. Table 3.5 illustrates how the concepts of "differences," "interdependence," and "societal control" have been developed in a recently developed social studies program for grades 1–8.[49] In short, these concepts serve as organizing "threads," and as such can be returned to in a variety of ways in each of the grades, though the factual data (persons, events, institutions, ideas, etc.) used to illustrate each of the concepts at different grade levels will be different. Concepts of similar power (e.g., cooperation, culture, power, values, conflict) can also be used, though all concepts would

[49]H. Taba, M. C. Durkin, J. R. Fraenkel, and A. H. McNaughton, *Handbook for Teaching Elementary Social Studies*, p. 21.

TABLE 3.4

*USING THE CONCEPT OF "CHANGE" AS AN ORGANIZING
THREAD IN SECONDARY SOCIAL STUDIES*

Grade Level	Subjects in Which the Concept is to Be Developed	The Concept of "Change"
XII	A comparative study of selected social problems in the U.S.	Alienation, crime, dissent, poverty, prejudice, discrimination, pollution, urban decay, drugs, alcoholism, campus unrest, propaganda, morality as causes and effects of changes in American life style.
XI	A comparative study of selected periods in United States History.	Changes brought about by immigration, wars, Presidential decisions, Congressional acts, political parties, expansion, inventions, international involvement, etc.
X	A comparative study of selected non-Western cultures.	Similar to Grade VII.
IX	A comparative study of selected geographic areas throughout the world.	How man both changes and is changed through interacting with his environment.
VIII	A comparative study of selected areas of the U.S.	Changing life-styles in different parts of the U.S.
VII	A comparative study of selected Western cultures.	Changes in man's traditions, customs, occupations, products, means of entertainment, family patterns, community structures, educational systems, political systems, beliefs, problems, values, etc.

not necessarily be developed to the same extent in every grade. Certain concepts might be developed more fully in one grade, course, or unit, other concepts more fully in another, depending once again on such factors as the objectives a teacher has in mind, his interests, knowledge, and abilities, the materials available or obtainable, and the needs and interests of the students involved. The essential point for teachers to consider, however, is the "connectiveness" that such powerful concepts can provide.

CHOICE INEVITABLE

It is probably obvious to you by now that choice cannot be avoided. A teacher cannot teach everything. He must, of necessity, choose certain content rather than another, no matter what subject he teaches. So that

TABLE 3.5

THE SPIRAL DEVELOPMENT OF THREE KEY CONCEPTS*

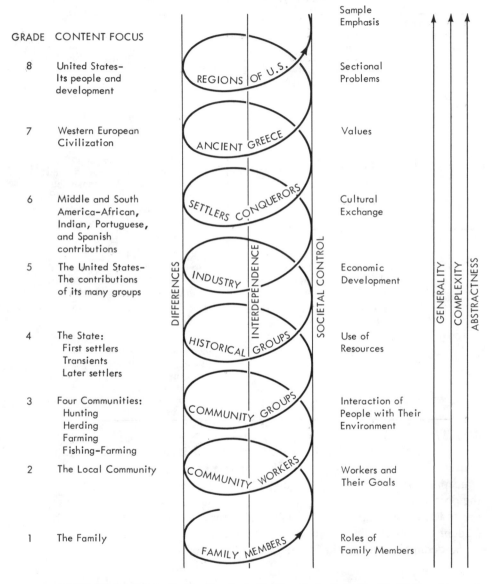

*Hilda Taba, Mary C. Durkin, Jack R. Fraenkel, Anthony H. McNaughton, A TEACHER'S HANDBOOK TO ELEMENTARY SOCIAL STUDIES, 2nd Edition, 1971, Addison-Wesley, Reading, Mass. Reprinted by permission.

rational choices can be made, however, criteria must be established. Criteria, however, arise out of one's views concerning the purpose of education, the nature of the social studies, the demands of society, the needs of learners, and a conception of reality, truth, and beauty. In short, out of one's educational philosophy. As Taba points out, "A different orientation to the task of the school in society, to the needs of the culture, and to learning will produce different objectives and a different set of criteria for a good curriculum."[50] The point to emphasize is that some criteria are necessary if rational choices are to be made, and if we are to ensure that positions and fads of the moment do not obscure more fundamental educational needs. What, then, might be some criteria which can serve as guidelines to the selection of content in the social studies? The following suggestions are presented for consideration:

* *Social studies content should emphasize the most fundamental or theoretical knowledge possible, drawing whenever possible upon the most powerful concepts and generalizations that the social science disciplines have to offer.* Earlier it was illustrated that concepts and generalizations are more fundamental than specific facts. "The more fundamental an idea, the greater will be its breadth of application, for the idea is 'fundamental' precisely because it has wide as well as powerful applicability. The history curriculum may be so studded with historic facts that no basic ideas about historic causation or of the essential nature of such movements as immigration in American history can emerge. . . . The more fundamental an idea is, the more likely it is to point to relationships between the subjects. . . . To explore the idea that specialization leads to greater productivity in work as well as to greater ennui in living, one needs to dip into economic as well as sociological and historical facts."[51]

Knowledge becomes significant when it offers important insights into how the world really is. Thus the idea "blondes have more fun," though amusing to contemplate, is not really significant since it does not help students gain in self and world understanding. "A nation's role in world affairs is affected by the resources, needs, values, desires, and prejudices of its people," on the other hand, reflects an insight into why certain nations are more prominent on the international scene than others. And thus it is more significant. The most abundant sources of fundamental ideas for social studies teachers at present are the disciplines of social science.

* *Social studies content should contribute to multiple objectives.* This criterion suggests that any content selected for study in the social studies should not only add to basic knowledge, but also help students think (e.g.,

---

[50]H. Taba, *Curriculum Development*, p. 267.
[51]*Ibid.*, pp. 269–270.

by being conducive to the tracing of relationships) and develop attitudes, feelings, and sensitivities. In short, social studies content should yield the greatest "mileage" possible. Porterfield illustrates the idea of mileage clearly in the following examples:

> Emphasis on the importance of steel in the modern world explains and ties together a wide range of phenomena. It underscores the high priority given to iron and coking coal among natural resources. It accounts for the location of many great cities and industrial areas. It explains why new nations, many of whom should be concentrating their energies elsewhere, all want steel plants. It accounts in part for the rise and fall of the United Kingdom. It throws light on the unique relationship (past hostility and present cooperation) between iron-rich France and coal-rich Germany. It bears on the creation of the Common Market. It justifies the use of the word "miraculous" as applied to the industrial giant Japan, which has little coal or iron. It goes far toward explaining the industrial superiority of the United States and the Soviet Union. It is in short, indispensable to an understanding of the "age of steel."

> By way of contrast, "the economies of the Eskimos and Laplanders, the details of tribal life in Afghanistan, the cultural conservatism of rural Iranians, the surviving remnants of Polynesian culture in the South Pacific—all these topics are exotic and awaken curiosity. As such they have a place in geographic study, but they do little— except by providing contrast—to throw significant light on the great environmental forces with which all youth will likely be influenced. They should be held in proper perspective.

> Spots on earth that have high strategic value will usually yield large rewards. The story of the Suez Canal, for example, can be used for vividly dramatizing an incredibly large range of important world information. A partial list includes the significant role of the Middle East in the cold war; the shifting from old concerns such as empire to modern ones such as access to petroleum; the world significance of Europe's petroleum poverty (and the development of Euratom among the "inner six"); the role of colonialism in the history of the Middle East; the rise of Middle East nationalism; the world effect of particularism and regional confusion among the Arab states; the disturbing, dynamic influence of Israel in the Mohammedan homeland; the international importance of Nasser; the story of East versus West in the building of the Aswan Dam; the background and significance of the 1956 and 1966 outbreaks in the Middle East; and how the United Nations, just because it existed, may well have prevented World War III in 1956. The Suez Canal repays extended attention.[52]

[52]John Porterfield, "Geography for Inner-City Youth," in *Strategies for Teaching in the Inner City* (Boston: Allyn & Bacon, in press).

• *Social studies content should be comparative in nature.* Today's world has shrunk tremendously as far as interaction and interdependence are concerned. Yet it is also composed of a veritable polyglot of nationalities, outlooks, attitudes, customs, and values. To present any one viewpoint or way of doing things as *the* way is shortsighted to say the least. When and wherever possible, therefore, life in one culture should continually be compared and contrasted with life in other cultures; life in one's own locale should continually be compared and contrasted with similar and different places around the world; life during one time period should be continually compared and contrasted with life in other time periods. In-depth studies of selected aspects of other cultures should be frequent, so that students will have ample opportunity to perceive the similarities as well as the differences which exist among the peoples of the world.

• *Social studies content should not be exclusively past oriented. It should emphasize the present.* Social studies content should continually emphasize the "here and now" *before* the past is delved into. As Taba suggests, too often the "background receives more attention than the foreground."[53] Students need to realize how present conditions are a change from past conditions. Unless they can be helped to understand what problems and promises such changes have produced, and thus deal more effectively with their present existence, studying the past "for its own sake" is, for most students, of little value.

• *Social studies content should be reality-oriented, dealing with real people, real emotions, real-life situations.* Students should have the opportunity to read about, hear, and see individuals *like themselves* living in places similar to their own and dealing with problems of concern to them as well. Lack of realism is one of the most pervasive criticisms which many students (if not most) attach to social studies content. Much social studies content is viewed as "phoney." The following dialogue illustrates why students view much of the content they are asked to learn as phoney. Here a teacher inquires further when a group of ninth-grade boys refuses to read some assigned material:

> T: What do you mean, "phoney"?
> S: Corny.
> T: What does "corny" mean? (no response)
> T: Can you give me an example of what isn't corny? On a TV program perhaps?
> S: "Naked City"
> T: Why isn't "Naked City" corny or phoney?

[53]H. Taba, *Curriculum Development*, p. 275.

S: Well, one Sunday you see a kid with his mother walking to church and the next day he gets in trouble.

T: Why isn't that phoney?

S: Because he isn't all bad or all good.
He isn't one way.

T: Are you saying then that a one-way character is phoney?

S: Yeah!

(Teacher writes "phoney" on the blackboard and under it "one-way character.")

T: What else do you see on TV that you don't think is phoney?

S: "Divorce Court"

T: Why isn't that phoney?

S: We don't know; it's just that they talk like real people. That's the thing about school books, they're not about life like we know it.

T: Would you agree, then, that another thing that makes books phoney is the fact that the characters and events or things that happen, aren't really believable to you?

S: Yeah!

("Unbelievable talk and events" are written on the blackboard.)

T: Suppose there was a science-fiction story about a man traveling to Mars. Would that be phoney?
(Some disagreement here by the class.)

S: It wouldn't have to be if the guy really acted like someone would act if he were really going.

T: So, you're saying that the situation wouldn't have to be real if the persons in it were acting in a believable way? (Agreement).[54]

• *Social studies content should be relevant to students' concerns.* All students today are caught up in the problems of their society. Indeed, they cannot avoid them . . . drugs, violence, discontent, anger, poverty, illegitimacy, discrimination, all impose themselves on student consciousness daily. "Most students are keenly aware they live in a world where conflict is the norm, where disharmonies prevail, and where justice is a disputed concept. They know about wars, political crises, labor struggles, racial animosities, thermonuclear weapons . . ."[55] As Fantini and Weinstein[56] suggest, most (if not all) students are exposed on television alone to realistic portrayals of crime, delinquency, illicit love, childbirth, mental illness, disease, violent

[54]Mario D. Fantini and Gerald Weinstein, *The Disadvantaged: Challenge to Education* (New York: Harper & Row, 1968), pp. 124–127.

[55]Ivor Kraft, "Social Studies: The Search for Meaning," *Social Education*, XXXI, November 1960, pp. 597–600; 604.

[56] M. D. Fantini and G. Weinstein, *The Disadvantaged: Challenge to Education.*

emotions (hate, anger, fear, passion). There is a great deal of horror and unpleasantness in the world, but students are exposed to violence and horror whether we like it or not, and whether we choose to face the fact or not. When we bypass the reality of the child of the ghetto, the Puerto Rican, the American Indian, we are in effect saying that his world does not really exist. We need to expose students to a wide variety of individuals, of all colors, sizes, shapes, and in all kinds of situations, interacting and reacting to real life, so that all students will have someone like themselves with whom they can identify. Real-life problems with which people in today's world are concerned should be identified, presented and discussed. For example, consider the following excerpt from a recently published book entitled: *The Drug Scene: Help or Hang-up?*

> The general consensus was that any and all drugs were "readily available" and that "almost anybody can get it for you."
>
> Almost everyone knew of someone at the high school level who uses drugs but the sources vary. Some felt that high school students or young adults in their 20's who had the mobility might provide drugs to a high school contact. Some students went up to the city (San Francisco) to the Haight-Ashbury and brought drugs back to the high schools. "We know the friends who get it from someone we may or may not know." The profit motive seemed not to be important "when you were dealing with your friends" but all felt that somewhere along the line, usually at the ultimate source, someone was making a profit. The cost of drugs depended on whom you were buying it from. A matchbox of marihuana, for example, cost from $3 to $5. A "lid" ranged from $7 to $15, though averaging about $10. A kilo or kilogram ranged from $75 to $90. The cost of LSD, though variable, was estimated at $3 per cap and $4 for a tab (you were lucky if in a cap you got 100 micrograms of LSD). A number of students did not know what "speed" was but one "authority" stated that for $3 you could buy enough "speed" (methedrine) or amphetamine usually to give you four or five trips. The prices of most other drugs were unknown to the youngsters.
>
> Without question the most commonly used drug was marihuana, with LSD second and speed or amphetamines considered the most likely candidate for third. Some students put prescription pills (like No-Doze or Dexedrine) as number three along with speed. One youngster considers sedatives as number four and almost all agreed that when glue was used, it was sniffed predominantly by youngsters below the 8th grade but that they themselves had little or no use for it. All denied using heroin.[57]

[57]"Almost anybody can get it for you," excerpted from the *Narcotics Inquiry Report*, San Mateo County (California) Juvenile Justice Commission, November 1967. Quoted in Walter L. Way, *The Drug Scene: Help or Hang-up?* (Englewood Cliffs, N.J.: Prentice-Hall, 1970).

The foregoing is but one of the many examples of relevant content which could be cited. Such problems as drugs, crime, military service, poverty, prejudice, alienation, dissent, air and water pollution, and urban decay impinge themselves repeatedly on young people's lives.[58] Yet in many instances such content is ignored and excluded from the social studies. How alive and vital the social studies could be if such content were included more frequently!

• *Social studies content should provide frequent opportunities for value inquiry and analysis.* Students should have frequent opportunities to gain insight into the actions and values of others; to see what other people in different situations and locations consider important and why; to appreciate the music, art, folktales, and dances of people in other cultures, and to increase their sensitivity to the common and uncommon needs and desires of people throughout the world. For example, consider the insights into values which the three excerpts cited below provide:

1

Richard Dixon, an ordinary man who wanted a home for his family, bought a house in the Sunset District two weeks ago. Someone didn't like Richard and Patricia Dixon and their three children having a home there because they are Negroes. Early yesterday morning that someone spelled out his hate.

He (or she or they) got a can of spray paint and, across the green center panel of Dixon's garage at 4430 Kirkham Street, he expressed his venom: "Nigger Go Home." It was signed "KKK" for the Ku Klux Klan.

"I'm not beating an integration drum," said the 30 year old mailman yesterday. "All my wife and I want is a house that's adequate to our family needs."

"It's such a sneaky thing to do. If this person would come and ring my doorbell, maybe I could talk to him. But he's not even giving me a chance this way."

"When we bought the house we didn't do it to prove anything. We don't feel we have to prove we're good Americans. Actions speak louder than words. Whoever did it certainly hasn't taken our actions into consideration. We saved years and years to buy this house."

"The neighbors have been very courteous," said Mrs. Dixon, "and the children haven't had any difficulty. They've been invited into other homes to play." Dixon, who, like his wife, is a high

---

[58]For other examples of reading material dealing with crucial social problems in the U.S., see the multi-volume series edited by the author and entitled, "Inquiry Into Crucial American Problems" (Englewood Cliffs, N.J.: Prentice-Hall, 1970). Problems considered in the series include Drugs, Poverty, Prejudice and Discrimination, Teen-Age Sex, Crime, Dissent, Urbanization, Propaganda, Military Service, Alienation, Education, Foreign Policy, Ecology, Population, Female Protest, and Violence.

school graduate, said that when he returned home from work Tuesday afternoon something illegible had been scrawled on his garage.

"I thought maybe it was just the kids," he said. "I wiped it off. But this morning—there was no mistaking it." Said Mrs. Dixon, petite and gently-spoken: "I feel a little sick and a little frightened."[59]

2

A young man who was holding his first position as a shoe salesman in a small city wrote an autobiographical statement in which he included the following instructions given him by the manager of the shoe store: "My job is to move out shoes and I hired you to assist in this. I am perfectly glad to fit a person with a pair of shoes if we have his size, but I am willing to misfit him if it is necessary in order to sell him a pair of shoes. I expect you to do the same. If you do not like this, someone else can have your job. While you are working for me, I expect you to have no scruples about how you sell shoes."[60]

3

Crime is increasing, says the most Reverend Fulton J. Sheen, because of a widespread and "false compassion" for criminals.

Bishop Sheen, leading philosopher of the Roman Catholic Church and the Bishop of Rochester, defines false compassion in these words: "A pity that is shown, not to the mugged, but to the mugger; not to the family of the murdered, but to the murderer; not to the woman who was raped, but to the rapist. . . ."

"Social slobberers" were deplored by the Bishop as those "who insist on compassion being shown to the junkies, to the dope fiends, the throat slashers, the beatniks, the prostitutes, the homosexuals, and the punks. Today the decent man is practically off the reservation."

Bishop Sheen noted that crime is increasing because "clemency of a false kind is shown to criminals."[61]

Certain kinds of content, such as the examples illustrated above, are especially rich in the opportunities which they provide for value investigation. (Strategies for identifying and analyzing values will be discussed in Chapter 6.) Through describing and analyzing the actions and decisions of a number of different people in similar situations, students not only gain

[59]"Message of Hate on a Negro's Home," San Francisco Examiner, Oct. 25, 1962. Quoted in Fred R. Holmes, Prejudice and Discrimination: Can They Be Eliminated? (Englewood Cliffs, N.J.: Prentice-Hall, 1970).
[60]Excerpted from Edwin H. Sutherland, White Collar Crime (New York: Dryden Press, 1949). Quoted in Jack R. Fraenkel, Crime and Criminals: What Can We Do About Them? (Englewood Cliffs, N.J.: Prentice-Hall, 1970).
[61]Excerpted from Bishop Fulton J. Sheen, "Too Much Compassion for Punks," U.S. News and World Report, Jan. 23, 1967. Quoted in Jack R. Fraenkel, Crime and Criminals.

insight into what others value and why they do, but also are helped to determine what they themselves value.

These criteria, like any criteria, rest on a certain set of value assumptions (among others, the beliefs that man can develop both mentally and emotionally through education; that thinking skills and value analysis can be taught; that students learn best when they actively pursue their interests; that the knowledge most transferable to new situations consists of concepts and ideas; and that the most important subject for man to study is man himself) that the writer considers important. Value assumptions, of course, vary from individual to individual. What is one man's nectar is another man's poison. What one person considers important, another disregards as insignificant. The possibility of any one set of values being adhered to by all teachers, therefore, is not only unlikely, but to this writer's way of thinking undesirable. The argument here, therefore, is *not* that any *one* set of values be established. If the search for criteria produces a wide variety of social studies courses and programs, so much the better. What is most essential, however, is that teachers determine what they do value so that they can establish (through development, selection, or some combination of each) a set of criteria which will enable them to select content to achieve their goals in the social studies.

SUMMARY

This chapter dealt with the problem of selecting content for inclusion in social studies courses. The main thesis of the chapter was that concepts and generalizations can be of considerable value as a means of simplifying the selection and organization of subject matter.

The terms "facts," "concepts," "generalizations" and "theory" were defined, discussed, exemplified, and their relationships and value explored. Criteria by which powerful concepts and ideas can be identified or formulated were presented.

The use of powerful generalizations as organizing foci around which to build teaching-learning units was discussed. Examples of such generalizations as conceptualized by selected social scientists were then presented.

The use of powerful concepts as organizing threads was described and illustrated. The value of such concepts as guidelines for use in preparing comprehensive lists of key questions for students to ask about the societies they study was discussed and illustrated.

Lastly, the point was made and argued that choice is inevitable in social studies (or any other) teaching. A variety of criteria that teachers can use to help them choose—to make their content selections—were therefore presented.

EXERCISES*

I. Listed below are several pairs of concepts or generalizations. Using the criteria identified on page 105 of this chapter, place an X in front of the concept or generalization that is the more powerful in each pair.

1. A. _____ urbanization
   B. _____ city

2. A. _____ change
   B. _____ democracy

3. A. _____ argument
   B. _____ dissent

4. A. _____ family
   B. _____ interdependence

5. A. _____ conflict
   B. _____ dispute

6. A. _____ Several cultures in Latin America influenced and were influenced by foreign conquerors.
   B. _____ Cultures change in varying degrees when they come in contact with another culture.

7. A. _____ The wide variety of characteristics found among the states of the United States of America reflect the varied cultural backgrounds of the peoples who settled in them.
   B. _____ Though all cultures possess certain unique features, they are also similar in a number of ways.

8. A. _____ Man's ways of living affect, and are affected by, the physical and social environment in which he lives.
   B. _____ Certain inventions of early man revolutionized his way of life.

9. A. _____ Societies sometimes punish those who question established values.
   B. _____ The daily activities of the ancient Greeks and Romans reflected their values.

*Author's suggestions are on page 399.

10. A. ____ The changes that occurred in Western Europe after the fall of Rome came about as a result of many interacting factors.

B. ____ Pressures for change develop from many sources.

11. A. ____ Men continually seek to improve their condition through obtaining those rights they consider essential to their welfare.

B. ____ Many groups in the American society have continually striven to promote their own well-being as they have defined it.

II.* Of the concepts listed below, place a "C" before those that are conjunctive, a "D" before those that are disjunctive, or an "R" before those that are relational. (If you aren't sure of the terms, refer to a good dictionary.)

1. ____ dog   **6.** ____ citizen

2. ____ "strike" in baseball   **7.** ____ reptile

3. ____ house   **8.** ____ causality

4. ____ interdependence   **9.** ____ dignity

5. ____ glove   **10.** ____ writing instrument

III.* Listed below are several statements. Place the letter "P" in front of these that are propositions, and the letter "D" in front of those that are definitions.

____ **1.** You have a pencil in your pocket.

____ **2.** Chairs are things to sit on.

____ **3.** If country X invades country Y, country Z will declare war on country X.

____ **4.** John F. Kennedy was the thirty-fifth President of the United States.

____ **5.** Grass is green.

____ **6.** There are 100 Senators in the United States Senate.

____ **7.** The life style of a culture is shaped by the contributions of the groups that make up that culture.

____ **8.** To be "just" means to be "right" or "fair."

____ **9.** A "junk" is a Chinese flat-bottomed boat.

____ **10.** Anything which picks up iron filings is a magnet.

IV.* Place the letter or letters of the term from Column I in the space in front of the appropriate definition in Column II.

<table>
<tr><td align="center">I.</td><td align="center">II.</td></tr>
</table>

A. fact

B. concept

C. generalization

D. frame of reference

E. rationale

F. thought system

G. theory

H. discipline

_____ **1.** An explanation of why a teacher considers a certain event, person, object, idea, or happening worth having students learn.

_____ **2.** A word which refers to the characteristics common to a set of experiences.

_____ **3.** Something which happened in the past or which actually exists today, and which can be verified as being true or false.

_____ **4.** A single statement expressing a relationship among two or more ideas, events, individuals, objects, or things.

_____ **5.** A propositional statement.

_____ **6.** A set of interrelated statements having considerable predictive power.

_____ **7.** A definitional statement.

V.* Place a YES in front of those statements below that represent arguments or positions supported in this chapter, and a NO in front of those statements that represent arguments or positions that were argued against or refuted in the chapter.

1. _____ Concepts are the end-products of an individual(s) abstracting from his (their) experiences certain characteristics that he or they perceive these experiences share in common.

2. _____ Though some concepts are more abstract than other concepts, this is not true of generalizations.

3. _____ Generalizations suggest relationships which appear to exist in the world.

4. _____ A powerful generalization may consist of a number of concepts.

5. ———— A powerful theory includes many interrelated generalizations.

6. ———— Concepts are discovered rather than invented.

7. ———— Facts represent statements which can be supported or refuted by recourse to observable evidence.

8. ———— Concepts represent statements which can be supported or refuted by recourse to observable evidence.

9. ———— Generalizations are true by definition.

10. ———— Using generalizations as a focal point around which to build teaching/learning units simplifies revision of the units at a later date.

11. ———— The social science disciplines are of value because they identify a tremendous amount of valuable information that all students should learn.

12. ———— Concepts exist in the minds of men, not in the external world.

13. ———— If a powerful concept is used as an organizing "thread" for planning social studies content through several grades, examples of the concept can be explored in many different ways, using different factual samples, in different grades.

14. ———— Choice is inevitable in the selection and organization of subject matter for students to learn.

15. ———— A judgment of fact and a "true" fact are not necessarily the same.

Now reconsider each of the statements presented above. Are they propositions or definitions? How would you verify or refute them? (Don't just take the author's word.)

VI. Read some of the sources listed at the bottom of page 110 and page 125. What generalizations do these writers identify? Prepare a list of several of them and then rank them using the criteria identified on page 105 of this chapter. Discuss with your classmates what content samples (specific periods, places, or events) might be studied in order to gather data to determine whether the generalization holds up—that is, whether it should be supported, refuted, or qualified in some way.

VII. Browse through a random selection of social studies textbooks (elementary or secondary) currently available. Do they try to develop concepts? generalizations? If so, which ones? What conclusions would you draw about the nature of social studies textbook writers? Explain your reasoning.

VIII. Select a generalization from one of the social science disciplines (again, consult the sources listed at the bottom of page 110) and see if you can outline some particular subject matter that you would have students study in order to investigate and determine the validity of the generalization. Use the outline on pages 120–21 as a model if you wish.

IX. Take a particular society or period in time in which you are especially interested and prepare a set of basic study questions that you would have students ask to help them understand the people in that society or period of time. Try to be comprehensive—that is, design your questions so that, if answered, conscientiously, they will give a well-rounded picture of what the people were like. Compare your questions with those of your fellow students. What differences do you notice? similarities? Try to draw up as a class a set of criteria that any balanced, comprehensive set of questions for studying a group of people should possess. Compare your list with the list presented on pages 127–28 of this chapter. What questions, have you included or ignored?

X. Reconsider the list of criteria for selecting social studies subject matter presented on pages 131–38. Would you add any criteria to this list? delete any? revise any? Why or why not? Explain your reasoning.

CHAPTER IV

THE SELECTION
AND
ORGANIZATION OF
LEARNING ACTIVITIES*

This chapter deals with the nature of learning activities. The main thesis of the chapter is that learning activities as well as subject matter must be considered if maximum student learning is to be accomplished.

The first section of the chapter defines learning, and then presents a brief description of three learning theories that affect current school practice. The fact that the social studies consist of both subject matter and learning activities is emphasized.

The second section offers a definition of the term "learning activity," presents several examples of such activities, and suggests that learning activities are a much more important ingredient in effective teaching than many have realized in the past.

The third section sets forth a number of basic factors which can serve as guidelines in the development and/or selection of learning activities, and presents examples of learning activities designed to illustrate each of these factors.

The fourth section suggests that there are at least four major types of learning activities in which students should be involved in the social studies, illustrates several examples of each type, and presents two learning activity sequences that include each type.

*Much of the material in this chapter has been adapted or taken directly from Jack R. Fraenkel, "Learning Experiences and the Social Studies," *The Elementary School Journal*, The University of Chicago Press, March 1968, pp. 301–311. Copyright © 1968 University of Chicago Press. Used by permission.

The last section then identifies a number of skills important for students to acquire if they are to engage in learning successfully, and presents several examples of each skill.

When you have finished reading this chapter, therefore, you should be able to do the following:

- *explain* why the reorganization of content (subject matter) by itself is insufficient to bring about effective curriculum reform in the social studies;
- *explain* what is meant by the terms "learning," "learning theory," and "learning activity";
- *state* several (at least five) factors which can be used as guidelines in selecting and/or developing learning activities, and *give* at least one example of a learning activity that would illustrate the meaning of each of these factors;
- *distinguish* among intake, organizational, demonstrative, and creative types of learning activities, and *name* several (five or more) examples of each type;
- *prepare in writing* a learning activity sequence which includes all four types of learning activities mentioned above;
- *distinguish* between academic and social skills, *explain* why both types of skills are important for students to master, and *list* several (at least five) examples of each type.

LEARNING AND LEARNING THEORIES

What does it mean to learn? In what ways is an individual different after he has learned than he was before? *Learning*, as defined here, refers to any change which takes place in an individual that is not due to maturation. When an individual learns, he thinks, feels, or acts in a manner that is somehow different from the manner in which he acted, felt, or thought before the learning took place. He may have acquired a new idea or insight, improved an old (or mastered a new) skill, be able to perform at a higher level of proficiency than before, or be able to do something that he could not do previously. Learning "may be a change in insights, behavior, perception, or motivation, or a combination of these."[1]

A *learning theory* is a carefully worked out set of interrelated propositions that attempts to explain *how* people learn. There are a number of theories of learning which influence (though often implicitly) the instructional practices of teachers.

[1]Morris L. Bigge, *Learning Theories for Teachers* (New York: Harper & Row, 1964), p. 1.

One such theory is that of mental discipline. Mental disciplinarians believe that an individual's "mind" contains a certain number of basic faculties or capacities—such as imagining, willing, reasoning, and remembering—which grow and develop when trained. The main task of education is to develop these faculties by training or "exercising" them through the acquisition of knowledge. One learns by acquiring knowledge. The more difficult this knowledge is to acquire, the better, since the mind will thus be "exercised" more thoroughly. For this reason, mental disciplinarians often argue that some subjects are more important to study than others (e.g., the "harder" ones such as mathematics, history, or foreign language) because they help to exercise the mind more effectively. Practice and drill are important for their value in helping to bring about such development. Though largely rejected as a psychological theory, the influence of mental discipline is reflected in the practices of many teachers who emphasize drill, rote memorization, and toughness for toughness' sake.

A second theory which affects school practice to a considerable degree is *associationism*. Associationists assume that individuals are a collection of specific responses (R) to specific stimuli (S). "Stimuli are features of the environment which act on an organism to cause it to respond. Responses are reactions of an organism to stimulation."[2] Every specific reaction that an individual makes is considered a response to a specific stimulus.

In this theory, learning is viewed as the forming of connections or associations between stimuli and responses. The earliest explanation as to how such connections were formed was that ideas or things became associated in our minds because they were connected in some way when we first experienced them. Aristotle observed that it was easier for a person to remember an idea if he associated it with another idea when he first learned it. He argued that three kinds of associations or connections were particularly effective in helping an individual to remember: contiguity, similarity, and contrast.[3] "Contiguity means being together. If a child is told about Eskimos and igloos at the same time, future mention of 'Eskimo' will help him recall 'igloo.' 'A tiger is a big kitty' uses the principle of similarity. If a person learns that pleasure is the opposite of pain, mention of 'pain' will aid him in thinking of 'pleasure.' "[4]

Later thinking suggested trial and error, reinforcement (e.g., saying "good" or smiling when a student gives a correct answer), and conditioning as the means by which connections occurred, as evidenced by the famous animal experiments of the Russian physiologist Pavlov. He put food before a hungry dog and sounded a bell. By repeating this procedure a number of

[2] M. L. Bigge, *Learning Theories*, p. 9.
[3] John S. Brubacher, *A History of the Problems of Education* (New York: McGraw-Hill, 1947), p. 143.
[4] M. L. Bigge, *Learning Theories*, p. 34.

times, he found that after a while the mere sounding of the bell would cause the dog to salivate. Thus students may learn to give a certain response (the answer, John F. Kennedy) to a certain stimulus (e.g., the question, "Who was the thirty-fifth President of the United States?") and be rewarded (i.e., reinforced) by approving teacher gestures or actions. Whether the student *understands* why a given answer is correct is another matter. Getting students to think about that which they are learning is secondary to establishing desired responses.

In contrast to associationist thinking is field psychology. Field theorists see learning not as the forming of connections between previously unrelated stimuli and responses, but as the discovery of meaning or insight within a given situation. These theorists assume that insight, intelligence, and other cognitive processes are the fundamental characteristics involved in the responses of human beings, evident in even the most simple perception of their environment. A fundamental characteristic of man is his capacity to perceive and to formulate relationships. The understanding of relationships is what guides man's actions.

The famous experiments of Köhler with chimpanzees and chickens illustrate this approach to learning. In one experiment, Köhler taught chickens to take food only from the darker of two pieces of paper placed side by side. He then substituted for the lighter of the two pieces of paper a piece even darker than the original dark one. In 70 percent of these instances, the chickens switched their preference from the originally preferred dark piece of paper to the new, even darker one, suggesting that they had achieved an insight. Bigge suggests that the chickens sensed the relationship between the color of the paper and the acquisition of food as a general principle; "If I go to the darker piece of paper, then I will get food."[5]

Bigge gives the following as another example of insightful learning:

> What is the answer to $\sqrt{(\text{dog})^2} = ?$ How did you know it was "dog"? Had you ever before worked with square root and dog at the same time? If you knew the answer was "dog," you had an insight into the problem. Perhaps you had never put the insight into words, but you knew that $\sqrt{x^2} = x$ and $\sqrt{4^2} = 4$. Your insight, when verbalized, would run something like, "The square root of anything squared is that thing." Conversely, you may have "learned"—memorized— "The square root of a quantity is that quantity" and still not know the answer to $\sqrt{(\text{dog})^2} = ?$[6]

Field theory suggests a concept of learning and instruction similar to that already explored in Chapter 3. The most productive kind of learning is that which helps students to perceive, develop, and validate generalizations

[5]M. L. Bigge, *Learning Theories*, p. 9.
[6]*Ibid.*, p. 106.

(relationships). Having students memorize isolated pieces of factual information, such as the dates of battles, the names of individuals, or the location of places, without also helping them to place such facts within the context of an organized relationship has little meaning "unless its (their) connection with some general principle or rule is made explicit."[7]

Teachers need to realize that everything they do in the classroom is influenced by the theory they hold. If a teacher believes that students learn by being conditioned step-by-step under his guidance, he will proceed accordingly. If he believes that students learn most effectively by attempting to perceive and understand relationships, he will proceed differently. A teacher who does not base his instructional decisions on theoretical underpinnings is operating haphazardly and trusting to chance for success. He has no logically defensible rationale for his actions. "A teacher without a strong theoretical orientation inescapably makes little more than busywork assignments. True, many teachers operate this way and use only a 'bag of tricks' without theoretical orientation. However, this muddled kind of teaching undoubtedly is responsible for many of the adverse criticisms of public education which we hear today."[8] The *professional* educator knows and can explain why he is having students study a specific topic, investigate a certain question, or engage in a particular learning activity. The responsible teacher will strive to learn as much as he can about various learning theories so that he can base his instructional procedures upon a logically and psychologically defensible rationale rather than chance alone.[9]

In recent years, not only teachers, but also many curriculum workers have neglected this advice. They have failed to link their curriculum and instructional designs to a logically defensible theory of learning. As a result, it has often been wrongly assumed that the key to curriculum reform in the social studies lay in the reorganization or rearrangement of subject matter. Many of the major curriculum projects sponsored by the United States Office of Education, along with professional organizations, private institutions, government agencies, most of the lay public, and many teachers seemed to accept this assumption. Operating under the same assumption, several organizations or groups of professional scholars in history and the social sciences have also tried to improve instruction in their fields at the public school level. A number of books[10] have been published in which

[7]Maurice P. Hunt and Lawrence E. Metcalf, *Teaching High School Social Studies*, 2nd ed. (New York: Harper & Row, 1968), p. 53.

[8]M. L. Bigge, *Learning Theories*, p. 6.

[9]Space prohibits an extensive treatment of the various learning theories here. A detailed treatment that teachers might consult is Morris L. Bigge, *Learning Theories for Teachers* (New York: Harper & Row, 1964).

[10]See American Council of Learned Societies and the National Council for the Social Studies, *The Social Studies and the Social Sciences* (New York: Harcourt

individual social scientists have presented their interpretations of the newer insights and understandings of their disciplines. Several major publishing houses not only have published the results of these curriculum efforts, but also are in many cases engaged in curriculum development efforts of their own.

As was illustrated in Chapter 2, most social studies content consists of facts, concepts, and generalizations, drawn, in one form or another, from the disciplines of history and the social sciences—anthropology, economics, geography, political science, psychology, and sociology.

The manner in which each of these various elements is arranged or put together is often called the *structure* of a discipline,[11] even though it appears that there is no "one" structure (at least at present) for any given discipline upon which all scholars within the discipline can agree. Theoretically, however, the concepts and generalizations (and ways of developing them) in one discipline (e.g., sociology or economics) differ from those in another (e.g., political science or geography).

As suggested in Chapter 3, we therefore find included in social studies courses, in both elementary and secondary schools, information that consists of concepts (e.g.—culture, family, services, topography, change); generalizations (e.g.—individual and group values influence people's behavior); and specific facts (e.g.—birth and death rates) from each of the social science disciplines, as well as from other sources. These constitute the "subject matter" of the social studies that students are expected to learn.

To focus on subject matter alone, however, as the key to instructional improvement in the social studies is to deal with only part of the problem. As suggested in Chapter 1, the social studies, like all subjects, consist of both content (e.g.—modern man's alienation) and process (e.g.—learning activities relating to the theme of alienation). They go hand in hand. Students cannot deal with subject matter without engaging in some learning activity, some mental or physical process by which they "engage" or "come in contact with" the content. Teachers always need to consider not only *what* students learn, but also *how* they learn it. The most revealing insight presented in a dull fashion has but little effect; the most absorbing tech-

Brace Jovanovich, 1962); Erling M. Hunt *et al., High School Social Studies Perspectives* (Boston: Houghton Mifflin, 1962); John U. Michaelis and A. Montgomery Johnston (eds.), *The Social Sciences: Foundations of the Social Studies* (New York: Allyn & Bacon, 1965); Raymond H. Muessig and Vincent R. Rogers (eds.), *Social Science Seminar Series*, 6 Vols. (Columbus, Ohio: Charles E. Merrill, 1965); Irving Morrissett (ed.), *Concepts and Structure in the New Social Science Curricula* (New York: Holt, Rinehart & Winston, 1967); and William T. Lowe, *Structure and the Social Studies* (Ithaca, N.Y.: Cornell University Press, 1969).

[11]Jerome S. Bruner, *The Process of Education* (New York: Random House, 1968).

niques do not make trivial data significant. Mayer put the point well when he said: "Weak content in a discipline cannot be seriously defended by the claim of good method—over the long run, method will be judged by the quality of content.[12]

Subject matter by itself provides only the basic knowledge that students need as a foundation on which to build an understanding of themselves and the world in which they live. Specific facts, generalizations, and concepts, regardless of their source, do not, in and of themselves, encourage students to think; do not change prejudices and dispositions; do not develop social and academic skills. These objectives are achieved primarily by the ways in which this basic content is translated into learnable tasks for students in the classroom.

What Is a Learning Activity?

Learning activities are experiences designed to involve students in the material at hand. The purpose of such involvement is to encourage students to think about and use the subject matter, to maximize their individual learning, and to stimulate their interest so that schooldays will be eventually succeeded by self-directed continuing education. While the selection and organization of social studies content serves to impart knowledge, the selection and organization of learning activities facilitates the use of such knowledge. It is through the learning activities by which students become both spectators and participants in life that they acquire the competencies to assimilate, understand, and work with knowledge.

It is apparent to anyone who has ever taught that individual students learn differently. Some learn easily, all or some of the time, through reading; others need to see, hear, or touch the objects with which they are working. Some are able, part of the time, to work effectively by themselves; others often need the stimulation of group participation. Some students understand more clearly if they can express what they have absorbed in an unusual form (for example, a "letter to the editor"); others group things more easily if they can organize their data into tabular or chart form.[13] It is important, therefore, that we take steps to insure that students have as many ways to learn as possible open to them.

A number of investigators[14] have demonstrated that reaction to incon-

[12]Martin Mayer, *Social Studies in American Schools* (New York: Harper & Row, 1963), p. 111.
[13]Hilda Taba, *Curriculum Development: Theory and Practice* (New York: Harcourt Brace Jovanovich, 1962).
[14]D. E. Berlyne, *Conflict, Arousal, and Curiosity* (New York: McGraw-Hill, 1960); Karl H. Pribram, "Neurological Notes on the Art of Education," in *Theories*

sistency seems to be a built-in feature of the nervous system and that individuals pay attention when there is a change in the events to which they are exposed. Exploration decreases when the same set of objects is presented repetitively. In experiments with five-year-old children as well as with advanced graduate students, Berlyne found that items that were incongruous, complex, surprising, or irregular in a series of items produced greater attention and study than the normally expected item did.[15] As familiarity increased, curiosity decreased.

Furthermore, we must pay attention to the fact that students need different types of learning activities for their self-development. Shy students need to participate in group activities. Talkative students often need the give and take of committee work. Those who tend to overgeneralize need the experience of gathering precise data, organizing it, and then offering reasonable analyses based on such data. Most important, students need to acquire a large number of intellectual and social skills so that they can continue to learn after their formal schooling has ended. The more varied the student's ways of learning, the better off he will be.[16]

All this seems to suggest that learning activities are far more important than many teachers and curriculum workers have realized. They need to be spelled out in much greater detail than they have been in the past and a number of factors taken into account. The factors which follow are especially important.

GUIDELINES TO THE DEVELOPMENT OF SIGNIFICANT LEARNING ACTIVITIES

JUSTIFIABILITY

Every learning activity should serve a justifiable function related to specific objectives (for example, increasing the student's ability to conceptualize, to draw inferences from data, to organize information for oral reporting, to co-operate with others on a group project). In other words, each learning activity should serve a distinct purpose. Otherwise, it is mere "busy work." The purpose should be clear to all involved—students, teachers, administrators, and parents. It is to be reemphasized, therefore, that teachers need to be very clear in their own minds about what it is that

---

of Learning and Instruction, Chap. 4. Sixty-third Yearbook of the National Society for the Study of Education, Part I. (Chicago: Distributed by the University of Chicago Press, 1964); E. N. Sokolov, in M. A. B. Brazier (ed.), The Central Nervous System and Behavior. Transactions of the Third Conference, Josiah Macy, Jr., Foundation, 1960.

[15]D. E. Berlyne, Conflict, Arousal, and Curiosity.

[16]H. Taba, Curriculum Development, p. 309.

they want students to learn, and how they expect to bring about such learning.

For example, suppose that one of a teacher's objectives is to increase student ability to form concepts. What kinds of activities will promote the accomplishment of this objective? In what kinds of experiences can the teacher involve students so as to give them practice in forming concepts?

Concept formation involves three essential tasks—listing, grouping, and labeling. Teachers can help students participate in these tasks by exposing them to a rich source of data from which they can select particular items which capture their attention; encouraging them to group (in various ways) the items which they have selected; and then asking them to label the groups which they have formed. Let us consider an example:

Suppose a teacher shows his students a film about the Boston Tea Party which occurred in 1773. After the showing is completed, he might ask the class: "What did you see?" or "What happened in this film?" All student responses can then be listed on the blackboard or a transparency. Students might say, "A ship was kept from landing its cargo," "A ship was refused permission to leave the harbor," "Men disguised as Indians boarded the ship and threw overboard all the tea they found." Students should be encouraged to offer as many observations as they can.

When the list seems fairly extensive, the teacher might ask: "Can you see any items here that might be placed together?" He thus encourages students to note similarities and differences, as they try to place similar items in the same group and perhaps combine some groups into larger groups. Some students, for example, might put the refusal to let the ship leave the harbor in the same group with throwing the tea overboard. Others might place refusing permission to land cargo with refusing permission to leave the harbor. Many different groupings of varying length are possible, and students should be encouraged to form as many groups as they can. (It is the students who need to do the grouping here, however, *not* the teacher.) When the students seem to have exhausted the possibilities for grouping, the teacher can ask: "What would you call each of these groups you have formed?" Students might thus describe the first two items (refusal to let the ship leave the harbor and throwing the tea overboard) as defensive actions, "aggression," "patriotic protest," "fighting," or what have you. The point to emphasize here is that it is not too important what students label their groups as long as they have fairly clear reasons for the labels they give. The teacher must take special care not to impose his labels.

Through this process of listing, grouping, and labeling, students are involved in a learning activity which encourages them to think and helps them develop the ability to do so. Not only do they see that several different kinds of items can all be classified together in the same category under a single heading, but they also learn that one item may fall into several categories. Such learning is useful. It helps students break down stereotyped thinking, makes them more flexible, and increases their ability to apply what they have learned to a wider variety of instances than they otherwise might be able to do.[17]

Let us consider a second illustration of the principle that learning activities should serve a distinct purpose. Our second example involves a teacher who has as one of his objectives getting students to think about values. In what kinds of activities can he involve students in order to bring this objective about? He decides on role-playing, and carefully structures a role-playing situation as follows:

"Bill, you play a counterman at a lunch counter in the South who has never served Negroes. You are behind the counter attending to some washing. Chuck and Mary, you play Negro teen-agers who have come to demand service." (After they have proceeded a bit) "Fred, you play a white person who enters the lunchroom and helps with the argument on the side that seems to be getting the worst of it."[18]

The opportunity to role-play situations of this kind involves students in an activity which allows them to take on a new identity in a protected situation, with the possibility that a host of new feelings and insights may result. (After students get the hang of such an activity, the situation need not be so carefully structured and the teacher can call for volunteers to fill roles.)[19]

MULTIPLE FOCUS

Note that each of the preceding examples serves a variety of functions. In the conceptualizing example, students are helped not only to conceptualize, but also to analyze and synthesize information. They are encouraged to look for relationships and then to express the relationships they find in their own words. The role-playing example is geared to help students identify with, and gain insight into, the feelings of others and to help promote an understanding of the difficulties underlying race relations in the United States today.

[17]Notice that the emphasis of a learning activity is what the *students* do—in this instance, selecting items from a data source, grouping in various ways those items selected, and then labeling the groups they have formed. But it is the student, not the teacher, who performs these tasks. To assist and encourage students, teachers ask certain questions in a given sequence. The strategy which such a sequence of questions represents will be discussed and illustrated in Chapter 5.

[18]Louis Raths *et al., Values and Teaching* (Columbus, Ohio: Charles E. Merrill, 1966), p. 121.

[19]For further ideas about the value of role-playing, see Mark Chesler and Robert Fox, *Role-Playing Methods in the Classroom* (Chicago: Science Research Associates, 1966), or Fannie R. Shaftel and George Shaftel, *Role-Playing for Social Values: Decision-Making in the Social Studies* (Englewood Cliffs, N.J.: Prentice-Hall, 1967).

The total sequence of learning activities to be presented—that is, the sum total of activities designed to develop a particular idea—should provide for the realization and the development of several objectives. These include the acquisition of knowledge, the encouragement of thinking, the increasing of social and academic skills, and the development of humanistic attitudes and sensitivity toward others. (Chapter 8 illustrates a set of sequentially developed learning activities designed to promote several objectives.)

SEQUENCE

Some objectives (for example, the development of attitudes and/or thinking) are attained over a considerable period of time. Others may be attained more quickly (for example, the absorption of specific facts). Learning activities, therefore, need to be sequentially structured to provide for continuity in learning. In short, each learning activity should not only serve as a prerequisite for learning activities to follow but also build on those that have come earlier. In addition, the idea of sequential ordering implies that learning activities should in general proceed from those that are concrete and specific (for example, reading or viewing to obtain specific information) to those that are more abstract (for example, drawing inferences from statistical data); from those which are experientially close (for example, describing one's own interests) to those that are experientially distant (for example, comparing and contrasting one's own interests with those of one's peers in another culture); from learning experiences that require relatively simple thought processes (for example, listing items of information in a picture) to learning experiences that require abstract and formal reasoning (for example, predicting what will happen in a new and unfamiliar situation).

Let us consider a few activities in order to understand more clearly the principle of sequential ordering of learning activities. In the example that follows, each activity is designed to be a prerequisite for the activities that follow as well as to build on activities that occur earlier in the sequence. The activities are designed in this case for use with a seventh-grade class. The idea or generalization to be investigated in this example is that all people have some body of beliefs by which they try to explain the world in which they live. A sequentially developed set of activities (though incomplete) is as follows:

(1) As an opening activity a teacher might present students with the following list of statements, duplicated, written on the board, or placed on a transparency:

Treat others as you would want to be treated.
All men are created equal.

An eye for an eye, a tooth for a tooth.

The sun is the wheel of a golden chariot that
   moves through the sky during the day.

If a black cat crosses your path, bad luck follows.

Love conquers all.

Respect your elders.

The pen is mightier than the sword.

Stars are the eyes of the gods of the night.

Eat, drink, and be merry, for tomorrow you may die.

He then can ask the class: "Can you think of any other statements like these that you might add to the list?" "What would you call these statements?"

Note that there are no right or wrong answers here. Students are simply being asked to think. As many responses as possible should be encouraged, but the activity should not be continued so long that it becomes boring. The aim is to stimulate thinking rather than just to foster discussion.

(2) As a first developing activity the teacher can then ask the class to prepare a list of other statements like those in (1) above from various sources, such as textbooks, other books, newspapers, and magazines, and to add these statements to those listed in the opening activity.

(3) For the second developing activity, students can be asked to pick any one statement from the enlarged list. The teacher then can ask: "Where do you think people get such ideas as these?" "How would you explain the differences in ideas?" (Responses should be recorded and saved for later comparison.)

(4) For the third developing activity, the following questions can be listed on the board:

How did the world come to be?

Where did fire and water come from?

Where is the wind when it does not blow?

Where did the first man come from?

What happens to people after they die?

The teacher can now say to the class, "We want to see how many different explanations to answer these questions we can list." (Story-telling should be encouraged but not silly or ridiculous stories.) The responses can then be listed, grouped, and labeled.

The skills of listing, grouping, and labeling (as illustrated earlier) require a number of items to group and some kind of basis by which to group them. If the students do not suggest that some of the items be placed under a heading during the listing, the teacher might ask, "Do some of these things seem to belong together?" Or "What else might go together?"

What is important, however, is that the students see the relationship between items and recognize that the same items can be grouped in many ways, not that a name be given to each grouping. The expressions of the students should reveal how sharply they see these relationships and the variety of possible relationships that exists. Their groupings may not be the teacher's. They may not even be adequate. Here the process is important, and, from the results, the teacher can judge how many further opportunities are needed to practice this skill.

(5) As a fourth developing activity, the class can read "Stone Age Religions" from *Our Beginnings in the Old World.*[20] The teacher can then ask the class: "With what kinds of questions do the people in this story seem to be concerned?" "Why do you think they are so concerned?"

The foregoing activities represent only the beginning of a complete learning activity sequence. They do suffice, however, to illustrate the principle of sequential ordering. Each activity in the sequence builds upon those which have preceded it, and serves as a prerequisite for those which are to follow. (See Chapter 8 for an example of a complete unit organized around sequentially ordered learning activities.)

In essence, a sequential ordering of learning activities is based on the idea of *incremental development*. As students progress through their lessons and units of study, they should learn to deal with subject matter that is new and increasingly difficult, and they should increase their ability to think and use the data they have acquired. Each step in learning should provide a bit more than the previous one and be intriguing enough to challenge the student, yet not so difficult that it is impossible for him to accomplish what is asked. Learning activities should encourage all students to make an effort, not discourage them from making any effort whatsoever.

TRANSFERABILITY OF ACQUIRED KNOWLEDGE

Learning activities should enable students to apply what they have learned in one situation to other new and different situations. To develop intellectually, students need to be constantly encouraged to use what they have learned in new settings—to explain some new occurrence, to predict possible outcomes of events, to hypothesize about what might happen. Through efforts of this kind, students develop the habit of learning to learn, a habit that will stand them in good stead in later years.

One way of getting students to use what they have learned previously in a new setting is to get them to hypothesize. Here is a partial example of a

[20]Harold H. Eibling, Frederick M. King, and James Harlow, *Our Beginnings in the Old World* (Sacramento, Calif.: State Department of Education, 1964), p. 21.

learning activity sequence designed to accomplish this objective, in this case designed for use with ninth and tenth graders.

(1) Organize the class into five research committees to collect basic information to compare certain fundamentals about five of the world's major religions. Give students the questions listed below as a basic guideline, but be sure to stress the importance of citing evidence to support answers. Some questions may have no answers. For questions of this kind, inform students that they will be expected to tell what they have done to try to find information before they decided there was none. Inform the class that these are basic questions to which we shall return several times.

Suggested study questions:

Where did or do the followers of this religion live?
When did these people live?
Who was the founder of the religion?
Who were the teachers, prophets, or leaders of this religion?
What is their holy book?
Describe the god or gods of this religion.
What conditions led to the spread of this religion?
What problems did it face?
What rules (ethics) did the followers have to help them in their religion?
What do the rules say about the treatment of animals, plants, money, and other things?
What do the rules say about the treatment of other people?
What rewards does the religion offer for obeying the rules?
What answers does the religion give to other important questions?
In what ways is religious knowledge different from scientific knowledge?

(2) After a sufficient period of research, let each committee exchange information with the balance of the class. Discuss with the class how they might condense the information reported for a comparison chart. (This chart can serve as a data retrieval chart in discussions.) The class might also want to make a large wall chart, or the equivalent, for display in the classroom.

(3) Show the film "Major Religions of the World."[21] Have the class refer to their study questions begun in Activity 1 and the chart begun in Activity 2. Have the class add to the chart any new (not already listed) information they obtain from the film.

[21]Encyclopedia Britannica Films, Inc., 1150 Wilmette Ave., Wilmette, Illinois (20 minutes).

(4) Pick from the chart in Activity 2 any belief shared by two or more religions. Do some people believe this in the same way today? Why might such an idea be important to people?

Notice particularly that the last listed activity asks students to hypothesize, drawing on models they have previously stored in their minds to suggest possible explanations for questions the answers to which cannot be proven empirically. It is not necessary to correct faulty hypotheses immediately. It is far more important that students get used to formulating hypotheses and then gathering additional data by which these initial hypotheses can be checked and re-evaluated.

OPEN-ENDEDNESS

Learning activities need to be open-ended so that they not only permit, but encourage, a variety of responses differing in quality and quantity. Such activities should permit a variety of approaches and, when necessary, modifications by skilled teachers. There is no "right answer" to the question: "What might have happened if Christian monasteries had not existed when they did?" Nor is there one "right" technique for the teacher to use to encourage students to respond to such a question.

SELF-CONFIDENCE IN ABILITY TO LEARN

Learning activities should help students increase their understanding of themselves and the world in which they live. Thus, the learning activities that teachers design should encourage and help students to inquire into the nature of themselves and their world, to inquire and think for themselves, to learn how to deal with difficulties and problems, and to try out their own ideas. Rather than providing answers, activities should help students learn how to find answers for themselves. (For example, asking students to compare and contrast the viewpoints of different authors by having them read selected passages helps them to arrive at their own ideas. Simply asking them to describe what one author said only gives them the ideas of others.)

PRINCIPLES OF LEARNING

Learning activities should be based on established principles of learning. As we have seen, many theories about learning exist. Unfortunately, there is as yet no coherent set of basic laws of learning to which teachers can refer. There are, however, many points that most theorists would agree can be considered, if not laws, at least descriptive principles about learning. These include:

- Individuals learn by responding to and interacting with their environment.
- Learning is essentially an active process whereby a change takes place in the ways in which individuals perceive and give meaning to their environment.
- Since every individual in a group has a unique set of experiences, needs, and perceptions, a variety of responses to any given stimulus is likely. Therefore, provision for individual differences in learning is crucial.
- The cultural environment in which an individual finds himself shapes to a considerable extent what he perceives and values.
- A major factor in man's capacity to modify his behavior is his ability to perceive abstract relationships.
- Learning is facilitated when an individual is motivated and interested in what is to be learned.
- Practice is important for many kinds of school learning.
- When a "dissonant" object or fact is inserted into any sequence of objects or facts, attention, curiosity, and interest often increase, thus affecting learning.
- The breakdown of a task into its component parts is often necessary if maximal learning of the task is to be accomplished.
- Transfer of learning is not automatic, but it is more likely to occur when an individual learns the underlying principles of a subject or problem and has practice in applying them in varied situations.
- Reward is usually preferable to punishment as a means of controlling learning.
- Meaningful materials and tasks are learned more readily then non-meaningful ones.
- Providing students with information about what constitutes a "good" performance, along with knowledge of mistakes and successful results, aids learning.
- A tolerance for failure can be developed best by providing a backlog of successful learning experiences to compensate for the failures a student experiences.

BUILDING LEARNING ACTIVITY SEQUENCES

Not all learning activities serve the same function. For example, some provide for *intake* of information. Activities of this kind may include reading, interviewing, observing, listening to records, and viewing films. These kinds of activities are essential for students, since they must have information to work with or think about before they can be expected to engage in intelligent action. They must have data before they can do anything with it. Raw data alone, however, is but perception. Data must be organized and internalized in anticipation of being used. Thus, the necessity for a second type of learning activity—which facilitates *organization* of the information. Examples of this type of activity include charting, note-taking, graphing, map-making, outlining, and preparing timelines. Such activities help students to organize the material to which they've been exposed.

A third type of learning activity helps students to *demonstrate* what they have learned. Such activities as discussions, sociodramas, murals, writing, and role-playing enable students to display the skills they possess, to demonstrate how well they can think, and to indicate how well they understand the actions, problems, and feelings of others.

A fourth type of learning activity encourages students to *express* themselves by *creating* or producing an *original* product. Examples of this type include composing a poem or song, writing an original essay, building an original model, illustrating an idea by means of dance or drawing. Though they often overlap to some degree, the essential difference between creative and demonstrative activities is that demonstrative activities ask students to illustrate the degree to which *they understand* data they have previously acquired and organized. Creative activities, on the other hand, encourage students to use their newly acquired understanding to create or produce *a new and different* product, or to render an original *performance* (see Table 4.1).

A realization of the idea that different kinds of learning activities serve different functions should help us design learning activities that will assist students to learn in a variety of ways.

In too many classrooms, students are engaged for the most part in the same kinds of activities every day—they listen to teachers talk (most teachers talk far too much[22]), they read, they write. These kinds of activities are obviously very important. But different students learn in different ways. And many students do not learn very well at all via talk and the printed word. They need to be more directly or actively involved. It is for this reason that activities such as field trips, role-playing, sociodramas, committee-work, drawing, painting, dancing, taking photographs, making maps, working in the community—in short, any and all activities that involve *doing* things as well as *receiving* information, are so important for students to experience as teachers develop new activities in class. Students need to learn from books and other printed materials, to be sure, but they also need

[22]Floyd tape-recorded 31 one-hour class sessions in elementary schools. He found that *71 percent* of all words spoken were by the teacher. See W. D. Floyd, "An Analysis of the Oral Questioning Ability in Selected Colorado Primary Classrooms." Unpublished doctoral dissertation, Colorado State College, 1960.

TABLE 4.1

EXAMPLES OF LEARNING ACTIVITIES IN EACH CATEGORY

Intake*

READING:
- books
- articles
- magazines
- newspapers
- dittoes
- labels
- advertisements
- circulars
- pamphlets
- handbills
- posters
- experiment

OBSERVING (looking, watching, seeing, photographing, etc.):
- films
- slides
- filmstrips
- pictures
- drawings
- paintings
- photographs
- people
- buildings
- television
- records

LISTENING TO:
- guest speakers
- lectures
- music
- debates
- discussions
- radio

TOUCHING:
- objects
- artifacts
- buildings
- natural environment

INTERVIEWING:
- speakers
- friends
- parents
- other adults (especially older adults, like grandparents)

TASTING:
- foods
- liquids

Organizational*
- outlining
- chart-making
- graphing
- mapping
- time-line building
- diagramming
- arranging
- note-taking
- filing
- question-answering
- question-asking
- stating
- re-stating
- building
- summarizing
- writing
- identifying
- categorizing
- choosing
- recording
- experimenting
- ordering
- sorting

Demonstrative*
- role-playing
- discussing
- writing
- drawing
- question-asking
- reporting
- explaining
- analyzing
- generalizing
- building
- singing
- dancing
- modeling
- describing
- debating
- photographing
- reacting
- story-telling
- preparing murals
- applying
- sketching
- choosing

Creative*
- solving problems
- inventing new uses for things
- composing songs or poetry
- writing essays or stories
- role-creating
- mimeing
- painting
- writing fiction
- question-forming
- cartooning
- hypothesizing
- predicting
- drawing
- singing
- dancing
- photographing
- proposing
- building
- creating a mural
- discussing

*Some activities legitimately fit into more than one category, depending on the purpose behind the activity.

161

to learn from audio-visual media, from discussing, from observing, from interviewing, from taking things and ideas apart, from putting things and ideas together, and from feeling. But all four types of activities—intake, organizational, demonstrative, and creative—are essential if learning is to take place.

Let us consider some examples. Imagine that a teacher and his class of upper elementary-grade students have decided to investigate the contemporary problem of alienation in the United States today. The teacher intends, as an initial objective, that students will be able to express orally or in writing their beginning impressions of how an alienated person feels. In what kinds of activities might he begin to engage students in order to fulfill this objective?

Problem: Alienation
Objective: Students will express orally or in writing their beginning impressions of how an alienated person feels.
Procedure:

1. Play the record "She's Leaving Home" from the album *Sgt. Pepper's Lonely Hearts Club Band*.[23] Ask the class if they can identify the artist and the song. (Intake)

2. Ask the class to listen to the record again, only this time to follow the lyrics that are reprinted in the beginning of Chapter I in *Alienation: Personal Problem or National Tragedy*.[24] Ask them to reflect on what the song is talking about and then answer in writing the following questions:
   a. What is the song about?
   b. Why is the girl in the song leaving home?
   c. How does she feel? What makes you think so?
   d. How do her parents feel? What makes you think so?
   e. How would you describe the relationship which exists between the girl and her parents?
   f. What might produce such a relationship? (Organizational)

3. Discuss each of these questions with the class, encouraging students to offer their opinions. Point out that there are no right or wrong answers to these kinds of questions. (Demonstrative)

4. Encourage the class to write a short passage of their own, compose a poem, draw a cartoon, or sketch, etc. in which they describe a situation in which they or someone they know has experienced feelings similar to the girl's. (Creative)

5. Summarize the class's response to questions e and f. Now ask the class to read the rest of Chapter I, pointing out that in the remainder of the Chapter are recounted two additional and somewhat different situations which, when considered along with the song, are both similar and different in several

---

[23]John Lennon and Paul McCartney, "She's Leaving Home," from the album *Sgt. Pepper's Lonely Hearts Club Band*. Copyright © 1967 Northern Songs, Ltd.
[24]Ronald V. Urick, *Alienation: Personal Problem or National Tragedy* (Englewood Cliffs, N.J.: Prentice-Hall, 1970).

ways. Ask the class, as they read, to look for some of these ways. (Intake and Organizational)

6. Have each student make a list of the similarities and differences that he has identified, and then ask the class to compare the lists. What differences do they notice? How would they explain these differences? (Demonstrative and Creative)

7. Now ask the class to hypothesize as to what factors encourage alienation in people. (Creative)

As a second example, this time at the primary level, consider the following sequence developed by a teacher desiring to help her students begin to develop a positive self-image and identity.

Problem: Self-identity
Objective: Children will identify voices of their classmates and themselves, speaking on a tape recorder.
Procedure:

1. Introduce the tape recorder to the children. Show how it operates. Talk into the microphone and record your voice, then play back the recording for the children. (Intake)

2. Let each child record into the tape recorder by first making body sounds— clapping, stomping, whistling. Play back the recording to children. (Organizational, Demonstrative)

3. Let each child hold the microphone and say his name into the tape recorder. Play back the recording immediately. (Organizational, Demonstrative)

4. Point out that there are no "right" or "wrong" voices. Point out the similarities and differences in people's voices. Emphasize the fact that each person has his own individual voice. (Intake)

5. Re-play the tape and have children point out some similarities and differences in the tone or sound of each other's voices. Record these differences by making a line graph. Using a piece of paper and crayon, have the children draw in one continuous line, making the line go up if the voice is high and down if the voice is low. (Organizational)

6. Let each child make up a story and record it on the tape without using his name. Play back the tape and use these stories to test the child's voice recognition. (Demonstrative, Creative)

Both of these learning activity sequences include all four categories of activities intake, organizational, demonstrative, and creative—described above. Each is but one example of how the objective in each case might be accomplished. The point to stress, however, is that each teacher helped students obtain data necessary for the task at hand (the intake), helped them to organize this data in their own way so that they could use it later, provided an opportunity for them to demonstrate (and the teacher to realize) their understanding of the data and what it meant to them, and then encouraged them to express their understanding in an original product, creation or task. In the past, many teachers have concentrated unduly on activities that provide for intake, while overlooking or minimizing organizing, demonstrating and creative opportunities. Teachers who expand their classroom repertory to include a rich mosaic of learning activities are likely to find their students enjoying the social studies more and becoming increasingly capable of varying their education experience.

SKILLS[25]

If students are to engage successfully in learning activities, they will need to master a variety of skills that will help them learn. Such skills fall somewhat logically into three fairly distinct categories—thinking skills, academic skills, and social skills. The development of thinking will be discussed in Chapter 5. Academic skills include:

Reading	books, articles, magazine excerpts, newspapers, reviews, appendices, and other printed matter
Viewing	films, filmstrips, pictures, transparencies, and the natural environment
Listening	to records, tapes, guest speakers, teachers, parents, and peers
Outlining	of information obtained from printed, oral, or visual sources
Note-taking	using study questions, during unstructured reading sessions, when the class exchanges information after a period of research, or upon listening to resource people. This involves in particular referring to a wide variety of source materials
Caption-writing	concise, accurate descriptions for bulletin boards or other classroom or report displays
Making Charts	for example, of the kinds of occupations and people in those occupations in a particular locality

[25]Much of the material in this section has been taken directly or adapted from Chapter VI of Hilda Taba, Mary C. Durkin, Jack R. Fraenkel, and Anthony H. McNaughton, *A Teacher's Handbook to Elementary Social Studies*, 2nd ed. (Reading, Mass.: Addison-Wesley, 1971).

Reading and Interpreting Maps	for example, noting the differences between South Vietnam and Viet Cong maps of territory held by each and learning how to interpret the validity of each set of information as well as gaining additional implied information (e.g., urban and rural population locations)
Diagramming	for example, of family and social structures in different cultures
Tabulating	for example, the votes of congressional members on foreign aid appropriations (this skill can be expanded to include several tabulations which produce a charting of votes over a period of time which would then require the interpretation of patterns that might result related to social, economic, political, geographical, and international factors)
Constructing Timelines	for example, of inventions or discoveries that have changed man's life for the better (or worse) from 1500 to the present, including significant events
Asking Relevant Questions	of guest speakers and other sources; this involves realizing that different questions serve different purposes. For example, to ask "Who was elected President of the United States in 1972?" brings forth but one answer and offers no insight into reasons. "What causes men to seek the Presidency?" requests an explanation of why certain men act as they do.

The most important academic skills are described briefly in the following paragraphs.

Reading. In our culture, reading is essential. Individuals must be helped to read as effectively and intelligently as their unique capabilities permit. Thus, opportunities for vocabulary development and enrichment (e.g., through being exposed to the usefulness of word-recognition techniques such as context clues, or known word elements such as prefixes and suffixes) must be provided. Students need to acquire additional meanings for words they already possess (such as cape, belt, source, level, and mouth) as well as to acquire new words. A continual effort should be made to relate words to individuals and events that students see or come in contact with in their own lives. They also need to learn how to read in different ways for different purposes. Thus, practice in skimming, reading to formulate questions to ask of a resource person, reading for details to answer study questions, and reflective reading for critical analysis all need to be cultivated.

Students should have some general idea of how books are organized. The organization of a book is indicated by its table of contents. Students need to know and be able to utilize this fact. In addition, they need to realize that the index serves a different function. It not only indicates specific references within the text as a whole but also gives references to pertinent maps, diagrams, and figures. Students who have learned how to use the page references which follow index entries can find all pertinent information on a given topic which a particular book contains. Realizing that different synonyms, such as farming and agriculture, may, in different indexes, be used to classify the same information is of further help.

Students need to know where different types of source materials may be obtained. Teachers should not take such knowledge for granted. In fact, if necessary, they should specifically instruct them in how to locate information in such sources as periodicals, government publications, and community resource files; how to use as resources films, filmstrips, slides, charts, posters, records, radio, and television; how to interview, observe, and survey; and what to look for on field trips.

Different types of source materials need to be approached in different ways. Visual materials may require students to "look at" data differently than printed or oral stimuli. Methods of using conventional text materials may be inappropriate for other printed matter. For example, while novels may reflect accurately the feelings of the characters of a particular time, they may distort the particulars described in the setting presented. Strictly factual accounts, on the other hand, may give no inkling of the affective mood of the times. Students need to know how to utilize such different types of materials.

Note-taking.   Students also need to develop their own schemes for organizing and connecting information which they obtain. This is especially important when many different texts and other data sources are used. The preparation of individual notebooks based on note-taking can serve as "data banks" for retrieval purposes in class discussions, and for use in various organizational activities.

Viewing.   Firsthand experiences such as field trips need to be provided in order to clarify concepts of abstract terms and relationships (for example, several trips to different neighborhoods and areas to gain a more direct sense of what the abstract concept "city" means). Continual efforts should be made to relate words to events (or individuals) that students see or hear in pictures, films, filmstrips, or on records and tapes.

Writing. Students must also be able to express themselves clearly in writing. Practice in writing individual and group reports can help develop this skill. Assigning many short papers (one page in length, no more, for example) is probably of more value in this regard than one large term report as a sort of cumulative activity. Here again, students need to be helped to avoid vague terms, to distinguish between statements of fact, inference, and judgment.

Speaking and Listening. Further, students need to learn how to speak and listen. Panel discussions, oral and written reports, interviewing opportunities, and role-playing all can help with regard to speaking and practice should be provided throughout the grades. Providing opportunities for students to listen is equally important. (Guest speakers, records, tapes, radio, television, poetry read aloud—all are listening resources.) Still further, students need to learn how to attend to, comprehend, and evaluate oral and written sources (for example, comparing and contrasting two or more speakers' comments on a given event or occurrence).

Reading and Interpreting Maps. Also important is developing a sense of place and space. Continual and frequent reference to maps and globes (e.g., through asking students to note directions, compute distances, locate places, and express relative location); explanation and use of scale and symbols, exposure to different kinds of projections; comparisons between different kinds of maps; and drawing inferences from maps are all important.

Constructing Timelines. Students need to develop a sense of time and chronology, and to realize that different concepts of time exist. (Thus primary children can master the telling of time through the use of clock mock-ups, calendars, placing events in order of occurrence, and relating dates to their personal life experiences. Older children can be exposed to a more in-depth study of a past culture in order to increase their sense of historical chronology, asked to make generalizations about time in terms of the development of social institutions, and then asked to apply their generalizations to new situations.)

Social skills include:

Planning with Others	for example, how to divide the tasks involved in preparing a group-written report, or how to decide who will search for answers to which of several study questions

Participating in Research Projects	a committee effort to research a problem of common concern, or working in two- or three-man small groups to investigate a particular topic
Participating Productively in Group Discussions	through developing confidence in one's ability to contribute ideas and information to others
Responding Courteously to the Questions of Others	through learning to listen to what others are asking and then to respond appropriately
Leading Group Discussions	through learning how to ask appropriate questions, how to encourage others to speak, and how to refocus and clarify others' responses
Acting Responsibly	through estimating what the consequences of a given action may be and taking responsibility for those actions which one initiates
Helping Others	through providing assistance when one has information which will make it easier for another to succeed in a given task

Social skills involve a concern for, and interaction with, other people. They are much broader in scope than academic skills and, accordingly, more difficult to implement. Social skills involve both facts and feelings; they are rarely learned completely and forever but continue to be developed throughout an individual's lifetime. As in the case of academic skills, however, certain factors appear basic to consider in developing these skills throughout a series of lessons and units.

Students need to be helped to identify with others in situations different from their own, to empathize with others' concerns, to "feel" as they do, and to see things from another's point of view. They may learn to do this by identifying how individuals in other cultures feel in a conflict situation, or by role-playing individuals trying to decide how to deal with a particular problem with which they are faced. They also need to realize that there are others in their own culture with whom they share ideals and points of view.

Students need to be helped to avoid using stereotypes as a means of classifying individuals (e.g., by learning to recognize and analyze propaganda techniques; by learning to distinguish between factual reports, inferences, and value judgments, and by learning that people in different cultures are individuals with unique perceptions and desires).

Students need to be helped to examine their own feelings, sensitivities, and values in order to understand themselves as thoroughly and honestly as possible (e.g., by writing essays on topics such as "What Makes Me Angry or Happy," through reacting and responding to others' opinions and others' critiques of their work, and by revising such work accordingly, when appropriate).

Students should be expected to assume responsibility for actions which they initiate. (For example, they should be able to plan with others, decide who will do certain tasks, and accept specific responsibilities on a group research project or committee investigation.)

SUMMARY

This chapter stressed the fact that learning activities *as well as* subject matter must be considered if maximum student learning is to be accomplished. The terms "learning," "learning theory," and "learning activity" were defined and exemplified. It was argued that learning activities are much more important than has heretofore been generally realized, and a number of basic factors to consider when selecting and/or developing learning activities were therefore set forth.

Four major types of learning activities were identified, examples of each type were described, and an example of two learning activity sequences incorporating each of the four types was then presented.

Various social and academic skills that are important for students to master in order to facilitate learning were identified and several examples of such skills described. The importance of engaging students in a variety of different kinds of learning activities so that multiple ways of learning are provided students was stressed.

EXERCISES*

I. Place the letter of the learning activity criterion from Column A in front of the statement or statements to which it refers in Column B.

*The author's suggestions are on pages 400–401.

A	B
a. Justifiability	**1.** ____ Learning activities should encourage a variety of responses differing in quality and quantity.
b. Incremental Development	
	2. ____ Learning activities should serve a distinct purpose.
c. Sequential Ordering	
d. Multiple Focus	**3.** ____ Each learning activity should not only serve as a prerequisite for the learning activities to follow, but also build on those learning activities that have come earlier.
e. Transferability	
f. Open-Endedness	
g. Principles of Learning	
	4. ____ Any sequence or set of learning activities should help students deal with content that is increasingly more difficult, abstract, and complex.
h. Self-Confidence in Ability to Learn	

5. ____ Any sequence or set of learning activities should provide for the realization of not only knowledge objectives, but also cognitive, affective, and skill objectives.

6. ____ Learning activities should help students apply what they've learned in one situation to other new and different situations.

II. Place the correct letter (or letters) from Column A in front of the proper examples to which it refers in Column B. (Some of the examples may represent examples of more than one type of learning activity, depending on how they are used.)

A	B
Intake **(I)**	**1.** ____ reading a chapter in a text
Organizational **(O)**	**2.** ____ taking notes on a guest speaker
Demonstrative **(D)**	**3.** ____ viewing a film
Creative **(C)**	**4.** ____ discussing an editorial
	5. ____ outlining an argument
	6. ____ composing a poem
	7. ____ interviewing members of the local council

8. _____ comparing and contrasting orally Hamilton's and Jefferson's views on the nature of government

9. _____ proposing an alternative explanation for student unrest today

10. _____ preparing questions to ask of a resource person

11. _____ grouping various periodicals in terms of their perceived political emphasis

12. _____ identifying the main idea(s) to be found in a paragraph

13. _____ writing an interpretive essay on the comparative effects of the New Deal and the Great Society

14. _____ seeing a filmstrip describing the underlying reasons behind the War of 1812

15. _____ participating in a debate on whether Andrew Jackson or Thomas Jefferson was the greater President

16. _____ restating an argument found in a text

17. _____ refuting an argument found in a text

18. _____ diagramming on the blackboard the steps a bill must follow in order to become a law in the United States

19. _____ drawing on a map the routes taken by frontiersmen to penetrate the Appalachian Mountains during the 1700s

20. _____ participating in a mock "Meet the Press" program in which the present Secretary of State (portrayed by a student) in interviewed by other members of the class as to his feelings about the nature and direction of U.S. foreign involvement in the years to come

III. Place the correct letter from Column A in front of the proper example or examples to which it refers in Column B.

A	B
Academic Skill **(A)**	**1.** _____ Outlining a chapter
Social Skill **(S)**	**2.** _____ Asking questions of a guest speaker
	3. _____ Skimming a paragraph in a textbook
	4. _____ Working as a member of a committee to investigate the problem of poverty throughout the world
	5. _____ Listening to a committee report
	6. _____ Leading a class discussion on the effects of drug usage among various segments of the population of the United States
	7. _____ Helping another student research a topic in the library
	8. _____ Watching a film
	9. _____ Preparing a series of overlay maps
	10. _____ Taking notes on information contained in an encyclopedia
	11. _____ Planning a group presentation with five other students
	12. _____ Role-playing an individual faced with a difficult choice

IV. Try to write a learning activity sequence yourself that you believe will help students attain one or more objectives. Try to include the four major types of learning activities (intake, organizational, demonstrative, and creative) described in this chapter. What difficulties do you encounter?

V. Review the examples of different kinds of learning activities presented in Table 4.1. What other examples could be added under each category?

VI. Is the I-O-D-C model presented and discussed on pages 159–64 a useful one for you? Would you modify the suggested sequence in any way? If so, when? how? Would you suggest any other categories?

VII. It has been said that a major difficulty for many students is that they have trouble organizing the large amount of data they come across in their studies; it becomes less and less meaningful, and they become more and more disinterested. Would you agree with this analysis? Would a consistent emphasis by teachers on organizational-type learning activities help such students? Explain your reasoning.

VIII. One of the major contentions of the author of this book is that a teacher should *never* engage students in two or more intake activities in a row, since this can too easily lead to "information overload." Two organizational, demonstrative, or creative activities in a row, on the other hand, are often necessary. Can you give any examples of where the latter might be the case?

IX. Can you suggest a learning activity that, in and of itself, might provide all four of the functions described on pages 159–64?

CHAPTER V

TEACHING STRATEGIES
FOR
DEVELOPING THINKING

This chapter deals with the nature and importance of encouraging students to think about data. A major contention is that an emphasis upon helping students to formulate their own concepts and ideas rather than only to learn the concepts and ideas of others has a number of advantages, the most important being that such an emphasis helps students learn to think for themselves.

The first section of the chapter defines the concept of teaching strategy, and points out that the heart of any effective teaching strategy lies in the questions that a teacher asks. A number of different kinds of questions are discussed, several examples of each type of question are presented, and the value of helping students to learn to ask as well as to answer questions is argued.

The remainder of the chapter describes and discusses strategies that teachers can employ to help their students think about data. Certain unwarranted and warranted assumptions about the nature of thinking are examined. Several generically applicable strategies are then presented, along with samples of dialogue by students engaged in the strategies in actual classrooms. Finally, practical suggestions are made as to how teachers can use the strategies.

When you have finished reading this chapter, therefore, you should be able to do the following:

- *define* the term "teaching strategy";
- *name* at least six types of questions that a teacher might ask to encourage students to think about data, *explain* how these types differ from one another, and give several (at least three) examples of each type;
- *describe* at least four ways by which a teacher can encourage students to ask different kinds of questions of themselves and others;

- *state* several (four or more) examples of warranted and unwarranted assumptions about the nature of thinking and *identify* several (at least four) different ways a teacher might test such assumptions;
- *identify* several (at least five) strategies that you can use to help students learn to "think," *describe* the steps involved in each of the strategies, *explain* how they encourage student thinking, and actually use the strategies in your own teaching.

It was argued in Chapter 4 that subject matter by itself, no matter how interesting, only provides the basic information that students need as a foundation upon which to build. Specific facts, concepts, and generalizations, regardless of their origin, do not, by themselves, encourage students to think, to feel, or to value. These latter objectives are accomplished only when students use the facts, concepts, and generalizations they acquire in some way. Thus the need for a variety of interesting, carefully thought out, and well-designed learning activities to involve or "engage" students in, or with, subject matter. It is worth repeating that the selection and organization of subject matter by itself only serves to impart knowledge. It is the selection and organization of learning activities that helps students to learn how to use such knowledge.

Both, however, are essential. As stressed in Chapter 1, it is impossible to learn subject matter of any sort unless one engages in some mental process at the same time. Students cannot, for example, understand the meaning of the concept of "region" unless they learn to identify the common characteristics which regions possess that non-regions do not. They cannot learn to compare and contrast unless they learn to search out and identify similarities and differences among various events, objects, individuals, or ideas.

As mentioned earlier, therefore, teachers need to consider not only *what* they expect students to learn (subject matter), but also *how* they expect them to learn it (learning activities). But subject matter and learning activities are only part of the total picture of learning. A teacher must also consider his own actions—what he needs to do in order to involve his students most effectively in subject matter and learning activities to help them learn. For example, if he desires that students compare and contrast various reasons that men have offered throughout history for exploring the unknown, he must ask himself what he needs to do in order to facilitate such comparing and contrasting. Thus there is not only a need for teachers to possess a considerable amount of knowledge themselves, and to be able to develop or select a variety of interesting learning activities, but also a necessity for teachers to master and have at their command a variety of precisely defined and carefully thought out teaching strategies applicable in a variety of different contexts.

WHAT IS A TEACHING STRATEGY?

Teaching strategies represent combinations of certain specific procedures or operations (such as carefully developed question sequences), grouped and ordered in a definite sequence, that teachers can use in the classroom to implement both cognitive and affective objectives (e.g., conceptualizing, generalizing, valuing, and exploring feelings). Whereas learning activities represent things which students do, or actions in which they engage, teaching strategies refer to operations a teacher performs in order to involve students in activities to help them learn. We shall discuss a number of such operations in the remainder of this and the next chapter. The heart of any effective teaching strategy, however, lies in the questions a teacher asks. Before we consider the strategies themselves, therefore, let us consider some aspects of teacher and student questioning.

THE IMPORTANCE OF GOOD QUESTIONS[1]

The essence of any effective teaching strategy lies in the questions a teacher asks. The importance of good questions is illustrated by the following anecdote:

> Max Lerner once described his passing the front of a small pawn shop where a sign in the window asked: "If you're so smart, why aren't you rich?" Admittedly fascinated by the sign, he returned to it again and again. "I couldn't answer the question," he remarked, "and what's more, I didn't know why I couldn't! Then it came to me. It was the wrong question!"[2]

Many teachers ask such "wrong questions"! Certainly every teacher needs to be able to ask the "right" questions. But what are the "right" questions? I am not speaking in an absolutist or totalitarian sense, where "right" refers to only one type of action, predetermined by some external source. Rather, I propose that there are several different types of questions which teachers may ask, depending upon what purposes they have in mind. In this sense, the "right" questions are those which assist the teacher in achieving a particular objective or set of objectives he considers important. Once again, the importance of a clearly thought out purpose, of a teacher knowing where he is going, is evident.

Teachers continually need to ask: "Why do I want students to learn this (fact, concept, generalization)?" By asking themselves this question, and

---

[1] Parts of this section appear in somewhat different form in Jack R. Fraenkel, "Ask the Right Questions," *Clearing House*, March 1966, pp. 397–401.
[2] *Ibid.*, p. 397.

arriving at a satisfactory answer (however temporary), they can determine what questions to ask their students. Teachers who know the "why" of a particular undertaking will more likely be able to justify to students the relevance of that which takes place in the classroom. If teachers do not know why something is important, certainly students cannot be expected to know. And if students are not convinced that what they are being asked to consider, think about, or deal with is important (i.e., relevant), they quite likely will not consider it at all.

Teachers must also ask themselves: "Where am I going?" "What do I want to accomplish?" "Why do I want to accomplish this?" "How can I most effectively accomplish what I wish to accomplish?" Answers to such questions will help decide what questions must be asked of students.

The questions a teacher asks reveal a great deal about the outcomes he has in mind. If primary interest is in having the students acquire factual knowledge, certain types of questions will tend to be asked. If teachers are interested in students' being able to organize or analyze the knowledge they have acquired, questions of a different order will be asked. Should they desire their students to be able to synthesize or evaluate the data they have acquired, yet other types of questions will be necessary. And finally, should the goal be the exercise of creative thought, queries of still a different nature will be needed.

Let me suggest a taxonomy of questions, which various purposes would require. Consider this classification in terms of the purposes which teachers might have, the actions required or desired of students, and the types of questions which teachers would accordingly ask. Such a classification would be similar to that shown in Table 5.1.

KINDS OF QUESTIONS

RECALL QUESTIONS

The purpose of recall questions is to determine if students have acquired or obtained a desired amount of factual information; teachers are asking them to remember certain specific information that they have learned beforehand. There is but one correct answer. Examples of such questions would be:

1. Who was the commander of the British forces during the Battle of Bunker Hill?
2. Who was the first black athlete to break into major league baseball?
3. What territory did the United States gain by the Treaty of Guadalupe Hidalgo?

TABLE 5.1

LEVELS OF QUESTIONING

Purpose	Type of Question	Student Action Desired
VI. Divergent thinking	Open-Ended	Gives many possible predictions
V. Evaluation as to the quality of a relationship or conclusion	Judgmental	Tells which of two or more alternatives is best according to clearly specified criteria
IV. Formation and/or identification of relationships and conclusions	Synthesizing or summarizing	States a relationship or connection among previously unrelated data
III. Analysis of the reasons behind an action	Explanatory	Gives reasons why a given individual or individuals acted in a certain way, a given event or events occurred as it (they) did, or a certain effect or effects resulted.
II. Organization of data	Descriptive or comparative	Describes, compares, contrasts, or compares and contrasts data
I. Acquisition of information	Recall or recognition	Gives correct answer

4. When did Pakistan and India become separate states?
5. What is the present population of the Soviet Union?
6. Where is the city of Prague located?
7. What classes of people were guaranteed rights under the Magna Charta?
8. When was John F. Kennedy inaugurated President of the United States?

Questions such as these are important ones, for by answering them students acquire information with which to think about, formulate, and verify conclusions and relationships. One cannot think if one has nothing to think about! Far too often, however, many teachers never go beyond this. If teachers want more from their students than simply the extent of factual knowledge which they have acquired, they must ask questions of a different sort.

DESCRIPTIVE QUESTIONS

Descriptive questions help students put together and organize the facts which they have gathered—to make some sense out of their data. It is assumed that some type of relationship exists, that there is some continuity or sequence within the material that can be identified. For example, students might be asked to describe, compare, contrast, or compare and contrast data. Students are still being asked to recall information previously learned, but they are also being asked to describe aspects of this information in greater detail. Examples of such questions are:

1. Describe the kinds of problems faced by immigrants to the United States in the 1920s.
2. Describe the characteristics of the five major vegetation zones of the Soviet Union.
3. How has African nationalism since 1945 differed from that prior to World War II?
4. How did the Whigs campaign in 1840?
5. Describe the effects of the Los Angeles earthquake of 1971.
6. Compare peasant life in the Soviet Union under Stalin with peasant life under Khrushchev.
7. Contrast Stokely Carmichael's views on race relations with the views of Martin Luther King.
8. Compare and contrast the traditional Iroquois sense of time with the sense of time more commonly accepted throughout the Western world.

In short, one answer (though often having many parts) is still desired and students still are asked to exercise their powers of recall. However, they are asked not only to remember, but also to organize and describe in detail the facts which they have learned. To explain *why* certain things occurred however, a third type of question, that of explanation, is necessary.

EXPLANATORY QUESTIONS

Explanatory questions ask students not only to remember and organize material, but also to make inferences and seek causes and effects. This type of question asks students to analyze data—to break information into its component parts, and then explain how these parts are related. Students must tell *why* they think as they do—in short, explain the reasoning behind their answers. Questions with these purposes in mind are typified by such requests as: "Explain what you mean by that, John!" "Why did you choose what you did, Susan?" "Why did these things happen?" "What other alternatives might exist?" Hence, questions such as these appear:

1. Why do you think the United States supported Pakistan rather than India in 1971?
2. Why do you think young people participated in the "Freedom Rides" of the early 1960s?
3. Why do you feel the South was irritated with the Abolitionists in the 1850s and 1860s.
4. Why do you think Russia is building more nuclear submarines?
5. Why might someone disagree (or agree) with this position?
6. What causes alienation?

Here many answers are possible as students reflect upon and analyze the data they have gathered. Notice that the focus of the question is very important, however. Simply asking "why" is not enough. For example, "Why was Richard Nixon defeated for the Presidency in 1960?" may result in students reciting a list of textbook "reasons." The teacher must take care to ensure that ready-made answers that students can memorize are not available, or he may inadvertently find himself requiring only recall or recognition rather than explanation. Teachers must also not push their own ideas, for they must encourage students to present and defend *their* reasons for thinking as they do. Unfortunately, far too few teachers ask questions that encourage these answers. Even fewer promote synthetic learning. And that brings us to the next category.

SYNTHESIZING QUESTIONS

The outcome hoped for here is to get students to suggest connections or relationships that they believe certain data support, and on what basis. Synthesizing questions require students to put things together, to combine, relate, or connect pieces of previously unrelated content. They are asked to seek out relationships, form connections, and draw conclusions. Questions which promote these objectives include "How would you sum up this author's argument?" or "What conclusion would you draw from this line of reasoning?" Examples of this kind of questioning include:

1. What conclusions have you come to regarding the foreign policies of Harry Truman and Lyndon Johnson?
2. How would you summarize the effect of Caesar Chavez's efforts to improve the lot of migrant farm workers in California?
3. What implications does the author's argument have for resolving present-day international tensions?

4. Under what conditions might an oppressed people be likely to revolt against their oppressors?

Once again, many answers are possible as students suggest various conclusions or relationships which they believe the data suggest. The more facts they can find to support such conclusions, the more warranted the conclusion becomes. Teachers can help students evaluate these conclusions, however, by encouraging and helping them to search for data to *refute* them.

JUDGMENTAL QUESTIONS

Judgmental questions require students to choose among alternatives, making a judgment as to which of two or more possibilities is best according to some previously established criteria. In short, we are asking students to choose or otherwise judge as to the quality of a relationship or conclusion, basing their choice on a certain set of characteristics or criteria possessed in greater degree by one of the alternatives in question. Thus we ask questions such as "Which way is quickest?" "What does the cleaner job?" or "Which alternative has the greatest money-making possibilities?" Further examples include:

1. Which statement most adequately explains all the data we have examined?
2. Should the author's position be defended or attacked? On what grounds?
3. Which author has the most empirical data in support of his position?
4. Which of the following conclusions is the most logical?
5. Which of the following alternatives would most likely result in a lowered birth rate in the United States?

The teacher must take care to ensure that criteria for judgment have been established. Students cannot judge effectively or fairly if they have no basis for evaluating the merits of particular alternatives. Too often such criteria, however, are *not* established. Even less frequently do teachers encourage divergent thinking as suggested by our final category.

OPEN-ENDED QUESTIONS

It is with this last level that teachers, in effect, enter the stratosphere. Teachers who ask open-ended questions are pretty rare birds. One study,[3] in fact, showed that over 90 percent of the questions asked by junior high school teachers required students only to reiterate information given in the textbook. Open-ended questions, however, require students to seek and

[3]J. G. Fowlkes, *The Wisconsin Improvement Program—Teacher Education and Local School Systems* (Madison, Wis.: University of Wisconsin, 1962).

determine for themselves what they consider to be acceptable answers. No answers are more acceptable than others. Guilford[4] referred to this type of activity as divergent rather than convergent thinking. In actuality, students venture out onto heretofore uncharted seas. Such questions include queries such as:

1. What might have happened if Hubert Humphrey had been elected President of the United States in 1968?
2. If you were inventing a language for Martians, where would you begin?
3. Why do some men become professional poets and others professional athletes?
4. What kind of world might exist if there were no sound?
5. How would you describe eternity?

In essence, students are asked to venture out onto their own, to make a creative leap into the unknown, to stretch both their imaginations and their intellects. The atmosphere produced by such questioning is a difficult one for many teachers to endure, for questions of this kind ask students to seek knowledge on their own initiative rather than to passively receive it from the teacher's hallowed lips. Torrance and Myers[5] have developed and published sets of these kinds of questions, which they classify as highly unconventional. They note that most adults find it very difficult to deal with such questions, since they usually interpret them literally. Questions like "Where is the Fourth of July in Mexico?" "Is a month a mile?" and "When is the sky?" produce frustration and anger, however, even in some children. Nevertheless, the value of this type of question is that it encourages students to search for and see relationships that are not obvious.

STUDENT QUESTIONING

The ability to ask significant questions is an important skill for *students*, as well as teachers, to possess, since it is an important key to effective learning. Torrance and Myers have suggested that students do ask many questions in school, and that the majority of these fall into one of four categories:

4See J. W. Getzels, "Creative Thinking, Problem-Solving, and Instruction," in *Theories of Learning and Instruction*, Sixty-third Yearbook of the National Society for the Study of Education (Chicago: University of Chicago Press, 1964), p. 247.

5E. Paul Torrance and R. E. Myers, *Creative Learning and Teaching* (New York: Dodd, Mead, 1970).

1. Questions regarding procedures (e.g., May I go to the lavatory? Can I have another piece of paper?).
2. Questions regarding tasks (e.g., When is this assignment due? Why do we have to have a test on that?).
3. Questions regarding information (e.g., How do you spell "vertical"? What's a pension?).
4. Questions regarding understanding (e.g., What do you mean by "texture"? Why do you invert the fraction? Why does carbon dioxide burn my hands?).[6]

These authors go on to point out that the kinds of questions that students ask reveal a good deal about their perception of the teacher's attitude and philosophy.

> For instance, if a class of pupils asks questions mostly concerning permission, they probably consider their teacher a babysitter or a warden. If most of their questions are about the ways in which they are to perform their tasks, children probably see their teacher as a boss or a supervisor; some may see him as a drill sergeant. It is likely that many children see their teacher as a repository of information when their questions are mostly of the factual type. If a preponderance of their questions concern the things in their lives they wonder about and want to understand, a group of children probably regards its teacher as a co-experiencer.[7]

You may or may not agree with the preceding analysis. But it seems logical to assume that by studying the kinds of questions students ask repeatedly, teachers can gain some insight into the kind of answers students desire (and perhaps think the teacher expects!) and, if necessary, revise or modify their instructional procedures.

Teachers certainly need to ask provocative questions, but these alone will probably not be enough. If they wish to help students learn how to ask better questions, they need to provide the kind of classroom atmosphere in which such questions are likely to come forth. Students need to be aware that different kinds of questions serve different functions, and indicate a request for different kinds of information. Much of a teacher's time, therefore, might well be spent in planning how to help students *ask* better questions of themselves and others. One technique that offers promise is to present students with an *answer* (e.g., a name, a concept, a generalization, a relationship, etc.), and then ask them to ask a series of questions that would enable them to arrive at that answer. Another possibility is to encourage students to query *themselves* (about what they'll need to find out)

[6]E. P. Torrance and R. E. Myers, *Creative Learning and Teaching*, pp. 226–232.
[7]*Ibid.*, p. 232.

before they begin work on a project or other activity. The old game of Twenty Questions, in which the teacher responds only with replies of "yes" or "no" to children's queries is yet another possibility. Or they can be helped to organize material into categories by learning to ask what Torrance and Myers[8] call "troubleshooting" questions, such as "Why was this type of problem so difficult this time and so easy last time?" or "Would this be more a problem of transportation or one of communication?" Encouraging students to ask questions like these helps them to think in terms of categories of data rather than isolated pieces of unrelated information.

A further possibility is to present students with patterns or sequences of questions like the taxonomy presented earlier, focused on a given topic, so that they may perceive the various kinds of replies and thinking that differently worded questions call for. For example, as described in Chapter 1, Bloom and his associates[9] suggest a sequence quite similar to the one presented earlier. It proceeds from questions that are primarily factual in nature up through questions of interpretation, analysis, synthesis, and evaluation.

Let us suppose, therefore, that a class has begun a study of poverty, its nature, causes, effects, and possible solutions. The teacher might place the following pattern (or one similar) on the board, *without* identifying the category (Factual, Explanatory, etc.) into which each question falls.

Factual Questions:
1. *Recall or retention:* How many families earn less than $3,000.00 per year in the United States?
2. *Comprehension:* What was the purpose of the "War on Poverty" initiated by the Johnson Administration?
3. *Description:* Under what conditions do poor people in Appalachia live?

Explanatory Questions:
4. *Analysis:* Why is it that many poor people in the United States cannot improve their status?
5. *Synthesis:* In what ways are poor people who live in the southern part of the United States different from poor people who live in the northern part of the United States? In what ways are they similar?

Judgmental Questions:
6. *Evaluation:* Which of the many agencies existing in the United States today to help the poor is most effective? (Be sure to explain what you mean by "effective.")
7. *Prescription:* Should the welfare program as administered by the Federal government be modified in any way?

---

[8]E. P. Torrance and R. E. Myers, *Creative Learning and Teaching*, p. 240.
[9]Benjamin S. Bloom *et al.*, *A Taxonomy of Educational Objectives, Handbook I: Cognitive Domain* (New York: McKay, 1956).

When all of the class has observed the pattern, the teacher can ask:

- What kinds of information does each question request?
- In what ways are these questions different? similar?
- How could you use each of these questions?
- What conclusion would you draw about the kinds of questions you can use to obtain information?

A final suggestion is the use of what Suchman[10] has called "discrepant events"—puzzling incidents or happenings that, on first glance, do not seem to make sense. Torrance and Myers cite an example of a teacher who instituted an "I" (for Inquirers) Club for students who successfully explained a puzzling event, and present the following example of how one teacher made use of a discrepant event to encourage students to ask good questions.

TEACHER: Several years ago a Japanese ship left port and headed for the open sea. When it had reached a spot about five hundred miles from the nearest point of land, the captain gave a signal and the crew spilled a half-ton of pearls over the side. What questions can you ask that might help you explain this apparently unreasonable (and true) happening? Ask only questions that can be answered by "yes" or "no." Each of you can keep up his questioning until he decides to "pass" to someone else.

VICKI: Were they crooks who were being chased by the police and wanted to get rid of the evidence—the pearls—so they wouldn't be jailed?

TEACHER: No.

VICKI: I pass.

HARRY: Was the captain driven crazy by a mysterious drug, and then he forced his crew to throw the pearls overboard?

TEACHER: No.

HARRY: I pass.

JENNY: Did the Russians break a Japanese code and then follow them in a sub, and then they surfaced and were about to get the pearls, and so the captain told the men to throw the pearls overboard?

[10]J. R. Suchman, "Inquiry Workshop: A Model for the Language of Education," *The Instructor*, 76, Aug./Sept. 1966, pp. 33, 92.

TEACHER:	No.
JENNY:	I pass.
MARY:	Were they doing anything illegal?
TEACHER:	No.
MARY:	Uhh . . . I pass.
JEFF:	Was the captain following orders from someone?
TEACHER:	Yes.
JEFF:	From the Japanese government?
TEACHER:	Yes.
JEFF:	Was it the war or defense department?
TEACHER:	No.
JEFF:	Was it the part that has to do with trade with other countries?
TEACHER:	Yes. That is, I believe so.
JEFF:	Was it because they had *too many* pearls?
TEACHER:	Yes. That's half of it. Can you get the rest?
JEFF:	Uhh. Gosh, I don't know.
TEACHER:	Go ahead—try another question.
JEFF:	Was it because they wanted to keep the price of pearls high?
TEACHER:	Yes. You're in the "I" Club.[11]

You now know how the purposes a teacher or student has in mind can influence the kinds of questions he asks. Purposes, in effect, can *indicate* the types of questions one needs to ask. Acquisition of information calls for one type; description and organization a second; analysis a third; synthesis a fourth; evaluation a fifth; divergent thinking a sixth. It is hypothesized here that if teachers both ask questions and encourage their students to ask them, continually seeking to move from questions of the order of Type I to those of Type VI, the teacher will be more likely to prevent the development of uncritical minds which readily and quickly accept all information without question. In the strategies that follow, look closely at the questions to be asked. Do they promote the purposes for which the strategy is intended?

[11] E. P. Torrance and R. E. Myers, *Creative Learning and Teaching*, pp. 241–242.

Encouraging Students to Think for Themselves

One of the major objectives professed by most social studies educators is to help students "learn to think." When pressed, however, many teachers have difficulty specifying exactly what it is that "thinking" involves, or what a teacher needs to do in order to obtain it. This lack of clarity and confusion over the nature of thinking rests to a large degree on a number of unfounded assumptions about learning, such as the argument that it is important for student understanding of a subject to "cover" the textbook in its entirety, or that many periods, topics, or problems must be broadly surveyed rather than a few investigated in depth. Examples of these unwarranted assumptions are especially evident when many educators talk about the nature of thinking and what it involves. One such assumption, for example, is that a great deal of factual information must be acquired by students before they will be able to think about such information (a corollary of this is the assumption that learning to think occurs as a by-product of memorizing the thoughts of other people). Another is that thinking skills are only learned through such so-called "intellectually demanding" subjects as mathematics or science. Still another is the view that thinking is a capacity which only some individuals, usually the very bright or "gifted," possess. Some would also claim that it is futile to attempt to manipulate the learning environment to improve thinking significantly, since the development of thinking skills is locked into a predetermined physiological growth process.

Research on critical thinking suggests just the opposite, however. Shaver, reviewing such research in 1962, drew the following conclusion:

> Probably the most conclusive suggestion supported by the research reviewed here is that we should not expect that our students will learn to think critically as a by-product of the study of the usual social studies content. Instead, each teacher should determine what concepts are essential—e.g., that of relevance—if his students are to perform the intellectual operations deemed necessary to critical thinking—such as, for example, the formulation and evaluation of hypotheses. Each of these should be taught explicitly to the students. Utilizing what is known about transfer of learning, a further step can be suggested: Situations as similar as possible to those in which the students are to use their competencies should also be set up in the classroom, and the students guided in application of the concepts in this context.[12]

Shaver's conclusions are supported by other theory and research,[13] as well as the fact that students find a classroom emphasis on thinking inherently interesting.[14] Encouraged in part by such theory and research, and in part by a basic belief that all children are desirous of putting things together in their own mind in order to learn how such things "work," many educators reject the assumptions stated above in favor of the following alternatives:

- Thinking skills can be taught.

- Thinking involves an active transaction between an individual and the data with which he is working. Data (information) becomes meaningful only when an individual performs certain cognitive operations upon it. Thus students must be involved and actively working with data if thinking is to be encouraged.

- The ability to think cannot be "given" by teachers to students. How well an individual thinks depends on the richness and significance of the content with which he works, his own interest and desire to participate in the endeavor, the processes he uses, and the initial assistance he is given in the development of such processes.

- All subjects offer an appropriate context for thinking.

- All children are capable of thinking at abstract levels, though the quality of individual thinking differs markedly.

- Since thinking takes many forms, the specific thinking processes which are being developed should be clearly differentiated in the teacher's mind.

- Precise teaching strategies can be developed which will encourage and improve student thinking.[15]

It is a basic contention of the author that a major purpose of the social studies (indeed, of all subjects) should be to help students learn to "think," that is, to use the information they obtain in as productive a manner as possible in order to make sense out of the world as they find it and to build better "worlds" than they do find. The preceding assumptions, therefore,

[12]James P. Shaver, "Educational Research and Instruction for Critical Thinking," *Social Education*, 26, Jan. 1962, 16.

[13]Hilda Taba, Samuel Levine, and Freeman Elzey, *Thinking in Elementary School Children*, Final Report, Cooperative Research Project No. 1574, U.S. Office of Education, April 1964.

[14]Norman E. Wallen, "How Much Structure in the Curriculum? An Old Problem Presented in a New Context." Paper presented at the 1968 Annual Convention of the Western Psychological Association, San Diego, Calif., March 1968.

[15]Norman E. Wallen and Jack R. Fraenkel, "A Partial Evaluation of the Taba Curriculum Development Project in Social Studies: Developing Children's Thinking Skills." Paper presented at the Forty-eighth Annual Meeting of the National Council for the Social Studies, Washington, D.C., Nov. 1968.

need to be tested in a variety of teaching-learning situations and with many different kinds of students. Let us now consider some strategies that you might use to test these assumptions.

The strategies which follow represent several examples of procedures that teachers can use to help students engage in various intellectual operations. These strategies give teachers a starting point for improving their own instructional efforts and in the planning of learning activity sequences. This list should not be viewed in any way as final or absolute. The strategies identified are not mutually exclusive, since many of the operations described in one strategy overlap or are parts of other strategies. Nor is the list a hierarchy of any sort, with the operations at the top of the list considered as being prerequisite to those listed at the bottom. The primary purpose of the list is to suggest *some* dimensions of the global concept "thinking" that teachers can emphasize in order to bring about an increase in the thinking "behaviors" of students in their classrooms. The operations to be discussed include:

Observing
Describing
Developing Concepts
Differentiating
Defining
Hypothesizing
Comparing and Contrasting
Generalizing
Predicting
Explaining
Offering Alternatives

OBSERVING

Instructional Objective: Given an array of data, students can *identify* various items (individuals, objects, events, or ideas) included in this array on the basis of certain objective characteristics which they possess.

Observing is a necessary prerequisite to all intellectual operations that involve thinking. Students must be brought into contact—that is, "engaged" with data before they can do anything with it. It is imperative, therefore, that teachers provide opportunities for students to read/view/ taste/hear/feel/smell/touch/participate—in short, become involved in as many different kinds of experiences as possible. Equally important here is the necessity for teachers not to structure or determine ahead of time what students are expected to observe (apart from perhaps providing a focus. For example, in a film about the Sioux Indians, students might be asked to look for evidence of how the Indians used the land). The teacher's job here is essentially one of providing and engaging students in different experiences so that they can come in contact with a large number of different kinds of ideas, events, individuals, or objects, and their differing characteristics. (Review Chapter 4 for ideas as to *how* teachers can so engage students.)

DESCRIBING

Instructional Objective: Given various items (individuals, objects, events, or ideas), students can *identify* the particular characteristics which the items possess that caused them to be noticed in the first place.

Observing is only a beginning. Once students have been motivated to engage in experience—to view, listen, smell, taste, or touch the world, they must be encouraged to describe as fully and richly as possible the characteristics of that which they have observed. The teacher's task in this regard, therefore, is to go beyond just involving students in a variety of experiences —it is to ask them to report back (through asking an open-ended question such as "What did you notice in this film?" or "What happened in this story we just read?") what it was that they (i.e., the students) actually did observe (i.e., touched, tasted, felt, heard, saw, or read) in their experience. By asking open-ended questions such as "What can you tell me about these data?" (be it a picture, a film, a diagram, a map, a record, a collection of artifacts, a story, or whatever), teachers can encourage students to describe their observations. Again, care must be taken to ensure that students report their own, rather than the teacher's, perceptions.

DEVELOPING CONCEPTS

Instructional Objectives: Given an array of data, students can *identify* certain characteristics which various items (individuals, objects, events, or ideas) included in the array have in common, *group* the items on the basis of these characteristics, and then *assign* logically defensible and abstract labels to these groups.

Students form concepts when they begin to sort different objects (ideas, events, etc.) that they have observed or identified into a meaningful set of categories so as to make some sense of order or pattern out of their diversity. The teacher's task is to get them to respond to questions which require them to: (a) observe a situation (read a book, watch a film, listen to a record, etc.); (b) describe that which they have observed (list items); (c) find a basis for grouping those listed items which are similar in some respect; (d) identify the common characteristics of the items in a group; (e) label the groups they have formed; (f) subsume additional items that they have listed under those labels; and (g) recombine items to form new groups and to create even larger and more inclusive groups.

When a large number of items have been reported and made accessible to the entire class (by listing the reported items on the chalkboard, for example), students can be asked to group together various items which they perceive as similar in some way, and then to attach a label or "name" to the groups which they have formed. As part of this process, they must differentiate in some way or another the various items before them, and then decide on the basis of the groups which they have formed what the labels for these groups are to be.

Let us consider an example. Suppose that a teacher wished to assess his class's familiarity with the suggested causes of urban decay in the United States today. He first needs to help them obtain information on the topic from various sources—books, films, records, or speakers—which contain information as to various contributing factors, and then to ask them to identify in class as many of the suggested factors as they can (describing). Possible responses the class might suggest include absentee landlords, apathy, greed, too many people for too little space, poor schools, inefficient or ignorant public officials, flight of many of the "middle class" to the suburbs, movement of expanding industries out of the city, vested interest groups, insufficient share by certain city departments in tax revenue, and/or insufficient yet high taxes. These factors can then be written on the chalkboard or a transparency for all to see.

When the list is fairly extensive, the class can be asked: "Looking at the list of factors on the board, do you see any factors which might be placed or grouped together?" Students are thus encouraged to note similarities and differences as they try to place the various factors with similar characteristics in the same group and perhaps even combine some groups into larger groups. Possible supportive questions at this point to get them thinking about similarities include "Why do you think these factors might be grouped together?" or to encourage multiple grouping "Does anyone see *another way* that some of these factors might be grouped together?" How the students group, however, is not as important as the fact that they learn to increase their capability to identify common characteristics which otherwise quite dissimilar factors possess.

When the class seems to have exhausted the possibilities for grouping and regrouping, they can then be asked: "What names can be given to these groups that you have formed?" It is important to emphasize here that teachers should accept the kind of relationship which the students suggest through their labels as long as the students have fairly clear reasons for them. This does not preclude a teacher suggesting or encouraging students to reconsider their labels in terms of a particular topic being focused on. But the essential point of the strategy is to gêt the students to formulate their own concepts rather than to accept the concepts of somebody else. What is most important is that *the students* perform the operations for themselves, that they see the relationships which exist among items, that they recognize a basis on which to group items, and then that they label the groups that they have formed. A teacher should not do these things for students.

It is also important for students to discover that any item has many different characteristics and, therefore, that it can be grouped in many different ways and placed under many different labels. (For example, the items absentee landlords, ignorant public officials, and vested interest groups all would legitimately fit under such varied labels as "personal causes," "misuse of public trust," or "irresponsibility.") Hence, students need to be continually asked: "In what other ways might these items be grouped?" "Are there any items which are in one group that might also logically be placed in another group as well?"

Once the groups are formed, and the labels attached, students can then be asked whether they would remove any items from any of the groups. If they suggest that certain items do or do not possess the common characteristics of the other elements in a group, and can explain why, a teacher has a fair idea that they understand what constitutes an example of the concept which they have formed.

The sequence of questions the teacher pursues in order to elicit the behavior necessary for students to conceptualize is illustrated in Table 5.2.

Notice that each of the developmental steps is a necessary prerequisite for the one following. The listing of items cannot take place until students have participated in some type of experience (e.g., reading or listening to a story, going on a field trip, or viewing a set of slides). Grouping cannot occur until there is a list of items to group and some basis for deciding how the items are to be grouped. Labeling cannot take place without groups to label, and the accompanying discovery of what goes together. The speed or ease with which students are able to engage in each of these activities varies considerably depending in part on intellectual ability, in part on familiarity with the particular content being studied, and in part on the practice students have had with the task of concept formation previously.

To repeat, it is most important that the students (rather than the teacher)

TABLE 5.2

DEVELOPING CONCEPTS*
(LISTING, GROUPING, AND LABELING)

The teaching strategy consists of asking students the following questions, usually in this order, after they have observed or been otherwise engaged in experience (reading, viewing, listening, or the like).

Teacher Asks:	Student:	Teacher Follow-through:
What do you see, (notice, find) here? (Listing)	Gives items	Makes sure items are assessible to each student. For example: chalkboard; transparency; individual list; pictures; item card; etc.
Do any of these items seem to belong together? (Grouping)	Finds some similarity as a basis for grouping items	Communicates grouping. For example: underlines in colored chalk; marks with symbols; arranges pictures
Why would you group them together?[1] (Explaining)	Identifies and verbalizes the common characteristics of items in a group	Seeks clarification of responses when necessary
What would you call these groups you have formed? (Labeling)	Verbalizes a label (perhaps more than one word) that appropriately encompasses all items	Records
Why? (Explaining)	Gives explanation	Seeks clarification if necessary
Could some of these belong in more than one group? (Recombining—seeking multiple groups for some items)	States different relationships	Records
Can we put these same items in different groups?[2]	States additional relationships	Communicates grouping
Can any groups be combined? (Subsuming)	States additional different relationships	Communicates grouping

[1]Sometimes you ask the same child "why" when he offers the grouping, and other times you may wish to get many groups before considering "why" things are grouped together.

[2]Although this step is important because it encourages flexibility, it will not be appropriate on all occasions.

*From DEVELOPMENT OF A COMPREHENSIVE CURRICULUM MODEL FOR SOCIAL STUDIES FOR GRADES ONE THROUGH EIGHT, INCLUSIVE OF PROCEDURES FOR IMPLEMENTATION AND DISSEMINATION, by Norman E. Wallen, Mary C. Durkin, Jack R. Fraenkel, Anthony H. McNaughton, Enoch I. Sawin. Final Report, Project No. 5–1314, U.S. Office of Education (Washington, D.C., Oct. 1969), p. 17.

perform each of the preceding operations. They need to identify the relationships which exist among items, formulate a basis on which to group items, and suggest the labels or names for these categories (groups). This is not to suggest, however, that the teacher should not on occasion, if students are bogged down, offer an alternative way of grouping items or suggest that a list of items be expanded. Various social science categories (concepts), for example, have a great power to explain (e.g., "causality" or "societal control"). Students may not create or formulate them out of their own thinking, and teachers should not hesitate, if they consider them useful as explanatory or synthesizing tools, to suggest them. (Review Chapter 3 for examples of such concepts.) The important thing to aim for is a climate in which teacher and students are working together to devise meaningful categories—where the teacher's suggestion is offered simply as another alternative to be considered. Admittedly, such a climate can only be established by careful thought and restraint.

As was mentioned earlier, it is also important for students to discover that the same item might legitimately belong in several different groups, since it possesses many different characteristics. Each of the many characteristics it possesses might be used as a basis for forming a new group. The ways in which students group items will suggest to the teacher how clearly and deeply they perceive relationships. For example, a ninth grader's statement that "land, labor, and capital could be classed as economic terms or productive resources" indicates an awareness of the possibility of multiple grouping. It suggests the possibility that the same items can be included in several different groups under different labels. If land, labor, and capital are perceived as productive resources, they can be placed under factors of production. If they are viewed as definitional terms that economists use to explain economic occurrences, they can be categorized as economic terms.

The following dialogue illustrates an example of listing and grouping as it actually took place in a tenth-grade discussion of the rise of Industrialism during the nineteenth century. The class had just read a number of excerpts from Samuel Hays, *The Response To Industrialism: 1885–1914*.[16] The teacher proceeded as follows:

(1) **TEACHER:**   Based on your reading, what comes to mind when I say "industrialism"?

(2) TOM: Cheap labor.

(3) BETTY: Lots of natural resources.

[16]Samuel P. Hays, *The Response to Industrialism* (Chicago: University of Chicago Press, 1957).

(4) PEG:	Nationwide transportation.
(5) JACK:	Yeah, railroad construction really boomed after 1850.
(6) ALICE:	Lots of farmers cashed in their money even to help pay for building railroads.
(7) JEAN:	Erie Canal
(8) **TEACHER:**	What other things come to mind?
(9) PHIL:	F. B. Morse
(10) JOHN:	Oh yeah, the telegraph,
(11) TOM:	and the telephone
(12) BETTY:	The rotary press
(13) AL:	Advertising
(14) **TEACHER:**	What else can you suggest?
(15) BILL:	Iron and steel
(16) JIM:	Carnegie
(17) TOM:	Blast furnaces.
(18) **TEACHER:**	Anything else?
(19) TOM:	Many European peasants were part of the labor supply.
(20) SUE:	Growth of cities.
(21) SAM:	People were more impersonal in their relationships.
(22) PEG:	Horrible working conditions in urban factories.

. . . . . (This listing continued until the blackboard was full of characteristics that the class identified with industrialism. Note that this is essential. Grouping will be unproductive unless students have a wide assortment of items—a rich "data bank" so to speak—from which to select, combine, and recombine.)

(23) **TEACHER:**	Now, what can we do with all of this data? Let me ask you to see if there are any here that might be placed or grouped together. What items might be grouped together?
(24) SUE:	The Erie Canal and railroads.
(25) **TEACHER:**	Why?
(26) SUE:	Because they are both forms of transportation.
(27) LARRY:	The telegraph and the telephone are both forms of communication.

(28) SAM:	I'd put working conditions, impersonal relationships, and European peasants together.
(29) **TEACHER:**	Why, Sam?
(30) SAM:	Because they all contributed to the kind of life that existed in the new cities that were growing up.
(31) ALICE:	I think we can add the rotary press to our communication group.
(32) **TEACHER:**	Okay. Are there any other groups we can form?
(33) PEG:	Cheap labor, European peasants, and horrible working conditions in the cities.
(34) **TEACHER:**	Why?
(35) PEG:	Because conditions were bad in lots of places because many employers exploited the peasants from Europe who were willing to work for almost nothing.
(36) ALICE:	They had to if they were going to live.
(37) PEG:	Maybe so, but that doesn't excuse it.
(38) **TEACHER:**	That's something we may want to investigate further.
(39) TOM:	I'd put iron and steel in Peg's group and also in Sam's group.

. . . and so on. This continued until the bell rang.

Notice a few things about this discussion. Students often tend to give the same *type* of response as offered by the first to volunteer, as is evident in the chain of responses numbered 4–6, 9–13, and 15–17. A variety of *different kinds* of responses are needed, however, if grouping is to be productive. To break up a line of such similar types of responses, the teacher needs to summarize the listing and/or then ask "What else can you suggest?" or "What else comes to mind?" as was done in responses numbered 8 and 18.

Students often will group and label simultaneously, as was done by Larry in response number 27. This is perfectly acceptable and probably, in many cases (and particularly with older students), inevitable.

The teacher is completely accepting of all responses. This is extremely important. Students must realize that the teacher is interested in, and desires, that they put things together in their own way according to the relationships which they perceive. The teacher must be careful not to "cue" the class that certain responses are less or more desirable than others by her voice inflection, facial gestures, or other mannerisms, or students will tend to relate items together because the "text" does or because they know the teacher would agree with such and such a relationship. The art of encouraging and accepting all student responses, no matter how unusual they appear to the teacher, is a difficult one to master. Being noncommittal does come with time, however, and the results of such mastery are highly rewarding in that they contribute to productive and individualized categorizing by students.

Multiple grouping began to occur in a number of instances. Peg (response 33) placed in a new group items that were already in a previously formed group, while Tom (response 39) simultaneously placed the same items in two different groups.

The teacher kept to the task at hand and refused to let herself go off on a tangent. When it appeared that Peg and Alice (responses 36 and 37) might get into an argument that would lead the class away from further grouping, the teacher accepted their responses, but merely stated that the "controversy might be something to investigate further," and then returned to asking students to continue grouping.

Grouping can be unproductive if the meaning of specific terms the class suggests are not clear. If students do not understand how an item is being used, they will have trouble deciding rationally on where it is to be grouped, and emotional arguments can easily result. If there is confusion over the meaning of a term, the teacher should seek clarification first before continuing.

In general, the following suggestions can be offered to help students group and categorize in a productive fashion:

1. When a category (group) is suggested by students, proceed to identify as many items as possible that fit within it.
2. Encourage students to look for a variety of categories into which *the same* item can be placed. This encourages flexibility of thinking, a quality which a number of theorists have argued plays an important part in cognitive development.
3. Encourage students to combine categories if possible. Thus items in a category of lesser breadth than another might be included in the broader category.
4. When the meaning of a category is not clear, ask the student who suggested it to explain what he means or to suggest other examples which belong in the category and then state the characteristics which these various examples have in common.
5. Encourage students to regroup and relabel all of the items they have listed and previously grouped. Oftentimes this can be done by simply erasing the formed groups but leaving the original list on the board for examination.

6. Realize that in many cases it is by no means necessary to insist upon closure, since the emphasis in concept formation is as much upon the processes involved as it is the content. An open and accepting attitude on the part of the teacher will enable students to offer items that are too difficult to deal with for the time being, or even irrelevant.

The power and applicability of the strategy described here is due to the fact that it provides a carefully worked out sequence of steps for teachers to utilize, but places no restriction on the kinds of responses that may be offered by students. When a teacher implicitly searches for particular kinds of responses, of course, he violates the nature and intent of the procedure. Concept formation exercises, if pursued in a climate of mutual investigation by a teacher who is open to, and accepting of, all student responses, can provide students with a number of opportunities to reflect upon their experience and to systematically deepen the meaning they can derive from it. A logical next step for a teacher interested in helping students build and investigate relationships is to have them compare their own groupings to the powerful concepts of the social science disciplines and to help them realize why the concepts of social science are superior to student-formed groups. As Hullfish and Smith[17] have suggested, examination will reveal that the concepts of social science are more explicit, precise, rigorous, abstract, general, and systematic than those of common sense. Students can then examine the different patterns of relationships that exist among the various groupings that have been formed and labeled, and make warranted statements about them in the form of generalizations. We shall discuss the formation of such generalizations later in this chapter.

DIFFERENTIATING AND DEFINING

> *Instructional Objectives:* Given a number of examples and non-examples of a certain concept, students can *state* which are examples and which are non-examples, and *tell why.*
>
> Having examined a number of examples and non-examples of a given concept, students can *state a definition* in which the essential attributes (characteristics) of the concept are presented.

During one classroom discussion on taxation that the author observed a student offered the following remark with which the balance of the class quickly agreed: "Taxes are much too high in this country and most people are suffering considerably as a result." Upon questioning various members

---

[17]H. Gordon Hullfish and Philip G. Smith, *Reflective Thinking: The Method of Education* (New York: Dodd, Mead, 1961), p. 73.

of the class, however, it became quickly evident that many students did not really understand just what a "tax" was. Before the teacher could attempt to get students to investigate further the allegation that most people in the country are suffering due to excessive taxation, he had to ensure that all members of the class understood (and hopefully could agree on) the meaning of the concept "tax" in the first place. How could this be done?

The teaching of a concept like "tax" can proceed in one of two ways, one inductive, the other deductive. Let us consider an inductive example first:

(1) The teacher must himself first research and form an adequate definition of the concept in order to determine its most important attributes. In this regard resort is often made to an official definition of the term if it exists. "Official definitions are those set forth by law, scholarship, religion, or some other authority. If we want to know what is meant by disease, we turn to the medical profession for an official meaning. The legal profession defines tort and contract for us."[18]

Broudy and his associates referred to the *Dictionary of American Politics* to obtain the following definition of tax: "A tax is a compulsory payment made to a government for its support or for the regulation or promotion of certain social purposes and levied according to law uniformly upon all taxpayers of a given class."[19]

(2) When a satisfactory definition has thus been obtained or developed, identify the larger class of which the concept is a part (e.g., in this case, the term "tax" is a part of the larger class of "payments") and then determine the most important attributes (in other words, the defining criteria) which a tax possesses that set it off from other kinds of payments.[20] Broudy and his associates illustrate the essential attributes which (according to the definition they obtained) a tax possesses by means of the following diagram:

---

[18]Maurice P. Hunt and Lawrence E. Metcalf, *Teaching High School Social Studies*, 2nd ed. (New York: Harper & Row, 1968), p. 90. As Hunt and Metcalf suggest, by having students obtain official definitions, teachers can avoid developing the idea that one definition is as good as another. There are generally accepted sources of scholarship to which students can turn for information. For example, they should learn what the medical profession means by coronary care rather than invent their own notion. This does not mean, however, that students cannot be expected and asked to try to clarify or otherwise improve on certain official definitions.

[19]Harry S. Broudy, B. Othanel Smith, and Joe R. Burnett, *Democracy and Excellence in American Secondary Education* (Skokie, Ill.: Rand McNally, 1964), p. 124.

[20]Notice that these criteria are not necessarily *all* of the attributes which the concept possesses, but rather *the most* important attributes (i.e., those necessary to distinguish examples from non-examples of the concept).

Category	Criteria (Attributes)
Major Category → Payments	1. Payment made to government
	2. Levied according to law
Sub-category → Taxes	3. Levied uniformly upon all payers of a given class
	4. Purpose is to support the government, or
	5. to regulate social purposes, or
	6. to promote social purposes[21]

(3) Present alternatively a variety of payments that are examples (e.g., sales, liquor, cigarette, and income taxes) and non-examples (e.g., fees, fines, mortgage payments, tariffs, ransoms, etc.) of taxes for students to examine.

4) As the class looks at the examples and non-examples that you have presented, point out which ones are taxes by saying "This is a tax" appropriately, and asking students to determine how they differ from the non-examples. This, in effect, requires students to look for and identify the essential attributes which all of the examples of taxes possess in common, but which the non-examples lack.

(5) Have the class state the major attributes which the examples all possess.

(6) Have the class state a definition of the concept by making a declarative statement which contains all of the major attributes ("A tax is . . .).

It is important that teachers not neglect this step. It points up the difference between an intensional and an extensional meaning of a concept. "The extension of a word is the set of things to which it is applied, according to a rule; the intension is the set of characteristics that things must have in order for the word to apply correctly to them. The extension of 'city' is London, Paris, New York, Berlin, Tokyo, Moscow, Nairobi, etc. The intension of 'city' is (roughly) the characteristic of being a politically independent area of high population density and large population total."[22] Thus intensional meaning refers to the definition of a concept; extensional meaning to examples of the concept. Though it is surely true that individuals can possess a concept without being able to verbalize it, the ability to explain what one means when one uses a word is extremely valuable. Many

---

[21] H. S. Broudy *et al., Democracy and Excellence,* p. 124.
[22] Monroe C. and Elisabeth L. Beardsley, *Philosophical Thinking: An Introduction* (New York: Harcourt Brace Jovanovich, 1965). Quoted in Hunt and Metcalf, *Teaching High School Social Studies,* p. 81.

inarticulate people experience considerable difficulty and frustration in attempting to communicate with their fellows because they possess few concepts and even fewer word-labels for the concepts they do possess.

(7) Present more examples and non-examples of the concept and ask students to identify which are taxes and which are not, telling why in each case.

(8) Have the students on their own find and identify new examples.

Notice that the essence of this strategy involves the identification of essential attributes through distinguishing between examples and non-examples of the concept in question. As students make such distinctions, they inductively realize what the essential attributes are. The strategy is summarized in Table 5.3.

A deductive alternative to the preceding approach is as follows: Once a satisfactory definition of the concept has been obtained from a dictionary or reputable source or developed, list the definition on the chalkboard or a transparency so that all students can see it. If possible, illustrate it if you can or perhaps compare it with other concepts the students already know. Then also list on the board the essential attributes which a tax possesses that set it off from other kinds of payments. Again present a variety of examples and non-examples of taxes (giving mostly examples at first), only now ask the class to examine them in light of the criteria that are before them on the board. Inform the class that if a given payment meets all of the criteria listed, it is a tax. If all of the criteria do not apply to a given payment, it is not a tax. As each example of a payment is given, ask: "Is this a tax?" rewarding those who correctly identify the examples and non-examples by saying, "Yes, you are correct, this is a tax," or "No, you are incorrect, this is not a tax" as is appropriate. Gradually include more non-examples, and then proceed as in the steps 7 and 8 given above.

As Broudy and his associates indicate, "To tell whether or not a given payment is a tax, the criteria must be applied to the payment. If a given payment meets all of the criteria, it is a tax. If it does not, the payment is not a tax, even though it may be made to the government. For example, an installment on a debt is a payment, but it meets none of the criteria and hence is not a tax. But what about fines, fees, and tariffs? These are all payments to the government. Are they to be called taxes? It depends upon whether or not they satisfy the remaining criteria. And . . . they do not. A fine is exacted as punishment for violation of the law and is not a tax. A tariff is designed to protect domestic industry and agriculture, and a fee is paid in return for services rendered directly to the individual. Neither meets the criteria and hence is not a tax."[23]

To broaden and deepen a student's understanding of a concept, exam-

[23]H. S. Broudy et al., *Democracy and Excellence*, pp. 124–125.

TABLE 5.3

*ATTAINING CONCEPTS
(DIFFERENTIATING AND DEFINING)**

Teacher	Student	Teacher Follow-through
Say the word after me[1] (Stating the concept)	Repeats word	Makes sure word is pronounced correctly
This is an . . .[2] This is also an . . . (Gives examples)	Looks at object or listens to description given, or reads statement which illustrates the concept	Checks for any students who may not be able to see or hear
This is not an . . .[2] (Gives non-examples)	Looks, listens to, or reads about new object which is not an example of concept but is similar to concept	Checks again
What characteristics does an . . . possess that enable you to recognize it?	States major attributes which all examples possess	Insures that all attributes are given
Tell me what you think an . . . is (Asks for definition)	States a definition of the concept	Has students write down their definition
Which of these describes[3] an . . . , *or* is this an . . . (Asks for identification)	Selects from one or more objects or descriptions	Shows additional objects or gives fresh descriptions to test
Show me an . . . (Asks for original examples)	Brings in new examples	Verifies correctness of example

[1]When proceeding deductively, the teacher writes the definition and the key attributes (the defining criteria) on the board initially.

[2]The teacher appropriately identifies each of the examples and non-examples that are presented. (These statements become questions—i.e., "Is this a . . ." when teaching the concept deductively.)

[3]Gradually more complex examples, that is, examples which possess additional defining attributes not originally displayed should be presented in order to broaden and deepen the student's understanding of the concept's dimensions.

*Adapted from A TEACHER'S HANDBOOK TO ELEMENTARY SOCIAL STUDIES: AN INDUCTIVE APPROACH (2nd ed.), by Hilda Taba, Mary C. Durkin, Jack R. Fraenkel, and Anthony H. McNaughton (Reading, Mass.: Addison-Wesley, 1971), p. 71.

ples which contain new attributes not contained in the original definition need to be presented, and students should be asked to compare these new examples with the examples they already know. They thus are helped to identify the new attributes. The new attributes should then be included in the definition of the concept, and students presented with a number of new examples and non-examples to help them clarify and understand the now expanded definition. They then can be asked to find on their own further examples which possess the now expanded list of attributes. It would certainly then be in order to ask the class to consider whether the definition of the concept might not be improved upon.

A final word about teaching concepts. As Jones[24] has suggested, though young children often have trouble identifying how an apple and a peach are alike, they may have little trouble telling how they are different. The difference in difficulty appears to be in the *level of abstraction* of the concept. To answer the question, "How are an apple and a peach different?" a child deals with characteristics (attributes) that are tangible and easily identifiable by the senses (i.e., fuzzy vs. smooth skin, seeds vs. a pit, and the presence vs. absence of a stem). When he is asked to answer the question "How are an apple and a peach alike?" he is required to deal with characteristics that are abstract—intangible attributes such as roundness, tartness, or the fact that they both are "fruit"—in itself an abstraction.

When categorizing concepts for instruction, therefore, teachers need to consider their level of abstraction. The more abstract a concept is, the less its distinguishing characteristics can be reduced to variations in physical dimensions, such as length, width, size, or color. This is simply another way of saying that more abstract concepts are more difficult for students to "see" than are those that are more concrete. Hence concepts like "house" or "reptile" are easier for students to learn than are concepts like "home" or "alike," while concepts like "honor" or "democracy" are the most difficult of all. Furthermore, the more abstract a concept, the more important a part language plays in learning it. The chief task for teachers in this respect is to find a *varied* number of concrete examples which illustrate the abstraction. To help students learn an abstract concept like "sharp," therefore, teachers need to present them with a number of different examples of objects all of which are sharp (e.g., needles, razors, splinters, knives, axes, saws, etc.), pointing out (or asking) all the while in what ways they are sharp and how all of the objects possess this quality of "sharpness" in common.

[24]J. Charles Jones, *Learning* (New York: Harcourt Brace Jovanovich, 1967), p. 96.

Evaluating Student Mastery of a Concept.   The degree to which a student learns or, to use Broudy's[25] term, "masters" a concept can vary considerably. Each of the following examples of concept learning, it would appear, might be considered as representing greater "mastery" of a concept.

1. Students can *state* a textbook definition of the concept verbatim from memory.
2. Students can *restate* a textbook definition in their own words.
3. Students can *state* from memory (or identify) rather common examples of the concept.
4. Students can *suggest their own examples* of the concept.
5. Students can identify (or suggest on their own) unusual *examples* of the concept.
6. Students can explain (tell why) various common and unusual items or instances are examples of the concept.
7. Students can relate (tell how) the concept to other concepts or ideas and explain how (tell why) the concept is related.

HYPOTHESIZING

Instructional Objective: Given relevant facts about an individual, society, or situation, students can *state* one or more logically sound but informally worded hypotheses (that they have not been given previously) about that individual, society, or situation today, in the past, or in the future.

A hypothesis is a statement offered and tentatively accepted in order to provide a basis for further investigation. By having students continually suggest hypotheses and then check them out (i.e., test them in the light of supporting or contradicting data), teachers can help them to inquire into their world in an orderly and more meaningful fashion, and to realize how reliable and valid information is obtained. Hypotheses help provide order to investigation. In the social studies, hypothesis formation and validation involves the following processes:

• identifying a problem to investigate;
• defining more precisely the particular aspects of the problem to be investigated (i.e., stating a question to consider);
• formulating a hypothesis (i.e., making a logical statement, usually in an "if-then" form as to what might exist or happen if such and such exists or happens);

[25]Harry S. Broudy, "Mastery," in B. Othanel Smith and Robert H. Ennis, *Language and Concepts in Education* (Skokie, Ill.: Rand McNally, 1961), pp. 72–85.

- gathering data (from reading, discussing, interviewing, observing, experimenting, etc.);
- organizing and evaluating the data (i.e., eliminating irrelevant material, categorizing the data which is relevant to the problem under consideration, checking the reliability and validity of sources);
- testing the hypothesis against the data (i.e., did such and such actually exist or happen as predicted?);
- drawing a conclusion (i.e., stating a generalization).

One sequence of questions a teacher can use to accomplish these processes is shown in Table 5.4.

Let us consider an example. Suppose that a number of students were interested in investigating the problem of alienation in the present-day society of the United States. They might be asked to read widely in a variety of sources in order to obtain some "feeling" for what it means to be alienated in the United States today. They could then be asked to define more precisely a dimension of the problem of alienation that they wish to investigate in greater detail. Suppose they wish to find out more about what *causes* alienation. A focusing question, to serve as the key to their investigation, can be formulated: "What do they think (hypothesize) at this time, based on their preliminary reading, causes alienation?" Various reading matter can now be identified and/or assigned. Personal interviews can be conducted. Field trips for observational purposes can be undertaken. The data they collect can be organized and evaluated as to adequacy, reliability, accuracy, relevance, etc., and their hypotheses "checked" against the data that they have collected and evaluated. What evidence is there to support their hypothesis? To refute it? To what extent is it supported or refuted? Should it be modified? If so, in what way(s), in light of the data they have obtained, should it be changed? The students can then be asked what qualification(s) have to be placed on the conclusion(s) (that is, in what areas or to what individuals would it not apply, and why?).

Whenever possible, students should be asked to proceed through the steps identified above. This does not mean that a teacher should assign the preceding steps to be laboriously and academically followed as a sterile exercise in investigating a textbook "problem." The problem must be of real concern to the student. Furthermore, actual investigation may well require that several of these steps be repeated since they are interactive in nature. For instance, as data are organized, it may become apparent that more information is needed, and thus necessitate further data-gathering; testing the hypothesis against the data may suggest new ways of organizing the acquired information. Investigation, in the social studies as anywhere

TABLE 5.4

HYPOTHESIZING

Teacher	Students	Teacher Follow-through
What bothers or concerns you about people or the world today? or What kinds of problems are of concern to you? or What are you worried about? etc.	Names problem area	Clarifies responses
Why is that a problem? or Why are you concerned about . . . ? or What about . . . might we investigate? etc.	Identifies and states a precise question or aspect of the problem to consider	Helps get question stated clearly
What causes . . . ? or If . . . continues, then what might occur? etc.	Formulates hypothesis to investigate	Helps get hypothesis stated and available for all to see. Clarifies terms
*Where can we obtain data that might help us come to some conclusions about . . . ?	Locates sources. Gathers data	Suggests additional sources to consult
How can we organize the data we've collected? or How might we group or categorize this data? etc. *	Organizes data into relevant categories. Regroups data into sub- and subordinate categories	Suggests additional categories to consider. Helps students place data into appropriate categories
* What data *can't* we use? Why?	Evaluates data as to relevance, accuracy, bias, etc.	Helps determine appropriate criteria by which to judge usefulness of data
What evidence is there to support our hypothesis (or hypotheses)? to refute it? To what extent is it supported or refuted?	Considers degree to which hypothesis is supported or refuted. Cites supportive or refuting evidence	Asks for evidence. Probes for inconsistencies. Places evidence so all can see
Should we change our hypothesis (hypotheses) in any way? If so, how? Why?	Modifies hypothesis if necessary. Gives reasons	Clarifies terms
What can we say about . . . (the problem) in light of the evidence we have obtained?	States generalization (conclusion)	Clarifies terms. Asks for estimate of degree to which conclusion is warranted, and on basis of what evidence

*As the investigation proceeds, it may be necessary to repeat several of these steps. For example, as data is organized, it may become apparent that more information is needed, and thus necessitate further data-gathering. Testing the hypothesis against the data may suggest new ways of organizing the acquired information.

else, does not proceed in neat little steps. Nevertheless, teachers can help students bring order to their investigations by continually asking them to define their problems as precisely as possible, to state hypotheses, to organize data into categories, to evaluate data, to check hypotheses against the data that they have acquired as a result of their investigation, and then to state generalizations which they can support with evidence.

COMPARING AND CONTRASTING

Instructional Objective: Given two or more different items (individuals, objects, events, or ideas), students can correctly *state* many of the similarities and differences which exist among the items.

Comparing and contrasting is an important part of thinking. Students cannot understand individuals, ideas, objects, events, locations, or characteristics clearly unless they can compare and contrast these phenomena in terms of their similarities and differences. Teachers can help students to compare and contrast by asking them to study similar aspects of previously unrelated content, and then to ask identical questions about this content. For example, suppose a teacher desires that students consider why different individuals in the United States (or around the world) do or do not use hallucinogenic drugs. A teacher might ask them to read (view, etc.) a number of accounts by individuals who have and who have not used drugs. He could then have them ask certain questions about each of the experiences they have read (viewed, etc.):

- What happened in this experience?
- Why do you suppose it happened as it did?
- In what ways are the descriptions you have read (viewed, etc.) similar?
- In what ways are the descriptions you have read (viewed, etc.) different?
- How would you explain these similarities and differences?

Notice that the same questions are to be asked of each account, and that they are arranged in a definite order. (See Table 5.5). This order is intentional. It is based on the assumption that students must understand what is occurring in each instance before they will be able to explain why it is occurring. They must decide on how two or more instances are similar or different before they will be able to explain why they are similar or different.

Let us consider another example. Suppose it were desired that students should be able to describe how Southern slaves felt during the period immediately preceding the American Civil War. They might be asked to read

TABLE 5.5

COMPARING AND CONTRASTING

Teacher	Students	Teacher Follow-through
What happened?	Summarizes facts of incident	Checks for accuracy and completeness Writes facts for all to see
Why?	Infers reasons for things happening as they did	Encourages responses Writes on chalkboard or transparency
In what ways are the descriptions you have read (seen, heard, etc.) similar? different?	Identifies similarities and differences	Encourages many replies Puts on chalkboard or transparency
How would you explain these similarities and differences?	Infers reasons for similarities and differences identified	Encourages replies; clarifies meaning
What does this suggest to you about _____ in general? or What conclusions can you draw about _____?	States a generalization	Places on chalkboard or transparency Encourages discussion as to how generalizations can be verified

various instances from two accounts of slave life, as experienced by two slaves each of whom had a different master. Questions similar to the foregoing could then be asked, as shown below:

• What happened to _____ in this instance?
• Why do you think this happened?
• How do you think each of these individuals felt? Why?
• In what ways are their feelings similar? Different?
• How would you explain these similarities and differences?
• Do these incidents remind you of anything else that you have heard or know about?

Suppose, however, that a teacher's purpose in using the two instances was to illustrate not how people's feelings differ, but how conditions within a particular institution may differ. Then a different question sequence would be in order, as follows:

- Describe the situation presented in each reading.
- What differences do you see?
- How would you account for these differences?
- What does this suggest to you about slavery in general?
- Do you know of any other institutions (e.g., religion, education, etc.) where differing conditions exist?

Notice here that the question sequence is designed to develop the concept of difference and to get students to form some conclusions about different situations, at first within the same institution, and then in general. Question sequences such as these are not incidentally determined, but need to be carefully thought out ahead of time by the teacher. The particular questions asked, however, and the order in which they are sequenced always depend on the objectives that a teacher has in mind.

Comparing and contrasting by students can be simplified somewhat if students are encouraged to place the data they acquire in the course of their investigations into some sort of organized form or arrangement in order to facilitate the identification of similarities and differences. One way of achieving this is by means of an organizational chart. An example of such a chart, from a seventh-grade unit dealing with ancient civilizations, is shown in Table 5.6. (The steps involved in planning the development of such charts are further discussed in Chapter 8.)

Notice the arrangement of data. Information pertaining to the same topics (resources, use of resources, major new ideas or inventions, and purposes or uses of these inventions or ideas) has been collected and organized so that comparisons and contrasts can be inferred fairly easily by students. The teacher's job is one of calling attention to one or more columns (depending on the sophistication and ability of the class) and asking (not telling) students to state any similarities and differences that they observe.

GENERALIZING

Instructional Objectives: Given a detailed list of items (individuals, objects, events, or ideas), students can *state* valid generalizations (that they have not been given previously) and, when asked, can *provide* the sources and limitations of the generalizations which they have formed.

If students are to use effectively the data which they acquire, they must be encouraged to establish connections and relationships among otherwise unrelated pieces of specific information. The ability to establish valid rela-

TABLE 5.6

EXAMPLE OF AN ORGANIZATIONAL
CHART ON ANCIENT CIVILIZATIONS*

People	Resources	Use of Resources	Major New Ideas or Inventions	Purpose or Use of Invention/Idea
SUMERIANS	Clay	Pottery	Cuneiform	Business contracts
	River	Brick buildings	Circle into 360°	
		Writing	Fractions, square root	Study of heavens
	People	Farmers, priests, rulers, slaves, craftsmen, soldiers	Wheeled vehicle	Many fights with neighbors
	Fertile soil	Crops for food, livestock	Ziggurat	Mountains touched heavens of gods
	Date palms	Baskets, ropes	12-month calendar	Study of stars
	Cattle	Leather goods	24-hour day	Gods
	Sheep	Rugs, tapestries	Weights & measures	Trade
		Metal goods	Enameled, baked brick	Temples & palaces for arches—no stone
		Ivory goods	Keystone	To keep gold & silver lumps—money
EGYPTIANS	Fertile soil	Crops for food	Hieroglyphics	Accounts for temple and stories of pharaohs
	River	Flax for linen		
		Irrigation		
	Papyrus	Livestock	Paper and ink	For scribes
		Paper	Shadoof	Lift water
			Mummifying	Keep soul alive after death
	People	Rulers, priests, slaves, farmers, craftsmen	Stone pyramids	Bury god—pharaohs
	Stone	Temples, pyramids, palaces	3 seasons of 4 months	When Nile would flood
			Surveying	Boundaries after flood
			Calendar—12 months	Study of heavens
			Shadow clock	Tell time—sun god

ASSYRIANS	Iron Clay People Horses	Chariots, weapons Books Soldiers, farmers, slaves, rulers	Protection from constant invasion To prevent revolt As a result of war One king liked learning To spread fear
		Iron weapons Wheeled rams Horse-drawn chariots Scattering captives First world empire First public library Advertising extreme cruelty	
MINOANS	Wood Stone People Water	Palaces Ships Crops for food Sailors, rulers, pottery	Inside-rooms Carry wastes to pits Earthquakes For royalty Bull-worship Trade and protection Comfort
		Light wells Drainage system Reinforced buildings Bathrooms Bull-vaulting First navy Hot and cold water in houses	

*From WESTERN CIVILIZATION: PERSPECTIVES ON CHANGE, by Jack R. Fraenkel. Grade Seven, Taba Social Studies Curriculum, Cooperative Research Project OE 6-10-182, U.S. Department of Health, Education, and Welfare, Office of Education, Washington, D.C., 1969 (distributed by Addison-Wesley Publishers, Menlo Park, Calif.), pp. 42-43.

tionships (i.e., statements supported by evidence) is essentially one of forming, using, and validating generalizations.

As Chapter 3 indicated, generalizations express a relationship among several concepts. The following statements, therefore, would all qualify as examples of generalizations:

- The daily activities of a people reflect their values.
- The life style of a culture is shaped by the contributions of the groups of people who live in that culture.
- Political change results from dissatisfaction with the status quo; many of the changes which occur attempt to deal with various causes of dissatisfaction.
- Man's ways of living affect, and are affected by, the physical and social environment in which he lives.

The word *generalization* is being used more and more frequently by curriculum writers and designers, and teachers would therefore be well-advised to become clear in their own minds as to what the term means. Most curriculum writers in the social studies appear to agree on the following points:

- powerful generalizations (as defined by the criteria identified in Chapter 3) can and should serve as organizing foci around which teaching-learning units can be built;
- the formation of warranted (i.e., supportable by evidence) generalizations is a skill worth developing in the social studies throughout the grades;
- students should be given frequent opportunity to generalize about what they see, hear, read, or otherwise experience, and then to support, refute, or modify (on the basis of supportive or contradictive evidence) the generalizations they have formed;
- teachers should spend more time than previously encouraging students (through carefully thought out and sequenced questions) to generalize for themselves and less time having students learn the generalizations which are the end-product of someone else's thinking.

Students generalize when they infer the similarities and differences in two or more situations or events. The teacher's task is to encourage students to respond to questions which require them to: (a) observe two or more incidents (read a story, view a film, listen to a speaker describing two or more similar yet different individuals, events, etc.); (b) describe what happened in the incidents they observed (i.e., recapitulate the situations or events as they occurred); (c) explain why they think the incidents occurred as they did; (d) look for similarities and differences; (e) attempt to explain these similarities and differences; (f) and then state a generalization that appears warranted on the basis of the data they have acquired and compared.

Getting students to make warranted generalizations, therefore, involves essentially three steps:

(1) They must look at two or more different samples of content with the same questions in mind. (For example, what are the reasons for refusing to serve in the armed forces offered by a number of dissenters?)

(2) They must then explain the data they have obtained. (For example, citing the different reasons offered by the dissenting individuals and explaining why various individuals differ in their reasons.)

(3) They must then offer a generalization by inferring what are the common factors and differences involved in a number of situations. (For example, in this instance, regarding the dissenter's reasons for refusing to serve in the armed forces.) The sequence of questions the teacher pursues to bring about these generalizations is illustrated in Table 5.7.

Getting students to generalize is not as easy as perhaps it seems, however. If they are to suggest relationships that are anything more than trivial truisms, they will have to make inferences which go beyond that which is directly given them in their reading (viewing, etc.). In the preceding example, they must not only identify and understand, but also generalize about the reasons for not serving offered by the dissenters, and finally, make further generalizations by comparing and contrasting the generalizations which different members of the class suggest. They might then obtain information about dissent in another area of American life (e.g., dissent by Catholic priests and nuns), and the process can be repeated. They may then be in a position to make generalizations about generalizations (over-arching generalizations) about the reasons for dissent in general throughout the United States. A schematic representation of this process is shown in Table 5.8.

Notice in this model that we begin with student concerns, the place where all classroom instruction and investigation should originate. We first ask students to think of an incident in which they themselves dissented (e.g., against a parental dictum), to state their reasons for so dissenting, and to describe how they felt about their action. They might then suggest a rather narrow statement (narrow in the sense that it only applies to themselves) as to why people dissent in a particular situation.

The class can now be assisted to broaden the applicability of their generalizations. Students can be asked to consider how other people might feel about dissent. Information can be obtained about various dissenters (for example, individuals who refuse to serve in the armed forces and former priests and nuns) through such learning activities as reading, interviewing, inviting speakers to class, etc.; their reasons for dissenting reviewed; and

TABLE 5.7

GENERALIZING*

This cognitive task requires the students to interpret, infer, and generalize about data. The teaching strategy consists of asking the students the following questions, usually in this order.

Teacher Asks:	Student:	Teacher Follow-through:
What did you notice? See? Find? What differences did you notice (with reference to a particular question)?	Gives items	Makes sure items are accessible, for example: Chalkboard Transparency Individual list Pictures Item card Chooses the items to pursue
Why do you think this happened? Or how do you account for these differences?	Gives explanation which may be based on factual information and/or inferences	Accepts explanation. Seeks clarification if necessary
What does this tell you about . . . ?	Gives generalization	Encourages variety of generalizations and seeks clarification where necessary

This pattern of inviting reasons to account for observed phenomena and generalizing beyond the data is repeated and expanded to include more and more aspects of the data and to reach more abstract generalizations.

*From DEVELOPMENT OF A COMPREHENSIVE CURRICULUM MODEL FOR SOCIAL STUDIES FOR GRADES ONE THROUGH EIGHT, by Norman E. Wallen, Mary C. Durkin, Jack R. Fraenkel, Anthony H. McNaughton, and Enoch I. Sawin. Final Report, Project No. 5–1314, U.S. Office of Education (Washington, D.C., Oct. 1969), p. 18.

their feelings about dissent considered. General statements about each of the different dissenting groups can be expressed, these generalizations compared, and then as inclusive and broadly applicable a generalization as possible suggested and evaluated (using the criteria suggested earlier in Chapter 3 on page 105).

The nature of the task of generalizing becomes increasingly complex as the scope of the discussion is increased to include more and more data. Let us illustrate this with a further example. Suppose a class were interested in investigating trade and government patterns in Latin America. A decision would first have to be reached as to what particular samples of content

TABLE 5.8

THE BUILDING OF GENERALIZATIONS

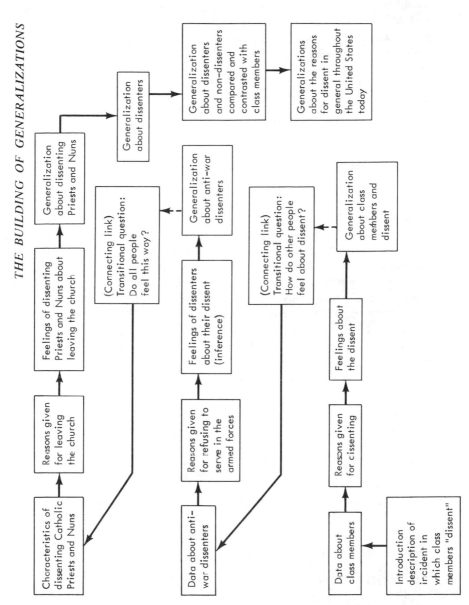

would be studied. Let us assume that the class decides on Brazil, Bolivia, and Mexico. One-third of the class will investigate each country. Each group would have to acquire information about its country, find out its major problems, obtain further information about each of the problems, exchange information, and then make inferences about the resulting government and trade patterns *in each country*. They then could generalize more broadly about trade *or* governmental patterns *in Latin America*, look for similarities and differences among these patterns, and finally make over-arching generalizations about similarities and differences *in government and trade patterns in Latin America*. The complexity of this building process is shown in Table 5.9.

The greatest difficulty which students have in learning how to make inferences and generalizations of anything more than a trivial nature lies in the fact that they have had little practice in the past in going beyond (i.e., inferring) what they find on the printed page. Many are literally conditioned to accept as gospel that which is on the pages of their textbooks and other sources, and discouraged from abstracting important ideas from those same pages. Often trained to settle for specific answers as found in the text, they are uneasy with going beyond the information given there. They have no model for interpreting and inferring. With practice and with assistance from the teacher, however, students can be encouraged and assisted to think about the possible implications of factual data, and to make reasonable interpretations and inferences in light of the data with which they are working. Here is an excerpt from a junior high school discussion in which a skillful teacher encourages students to draw conclusions and make inferences. The class had previously been studying life in various selected Latin American countries:

(1) **TEACHER:**   Now, let's get back to intermarriage. You said that intermarriage was so important. What about that?

(2) SETH: They marry freely, whoever they want to. They just pick. If they want to marry a Negro, an Indian, or a white person, they just do. It doesn't seem to bother them.

(3) **TEACHER:**   What do you have to say about that?

(4) CATHY: In Argentina they marry very young, and they are restricted and can't go out on dates. I mean free dates.

(5) **TEACHER:**   Let's get back to this intermarriage. What does that show about the country of Brazil?

(6) TOM: People aren't prejudiced and for segregation.

(7) **TEACHER:**   Why do you suppose they are not prejudiced?

TABLE 5.9

THE BUILDING OF GENERALIZATIONS ABOUT SIMILARITIES AND DIFFERENCES IN TRADE AND GOVERNMENT PATTERNS IN LATIN AMERICA*

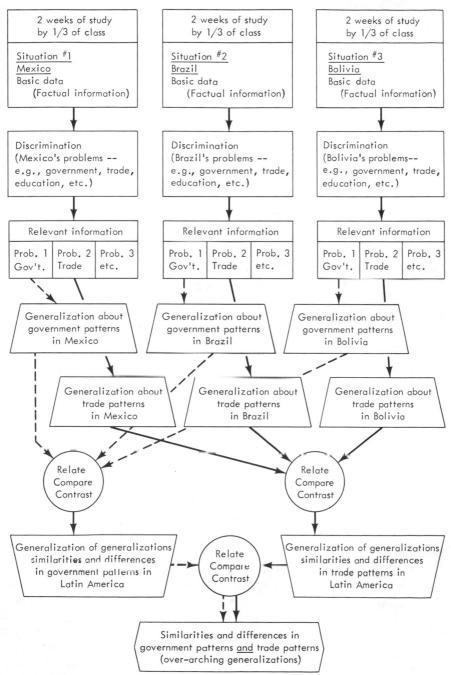

*From Hilda Taba, TEACHER'S HANDBOOK FOR ELEMENTARY SOCIAL STUDIES (introductory edition), 1967, Addison-Wesley, Reading, Mass. Used by permission of the Publisher.

(8) BOB: I think because they did it before.

(9) AMY: And there are more percentage of Indian and Negro than there are in different countries.

(10) **TEACHER:**   All right, do you want to carry that a little further? You thought that was a good idea, didn't you, when we talked about it?

(11) KARL: When the Portuguese came over to colonize they married. They found out that the Indians were there many hundreds of years before and they married them freely, and then there was an intermingling of bloods.

(12) **TEACHER:**   All these different peoples, and they seem to get along together . . .

(13) AMY: In Argentina there are not very many Indians because of the war of 1888.

(14) **TEACHER:**   What happened to the Indians then?

(15) AMY: They were almost wiped out because of the war. They were against the people and they were almost wiped out.

(16) KARL: The intermarriage came in places that are lightly settled.

(17) **TEACHER:**   Why is that?

(18) SETH: Because there is not very many to pick from.

(19) KARL: They use what is around

. . . . . .

(20) GWEN: Well, intermarriage shows that everybody is created equal.[26]

Notice that the teacher keeps the discussion moving by continually asking students to reflect on what they've said and to offer explanations for their interpretations—in short, to "go beyond the data." He also keeps the conversation focused on the topic at hand—intermarriage—by not allowing the class to go off on the tangent of "dating" introduced by Cathy (statement 4). As the discussion continues, Karl (statements 11 and 16); Seth (statement 18); and Gwen (statement 20) all offer interpretive generalizations based on the evidence the teacher has helped them (through the openness of his questions) to consider. If you were this teacher, how would you now attempt to get students to check out (i.e., support, refute, or modify) these generalizations?

[26]H. Taba, *Teacher's Handbook for Elementary Social Studies* (Introductory Edition), pp. 106–107.

You now realize the value of providing frequent opportunities for students to generalize about the data that they come across and work with in their study and learning. The formulation and testing of generalizations is of value in a number of ways. It encourages students to think about the possible relationships which may exist among various aspects of the world they experience; to "put things together" or establish connections in their own minds; and to consider what meaning (if any) such relationships or connections may have for human affairs in general and themselves in particular. In short, generalizing is one process that people use to make sense out of the world in which they live and to give meaning to their lives. The more warranted the generalizations are (supported by evidence), the more useful they are as guides. It is for this reason that the processes of forming and testing generalizations are so important to emphasize in school.

Teachers play an important role in these processes, however. They must provide an atmosphere in which student interpretations and inferences are not only accepted but encouraged, no matter how "unusual" or "odd" they may at first appear. This is essential. If students fear that only certain kinds of answers or conclusions will be accepted, original and creative thought is stifled. This is not to imply, however, that any and all generalizations are to be accepted as truth, nor that one generalization is as good as any other. Students must also be encouraged to check out or validate their generalizations against empirical evidence; to modify their ideas when and where appropriate; to refute ideas when the evidence so warrants. A significant help in this regard is to remind students continually that all generalizations are tentative and probabilistic in nature. This can be done by frequently asking: "Can you tell me that from the data we have accumulated to date?" or "Can you think of a situation where this idea would not apply?" On the other hand, they should also realize that the more evidence (i.e., data of various kinds) there is to support a generalization, the more warranted the generalization becomes. It is worth repeating at this point, therefore, the criteria suggested in Chapter 3. Students can be continually asked to check out the generalizations that they form against the following:

- To how many varied areas, events, peoples, ideas, objects, etc. does the generalization apply? (Applicability)
- How likely is it that the relationship which the generalization suggests does indeed exist in actuality? (Accuracy)
- To what degree does the generalization, as stated, lead on to other insights? (Depth)
- To what extent does (do) the relationship(s) which the generalization suggests describe important aspects of human behavior and explain important segments of today's world? (Significance)
- How much information does it encompass? (Breadth)

- How many powerful (complex) concepts does it include? (Conceptual strength)

It is crucially important, however, that students realize the tentative nature of *all* generalizations.

PREDICTING AND EXPLAINING

> *Instructional Objectives:* Given a generalization previously developed or acquired and given a new situation, problem, or question to which the generalization applies, students can *make a statement* or take other action that (in the judgment of a disinterested observer) represents a defensible use of the generalization in analyzing or coping with the situation, in solving the problem, or in answering the question.
>
> Given a set of events occurring or positions presented (one of which is identified as the event or position to be explained) in a social setting, students can *give* a plausible and logically sound explanation of the chains of cause-and-effect relationships that resulted in the occurrence of the event or the presentation of the position.

Helping students to form generalizations, however, is only part of what needs to be done if we are to encourage and assist student thinking. Students should also be encouraged to try out or apply the generalizations they have formed in one situation to another situation new and different. Such application allows students to demonstrate (and make clear to themselves) how well they understand the essence of an idea they have formed (or obtained) previously by determining its applicability in another situation that is somewhat similar in form yet different in particulars from the one in which the idea originated.[27]

In brief, then, the process of applying generalizations involves asking students to (a) make inferences based on their application of an idea they have previously formed as to what might happen in a new situation (i.e., what consequences might follow from certain already known conditions); (b) explain (on the basis of evidence or logical reasoning) why they think this would happen; (c) identify what facts would necessarily have to exist for the inference offered in (a) to indeed be true; and (d) to make further

---

[27]There is some research to indicate that the ability of students to use a previously formed generalization in a new and different situation depends on the amount of similarity there is between the situation (event, occurrence, etc.) in which the generalization originated and the one to which it is being applied, and also on the degree to which they see the new situation as similar in certain respects to another situation. See Irving Sigel, *A Teaching Strategy Derived from Some Piagetian Concepts*, Publication #113 (Boulder, Col.: Social Science Education Consortium, 1966).

inferences as to what might then follow. The sequence of questions the teacher pursues in order to encourage the above is illustrated in Table 5.10.

TABLE 5.10

*APPLYING GENERALIZATIONS
(PREDICTING AND EXPLAINING)**

This cognitive task consists of applying previously learned general-izations and facts to explain unfamiliar phenomena or to infer con-sequences from known conditions. It encourages students to support their speculations with evidence and sound reasoning. The teaching strategy consists of asking the following questions, usually in this order.

Teacher Asks:	*Student:*	*Teacher Follow-through:*
(Focusing question) Suppose that a partic-ular event occurred given certain conditions, what would happen?	Makes inferences	Encourages additional in-ferences. Selects in-ference(s) to develop
What makes you think that would happen?	States explanation; identifies relationships	Accepts explanation and seeks clarification if necessary
What would be needed for that to happen?	Identifies facts necessary to a particular inference	Decides whether these facts are sufficient and could be assumed to be present in the given situation
(Encouraging divergency) Can someone give a different idea about what would happen?	States new inferences that differ in some respects from pre-ceding ones	Encourages alternative inferences, requests explanations and neces-sary conditions. Seeks clarification where necessary
If, as one of you pre-dicted, such-and-such happened, what do you think would happen after that?	Makes inferences related to the given inference	Encourages additional inferences and selects those to pursue further

This pattern of inviting inferences, requiring explanations, identify-ing necessary conditions, and encouraging divergent views is con-tinued until the teacher decides to terminate the activity.

*From DEVELOPMENT OF A COMPREHENSIVE CURRICULUM MODEL FOR SOCIAL STUDIES, by Norman E. Wallen, Mary C. Durkin, Jack R. Fraenkel, Anthony H. McNaughton, and Enoch I. Sawin. Final Report, Project No. 5–1314, U.S. Office of Education, Washington, D.C., Oct. 1969, p. 19.

It is probably obvious to you by now that students must have already acquired a body of information and developed some generalizations (at least implicitly) if they are to apply them. For example, if students understand the implications of poorly trained police forces in large cities, they can predict what might happen if a riot were to break out on a college campus located in an urban area. If they understand how certain inventions have changed man's life, they can make inferences about what might happen if a cure for cancer were discovered. In sum, students are encouraged to use what they already know in order to predict in a conditional form (if such and such, then such and such) the consequences that might occur (and under what conditions) in a new situation.

Let us consider an example. Suppose students have been considering the concept of change and have previously drawn a number of conclusions about the changes which certain discoveries have had on men's lives, having studied in particular the effects of the discovery of metal on man. Reviewing the procedure outlined in Table 5.10, the first step is to encourage students to make inferences based on the ideas they have previously formed. Thus a teacher might ask: "What might happen if a new metal, harder yet more malleable than any yet known, were discovered today?"

The second step is to get students to explain and support the inference(s) they have made. For example, a student might infer that a number of entrepreneurs might try to buy up all the land around the area where the metal was discovered. The teacher needs to help the student make explicit the chain of causal links that leads from the discovery of the metal to the buying of the land so that the class as a whole may perceive the connection (and thereby build on it to make further connections).

The third step is one of identifying conditions that would be necessary to make the inference plausible. Why would these individuals want the land? Would the land be available? Could sufficient money be acquired? Who else might want it? For what purposes? Would the government permit the purchase? Students must be encouraged to determine the limits of their predictions. (It is important that the students, *not* the teacher do this, though the teacher may well assist students in this regard by suggesting various factors to consider.)

The fourth step extends the preceding step, the essential difference being that the teacher now encourages the students to build on their previous inferences. Thus he might ask: "If certain individuals did indeed purchase such land, what then might happen?"

Encouraging students to apply previously formed generalizations is an exercise in divergent thinking. It allows students to use information in an original way rather than simply encouraging its passive absorption. The teacher must take care, however, to be aware of the variety of possible predictions that he may obtain. Otherwise it would be easy for him to limit the discussion to only the most obvious or likely possibilities. This would suppress any incipient creative or unusual kinds of connections that the students might perceive, and once again imply that the teacher really wants what he considers to be "right" answers. This danger is particularly likely when students branch out into areas of content that are unfamiliar to the teacher (as inevitably happens at one time or another). On the other hand, divergent predictions can be carried to the point of sheer fantasy, with little, if any, link to what most of us perceive as reality. It is important, therefore, for teachers not only to see that students are challenged to produce factual and logical support for their ideas but also to be alert that certain examples may have considerable potential to develop in depth, and to encourage students to pursue an idea (by asking "why?" after each response) as far as they are able.

OFFERING ALTERNATIVES

Instructional Objective: Given a discussion or other setting in which generalizations, predictions, or explanations have been stated, students occasionally *suggest* that additional evidence or a different line of reasoning might lead to changes in one or more of the generalizations, predictions, or explanations.

Implicit in many of the foregoing strategies has been the need for teachers not only to suggest, but also to *encourage* students to seek out and offer alternative suggestions, viewpoints, and possibilities. To bring this about, the teacher must *continually* ask students to consider additional and different ways of thinking, perceiving, feeling, and acting. For example, as students report the details of their observations, they can be asked questions such as "What *else* did you notice?" When they are involved in a listing, grouping, and labeling exercise, they can be asked "Does anyone see *another way* that some of these things can be grouped together?" or "What *other* name might we give to this collection (group) of data?" Students can be regularly encouraged to suggest *additional* hypotheses and explanations. As they compare and contrast data, questions such as "In what *other* ways are they different?" or "What *other* similarities do you notice?" suggest themselves. When they generalize, alternative possibilities can be encouraged through such queries as "What *other* conclusion can you draw?" or "What *else* can you suggest?" Alternative predictions can be fostered by asking "What *else* might happen if such and such occurred?"

The foregoing may appear to belabor the obvious, but the examination of alternatives is essential if teachers expect students to do something other than uncritically accept the views of others (especially the statements of "authorities"). Much of the data that students encounter on critical issues (e.g., foreign policy) is one-dimensional in nature—that is, it presents but one viewpoint on the issue in question. If students are to be helped to make up their own minds on such issues, they must be encouraged to seek out and consider a variety of views as a matter of course. The active pursuit, presentation, and discussion of alternative ways of thinking, believing, feeling, and acting as a regular feature of classroom life can help to bring about the development of critical minds.

SUMMARY

This chapter introduced the concept of "teaching strategy," and argued that appropriate teaching strategies, as well as subject matter and learning activities, must be considered by teachers if desired objectives are to be attained.

The first part of the chapter suggested that the heart of any effective strategy lies in the questions it contains, and identified a number of different kinds of questions that teachers can ask for different purposes. Several examples of each type were given, and an argument was made for encouraging and helping students to learn how to ask as well as to answer several different kinds of questions in order to obtain different kinds of information.

The remainder of the chapter argued that thinking skills can be taught. Several generically applicable teaching strategies that teachers can employ to encourage student thinking were described and discussed. These strategies included *observing; describing; developing concepts*, in which learners list, group, and label items selected from an array of data; *differentiating and defining*, where students determine what attributes or characteristics they need to look for in order to decide whether particular examples are or are not instances of a concept; *hypothesizing*, in which students formulate and try to verify "if-then" statements; *comparing and contrasting*, in which students search for similarities and differences; *generalizing*, in which students suggest relationships; *predicting*, in which they test out generalizations previously formed; *explaining*, in which they suggest reasons for various occurrences; and *offering alternatives*, where they are encouraged to search for alternative possibilities. Examples of responses by students engaged in developing concepts and generalizing in real-life classrooms were presented. In general, the importance of helping students to think for themselves was stressed.

EXERCISES*

I. A number of questions are listed below in Column B. In the space provided, write the correct word from Column A that correctly identifies the category to which the question in Column B belongs.

A	*B*
Open-ended	_____ **1.** What kind of campaign tactics did Richard Nixon use during the election of 1968?
Judgmental	
Synthesizing	_____ **2.** In what ways, if any, do the causes of the Russian Revolution resemble those of the American and French Revolutions?
Explanatory	
Descriptive	
Recall or Recognition	_____ **3.** When did the Democrats last have control of the governorship of California?
	_____ **4.** Which book—*Moby Dick* or *Huckleberry Finn*—is the greater novel?
	_____ **5.** What might happen if a vast reservoir of water were located smack in the middle of the Sahara Desert?
	_____ **6.** Who invented the bifocal lens?
	_____ **7.** Why do you say that the United States should not get out of Vietnam?
	_____ **8.** What reasons would you offer to support your position?
	_____ **9.** How far is up?

II. What kind of question would you ask to obtain information about the items listed in Column B? In the space provided, write in the word from Column A that represents the kind of question called for.

*The author's suggestions are on pages 401–2.

A	B

A

Open-ended

Judgmental

Synthesizing

Explanatory

Descriptive

Recall or Recognition

B

_____ 1. The name of the present Prime Minister of England.

_____ 2. The best way to write a research report.

_____ 3. The reasons why a certain individual believes *Moby Dick* to be the greatest American novel.

_____ 4. A summary of the effects of a certain governmental action on America's image abroad.

_____ 5. The location of the capital of Brazil.

III. Try to write some questions of your own, using either of the category systems presented in this chapter. Have several other individuals read your questions and see if they would agree as to the *purposes* of each. What difficulties, if any, do you encounter in reaching agreement? How might such difficulties by resolved?

IV. Can you suggest any other types of questions not covered by the category systems presented in this chapter? Give an example of such questions.

V. The steps involved in the strategies of concept formation (Developing Concepts) and concept attainment (Differentiating and Defining) have been scrambled below. Indicate the correct order by numbering each statement in the order it belongs (i.e., place a "1" before the first step involved in the strategy, a "2" before the second step, etc.).

Developing Concepts

a. _____ Labeling

b. _____ Listing

c. _____ Explaining

d. _____ Grouping

e. _____ Recombining

Attaining Concepts

a. _____ states a definition of the concept

b. _____ repeats word

c. _____ views examples and non-examples

d. _____ brings in new examples

e. _____ selects from array of examples and non-examples

f. _____ states major attributes which all examples of the concept possess

VI. The steps involved in the tasks of hypothesizing, generalizing, and applying generalizations have likewise been scrambled below. Indicate the correct order of the steps in each task by numbering each in the proper order (i.e., similarly to what you did in IV above).

Hypothesizing

a. _____ gathering data
b. _____ defining aspects of the problem
c. _____ drawing a conclusion
d. _____ formulating a hypothesis
e. _____ identifying a problem for investigation
f. _____ testing the hypothesis against the data
g. _____ organizing and evaluating data

Generalizing

a. _____ describing what happened
b. _____ explaining reasons for actions
c. _____ stating a generalization
d. _____ explaining similarities and differences among incidents
e. _____ observing two or more incidents
f. _____ looking for similarities and differences among incidents

Using Previously Formed Generalizations in Situations New and Different

a. _____ explain why a given prediction might happen
b. _____ infer what might happen given a previous line of prediction and explanation
c. _____ suggest what might happen in a new situation (basing their suggestion on an idea previously formed)
d. _____ identify facts necessary to exist for a given prediction to be true.

VII. Try out the strategies described in this chapter with a group of students. What difficulties do you encounter? What suggestions would you make for improving the strategies?

VIII. Now try to devise some strategies of your own. Think of some aspect of thinking that you would like to emphasize with students and then attempt to formulate and sequence the necessary questions to engage students accordingly. What difficulties do you encounter?

CHAPTER VI

TEACHING STRATEGIES FOR DEVELOPING VALUING

This chapter deals with the nature of values and the process of valuing. A basic contention is that value development is unavoidable in education.

The first section of the chapter suggests a number of reasons why many teachers are reluctant to deal explicitly with values in their daily classroom endeavors, but points out that matters of value are indicated or implied all the time in the social studies.

The second section defines the term "value," and suggests criteria to use in order to determine if a value exists.

The third section illustrates several strategies that teachers can use to help students deal with values and valve conflicts. These include helping students to identify their own and others' values, to explore value conflicts, to understand and empathize with individuals caught in situations in which two or more values are in conflict, and to define various value terms more explicitly.

The fourth section discusses the teaching of particular values, suggesting when and how the teaching of such values is justified. A strategy that teachers can use to help students explore and evaluate various questions of personal and public policy is presented.

The last section discusses the development of moral reasoning, and presents examples of six stages of moral reasoning suggested by recent research as existing in all cultures. Procedures whereby teachers can encourage the development of higher levels of moral reasoning are suggested.

When you have finished this chapter, therefore, you should be able to do the following:

- give a definition of the term "value"; and apply a given set of criteria in order to determine if a value exists;

- *describe* the steps involved in helping students to identify their own and others' values, to explore value conflicts, to empathize with individuals caught in value-conflict situations, and to define value terms more precisely, *explain* how these steps help students to deal with values, and actually *use* the strategies containing these steps in your own teaching;
- *discuss* when it is and when it is not justifiable to teach a particular value;
- *describe* the steps involved in helping students explore and evaluate the consequences of various questions of personal and public policy, *explain* how these steps help students to do such, and then *use* this strategy in your own teaching;
- *identify* examples of student statements which illustrate different levels of moral reasoning, and *describe* procedures you can undertake in order to encourage the development of higher levels of moral reasoning on the part of your students.

One of the most neglected areas in social studies teaching is that of value analysis and development. It is probably no exaggeration to state that the explicit consideration of value questions in most social studies classrooms is largely ignored. Objectives, content, learning activities, teaching strategies, and evaluative measures all tend to be selected, organized, and developed more to promote learning in the cognitive domain than in the affective domain. Though the recent awakening to the ills of education in the United States produced a large variety of materials and suggestions towards reorganizing course content and improving students' thinking abilities, only a few writers have addressed themselves seriously to the question of values education.[1] The reasons for this are many and varied. Many teachers regard questions of value as essentially private matters with which they should not interfere. Furthermore, parents and other forces in the community often resist having controversial issues discussed and ques-

---

[1] William Glasser, *Schools Without Failure* (New York: Harper & Row, 1969); Maurice P. Hunt and Lawrence E. Metcalf, *Teaching High School Social Studies* (New York: Harper & Row, 1968); Richard M. Jones, *Fantasy and Feeling in Education* (New York: New York University Press, 1968); Lawrence Kohlberg, "Moral Education in the Schools: A Developmental View," *School Review*, Spring 1966, pp. 1–30; Jerold R. Coombs, Milton Meux, and James R. Chadwick, *Values Education: Rationale, Strategies, and Procedures*, Lawrence E. Metcalf, ed., Forty-first Yearbook of the National Council for the Social Studies (Washington, D.C.: NCSS, 1971); Fred M. Newmann, with Donald W. Oliver, *Clarifying Public Controversy* (Boston: Little, Brown, 1970); Donald W. Oliver and James P. Shaver, *Teaching Public Issues in the High School* (Boston: Houghton Mifflin, 1966); Louis E. Raths, Merrill Harmin, and Sidney B. Simon, *Values and Teaching* (Columbus, Ohio: Charles B. Merrill, 1966); Michael Scriven, *Student Values as Educational Objectives* (Boulder, Col.: Social Science Education Consortium, Pub. #124, 1966).

tions of value often involve controversy. Others, believing that values should be "caught" rather than taught, question the propriety of any program specifically designed for their development. Besides, they argue, the family, church, and other institutions are better equipped to deal with such matters. Some feel that any attempt on the part of teachers to influence or develop values in the young smacks of totalitarianism or "brainwashing." Some admit freely that their primary concern lies in trying to teach subject matter without having to worry about values.

Value education, however, is unavoidable. All of us engage in valuing. A teacher's actions, sayings, discussion topics, choice of reading assignments and materials, class activities, and examinations suggest that he believes certain ideas, events, individuals, or other phenomena are more important than others for students to consider. Indications of value are suggested all the time in the social studies: ". . . in the problems that are chosen to be discussed, in the manner in which they are discussed, in the historical documents and events that are emphasized, as well as in the leaders that are chosen to illustrate the important and the worthy and the unimportant and the unworthy in the affairs of man."[2] The social studies, by their nature, incorporate certain special values of their own: The "attempt to be objective, to look at oneself or one's own group dispassionately; to recognize how stubborn the diversities between different individuals and between different groups are; to distrust simple formulas and simple solutions in the government of human affairs."[3] As Childs has pointed out, the very organization of a system of schools represents a moral enterprise, for it signifies the deliberate attempt of a human society to control the pattern of its own evolution.[4]

Nevertheless, it must be admitted that in many instances whatever value education there is in a given social studies unit or course occurs implicitly (e.g., through the accidental use of certain books and materials) rather than explicitly through careful planning and design. A key question for all teachers to ask themselves is whether they want values to develop haphazardly in students without any conscious and specific involvement on their (i.e., the teacher's) part, or whether they intend to help students explore and come to some conclusions about values (both their own and

[2]John Childs, *Education and Morals* (New York: Appleton-Century-Crofts, 1950), pp. 17–19. Quoted in Van Cleve Morris, *Philosophy and the American School* (Boston: Houghton Mifflin, 1961), p. 289.

[3]Charles Frankel, "Needed Research on Social Attitudes, Beliefs, and Values in the Teaching of Social Studies," in Roy A. Price, ed., *Needed Research in the Teaching of the Social Studies*, Washington, D.C.: National Council for the Social Studies, Research Bulletin #1, 1963, p. 35.

[4]J. Childs, *Education and Morals*, p. 2.

those of other individuals in a wide variety of settings and cultures) explicitly.

The accomplishment of the latter is extremely important and badly needed in the social studies today. The apathy and lack of concern of large numbers of the American populace for other human beings of a different color, origin, area, or social class has been widely documented, not only in the most scholarly of professional journals and reports, but also in the daily press, popular magazines, and on radio and television.[5] Relatively few adults find themselves able, or willing, to speak out on issues of social concern.[6] Young people are continually bombarded by a variety of conflicting value-claims and urgings which leave many (if not most) uncertain and confused about what values, if any, to endorse. Certainly the increasing number of acts of violence—often for which there seems no readily identifiable "cause" or "reason"—suggests the inability of many individuals to resolve their own inner and interpersonal conflicts (not to mention the incapacity on a much larger scale of many nation-states to resolve their international disputes) by means other than a resort to force and weaponry.

Values underlie most (if not all) human behavior, though honest men can, and often do, differ as to the values they hold. The issue, therefore, is not whether values should be taught, for teachers cannot avoid teaching values. More relevant concerns involve helping students to identify their own and others' values, helping them to deal with value conflicts, justifying certain values to teach, and deciding how to teach them. Let us consider each of these tasks in turn.

WHAT IS A VALUE?

Values are concepts. Like all concepts, they do not exist in experience, but in the minds of men. They represent the quality of worth or merit which men place on various aspects of their experience. The study of values is usually divided into the areas of aesthetics and ethics. *Aesthetics* refers to the study and justification of what men consider beautiful—what they enjoy. *Ethics* refers to the study and justification of conduct—how men

[5]For example, examination of the Kerner and Eisenhower reports reveals that few of their recommendations are being put into practice. See U.S. President's National Advisory Commission on Civil Disorders, *Report of the National Advisory Commission on Civil Disorders* (New York: Dutton, 1968); U. S. President's National Commission on the Causes and Prevention of Violence, Washington, D.C.: Superintendent of Documents, Government Printing Office, Oct. 1969.

[6]See Rodney Stark, Bruce D. Foster, Charles Y. Glock, and Harold Quinley, "Sounds of Silence," *Psychology Today*, 3, No. 11 (April 1970), 38–41; 60–61.

act. At the base of the study of ethics is the question of morals—the reflective consideration of what is right and wrong.

Values are not things. They are standards of conduct, beauty, efficiency,
or worth that a person endorses and that he tries to live up to or maintain.
They do not exist in and of themselves, but are reflected in specific *value
judgments* or *claims* that individuals make. When a person claims that a
certain idea, individual, object, act, policy, or way of behaving is good,
right, ought to be supported, or should be carried out, such standards are
often revealed in the reasons he gives for his claim. For example, an individual might argue that capital punishment should be abolished (value
judgment) because it is ineffective (value = effectiveness), or that a particular politician should be supported (value judgment) because he is honest
(value = honesty).

As evidence that a value exists, Raths and his associates suggest the following criteria. When a person values something, he:

Chooses:	(1)	freely
	(2)	from alternatives
	(3)	after thoughtful consideration of the consequences of each alternative
Prizes:	(4)	cherishes, is happy with the choice he has made, and is
	(5)	willing to affirm the choice publicly
Acts:	(6)	does something with his choice
	(7)	repeatedly, in some pattern of life.[7]

Things that are similar to values, only somewhat weaker or less intense
and which do not meet the seven criteria above they call "value indicators."
Value indicators include such things as goals, aspirations, attitudes, interests, feelings, beliefs, activities, and worries.[8]

HELPING STUDENTS TO VALUE

IDENTIFYING VALUES

Many students are unaware of what their values are, or even if they
have any. One task for a value-education inclined teacher, therefore, is to
help students identify those things (acts, objects, procedures, individuals,
ideas) that they do consider important and then to help them reflect on why
they do. One way to bring such identification of values about is to ask stu-

[7]L. E. Raths, M. Harmin, and S. B. Simon, *Values and Teaching*, p. 30.
[8]*Ibid.*, pp. 30–33.

dents to recall from previous study (of a story, film, real-life incident, etc.) information about the behavior of a certain individual or group, to explain why they think such behavior occurred as it did, and then to make inferences about the values of the individual(s) involved. They then can be asked to hypothesize about their own behavior and values, and to make comparisons among the various values which have been identified and discussed. The objectives involved in this strategy are the following:

Instructional Objectives: Given a certain amount of previous information contained in a story, film, or other source of data dealing with values, students can:
   a. describe what the key figure(s) in the data did;
   b. give at least one possible reason the key figure(s) might have had for doing what he (they) did;
   c. suggest (infer) at least one possible value the key figure(s) might hold;
   d. hypothesize about their own actions and values in a similar situation;
   e. identify some (at least two) differences and similarities among the various values which have been identified and discussed.

Here is an example of the kind of story that can be used in this regard:

THE INVISIBLE MAN[9]

I am an invisible man. No, I am not a spook like those who haunted Edgar Allan Poe. . . . I am a man of substance, of flesh and bone, fiber and liquids—and I might even be said to possess a mind. I am invisible, understand, simply because people refuse to see me. . . . When they approach me they see only my surroundings, themselves, or figments of their imagination—indeed, everything and anything except me. . . .

That invisibility to which I refer occurs because of a peculiar disposition of the eyes of those with whom I come in contact. A matter of the construction of their *inner* eyes, those eyes with which they look through their physical eyes upon reality. . . . You're constantly being bumped against by those of poor vision. Or again, you often doubt if you really exist. You wonder whether you aren't simply a phantom in other people's minds. . . . It's when you feel like this that, out of resentment, you begin to bump people back. And, let me confess, you feel that way most of the time. You ache with the need to convince yourself that you do exist in the real world, that you're a part of all the sound and anguish, and you strike out with your fists, you curse and you swear to make them recognize you. And, alas, it's seldom successful.

One night I accidentally bumped into a man, and perhaps because of the near darkness he saw me and called me an insulting name. I sprang at him, seized his coat lapels and demanded that he apologize. He was a tall blond man, and as my face came close to his he looked insolently out of his blue eyes and cursed me, his breath hot in my face as he struggled. I pulled his chin down sharp upon the crown of my head, butting him as I had seen the West Indians do, and I felt his flesh tear and the blood gush out, and I yelled, "Apologize. Apologize!" But he continued to curse and struggle, and I butted him again and again until he went down heavily, on his knees, profusely bleeding. I kicked him repeatedly, in a frenzy because he still uttered insults though his lips were frothy with blood. Oh yes, I kicked him! And in my outrage I got out my knife and prepared to slit his throat, right there beneath the lamplight in the deserted street, holding him by the collar with one hand, and opening the knife with my teeth—when it occurred to me that the man had not *seen* me, actually; that he, as far as he knew, was in the midst of a walking nightmare! And I stopped the blade, slicing the air as I pushed him away, letting him fall back to the street. I stared at him hard as the lights of a car stabbed through the darkness. He lay there, moaning on the asphalt; a man almost killed by a phantom. It unnerved me. I was both disgusted and ashamed. I was like a drunken man myself, wavering about on weakened legs. Then I was amused. Something in this man's thick head had sprung out and beaten him within an inch of his life. I began to laugh at this crazy discovery. Would he have awakened at the point of death? Would Death himself have freed him for wakeful living? But I didn't linger. I ran away into the dark, laughing so hard I feared I might rupture myself. The next day I saw his picture in the *Daily News*, beneath a caption stating that he had been "mugged." Poor fool, poor blind fool, I thought with sincere compassion, mugged by an invisible man!

Once the activity (story, film, role-playing, etc.) is completed, the teacher can then ask the class the following questions:

1. What did the (key figures) do in the story?
2. What do you think were their reasons for doing what they did?
3. What do these reasons you've identified tell you about what is important to them?
4. If you did such and such (teacher specifies a similar situation) what would you do? Why?
5. What does this show about what you think is important?
6. What differences do you see in what all these people think is important? Similarities?

This question sequence represents one example of a strategy that teachers can use to help students identify their own and others' values. In question 1, students are asked to recall the actual behavior of certain individuals in a situation where their values come into play. In questions 2 and 3 they make inferences as to the reasons and values underlying this behavior. Question 4 asks them to explain their own behavior in a similar situation, while in question 5 they make inferences about their own values. Lastly, question 6 requires them to make comparisons among the many reasons and values they have identified.

The strategy is further described in Table 6.1.

The assumption underlying this strategy is that by making inferences about what they and other individuals consider important (i.e., their

TABLE 6.1

*IDENTIFYING VALUES**

	Teacher	Student	Teacher Follow-through
	What did they do . . .	Describes behavior.	Sees that description is complete and accurate.
A	What do you think were their reasons for doing/saying what they did?	States inferences as to reasons.	Accepts, seeks clarification, if necessary.
	What do these reasons tell you about what is *important* to them?	States inferences regarding values.	Re-states or asks additional questions to ensure focus on values.
B	If you . . . (teacher specifies similar situations directly related to student, e.g., "If you accidentally tore a page in someone else's book, what would you do? Why?")	States behavior and gives explanation.	Accepts, may seek clarification.
	What does this show about what you think is important?	States inferences about his own values.	Accepts, seeks clarification, if necessary.
	What differences do you see in what all these people think is important?	Makes comparisons.	Ensures that all values identified are compared.

^AThis sequence is repeated for each group or person whose values are to be analyzed. Each group specified by the teacher, however, must have been previously studied.

^BThis sequence is repeated in order to get reactions from several students.

*This strategy is an adaptation of one developed as part of the Taba Curriculum Development Project at San Francisco State College. See N. E. Wallen, M. C. Durkin, J. R. Fraenkel, A. H. McNaughton, and E. I. Sawin, *Development of a Comprehensive Curriculum Model for Social Studies.*

values), students will be more likely to reflect (and hopefully act) upon and consider what it is that they do value.

Some of the most provocative work in the area of value identification and clarification has been done by Raths, Harmin, and Simon.[10] Two of their most usable suggestions involve what they call the "clarifying response" and the use of a "value sheet." Let us look at examples of each.

A clarifying response is a response made by a teacher to what a student says or does that encourages the student to think about his statements and/or actions. Raths and his co-workers discuss this kind of response as follows:

> Imagine a student on the way out of class who says, "Miss Jones, I'm going to Washington, D.C., this weekend with my family." How might a teacher respond? Perhaps, "That's nice," or "Have a good time!"
>
> Neither of those responses is likely to stimulate clarifying thought on the part of the student. Consider a teacher responding in a different way, for example: "Going to Washington, are you? Are you glad you're going?" To sense the clarifying power in that response, imagine the student saying, "No, come to think of it, I'm not glad I'm going. I'd rather play in the Little League game." If the teacher were to say nothing else at this point other than perhaps "Well, we'll see you Monday," or some noncommittal equivalent, one might say that the student would be a little more aware of his life; in this case, his doing things that he is not happy about doing. This is not a very big step, and it might be no step at all, but it might contribute to his considering a bit more seriously how much of his life he should involve in things that he does not prize or cherish. We say it is a step toward value clarity.[11]

Here is another example of a teacher-student exchange involving a clarifying response:

TEACHER: Bruce, don't you want to go outside and play on the playground?

STUDENT: I dono. I suppose so.

TEACHER: Is there something that you would rather do?

STUDENT: I dono. Nothing much.

TEACHER: You don't seem much to care, Bruce, is that right?

[10]Louis E. Raths, Merrill Harmin, and Sidney B. Simon, *Values and Teaching.*
[11]From Louis E. Raths, Merrill Harmin, and Sidney B. Simon, VALUES AND TEACHING, pp. 51–52. Copyright © 1966 by Charles E. Merrill Books, Inc. Used by permission of the publisher.

STUDENT: I suppose so.

TEACHER: And mostly anything we do will be all right with you?

STUDENT: I suppose so. Well, not anything, I guess.

TEACHER: Well, Bruce, we had better go out to the playground now with the others. You let me know sometime if you think of something you would like to do.[12]

In short, clarifying responses represent an attempt by the teacher to get a student to look at and think about his own behavior and ideas, and hopefully to decide what is important for him. Moralizing is deliberately avoided.

A *value sheet* is a thought-provoking statement, story, or set of questions which contain value implications for students to consider and write about. Here are two examples of such value sheets:

FRIENDSHIP

1. What does friendship mean to you?
2. If you have friends, did you choose them or did they get to be your friends by accident?
3. In what ways do *you* show friendship?
4. How important do you think it is to develop and maintain friendships?
5. If you plan to make any changes in your ways, please say what changes you will make. If you do not intend to make any changes in your ways, write "No Changes."[13]

HOME OF THE BRAVE?

I used to be an idealist. When there was a picket line, I would picket. When there was a sitdown, I would sit. When there was a demonstration, I would demonstrate. I sat for two days in front of a store that wouldn't hire "minority-type" people—I felt that they should have a fair chance in the land of opportunity, that all men are created equal. They told me to go to Russia. I was born in Brooklyn!

Then there was the time I marched around the U.N. and handed out leaflets saying that we shouldn't use bombs to kill each other, and that man should study war no more. They called me an atheist!

Once I was arrested for going into a school with a sign saying that

---

[12]From Louis E. Raths, Merrill Harmin, and Sidney B. Simon, VALUES AND TEACHING, pp. 52–53. Copyright © 1966 by Charles E. Merrill Books, Inc. Used by permission of the publisher.

[13]From Louis E. Raths, Merrill Harmin, and Sidney B. Simon, VALUES AND TEACHING, p. 95. Copyright © 1966 by Charles E. Merrill Books, Inc. Used by permission of the publisher.

all children are entitled to an equal opportunity to education, like the Supreme Court says the Constitution means. They called me a Communist!

Soon I got tired of being called all these names, so I gave up. I don't care if half of them starve. I don't care if they don't all get educated. I don't care if they kill each other with bombs. I don't care if their babies die from radiation. Now I'm a good American.

To think on and write on:

1. What is this writer for and what is he against?
2. Have you had any experiences like his?
3. Who are some people who should be concerned about the problems he mentions?
4. Are there any things which *you* are working to change, to set right, to improve? Discuss briefly.[14]

Raths and his co-workers suggest that value sheets can be used in a variety of ways. Students can discuss their answers in small groups without the teacher present. They can turn in their responses for later reading by the teacher of selected excerpts that are especially illustrative of a particular viewpoint (without identifying the writer, though the writer may claim credit if he wishes). Individual students who so desire can place particular thoughts on the bulletin board for reflection by others.[15] The reader should refer to this work for many thought-provoking and useful ideas about value identification and clarification.

EXPLORING VALUE CONFLICTS

As students begin to identify their own and others' values, they will soon realize that they (like the rest of us) have acquired, in the process of growing up, many values which conflict.

Many of the values of our society themselves conflict. For example, consider the values ingrained in an American creed identified by Myrdal[16] in the 1940s and cited by Oliver and Shaver[17] and Newmann.[18]

[14]From Louis E. Raths, Merrill Harmin, and Sidney B. Simon, VALUES AND TEACHING, p. 100. Copyright © 1966 by Charles E. Merrill Books, Inc. Used by permission of the publisher.

[15]*Ibid.*, pp. 105–111.

[16]Gunnar Myrdal, *An American Dilemma: The Negro Problem in Modern Democracy* (New York: Harper & Row, 1944).

[17]D. W. Oliver and J. P. Shaver, *Teaching Public Issues in the High School.*

[18]F. M. Newmann, with D. W. Oliver, *Clarifying Public Controversy.*

the worth and dignity of the individual
equality
inalienable rights to life, liberty, property, and pursuit of happiness
consent of the governed
majority rule
rule of law
due process of law
community and national welfare
rights to freedom of speech, press, religion, assembly, and private
    association[19]

Newmann points out that such values are basic to the American political system, forming the nucleus, in fact, of what might be viewed as America's "constitutional morality." Other, less constitutionally oriented values in the creed include:

brotherhood
charity
mercy
nonviolence
perseverance, hard work
efficiency
competence and expertise
competition, rugged individualism
compromise
cooperation
honesty
loyalty
integrity of personal conscience[20]

As Newmann suggests, the list of values included in Myrdal's American creed contains a number of conflicting commitments, such as an emphasis on competition and rugged individualism on the one hand as opposed to a concern for cooperation and compromise on the other. To further the confusion, people often justify widely different positions by showing that they are consistent with one or more abstract values, such as those mentioned in the creed. Newmann offers as an example the following exchange between two students, who have been discussing whether a religious minority like the Amish should be exempt from compulsory school attendance and social security laws.

Jack: "In this country we believe in majority rule and the majority of the people in Pennsylvania think the Amish should go to public school. Therefore, they should not be excused."

[19]Newmann, *Clarifying Public Controversy*, p. 11.
[20]*Ibid.*, p. 12.

> Marion: "No, they should be excused. The Amish are a religious minority and our country was founded on a belief in preserving the rights of religious minorities, even though the majority have different views."[21]

Conflicting values often cause us considerable discomfort and even anguish. Hunt and Metcalf[22] cite the story of a secretary who had developed strong feelings of loyalty for her employer. He had provided good working conditions, liberal vacations, raised her salary several times, and even provided financial help for her aged mother. The secretary had recently discovered, however, that he had falsified his income tax returns. She thereupon sought advice from a local news columnist who gave advice to the lovelorn. She wanted to know what she should do—remain loyal to her employer and keep her mouth shut, or whether she should be honest and report him to the tax authorities. She was faced with a conflict between two values, both of which she endorsed.

How can we help students to deal with this kind of value conflict? As Hunt and Metcalf[23] suggest, to be told that one should always value both honesty and kindness doesn't help much when the two conflict.

Here is one strategy to consider:

Instructional Objectives: Given a certain amount of previous information contained in a story, film, or other source of data dealing with value conflict, students can:

   a. *state* the alternatives open to the central character(s) in the story;
   b. *describe* at least two things that might happen to the central character(s) depending on what course of action he (they) decides to pursue; *state* what they think the key figure(s) should do, and *explain* why they think so;
   c. *identify* a similar experience of their own, and *describe* what they did in that situation;
   d. *evaluate* (i.e., tell) whether their action at that time was good or bad, and why;
   e. *state* what else they believe they might have done in that earlier situation.

In this strategy, the teacher asks students to read a story (view a film, watch a role-playing sequence, etc.) in which lifelike individuals are faced with a choice between two (or more) conflicting alternatives. For example, here is one such story that might be used with first graders:

---

[21]F. M. Newmann, *Clarifying Public Controversy,* p. 13.
[22]M. P. Hunt and L. E. Metcalf, *Teaching High School Social Studies,* p. 124.
[23]*Ibid.,* p. 124.

Willie Johnson was in trouble! He had thrown his paint water at Sue Nelligan and the teacher had become angry with him. "Why did you do that Willie?" she had asked. Willie couldn't tell her, because he really didn't know why himself. He knew that Sue had teased him a little, but that wasn't the real reason. He just didn't know! The whole thing put him in a bad mood. From then on, the entire day just went to heck.

In the afternoon he had pushed Tommy Grigsly in the recess line. He also stamped his foot and yelled at the teacher. The teacher had become angry with him again. But this time she had pinned a note to his mother on his jacket.

That note! Willie knew it was about his behavior in class during the day. He felt he should obey the teacher, but he also knew that the other kids would think him a sissy if he just gave in without any protest. He knew that when he got home his mother would read the note and give him some kind of punishment. Then his father would find out about it and he'd really get it!

On his way home from school Willie was thinking about what his father would do to him. Oh brother!

"Wow!" he thought. "I'll get killed, if I bring this note home. I'd better take it off and throw it away."

He was just about to do that when he remembered how his mother had felt once before when she found out that he had lied to her. She kept saying he had let her down and he had felt terrible. He didn't want that to happen again!

Wow! He couldn't give the note to his mother, he couldn't throw it away. What should he do? He had a problem, all right. He had to make a choice, but how should he choose. No matter what he did, the outcome didn't look too good! What should he do?

Another example, for use with older students, is suggested by Shaver:

A man is upon a soap box giving a fiery harangue. A crowd begins to gather, and the police who are present are faced with a decision. It looks like there may be violence; what should they do? Should they disband the crowd or try to hold them back, or should they pull the fellow down from the soap box and haul him to jail.[24]

Upon completion of such readings, the teacher can then ask the class the following questions:

1. What is this story about?
2. What different things might the key individuals involved do (what alternatives are open to them)?

[24]James P. Shaver, "Values and the Social Studies," in Irving Morrissett, ed., *Concepts and Structure in the New Social Science Curricula* (New York: Holt, Rinehart & Winston, 1967), p. 12.

3. What might happen to them, if they do each of these things?
4. What might happen to other people?
5. What do you think he (they) should do?
6. Why?

This question sequence is an example of a teaching strategy that teachers can use to help students explore value conflicts. Question 1 asks students to describe what happened in the story they have read. Question 2 asks them to determine what alternatives are open to an individual placed in an uncomfortable situation. No matter what the key individuals (in the first example, Willie; in the second, the policemen) do, the consequences may be rather unpleasant. The individuals involved are in a dilemma, however, since underlying values are in conflict. Willie values obeying the teacher and not hurting his mother, but also not being considered a sissy. The policemen are torn between maintaining order and permitting freedom of speech. Thus the similarity to real life, for who among us has not been at one time or another in a somewhat similar predicament? Students are not only asked to analyze alternatives, however. They are also requested to predict consequences (questions 3 and 4), to make a value judgment as to which alternative should be pursued (question 5), and to give their reasons for choosing a particular alternative over others (question 6).

As Shaver[25] points out, students will come up with different solutions to these kinds of predicaments based on differing and usually unexamined, commitments. Along with others, Shaver has suggested using analogy to help students clarify these commitments. For example, in the freedom of speech example given above, analogous situations can be developed along a continuum, at one end of which freedom of speech is viewed as being most important relative to property damage, and at the other end of which property rights are viewed as more important. He goes on to discuss the use of such analogous cases as follows:

> For example, if a student replied that in the soapbox case, cited above, the police should stop the speaker, the teacher might query: "What if a presidential candidate who was very unpopular in your community was scheduled to speak and it became clear that feelings were so strong that a serious disturbance would occur unless action is taken. Should the candidate be told that he could not speak?" The analogy between the two cases lies in the confrontation between the principles of free speech and freedom and order. However, when the speaker is not a "rabble-rouser," freedom of speech takes on greater salience and most students would insist on police protection. (Whether it could be provided would likely be questioned—a

[25]*Ibid.*, p. 121.

factual question upon which the value choice might hinge.) When two such cases elicit contradictory responses, the examination of relationships between the situations affords a way of getting students to see that the values do conflict, and how they conflict, and of helping them determine at which point the nature of the situation has changed sufficiently so that they are willing to shift from supporting one value to supporting one or more others being violated.[26]

After a sufficient amount of discussion as to the values and consequences involved has taken place, the teacher can help students to consider their own behavior in similar situations that they have experienced. This is accomplished by focusing on a *particular* action suggestion and then asking the following additional questions of the class:

7. Has anything like that ever happened to you?
8. What did you do?
9. As you think back now, was that a good or bad thing to do? Why?
10. What else could you have done?

Questions 7 and 8 now ask students to recall their own actions in a similar experience, while question 9 asks them to evaluate the alternative they chose in that instance. Question 10 then asks them to consider other alternatives that they might have pursued at that time.

The intent of this strategy is that students consider seriously the alternatives open to them rather than simply give what they consider to be the "solution" desired or considered "good" by the teacher. The giving of such "acceptable" responses is particularly likely to happen when students are asked to evaluate their own (recalled) behavior (question 9 above). It is crucial at this point, therefore, that teachers *not* approve or disapprove of various student responses, but accept any and all of their replies (even the most anti-social) at face value and then encourage them to consider the consequences of each.

The complete strategy is further described in Table 6.2.

The assumptions underlying this strategy is that through realizing, discussing, and evaluating alternative courses of actions, along with the consequences of these alternatives, students will become more aware of their own values, realize that all of us hold values which at times will conflict, be willing to shift from supporting one value to supporting one or more others they believe more worthy of support, realize that there are many different ways of dealing with a particular problem, and possibly become more willing in the future to search for a variety of solutions rather than insisting on only one.

[26]*Ibid.*, p. 122.

TABLE 6.2

EXPLORING VALUE CONFLICTS*

	Teacher	Student	Teacher Follow-through
	1. What happened? Or what did . . . do?	Describes events.	Insures that all events are given; tries to get agreement or, if not possible, a clear statement of differences in perception of what occurred.
	2. What different things might . . . do?	Suggests alternatives open to central figure(s).	Insures that all alternatives open to central figure(s) are given.
	3. What might happen to him if he does each of these things? What might happen to other people?	Suggests various consequences of each alternative to people involved.	Encourages exploration of possible consequences.
A	4. What do you think . . . (the central figure) should do?	Makes value judgment.	Accepts response, seeks clarification where necessary.
	5. Why?	Gives reasons for choosing particular course of action.	Accepts. Seeks clarification, if necessary.
B	6. Has something like that ever happened to you?	Relates similar event in his own life.	Provides support, if necessary.
	7. What did you do?	Relates recalled behavior.	Clarifies, if necessary.
	8. As you think back now, do you think that was a good or bad thing to do?	Judges past actions.	Encourages student to judge his own past actions. The teacher may need to prevent others from entering the discussion at this point.
C	Why do you think so?	States reasons.	Accepts reasons. If necessary, asks additional questions to make clear the criteria or values which the student is using in judging his actions (e.g., "Can you tell us how you decided?").
	9. What else could you have done?	Offers alternative behavior.	Accepts. Asks additional questions to point up inconsistencies where they occur (e.g., "How does that agree with the reasons you gave earlier?").

[A]These questions are repeated in sequence several times in order to obtain a variety of responses.

[B]A considerable exploration of questions 4 and 5 should be encouraged here by the teacher before going on to question 6.

[C]These questions are repeated in sequence several times in order to obtain a variety of inferences and personal experiences.

*This strategy is an adaptation of one developed as part of the Taba Curriculum Development Project at San Francisco State College. See Norman E. Wallen, Mary C. Durkin, Jack R. Fraenkel, Anthony H. McNaughton, and Enoch I. Sawin, DEVELOPMENT OF A COMPREHENSIVE CURRICULUM MODEL FOR SOCIAL STUDIES FOR GRADES ONE THROUGH EIGHT, Final Report, Project No. 5–1314, Washington, D.C.: U.S. Office of Education, Oct. 1969.

DEVELOPING EMPATHY

To be *able* to identify and appraise the consequences of various alternatives, however, students need to be helped to identify and *empathize* with the individual who is faced with the conflicting alternatives. To help students identify and empathize with others (especially with those of dissimilar ethnic or socioeconomic backgrounds) teachers need to increase student sensitivity to the worth and dignity of other individuals, especially those unlike themselves. "To extend sensitivity, students need an opportunity to react with feelings and to identify with feelings of other people, whether in the reality of actual experiences or as described in fiction."[27] It is also to be stressed that "feelings, values, and sensitivities are matters that need to be discovered rather than taught."[28]

How can we help students explore feelings in a constructive sense? The following objectives indicate one strategy that might be used.

Instructional Objectives: Given a certain amount of previous information contained in a story, film, or other source of data dealing with people's feelings, students can:

  a. *describe* how they think the central figure in the story feels;
  b. *explain* why they think he feels as he does;
  c. *describe* how they think they would feel in a situation similar to that of the central figure;
  d. *state* what they believe is a warranted generalization about people and how they behave.

Students can be asked to read, view, or role-play excerpts from powerful, moving literature in which characters that are as real-life as possible express their feelings and show their emotions about other people, events, or ideas. Here is one such story, for example, that can be used with junior and senior high school students:

RALPH RAMIEREZ[29]

Okay, my name is Ralph Ramierez, why should that mean I'm dumb? Yea, I get put in the back seat and told to shut up ever since I was in first grade. Why? I'll tell you why if you'll let me. Sure, I don't have the good speech that you do, so most my life I've been told to shut up or been laughed at. Why don't you "Anglos" let us talk—maybe if you'd let us try to tell you how it feels, we could.

[27]Hilda Taba, *Curriculum Development: Theory and Practice* (New York: Harcourt Brace Jovanovich, 1962), p. 279.
    [28]*Ibid.*, p. 224.
    [29]From PREJUDICE AND DISCRIMINATION by Fred R. Holmes of the INQUIRY INTO CRUCIAL AMERICAN PROBLEMS Series © 1970 by Prentice-Hall, Inc., Englewood Cliffs, N.J. Reprinted with permission.

Sure, we don't use big words and good sentences—how can we, we speaked Spanish for five years till the first grade. Maybe if you only listen you'd be able to feel why I'm angry and mad and—and—all screwed up.

In the first grade I couldn't speak hardly any English. I didn't hardly know what the teacher was saying, and I couldn't answer questions. So what I do? What would you do? I shut up. A lot of us do. Then they gave us those tests! What a laugh—they didn't teach me to read yet.

Then they put us all together and told us we were dumb. Yea, some of them teachers told us right out that we was dumb. Those that didn't, treated us like we were dumb. Well, why didn't you teach us to read and talk before you called us dumb. Sure, all the "Anglos" thought the same thing. And when they grew up they re-membered. Ever have a cop yell at you "Hey, Mexican, get out of that car," and then when you started to tell him his question, he say, "shut up, Wetback," and phone in to the office to see if you had stolen your own car!

That's why we drop out of school; you never gave us a chance— bad teachers, never did go to a play—they only took the smart Anglos! Never got any new books. Nobody ever let us talk long enough in our bad English to know whether we believed in any-thing. So finally I turned it all off. Yea, that whole damn thing. Well, I got to sophomore year in college now because a hip girl talked me into going back. They took the time to listen up there— but now, right here today, what are you doing, I feel it; I see it in your faces; I hear it in your voices. You guys trying to put off a poor, dumb Mex! Why don't you help—that's all we want. Help us to read—take a poor, dumb Mex kid to a play. You sure as hell draft him into the army fast.

Upon completion of the reading, viewing, or role-playing, the teacher can then ask the class the following questions:

1. What is this story about? What happened in this story?
2. How do you think _____ (the key figure in the story) felt?
3. Why do you think he felt this way?
4. Has anything like this ever happened to anyone you know? In a story you've read? To you?
5. How did you feel? (Or why do you think people sometimes do things like this?)
6. After reading (viewing, etc.) a story like this and talking about it, what can you say about people and how they feel in situations like this?

The question sequence presented above offers a further example of a teaching strategy that teachers can use, in this case to help students explore feelings. Students are asked in question 1 to describe what actually happened to an individual in a specific situation. In questions 2 and 3 they describe and explain how they think the individual felt about the situation. Questions 4 and 5 then encourage the student to try to determine what his own feelings in a similar situation might be, and then question 6 asks students to try to draw some conclusions about the feelings of people in such situations. The strategy is further described in Table 6.3.

The assumption underlying this strategy is that by forming and comparing inferences about their own and others' feelings in certain instances, students will become more aware of the *similarities* (*as well as* the differences) in feelings which different people possess in various situations, and thus be more able to understand why people act as they do.

Role-playing.   A few words about role-playing are in order here, since it is a technique that teachers and students can use to advantage to gain insight into values and feelings. Role-playing requires students to take on and act out the roles of real or imaginary individuals in various situations. As described by Shaftel, it involves the following steps:

1. Warm-up (teacher introduction and reading of the story)
2. Selecting role-players
3. Preparing the audience to observe
4. Setting the stage
5. The enactment
6. Discussion and evaluation
7. Further enactments
8. Further discussion
9. Generalizing[30]

To engage students in role-playing, the teacher (or a student) reads a story (shows a film, plays a record, etc.) in which an individual (or individuals) is faced with a problem that is personally important, and relevant to the concerns of students in the classroom. Fantini and Weinstein argue that all students are concerned about and have a need to establish a positive self-image, a feeling of connectedness with the rest of society and each other, and a feeling of control over their own lives.[31] It is my experience

[30]Fannie R. Shaftel and George Shaftel, *Role-Playing for Social Values: Decision-Making in the Social Studies* (Englewood Cliffs, N.J.: Prentice-Hall, 1967), p. 84.

[31]Mario D. Fantini and Gerald Weinstein, *The Disadvantaged: Challenge to Education* (New York: Harper & Row, 1968), pp. 367–368.

TABLE 6.3

EXPLORING FEELINGS
(DEVELOPING EMPATHY)*

	Teacher	Student	Teacher Follow-through
A	What happened?	Re-states facts.	Insures that all facts are given and agreed upon. If students make inferences, asks that they be postponed.
	How do you think . . . felt?	Makes inference as to feelings.	Accepts inference.
	Why do you think he would feel that way?	Explains.	Asks student for clarification if necessary.
	Who has a different idea about how he felt?	Makes alternative inferences and explanations.	Seeks variety if necessary. Asks for reasons if necessary.
	How did . . . (other persons in the situation) feel?	States inferences about the feelings of additional persons.	Seeks clarification if necessary. Encourages students to consider how other people in the situation felt.
B	Have you ever had something like this happen to you?c	Describes similar event in his own life.	Ensures description of event.
	How did you feel?	Describes his feelings. May re-experience emotions.	Seeks clarification if necessary. Provides support if necessary.
	Why do you think you felt that way?	Offers explanation. Attempts to relate his feelings to events he has recalled.	Asks additional questions, if necessary to get beyond stereotyped or superficial explanation.

ᴬSometimes only certain of the questions are asked. The teacher should omit questions if students have answered them spontaneously.

ᴮThese questions are repeated in sequence several times in order to obtain a variety of inferences and personal experiences.

ᶜIf students have difficulty responding, you may wish to ask: "If this should happen to you, how do you think you would feel?" or "Has something like this happened to someone you know?" Another useful device is for the teacher to describe such an event in his own life.

*This strategy is an adaptation of one developed as part of the Taba Curriculum Development Project at San Francisco State College. See Norman E. Wallen, Mary C. Durkin, Jack R. Fraenkel, Anthony H. McNaughton, and Enoch I. Sawin, DEVELOPMENT OF A COMPREHENSIVE CURRICULUM MODEL FOR SOCIAL STUDIES.

that most students find stories, films, recordings, newspaper and magazine accounts, etc. that deal with such concerns interesting and worth discussing. The crucial variable, however, is that the incident being described must deal with real people or realistic characters faced with a believable dilemma in which a choice must be made between two or more alternatives. The stories on pages 241 and 245–46 are examples of such stories. Here are some other suggestions:

- You are a class of all black students and a new student, who is white, is enrolled. You want to make him feel at ease. What do you do?
- Your parents don't approve of some of your friends. You feel that they have misjudged them. You want to convince them otherwise. What do you do?
- One of your friends has copied from your paper during an examination without your realizing it. The teacher has asked you both to explain the fact that your papers are identical, even to some crossed-out words. What do you do?
- A group of your friends want to "rough up" and "work-over" another student that they feel is a "stool-pigeon" and "teacher's pet." They want you to join them, and suggest you're a "chicken" if you do not. What do you do?
- A student whom nobody likes is questioned by the teacher about stealing a book. You know that one of your friends is the actual thief. What do you do?
- Your school has a regulation against hair that extends beneath the top of the shirt collar. Your hair will be that long in a couple of weeks. Furthermore, you have been asked to join a rock band that requires long hair of its members. What do you do?[32]

Here are some further suggestions for involving students in role-playing, many of which are expanded upon by Shaftel:[33]

- Read the story (show the film, etc.) up to the moment of decision and then ask the class: "What do you think _____ (the character(s) will do?" or, "What do you think will happen now?"
- Allow individuals who seem to have identified with the various characters in the story to assume their roles. Students will usually indicate such identification by the remarks they make as to what they think may happen or what they think particular individuals will do. If necessary, ask for volunteers. Shaftel suggests, however, that students who have been volunteered for roles *by others* should *not* be assigned such roles, since the reasons behind the

[32]For further suggestions and examples, see Shaftel and Shaftel, *Role-Playing for Social Values;* Mark Chesler and Robert Fox, *Role-Playing Methods in the Classroom* (Chicago: Science Research Associates, 1966); or Muriel Crosby, ed., *Reading Ladders for Human Relations*, 4th ed. (Washington, D.C.: American Council on Education, 1963).

[33]Shaftel and Shaftel, *Role-Playing for Social Values*, pp. 74–81.

volunteering may be punitive or the suggested student may not see himself or herself in such a role.[34]

- Allow the role-players time to plan briefly what they will do and how they will do it.

- Prepare the rest of the class (the audience-to-be) to be participating observers. To enhance awareness of what the role-players are doing, to increase sensitivity to the role-players' efforts, and to encourage consideration of alternative possibilities for dealing with the problem under study, the remainder of the class can be assigned to various observer tasks. They can be asked to judge the degree to which they believe the roles depicted are realistic, or how they think various role-played individuals felt as the action progresses. Shaftel suggests that it is wise to warn a beginning group that has had few or no previous role-playing experiences that laughter spoils the role-playing but that attentive observation helps it.[35]

- Enact the role-playing. Shaftel points out here that role-players are not to be condemned or praised for their portrayals; students are not being evaluated on their acting ability.[36] The purpose of role-playing is to help students gain insights into the feelings and values of others.

- Discuss what took place. How realistic was the role-playing? How likely is it that the consequences as depicted would actually occur? The questions on pages 241–43 and 246 can be helpful here.

- Re-enact the dilemma. After a discussion of the first enactment has taken place, the role-players may wish to re-enact their roles, or roles can be switched, or new students may assume the roles in order to present new interpretations of what might happen.

- Discuss the new enactments.

- Encourage the class to draw some conclusions about what they observed and felt, and then to discuss these conclusions. Questions like "Why do people in situations like this act the way they do?" are helpful here. (Review the strategy for helping students to generalize that is described on pages 209 to 220 at this point.)

In all of the strategies presented so far, teachers must be careful *not* to approve or disapprove of various student responses, but to accept all replies as legitimate expressions of student feelings. Acceptance or non-acceptance can be shown in many ways, including any number of body movements and facial mannerisms (e.g., smiles, frowns, eye contact, etc.). Students learn quite early in the educational game to check out what the teacher "wants" and then to try and provide such, often at the expense of increasing their own understanding and gaining insight as to their own feelings. If teachers do not plan ahead of time and think carefully about the kind of responses they wish to encourage, students may come to view

[34]*Ibid.*, p. 76.
[35]*Ibid.*, p. 78.
[36]*Ibid.*, p. 79.

classroom "success" as the giving of teacher-"approved" answers or of saying the "right" words, even though these words or answers do not express their real feelings.

A teacher must think seriously, therefore, about his own manner of responding to student expressions. There are a variety of ways by which a teacher can show acceptance. He can listen carefully and respond in a somewhat noncommittal manner (e.g., by saying "I see" or "I understand"). He can restate what a student has expressed, but indicate that he understands what the student is trying to express (e.g., "You said that you felt very uncomfortable when you moved to a new town and began your freshman year in high school away from home. I can understand that kind of feeling"). He can verbally support the feelings expressed by students (e.g., "I know what you mean, Sam. I've felt that way myself").

The point being argued here is that the teacher is to do his best not to judge. There are no "right" or "wrong" answers when students are expressing and discussing their feelings. The personal reactions that students express concerning their experiences in the world are uniquely personal and private. A student's feelings, as long as they do not impose on someone else, are his alone, and should be respected as such. The teacher may not agree with a student's feelings, but he needs to accept them if he is to help all his students realize the different kinds of feelings that people in the same or similar situations may experience. This is *not* to say that teachers should not do their best to engage students in a rich variety of experiences so that they can continually expand their understanding of what the world includes. No teacher has the right, however, to dictate how any student should feel *about* these experiences. Bond illustrates how some teachers do attempt to dictate how students should feel, however.

TEACHER: Now I want you to listen to some Stravinsky. You'll find this is much more beautiful than Sibelius. (Teacher plays "Rite of Spring.")

TEACHER: As you heard, Stravinsky is much more intense—he gives you more feeling.

GEORGE: I got more feeling from Sibelius.

TEACHER: From Sibelius?

GEORGE: Yeah, I like him better. He makes me feel excited inside.

TEACHER: Well, that doesn't make sense. His music isn't as vibrant, or challenging.

GEORGE: Well, I still like Sibelius. In fact, I don't like Stravinsky at all.

TEACHER: Well, that's not true. And George, when I ask you which music is more vibrant on the exam, the correct answer will be Stravinsky.[37]

Should a student (or someone else) claim that what he finds good is also good for everyone else, however, it is a different matter. The student has made a value-claim, and it is part of any teacher's professional responsibility to ask and to help him to support (i.e., present evidence for) this value-claim if such exists. (The nature and importance of evidence is discussed further on pages 262 to 267.)

If individuals are to choose intelligently from among competing alternatives, they must be clear as to what the alternatives are. For example, if someone remarks that John is an excellent worker, we need to know what he means by excellent (i.e., what qualities, skills, etc. an excellent worker possesses) before we can assess John's work. Many value disputes arise, in fact, because people have different meanings in mind for the value terms they use. Many value disputes, however, can be settled by rational discussion. We would all agree that some workers, teachers, composers, football players, products, ideas, actions, and ways of doing things *are* better than others. Why? Because the individual, object, idea, action, or procedure judged superior to others possesses certain characteristics that those judged inferior lack. One problem is to identify and gain agreement on what these characteristics are. An appropriate instructional objective in this regard, therefore, is as follows:

> *Instructional Objective:* Given various value terms, students can define the term more precisely by stating the essential characteristics or attributes that the term represents.

Suppose a student claims in class that John F. Kennedy was a great man. If the class is to discuss and assess this claim, the meaning of the value term (i.e., "great") involved must be defined. What characteristics or attributes do "great" individuals possess? The teacher's job is to encourage and assist students to define the value term, and then to help them decide whether a particular individual (in this case, JFK) in a given situation would logically fall within the definition—that is, would possess the characteristics. The problem here lies in arriving at an agreed-upon definition of "great." Words like "great," being abstractions, are very difficult to pin down to a precise definition. The argument here however, is that teachers need to

---

[37]David J. Bond, "The Fact-Value Myth," *Social Education*, Feb. 1970, pp. 186–190.

encourage and assist students to make the attempt so that the meaning of various alternatives becomes clearer.

A student might define a term like "great" in several ways. He might translate it into terms more easily understood (e.g., "great" means "renowned the world over"). He might point to an example or examples of several individuals or actions whom he considers as being great, indicating the characteristics or attributes that they possess that make them great. The more characteristics identified, the better, since they enable us to determine more clearly whether a given instance does or does not warrant the label in question. Thus greatness can be defined as a person who (a) holds a high office, (b) is recognized for high achievement by authorities in his field, (c) has contributed to the betterment of mankind. According to this definition, a person would have to meet all three criteria in order to be considered great. Newmann[38] suggests three attributes that can be used to determine if a particular definition is adequate. It should be non-circular, that is, it should not simply define itself (e.g., defining excellent as "possessing the quality of excellence"). It should be convertible, that is, the term to be defined should "equal" the definition. Thus the definition of a slave as a human being who is the legal property of another is equally true when reversed

a human being who is the legal property of another = a slave

The definition "a slave is a man," on the other hand, is not convertible. Thirdly, an adequate definition should be sufficiently precise to differentiate among examples that differ in subtle ways. The specification of multiple attributes is most helpful in this regard.

Regardless of how a student defines a term, however, other students may disagree with this definition. What then? One possibility is to consult an authoritative source, such as a dictionary or official definition (e.g., to determine the meaning of "heart attack," we would be wise to go by the official definition of a heart specialist rather than relying on our own definition). A second possibility is to *stipulate* a meaning—that is, to agree among ourselves that the term means such and such in this particular instance (though not necessarily beyond this instance) so that discussion may proceed. If students are unable to agree on a definition, further discussion of the value-claim is likely to be unprofitable, since communication about the term in question will be impossible. Students will have no choice but to "agree to disagree" and to consider the statement as reflecting a matter of personal preference or feeling.

[38]F. M. Newmann, *Clarifying Public Controversy*, pp. 53–54.

THE TEACHING OF VALUES

PEDAGOGICAL VALUES

Beyond helping students to identify values, deal with the conflicts which opposing values produce, and define value terms more precisely, can we justify the teaching of *particular* values in the classroom? Can we justify a teacher requiring that certain rules of order be obeyed? punishing students? expelling them? What about particular ways of thinking? What about the teaching or non-teaching of certain subject matter (e.g., sex education or comparative political philosophies)? If so, on what basis?

The teaching of many values can be logically and empirically justified if teachers are to do their jobs. Specific rules of order in the classroom, for example, must be established if teachers are to teach at all. As Scriven has remarked, "the idea of public education does not merely *encourage*, it *presupposes* sufficient discipline to enable the teacher and pupils to perform their assigned roles—and so of course it requires the imposition on the student by the teacher of a very definite behavioral value-system. And either expulsion or corporal punishment of the trouble-makers *may* have to be part of the teacher's repertoire if he or she is to discharge this fundamental obligation to the other students and the society. The justification of this kind of value-conclusion, in certain circumstances, is perfectly straightforward."[39]

The teaching of certain procedural values, such as logical or critical thinking, is also essential to pedagogical effectiveness. If we want students, for example, to be able to evaluate rationally various conclusions and recommendations to which they are exposed during their lifetime, we must of necessity teach them the value of rational analysis, since it is pretty unlikely that they will learn this elsewhere. If we want them to base their actions on empirically-supported conclusions (i.e., those conclusions for which the most supporting facts exist), we must of necessity teach them the value of objectivity (as opposed to intuition, revelation, common-sense, etc.) as the best means of arriving at such conclusions.

Teachers must be clear in their own minds, however, as to *why* they are insisting that certain ways of proceeding or behaving be followed or practiced rather than other ways if they are to justify these procedures or behaviors to students. It is certainly conceivable (and likely) that different teachers will choose differently. The important thing for any teacher, however, is to be clear about *why* he has chosen certain behaviors and/or procedures over others, and to be able to give logical and just (i.e., fair) reasons for his choice. If a teacher cannot explain the reasoning behind a

[39]M. Scriven, *Student Values as Educational Objectives*, p. 12.

chosen procedure or behavior that he is requiring of students, it seems unlikely, to say the least, that doubting students will accept the procedure or
behavior as having value for them.

The procedures or behaviors a teacher endorses, however, must not only
be defended, but defensible. Now no one, at least not yet, has ever been
able to justify basic principles or ends in any "absolute" or "final" sense.
Both Scriven and Kohlberg, however, have argued cogently and clearly
that there is one fundamental principle that offers considerable potential
as a basis for justifying the desirability of other values and specific acts.[40]
It is the principle of prima facie equality of rights or justice. Scriven argues
that this principle can be justified both politically and directly—politically
in terms of the fact that we, as a nation, are committed to it. It is listed
first among the values identified in the Preamble to the United States Constitution ("We, the people of the United States, in order to form a more
perfect union, *establish justice* . . ."), and cited in most systems of religious
ethics (Treat others as you would like to be treated); and directly, by comparing the advantages and disadvantages of an equal allocation of rights
with any and all alternatives in terms of their effects upon the individuals
in any society or group which embraces these alternatives.[41]

The principle of equal rights means that all parties to a dispute or disagreement have an equal claim to consideration, though not necessarily to
equal treatment. Unequal treatment, however, can be justified only when
it can be shown to be necessary to protect the claims of all the individuals
involved. Equal rights means equal consideration of one's position or argument, not necessarily equal treatment in a specific situation, since there
may be good reasons for giving greater preference to some rather than to
others. "When the constitution of a country or of an organization of countries talks about all people being equal, it does not imply that they are all
equally strong, intelligent, or virtuous, and it does not imply that they
should receive equal incomes; it simply means that they have equal rights,
i.e., they must be given equal consideration in the formulation and application of the law of the land and the actions of its government and people."[42]

The principle of equal rights therefore, does not mean that every student
is to be *treated* equally. Some, depending on their ability or aptitude, may
need less or more attention than others. This *is* unequal treatment. But if
such treatment is a result of equal consideration, it may be viewed as fair.
It would not be fair for a teacher to spend as much time with a student who
does not need his assistance as with one who does.

[40]M. Scriven, *Student Values as Educational Objectives*; L. Kohlberg, "Moral Education in the Schools . . . ," *School Review*, Spring 1966, pp. 1–30.
[41]M. Scriven, *Student Values as Educational Objectives*, p. 8.
[42]Michael Scriven, *Primary Philosophy* (New York: McGraw-Hill, 1966), p. 242.

If one accepts justice as a fundamental principle to guide value education, specific procedural or behavioral values then become defensible, but only to the extent that they provide for equal consideration; only if they do not conflict with other values of the teacher that he considers more just; and only if they do not conflict with any values of students which are themselves more just. Given these stipulations, the teaching of such values is justified.

This does not mean, however, that we teach students to accept our conclusion that a particular way of behaving or proceeding is good because we tell them that it is. As was urged in Chapters 3 and 5, teachers should encourage and expect students to assess for themselves the validity of a given conclusion in terms of the amount and kind of evidence that exists to support it. Conclusions of value are no exception. Teachers should encourage and expect students to want to know the reasoning behind *any* assertion.

This is especially important with regard to values, because conclusions presented "without understanding of the arguments for them are rejected as soon as they conflict with inclinations. This is the distinction between teaching and brainwashing, and it can only be implemented gradually, since some values—a degree of obedience to parental commands, for example—must be indoctrinated in the infant before he can understand the reasons for them."[43] As students grow older, however, they become increasingly capable of understanding and evaluating rationally the reasons for various conclusions and recommendations.

It is in this regard that teaching students to distinguish among different types of value-claims becomes important. A value-claim is, as indicated earlier, a statement that a certain idea, object, act, policy, or way of behaving is good, right, ought to be supported, or should be carried out. There are three kinds of such claims to which students will frequently be exposed. They are personal value-claims, (what individuals prefer as a matter of taste); market value-claims (what groups of people like); and real value-claims (estimates of worth based on a certain set of applicable criteria).[44] Let us consider each of these types of claims a bit further.

Personal value-claims, as reflected in the statement "I prefer chocolate ice cream to other kinds of ice cream" are indications of taste. When an individual states that he prefers chocolate ice cream to other kinds of ice cream, he is not claiming that everyone should think so, he is merely indicating what he personally prefers.

Market value-claims refer to the kind of statement a person makes when he is trying to convey what a certain object (a stamp, a house, a painting) is

---

[43]M. Scriven, *Student Values as Educational Objectives*, p. 17.
[44]This is only a brief description. See Michael Scriven, *Value Claims in the Social Sciences* (Boulder, Col.: Social Science Education Consortium, Pub. #123, 1966).

worth in the open marketplace of buyers and sellers at a particular time. It is a generalized estimate *of the probability* that somebody will come along who will pay a given price (or close to it) for the object. It is of course possible that no one will come along to pay this price (e.g., $150,000 for an original Renoir). It is also possible that the generalized estimate of what the object is worth will change over time (e.g., the market value of a particular house may fluctuate over time). But market value-claims are not merely matters of taste or matters of opinion. The market value of an object is determined by comparing the prices at which objects with similar characteristics have (or have not) sold in the market. Such claims tell us something about the inclination of fairly large groups of people to pay a certain amount of money in order to obtain things for which they have a liking.

Real value-claims assert that a certain thing is better (i.e., of greater worth or merit) than other conceivable and available alternatives according to a particular set of criteria (e.g., money, energy, time, some combination of these, etc.) An individual making such a claim is not referring to the common (or even expert) opinion of what a particular thing is worth, nor is he merely expressing a personal opinion. He is claiming that a certain item or idea (or group of items or ideas) is better than another item or idea because all things considered, it outweighs its alternatives in terms of explicit criteria deemed important. Hence, the statement that the finest kind of leather is Brand X represents a real value-claim. So when a teacher claims that discussion is a better method of teaching social studies than lecture because (students stay attentive longer, interest is higher, etc.) he is claiming something for the discussion method that the lecture method does not possess. He is not merely stating a personal preference, nor is he expressing what teachers as a whole like.

Moral value-claims represent a particular kind of real value-claim claims involving the area of morality. "The domain of morality is simply the domain which is concerned with assessments of actions, attitudes, and behavior that may affect other people, judged from a particular point of view."[45] This point of view is, as argued earlier, the point of view of equal consideration, defensible both politically and practically.

A realization that people claim things to be of value for different reasons can help students determine the most appropriate means by which to validate various value-claims, and accordingly determine the appropriateness of these claims for themselves. The responsible (and wise) teacher will accordingly help students develop and acquire the necessary skills (by use of the strategies in this chapter as well as others) so that they can evaluate

[45]Michael Scriven, "Values and the Valuing Process," Unpublished paper prepared for the Diablo Valley Education Project, Orinda, California, Feb. 1971, p. 12.

various recommendations and conclusions in order to determine if they are worth endorsing themselves. As Scriven has suggested, it is not only immoral (i.e., unfair), but also unwise (i.e., impractical) to force on others views which they are given no chance to assess.[46]

NON-PEDAGOGICAL VALUES

The argument for procedural and behavioral values applies to non-pedagogical values as well. Teaching students simply to accept the conclusions of others without understanding the reasons behind these conclusions has a long history of ineffectiveness in schools. Techniques such as emotional pleas, appeals to conscience, slogans, preaching, rewards ("gold stars"), and setting "good examples" as a means of convincing others that something has merit or is worth doing simply don't work very well. "If admonition, lecture, sermon, or example were fully effective instruments in gaining compliance with codes of conduct, we would have reformed long ago the criminal, the delinquent, or the sinner."[47] The sad fact is that exhortation rarely produces committed, actively involved individuals. Essentially, it involves one-way communication, yet several studies have indicated that one-directional, persuasive communications are relatively ineffective.[48]

Hartshorne and May,[49] for example, found out some forty-odd years ago that didactic kinds of instruction had no effect on moral conduct, as measured by the degree to which experimental subjects cheated. Simply learning verbal rules about honesty had nothing to do with how these students acted. Those who cheated expressed as much of a belief in honesty as those who didn't.

Festinger[50] cites a study in which the use of fear and fear-arousing elements was introduced during training on oral hygiene. High school students were divided into four groups, with three of the groups hearing appeals

[46]M. Scriven, *Student Values as Educational Objectives*, p. 17.

[47]Solon T. Kimball, "Individualism and the Formation of Values," *Journal of Applied Behavioral Science*, 2, 1966, p. 481.

[48]Leon Festinger, "Behavioral Support for Opinion Change," *Public Opinion Quarterly*, 28, Fall 1964, pp. 404–417; Gordon W. Allport, *The Nature of Prejudice* (Reading, Mass.: Addison-Wesley, 1954); Elliott McGinnies, "Cross-Cultural Studies in Persuasion: An Attempt to Induce Both Direct and Generalized Attitude Change in Japanese Students," *Journal of Social Psychology*, 70, 1966, pp. 69–75; A. J. Sykes, "A Study in Attitude Change," *Occupational Psychology*, 40, 1966, pp. 31–41; H. Hartshorne and M. A. May, *Studies in the Nature of Character: Studies in Deceit*, Vol. I; *Studies in Self-Control*, Vol. II; *Studies in the Organization of Character*, Vol. III (New York: Macmillan, 1928–1930).

[49]H. Hartshorne and M. A. May, *Studies in the Nature of Character.*

[50]L. Festinger, "Behavioral Support for Opinion Change," *Public Opinion Quarterly*, pp. 404–417.

which attempted to persuade them to use proper methods of oral hygiene. The appeals were characterized as strong, moderate, and minimal. The strong appeal contained fear-arousing elements while the other two were more objective presentations of the facts. There were follow-up questionnaires to determine how many students had changed their practices to conform to the oral hygiene methods recommended. The relation between behavior and the degree to which students were made to feel concerned about oral hygiene was actually *in the reverse direction* from what one would expect from any simple relationship between attitude change and behavior. Festinger summed up his findings as follows: "All in all, we can detect no effect on behavior or even a clear and persistent change in opinion brought about by a persuasive communication."[51]

When we teach students that a particular action, idea, or way of thinking is good (or bad) without helping them to understand why we think it so, we do them a disservice, since we are not helping them to learn how to evaluate the conclusions of others in order to assess their applicability to themselves. As Hunt and Metcalf point out, when students are simply exposed to democratic practices without analysis of those practices, they "are inducted into democratic behavior without learning conceptually what democracy means. Such students cannot cope with criticisms of democracy, and when democracy conflicts with undemocratic alternatives, they cannot make rational choices. They also have difficulty in applying democratic attitudes to new situations.[52]

If teachers wish to help students learn to evaluate conclusions for themselves rather than blindly to accept them because their source is one of friendship, power, or prestige, therefore, they will not teach students that a particular value-claim (e.g., that schoolchildren should be bused, or that war should be eliminated) is good or bad, right or wrong, because we think so. They will teach students to seek out *the reasons why* the advocates (whomever they are) of a particular claim think a specified idea or action is good or bad (i.e., to identify the consequence or outcomes the advocates believe will occur as a result of the idea or action). They will also teach students to search for evidence, both pro and con, past and present, in order to determine the probability or degree to which the outcomes or consequences predicted are likely to happen. They will teach students that a particular action (recommendation, conclusion) is never good or bad in and of itself, but depends upon the circumstances under which it occurs and the degree to which the action, *under those circumstances and in that situation* is just or not. An action unjust at one time may be just at another.

[51]*Ibid.*, p. 410.
[52]M. P. Hunt and L. E. Metcalf, *Teaching High School Social Studies*, pp. 122–123.

Hence, lastly, they will teach students the meaning of justice, the fact that it is the basic principle upon which our society is based, and its potential usefulness as a universally applicable principle. Kohlberg is most clear in this regard:

> Justice is not a rule or a set of rules, it is a moral principle. By a moral principle, we mean a mode of choosing which is universal, a rule of choosing which we want all people to adopt always in all situations. We know it is all right to be dishonest and steal to save a life because it is just, because a man's right to life comes before another man's right to property. We know it is sometimes right to kill, because it is sometimes just. The Germans who tried to kill Hitler were doing right because respect for the equal values of lives demands that we kill someone murdering others in order to save their lives. There are exceptions to rules, then, but no exceptions to principles. A moral obligation is an obligation to respect the right or claim of another person. A moral principle is a principle for re-solving competing claims, you versus me, you versus a third person. There is only one principled basis for resolving claims, justice or equality. Treat every man's claim impartially regardless of the man. A moral principle is not only a rule of action but a reason for ac-tion. As a reason for action, justice is called respect for persons.[53]

But how? How can we teach these objectives? Let us consider an exam-ple. Many value-claims take the form of policy statements which contain words like "should," or "ought," and which advocate that a certain action or policy should (or should not) be done or put into effect. Capital punish-ment should be abolished. Marijuana should not be legalized. The United States should get out of Southeast Asia. Such statements also involve deci-sions of a highly personal nature and often are expressed in question form. Should I refuse induction into the armed forces? Should I drop out of school? Should I try marijuana? How can a teacher help students to evaluate such questions in the classroom? Here is one strategy, based on the work of Hunt and Metcalf,[54] that teachers can use. The instructional objectives in this regard are as follows:

Instructional Objectives: Given various policy questions or statements, students can:
   a. *define* the value terms involved as to their essential characteristics;
   b. *predict* consequences that might result if the policy in question is followed;
   c. *appraise* these consequences in the light of specified criteria; and
   d. *justify* the criteria used.

[53]Lawrence Kohlberg, "Education for Justice: A Modern Statement of the Platonic View," Ernest Burton Lecture on Moral Education, Harvard University, April 23, 1968, pp. 14–15 (mimeographed version).
[54]M. P. Hunt and L. E. Metcalf, *Teaching High School Social Studies*, pp. 133–139.

Suppose that a student argues that the intervention by the United States into the affairs of another nation is often justified. Other students disagree, arguing that such intervention is never justified. If the merits of the argument are to be understood and assessed by the rest of the class, the teacher will have to engage the class in a number of operations. The value term involved in the statement must be clearly defined, and the consequences of following this particular policy assessed. Accordingly, the first task of the teacher is to help students analyze and arrive at a clear definition of the term "intervention."

The teacher can ask students for *examples* of intervention. Was the sending of troops by the United States to the Dominican Republic in 1965 an example of intervention? What about Russia's sending tanks and troops into Hungary in 1956? Or India's sending of troops into East Pakistan in 1972? Are such efforts as the Marshall Plan or the Truman Doctrine examples? The Peace Corps? The activities of medical missionaries such as Albert Schweitzer or Tom Dooley? How about the actions of the United Nations in the Congo in 1960? What about the expansion of U.S. business interests into other countries? The teacher can also ask students for the defining *characteristics* of intervention (e.g., must a nation actually send troops into another country for an action to be considered intervention?).

These two procedures represent essentially an exercise in differentiating and defining as discussed in Chapter 5. Students are encouraged to differentiate between examples and non-examples of a concept (intervention) and to identify the essential characteristics which the examples of the concept possess. As Hunt and Metcalf[55] suggest, the method of comparison and contrast is particularly effective in this regard. Students can be helped to pin down the meaning of intervention as they compare and contrast examples of actions that represent intervention with examples of similar actions that do not represent intervention.

When the meaning of intervention is clear (at least in this instance), the question of consequences needs to be pursued. The teacher's task at this point is to encourage students to consider where a given policy might lead. This is essentially a question of fact. What might happen if the policy in question—in this instance, intervention—is followed? What consequences might result? Let us assume that the class agrees that invasion (the actual sending of troops across another nation's borders) constitutes one example of intervention. What might happen if invasion occurs? Will the invaded country benefit in some way? If so, how? What happens to the people of the country being invaded? What will be the repercussions for the United States? What effect will invasion have upon the rest of the world? What about long-range consequences, such as 20 years from now?

[55]*Ibid.*, p. 135.

Students often predict only certain kinds of consequences depending on their previous disposition toward the policy in question. Thus, those who favor intervention as a policy would predict consequences of a positive nature; those who are against intervention would predict negative consequences. Furthermore, many times students are not aware of what has resulted from the exercise of a given policy. When students suggest a very narrow or limited range of consequences, the teacher can help them expand their awareness by presenting them with evidence himself of various consequences that have resulted due to the carrying out of a particular policy. He needs to call to their attention any and all evidence that is more or less undeniable.

THE IMPORTANCE OF EVIDENCE

When a student argues that a particular policy will lead to certain consequences, the teacher's job is to encourage and assist the class to look for and present *evidence* of one sort or another that will enable them to judge whether the predicted consequences are likely to occur.

There are a number of kinds of evidence which students can present to support (or refute) their contention that certain consequences will occur as the result of following a particular policy. Suppose, for example, that a student argues that it is important for the United States to invade a certain country because such invasion will lead to a greater amount of internal order and stability within the country being invaded. What kinds of evidence could he and other students use to support (or refute) this contention?[56]

Personal Belief: One kind of evidence a student might offer is that he *personally* believes that invasion will lead to a greater amount of internal order and stability within the country being invaded. The student is indicating a personal preference or feeling. His evidence in support of invasion is his own personal, unique, subjective assessment. When pressed to defend his claim, the student may fall back on *intuition*—that is, he intuitively "knows" or "feels" that what he claims is so. The problem with this sort of evidence, however, is that it is essentially private—there is no way the student can demonstrate his intuitive knowing (feeling, etc.) so that others may substantiate or also experience it.

Group Consensus: A second kind of evidence that a student might offer is the consensus or agreement of others besides himself. He might find

[56]This is only a brief treatment. For a more extensive discussion, see the significant work done in this regard by D. W. Oliver and J. P. Shaver, *Teaching Public Issues in the High School*, and F. M. Newmann, *Clarifying Public Controversy*.

others (the more the better, at least in theory) who also believe that invasion is desirable, and offer their views in support of his claim. Much of the strength of this kind of evidence, however, depends on who the "others" are whose opinion he is offering in support of his own assertion that invasion will bring more internal order and stability to the invaded country (e.g., we probably would be more impressed if he presents the views of several noted political analysts or students of political affairs than if he presents the views of the local grocer).

Authoritative Opinion: A third source of evidence that students might use to support their claim, therefore, is the opinions of experts or "authorities" in the field to which the claim refers. The critical question here then becomes one of the degree to which we are willing to accept (and justified in accepting) the opinions of the experts. Whenever a student offers the opinion of experts or authorities to buttress his claim that certain consequences will result from following a certain policy, we are faced with the question of the authority's reliability. What makes an authority reliable? Oliver and Shaver suggest the following questions to ask of any authority in order to gain some idea of his reliability:

- Did the authority observe firsthand the event or events about which he speaks—that is, did he actually *witness* them in person?
- If the authority was not a firsthand observer, does he tell us *who told him* of that which he is suggesting—that is, the *original source* from which he got his data?
- Is the authority an expert on the subject or matter about which he is speaking—that is, what credentials (education, training, experience, etc.) does he possess which qualify him to speak authoritatively?
- Does any information exist about this authority that would cause us to question what he says—that is, is he personally *biased* in favor of or against that of which he is speaking?
- Does the authority contradict himself at any point—that is, is he consistent throughout in his reasoning?
- Is what the authority says supported by other authorities in his field?[57]

The preceding questions can help us judge the reliability of authorities, and in turn the reliability of their arguments that certain consequences are (or are not) likely to result from following a given policy.

The major weakness with authoritative evidence lies in the fact that authorities can be wrong too. In the fifteenth century, for example, the most noted authorities of the day agreed that the world was flat. In Gali-

[57]D. W. Oliver and J. P. Shaver, *Teaching Public Issues in the High School,* pp. 106–108.

leo's day, experts were convinced that the earth was the center of the universe. Medical authorities until only recently were "sure" that there were 48 chromosomes in the human body. Just because an expert "knows more" than a layman does not make him infallible. A key question to ask of any individual, be he layman or expert, therefore, is: "Upon what do you base your opinion or belief? Personal feelings? The consensus of other authorities? Documents or other written or audio sources produced by authorities? Your own observations or experiments?" This last query suggests another kind of evidence which students might present.

Public Verifiability. A fourth kind of evidence that a student might suggest is that he has personally observed, or otherwise experienced, the consequence that he is arguing will occur and that anyone else, if they will perform the same actions, with the equipment, conditions, personnel, and anything else involved as similar as possible, can observe or otherwise experience it as well. This kind of evidence, of course, is very powerful. The problem here is establishing the experiment or conditions so that observation can be repeated in a manner as similar to the first try as possible. This kind of evidence, though most convincing in certain situations, is much more difficult to come by in many others. In the intervention example discussed above, the teacher would need to encourage students to examine as many other similar situations in the past as they can find or he can suggest to determine how often, to what extent, and under what conditions the invasion of one country by another did, *in actuality*, lead to a greater amount of internal order and stability within the invaded countries.

The preceding are a few examples of different kinds of evidence that students might use to support or refute an assertion that certain consequences will occur as a result of following a given policy. Once a student has presented his evidence (no matter what kind it is), we are faced with the matter of *verification*. Does the evidence presented actually support, to the class's satisfaction, the likelihood that the predicted consequences will occur? If the supporting evidence offered is personal or authoritative judgment, the individual's reliability must be determined, and then his arguments either logically or empirically supported or refuted. If the supporting evidence consists of a set of defining characteristics, we check to see if such characteristics exist. If the supporting evidence consists of certain actions that would be performed or certain accomplishments that would be achieved, we check to see whether the alleged actions were indeed performed or the accomplishments indeed achieved in similar situations.

Before any profitable discussion can take place, however, the class must realize that the acceptance of different kinds of evidence may result in quite different assessments. Different individuals may come to quite different decisions depending on the kinds of evidence they accept. Teachers can help students realize that since there are different kinds of evidence that individuals can use to support or refute a claim, different people can view certain kinds of evidence as more acceptable than other kinds. What kind is most convincing and why? Honest men may legitimately differ as to the consequences they predict, but the man who will most often be correct in his predictions is the one who has the most evidence to support his predictions.

Appraisal of Consequences.   Once the consequences of a given policy have been determined, students must consider whether these consequences are desirable or not. Suppose that the class has amassed a considerable amount of evidence to indicate that intervention by one nation into the affairs of another under certain conditions would result in a greater amount of internal order and stability within the invaded country. Would such order and stability be good or bad?

As argued earlier, a defensible principle by which the desirability of any specific action or outcome can be justified is that of justice (equal consideration). Hence we ask students to consider if the rights of all the individuals concerned in this instance will be equally considered through the establishment of order and stability. What may be the short- and long-term effects of establishing such order on the people of the country being invaded? Of maintaining order? Are individual rights likely to be enhanced? restricted? Does it seem likely that the rights of all will be equally considered? If not, why not?

The teacher's job here is to encourage students to ask such questions, helping them to apply the criterion of justice consistently to all consequences that logic and empirical evidence seem to indicate are likely to occur should a given policy be carried out. Certain consequences may then be criticized as unjust (and thus not supportable) if other humanly possible alternatives exist that would be more likely to insure justice. If a particular real value-claim, therefore, can be shown on the basis of logic and considerable supporting evidence, along with a lack of much evidence to the contrary, to result in unjust consequences (e.g., the hoarding of food when people nearby are starving) at a particular time and place then we quite properly may consider and teach it to be a bad or wrong claim.

It is to be emphasized, however, that we teach as facts only those claims which really can be objectively established, such as the ineffectiveness of the death penalty; other claims we teach as hypotheses. This allows us to teach the truth or falsity of a given real value-claim (depending on the

TABLE 6.4

EXPLORATION OF POLICY QUESTIONS

Teacher	Student	Teacher Follow-through
What do you mean by _____? (the value term being used) or Can you give me an example of _____?	Describes characteristics or attributes of value term, and/or gives examples.	Lists characteristics on chalkboard for all to see. Seeks additional characteristics and/or examples if necessary.
What might happen if _____ took place? or What might be the consequences of _____ in this instance? in later years?	Suggests possible consequences.	Lists consequences on chalkboard or transparency. Suggests additional possible consequences.
What makes you think that _____ (consequence) will occur?	States reasons. Offers other evidence.	Lists evidence for all to see.
Does this evidence support the possibility of _____ (consequence) occurring? To what extent?	Evaluates adequacy, accuracy, relevance of evidence.	Helps evaluate evidence presented. Suggests additional evidence to consider.
Suppose _____ (consequence) is likely to occur. Would this be desirable? Would we want it to happen? Why?	Determines criteria by which to assess desirability of suggested consequences. Assesses each consequence predicted in terms of these criteria.	Helps determine criteria. Suggests additional criteria. Checks to insure that all consequences are checked against some criteria.
How do you justify defending (or not defending) _____ (consequence) as being a good (or bad) thing?	Discusses justification.	Encourages discussion.

extent to which it is supported or refuted by evidence available to all) without violating the rights of students to choose among conflicting claims when the evidence is not known or conclusive. (A summary of the steps involved in the preceding strategy is presented in Table 6.4.)

This, of course, does not mean that an action considered good (or bad) now may not be reversed in the future, should evidence as yet undiscovered so indicate. As Scriven points out, "the death penalty and the use of cigarettes may have to be reassessed in the light of new evidence, but that in no way justifies tentativeness in discussing their present status, which is exceptionally clear and well documented with respect to many (though naturally not all) of the most important questions about them."[58] Those claims for which *no* evidence exists at present to indicate that one alternative is better than another, we teach as hypotheses to be investigated and then accepted or rejected, depending on whether supportive or refutative evidence is eventually found. We openly admit that neither the claim nor its alternatives can be supported or refuted *at this time*, pointing out that data not presently in existence are needed before we can make a recommendation and suggesting that empirical trials of each alternative be carried out forthwith.

THE TEACHING OF JUSTICE

Kohlberg has argued that the schools are legally responsible for transmitting the value of justice. He writes:

> I am arguing that the only Constitutionally legitimate form of moral education in the schools is the teaching of justice, and that the teaching of justice in the schools requires just schools. It has been argued that the Supreme Court's Schemp decision calls for the restraint of public school education since such education is equivalent to the state propagation of religion, conceived as any articulated value system.
>
> The problems as to the legitimacy of moral education in the public schools disappear, however, if the proper content of moral education is recognized to be the values of justice which themselves prohibit the imposition of beliefs of one group upon another. The requirement implied by the Bill of Rights that the schools recognize the equal rights of individuals in matters of belief or values does not mean that the schools are not to be "value oriented." Recognition of equal rights does not imply value neutrality, i.e., the view that all value systems are equally sound. Because we respect the individual rights of members of particular groups in our society, it is sometimes believed that we must consider their values as valid as our own. Because we respect the rights of an Eichmann, however, we need not treat his values as equal to that of the values of liberty and justice. Public education is committed not only to maintenance of the rights of individuals but to the transmission of the values of respect for individual rights. The school is no more committed to value neutrality than is the government or the law. The school, like the government, is an institution with a basic function of maintaining and transmitting some, but not all, of the consensual

[58]M. Scriven, *Student Values as Educational Objectives*, p. 17.

values of society. The most fundamental values of a society are termed moral, and the major moral values in our society are the values of justice. According to any interpretation of the Constitution, the rationale for government is the preservation of the rights of individuals, i.e., of justice. The public school is as much committed to the maintenance of justice as is the court. Desegregation of the schools is not only a passive recognition of the equal rights of citizens to access to a public facility, like a swimming pool, but an active recognition of the responsibility of the school for "moral education," i.e., for transmission of the values of justice on which our society is founded.[59]

Note that Kohlberg emphasizes that the teaching of justice in the schools requires just schools in the first place. There is considerable evidence, however, that in many cases the schools are not just. Kozol[60] has described a school environment which represented the very antithesis of a democratic society and in which the rights of students were not equally considered. Glasser has presented a carefully documented case showing how the procedural, civil, and personal rights of students are continually violated by school practices and policies. He points out that "there are only two institutions in the United States which steadfastly deny that the Bill of Rights applies to them. One is the military and the other is the public schools. Both are compulsory. Taken together, they are the chief socializing institutions of our society."[61]

Kohlberg points out that any attempt at genuine moral education requires "full student participation in a school where justice is a living matter."[62] As an example of such a school, he quotes from the brochure of a boarding school in Rindge, New Hampshire:

> The sense of community is most strongly felt in the weekly meeting, consisting of faculty, their families and students. Decisions are made by concensus rather than by majority rule. This places responsibility on each member to struggle to see through his own desires to the higher needs of others and the community, while witnessing the deepest concerns of his conscience. The results of these decisions are not rules in the traditional sense, but agreements entered into by everyone and recorded as minutes.[63]

[59]L. Kohlberg, "Education for Justice: A Modern Statement of the Platonic View," pp. 11–12.

[60]Jonathan Kozol, *Death at an Early Age* (Boston: Houghton Mifflin, 1967).

[61]Ira Glasser, "Schools for Scandal—The Bill of Rights and Public Education," *Phi Delta Kappan*, Dec. 1969, p. 190.

[62]L. Kohlberg, "Education for Justice: A Modern Statement of the Platonic View," p. 26.

[63]*Ibid.*, p. 26. (This reference is to The Meeting School in Rindge.)

This is not to say that all schools must be like this one. It does suggest that the school described above might serve as a challenge to many teachers and administrators to think again about their own efforts to develop an understanding of the meaning of justice and to help students become more just themselves.

THE DEVELOPMENT OF MORAL REASONING

Kohlberg argues further that the concept of justice exists in all cultures, though individuals will differ in terms of the *reasons* they give for considering a particular action as good or bad, right or wrong. This difference in reasoning indicates a difference in levels of moral development. Using hypothetical situations (e.g., "Should the doctor 'mercy kill' a fatally ill woman requesting death because of her pain?"), he interviewed children and adults in the United States, Taiwan, Turkey, Malaysia, Mexico, and the Yucatan and classified their responses into one of six groups in terms of their reasoning with regard to one of 25 basic aspects of morality. In all the cultures he studied, he identified three levels of moral development, each of which contains two stages for a total of six forms of moral reasoning. These stages were found to exist in the same sequence in every culture, with each succeeding stage representing a higher level of reasoning than the one immediately preceding it. Kohlberg came to this conclusion due to the fact that no subject found to be at stages 1 through 4 had gone through stages 5 or 6, while those subjects at stages 5 and 6 had gone through stages 1 through 4. These six stages are summarized below:

LEVEL I—PREMORAL

Stage 1.—Obedience and punishment orientation. Egocentric deference to superior power or prestige, or a trouble-avoiding set. Objective responsibility.

Stage 2.—Naïvely egoistic orientation. Right action is that instrumentally satisfying the self's needs and occasionally other's. Awareness of relativism of value to each actor's needs and perspective. Naïve egalitarianism and orientation to exchange and reciprocity.

LEVEL II—CONVENTIONAL ROLE CONFORMITY

Stage 3.—Good-boy orientation. Orientation to approval and to pleasing and helping others. Conformity to stereotyped images of majority or natural role behavior, and judgment of intentions.

Stage 4.—Authority and social-order-maintaining orientation. Orientation to "doing duty" and to showing respect for authority and maintaining the given social order for its own sake. Regard for earned expectations of others.

LEVEL III—SELF-ACCEPTED MORAL PRINCIPLES

Stage 5.—Contractual legalistic orientation. Recognition of an arbitrary element or starting point in rules or expectations for the sake of agreement. Duty defined in terms of contract, general avoidance of violation of the will or rights of others, and majority will and welfare.

Stage 6.—Conscience or principle orientation. Orientation not only to actually ordained social rules but to principles of choice involving appeal to logical universality and consistency. Orientation to conscience as a directing agent and to mutual respect and trust.[64]

Examples of student reasoning with regard to one of the 25 basic aspects of morality considered at each stage—the motivation for moral action—are shown below:

Stage 1.—Obey rules to avoid punishment. Danny, age ten: (Should Joe tell on his older brother to his father?) "In one way it would be right to tell on his brother or his father might get mad at him and spank him. In another way it would be right to keep quiet or his brother might beat him up."

Stage 2.—Conform to obtain rewards, have favors returned, and so on. Jimmy, age thirteen: (Should Joe tell on his older brother to his father?) "I think he should keep quiet. He might want to go someplace like that, and if he squeals on Alex, Alex might squeal on him."

Stage 3.—Conform to avoid disapproval, dislike by others. Andy, age sixteen: (Should Joe keep quiet about what his brother did?) "If my father finds out later, he won't trust me. My brother wouldn't either, but I wouldn't have a *conscience* that he (my brother) didn't." "I try to do things for my parents; they've always done things for me. I try to do everything my mother says; I try to please her. Like she wants me to be a doctor, and I want to, too, and she's helping me to get up there."

Stage 4.—Conform to avoid censure by legitimate authorities and resultant guilt. Previous example also indicative of this.

Stage 5.—Conform to maintain the respect of the impartial spectator judging in terms of community welfare or to maintain a relation of mutual respect. Bob, age sixteen: "His brother thought he could trust him. His brother wouldn't think much of him if he told like that."

Stage 6.—Conform to avoid self-condemnation. Bill, age sixteen: (Should the husband steal the expensive black-market drug needed to save his wife's life?) "Lawfully no, but morally speaking I think

---

[64]L. Kohlberg, "Moral Education in the Schools: A Developmental View," *School Review*, Spring 1966, p. 7.

I would have done it. It would be awfully hard to live with myself afterward, knowing that I could have done something which would have saved her life and yet didn't for fear of punishment to myself."[65]

Kohlberg argues that the concept of stages implies sequence—that is, that all children in all cultures must go through these stages in order, though it is possible for a student to be "fixated" at a particular stage.

The implications for value education in this regard suggest that the development of individuals able to *act* justly (i.e., give equal consideration to the claims of others) requires the development of their moral reasoning so that they are able to *perceive* and *understand* what the claims of others are and that this lies not in having students memorize the rules or values of others, but in the development of individuals capable and desirous of reasoning at stages 5 and 6.

Kohlberg's research in this regard suggests that when individuals are thinking at the level of stages 5 and 6, they are more likely to act justly, that is, to consider the rights of others. One study of cheating, involving 100 sixth-grade children, the majority of whom were at the first four stages of moral reasoning, showed that 75 percent of these children cheated, while only 20 percent of the students at stages 5 and 6 cheated. In this instance, cheating, "the critical issue is recognition of the element of contract and agreement implicit in the situation, and the recognition that while it doesn't seem so bad if one person cheats, what holds for all must hold for one."[66] Another study showed that principled college students (those at stages 5 and 6) were more likely to engage in an act of moral courage or resistance when an authoritarian experimenter ordered them to inflict pain on another subject.[67]

Kohlberg also found, in a series of other experimental studies, that children and adolescents *prefer* the highest level of moral thinking that they can understand. They are able to comprehend all stages lower than their own, often one stage higher than their own, and occasionally, two stages higher than their own. Important in its implications for value education here is that once students understand the stage that is one higher than their own they tend to prefer it to their own. Just as important in terms of its implication for classroom instruction is the finding that students with extensive peer-group participation (e.g., discussion of moral dilemmas) advance more quickly through the stages than students without such participation.[68]

[65]L. Kohlberg, "Moral Education in the Schools: A Developmental View," p. 8.
[66]L. Kohlberg, "Education for Justice," p. 21.
[67]*Ibid.*
[68]L. Kohlberg, "Moral Education in the Schools," p. 17.

These findings suggest the following procedures for teachers to consider, therefore, if they wish to advance moral thinking of the kind illustrated by the examples of student reasoning at stages 5 and 6:

1. Provide frequent opportunities for students to discuss moral dilemmas similar to the ones used by Kohlberg, or like the one presented on page 241 of this chapter. There are a number of sources which include such dilemmas that teachers might consult.[69]
2. Try to determine the level of moral thinking at which various students are operating. This can be done by selecting a number of statements or actions from various dilemma situations and asking students to analyze them as to whether they are justifiable or not and then to give their reasons as to why they think they either are or not. Notice that it is not important for our purposes here *whether* they think a given statement or action is right or wrong, but *why* they think this.
3. Encourage and promote discussion between students who are operating at one stage of moral reasoning with other students operating one stage higher. When students appear to understand a higher level and to be reasoning on that level, engage them in discussion with individuals reasoning at the next higher stage.

The development of moral character, however, is also related to the development of the student's ego strength, which includes the development of such cognitive abilities as the intelligent prediction of consequences, the tendency to choose a greater long-term reward over a lesser but more immediate short-term reward, the ability to keep one's attention focused on a given topic or item for a fairly extended period of time, as well as many of the abilities described in Chapter 5.[70] Whereas the development of the student's moral reasoning increases his ability to make distinctively moral judgments, the development of the student's ego abilities increases his ability to apply his judgmental capacities to guide and criticize his own actions. The strategies described in Chapter 5 are designed so as to encourage the development of many of these ego abilities. As Kohlberg points out, "the problem of insuring correspondence between developing moral judgments and the child's action is not primarily a problem of eliciting moral self-criticism from the child. (It is) the development of the ego abilities involved in the non-moral *or cognitive tasks* upon which the classroom

[69]See any or all of the following: Jack R. Fraenkel, ed., *Inquiry into Crucial American Problems*, 16 vols. (Englewood Cliffs, N.J.: Prentice-Hall, 1970); Donald W. Oliver and Fred M. Newmann, Directors, *AEP Public Issues Series*, 24 vols. (Columbus, Ohio: American Education Publications, 1968–1970); Charles N. Quigley and Richard P. Longaker, eds., *Conflict, Politics, and Freedom* (New York: Ginn, 1968); William Goodykoontz, ed., *Law, You, the Police, and Justice* (New York: Scholastic, 1968).

[70]L. Kohlberg, "Moral Education in the Schools," p. 6.

centers. As an example, an experimental measure of high stability of attention (low-reaction time variability) in a simple monotonous task has been found to clearly predict resistance to cheating. . . . The encouragement of these attentional ego capacities is not a task of moral education as such but of general programming of classroom learning activities."[71]

In short, then, a variety of research suggests that conventional didactic kinds of value education efforts (e.g., exhortation, praise, and punishment) have little effect on the development of moral individuals. The development of moral character is directly related to two factors—the development of the student's moral reasoning and the development of the student's ego strength. The strategies presented in this chapter can help teachers with regard to the former and the strategies described in Chapter 5 can help them with regard to the latter.

The strategies presented in this chapter rest on the author's convictions that it is important (i.e., of value) to help students to identify their own values, to deal rationally with value conflicts, to empathize with individuals caught up in a value conflict, and to reflect upon the consequences of certain actions in terms of the degree to which they promote justice.

A further conviction is that the use of strategies like the ones presented in this chapter can help teachers become more systematic in helping students explore their own and others' values, and that this too is good. Teachers must first think about their objectives, of course. They must also provide relevant learning activities (e.g., films which present value conflicts, open-ended filmstrips, panel and class discussions on moral dilemmas, guest speakers, student field trips, essays on open-ended topics like "What makes me angry," role-playing, sociodramas, and the like) that will encourage students to discuss and analyze value matters. But the accomplishment of value education cannot be left to learning activities alone (no matter how varied and exciting they may be). Teaching strategies that identify specific procedures (such as the examples presented earlier) that teachers may use to help students identify and reflect upon their own and other's values must also be designed if we are to encourage value analysis and development in social studies classrooms.

SUMMARY

This chapter dealt with the nature of values and value conflicts. The main thesis of the chapter was that the teaching of values in social studies classrooms is not only unavoidable, but justifiable, provided that the values to be taught are consistent with the principle of justice. Several strategies

[71]*Ibid.*, p. 26. (Italics added.)

that teachers can use to help students deal with values and value conflicts were discussed, and examples of the kinds of materials that can be used to employ these strategies were presented. The development of moral reasoning was then briefly discussed, and procedures that teachers might use to develop higher levels of moral reasoning were suggested.

EXERCISES*

I. Listed below are several objectives. Some of these statements suggest specific examples of behavior that a teacher might look for as some evidence that students are acquiring one or more particular values. Which ones? If students displayed these behaviors, would we be justified in saying that a particular value then exists? Why or why not? What value? How can we tell when a value exists?

a. Given a discussion setting or other situation in which students can express their ideas without censure or ridicule, students make statements that describe in the opinion of a disinterested observer the probable feelings or other thoughts of people previously studied.

b. Given a discussion setting in which students are encouraged to speak out on a variety of issues of concern to them, students respect the viewpoints of others.

c. Students appreciate a considerable diversity of opinion.

d. Given a situation in which he is encouraged to express his own thoughts, a student shows a recognition and acceptance of the merits of different ways of life.

e. Given a situation in which he is encouraged to express his own thoughts, a student responds to statements of other students and the teacher in ways that the teacher judges to be fair toward the people involved and that show recognition and acceptance of the merits of different ways of life and points of view.

f. Students challenge derogatory or belittling statements about people of different cultures or about people who exhibit unusual behavior.

g. Given a context in which ideas and/or explanations have been stated, a student occasionally suggests that additional evidence or a different line of reasoning might lead to changes in one or more of the ideas or explanations and/or gives evidence that he recognizes the tentativeness of many ideas that he or others offer.

*The author's suggestions are on pages 402–3.

II. Listed below are a number of statements. Place a "VJ" in front of those which are value judgments, a "D" in front of those that are definitions, and an "F" or "G" in front of those that are statements of fact (F) or generalization (G).

   _____ **a.** An excellent teacher is one who inspires his students to want to learn.

   _____ **b.** Dwight D. Eisenhower was a decent man.

   _____ **c.** Sacramento is the capital of the state of California.

   _____ **d.** Good berry pickers can pick at least seven full bushels of berries per hour.

   _____ **e.** Chairs are things to sit on.

   _____ **f.** Mary Jameson is a beautiful but rather lazy woman.

   _____ **g.** A man who works mechanically and does not think for himself is nothing but a robot.

   _____ **h.** James Michener is the author of *Sayonara*.

   _____ **i.** Marijuana should be legalized.

   _____ **j.** Man's ways of living are affected by the social and physical environment in which he lives.

III. Which do you think would be the more adequate way to determine what a person values—by what he says or what he does? Why?

IV. The steps involved in the strategies of identifying values, exploring value conflicts, and developing empathy have been scrambled below. Indicate the correct order by numbering each statement in the order in which it belongs (I.e., place a "1" before the first step involved in the strategy, a "2" before the second step, etc.)

Identifying Values

   a. _____ explaining why the behavior of a certain individual or group occurred as it did

   b. _____ identifying similarities and differences among values identified and discussed

   c. _____ recalling from previous study the behavior of a certain individual or group

   d. _____ making inferences about the values of others

   e. _____ making inferences about one's own values

   f. _____ identifying one's own behavior in a similar situation

Exploring Value Conflicts

a. ———— predicting consequences of various alternatives an individual might follow

b. ———— determining which of two or more possible alternatives should be pursued

c. ———— recalling one's own actions in a similar experience

d. ———— stating alternatives open to the key figure in a story or film

e. ———— explaining why a certain alternative should be pursued in reference to others

f. ———— considering other alternatives that might have been pursued in a given situation

g. ———— evaluating one's own choice of alternatives

Developing Empathy

a. ———— offering reasons as to why an individual felt a certain way in a particular situation

b. ———— recalling a similar situation in which another individual has experienced similar feelings

c. ———— offering some conclusions about the feelings of people in various situations

d. ———— inferring how an individual felt in a certain situation

e. ———— describing one's own or another's feelings in a similar situation

f. ———— describing what happened during a fictitious or real event

V. The steps involved in helping a student evaluate a policy decision are likewise scrambled below. Indicate the correct order by numbering each statement as to the order in which it belongs by placing a "1" before the first step a teacher needs to take, a "2" before the second step, etc.

    a. ———— Evaluate consequences of proposed policy.

    b. ———— Define nature of policy to be evaluated.

    c. ———— Justify the criteria by which consequences are assessed.

    d. ———— Determine criteria by which to evaluate consequences.

    e. ———— Predict consequences of following the proposed policy.

VI. Try out some of the strategies described in this chapter. What difficulties (if any) do you encounter? What suggestions would you have for improving the strategies?

VII. Listed below is a statement written by Martin Luther King, Jr. while in jail in Birmingham, Alabama, which, according to Kohlberg's six-stage scale, typifies stage 6 moral reasoning.

There is a type of constructive non-violent tension which is necessary for growth. Just as Socrates felt it was necessary to create a tension in the mind so that individuals could rise from the bondage of half-truths, so must we see the need for nonviolent gadflies to create the kind of tension in society that will help men rise from the dark depths of prejudice and racism.

One may well ask, "How can you advocate breaking some laws and obeying others?" The answer lies in the fact that there are two types of laws, just and unjust. One has not only a legal but a moral responsibility to obey just laws. One has a moral responsibility to disobey unjust laws. An unjust law is a human law that is not rooted in eternal law and natural law. Any law that uplifts human personality is just, any law that degrades human personality is unjust. An unjust law is a code that a numerical or power majority group compels a minority group to obey but does not make binding on itself. This is difference made legal.*

Examine several weekly news-magazines and the daily newspaper and select a number of statements made by various public figures. Using the Kohlberg scale on pages 269–70, try to determine what level of moral reasoning the statements typify.

VIII. Select a number of statements made by one particular public figure over a period of time. At what level of moral reasoning is he operating?

---

*Martin Luther King, Jr., "Letter from a Birmingham Jail," in *Why We Can't Wait* (New York: New American Library, 1965). Quoted in Lawrence Kohlberg, "Education for Justice: A Modern Statement of the Platonic View," Ernest Burton Lecture on Moral Education, Harvard University, April 23, 1968 (mimeographed copy).

CHAPTER VII

SUMMATIVE
EVALUATION

Assessment of student progress toward desired objectives is essential if teachers are to help students learn. Subject matter, learning activities, and teaching strategies are to no avail if teachers have no systematic idea of student progress. Thus the need for summative evaluation devices.

The first section of the chapter discusses a number of basic characteristics that all tests should possess and suggests certain basic rules of test construction that are helpful in preparing tests which have these characteristics.

The second section discusses the measurement of understanding. Similarities and differences that exist between objective and essay tests are presented and certain conditions that are especially appropriate for using each type identified. Examples of poor and improved objective and essay questions are presented. Common errors to avoid in order to write good questions in each category are discussed. A method for scoring student responses to essay questions is illustrated.

The third section discusses the measurement of thinking. Sample test items designed to measure a number of intellectual abilities and skills are presented.

The fourth section discusses the measurement of non-cognitive objectives. Several devices for measuring such objectives are presented and discussed.

The fifth section discusses the measurement of social and academic skills. Several examples of test items or procedures that teachers can use to assess these kinds of objectives are presented.

Lastly, the sixth section of the chapter briefly describes five basic steps for teachers to consider in order to increase the adequacy of their evaluation efforts.

When you have finished reading the chapter, therefore, you should be able to do the following:

- *define* what is meant by the terms "validity," "reliability," and "objectivity" with regard to test items, and *describe* at least five rules of test-making considered basic by experts that teachers can use to prepare valid, reliable, and objective tests;

- *state* a number of similarities and differences that exist between objective and essay type tests, and *describe* at least five conditions that are especially appropriate for using each type;
- *identify* a poor objective or essay test question, and *describe* a number of errors to avoid in order to write good objective and essay test items;
- *explain* how to score an essay test objectively;
- *distinguish* between test items designed to measure the attainment of knowledge, and test items designed to measure other, "higher," intellectual abilities and skills; and *write* test items yourself in each category;
- *name* several (at least seven) devices that a teacher can use to measure the attainment of non-cognitive objectives, and actually *use* such devices yourself;
- *describe* at least five basic steps that teachers might consider in order to increase the adequacy of their evaluation efforts.

As was discussed in Chapter 1, education represents a process whereby teachers (and often students) seek to help students change in certain ways they consider desirable. These changes include not only the acquisition of knowledge, but also the development of thinking and other types of skills, the formation of attitudes, the understanding and exploration of feelings, and the development of values. Such changes represent objectives of instruction. Evaluation (more precisely *summative* evaluation) "designates a process of appraisal which involves the acceptance of specific values and the use of a variety of instruments of observation, including measurement, as the bases for value judgments."[1] When teachers evaluate student progress, they are judging whether certain changes have occurred, or certain objectives have (at least to some extent) been attained.

Chapter 2 identified and discussed a number of informal diagnostic tools that teachers can use to gather evidence about their students' ability and characteristics both before and during instruction. Many of these devices can also be used for evaluating student achievement once a certain amount of instruction has been completed. The major part of this chapter, however, will concentrate on discussing the construction and improvement of the more traditional means of evaluation—pencil-and-paper tests. Before we can discuss and present examples of different types of items that could be used in such tests, however, we shall discuss a number of basic characteristics that all tests should possess.

[1]Ralph W. Tyler, "The Functions of Measurement in Improving Instruction," in E. F. Lindquist, ed., *Educational Measurement* (Washington, D.C.: American Council on Education, 1951), p. 48.

VALIDITY

The most important characteristic that any test should possess is that of validity. The usual definition of a valid test is that it measures what it is supposed to measure. If we are measuring changes in student behavior, for example, we want an evaluative device that will indicate to some degree whether any change, of the kind we are interested in bringing about, has occurred.

A valid achievement test, therefore, would actually measure the kinds of changes identified in an instructional objective. If one objective of instruction is that students will be able to compare and contrast family structures in different cultures, then a test item, to be valid, must actually require students in some form or another to do such comparing and contrasting. For example, consider the following:

> *Instructional Objective:* Given appropriate data, students can apply previously acquired information to draw a correct conclusion that is based on the data they are given.
> *Evaluative Item:*
>   In country A, 50 percent of national income is spent on food, while in country B only 25 percent is so spent. Which of these is a reasonable conclusion to draw from these figures?
>   1. A smaller percentage of the population is engaged in agriculture in A than in B.
>   2. Per capita income is higher in B than in A.
>   3. A is considerably better fed than B.
>   4. B is less highly industrialized than A.[2]

Is the foregoing a valid item? Yes, it is, because it asks students to demonstrate that they can perform as the instructional objective requests, in this case, to apply previously learned information to draw a correct conclusion from data.

The concept of validity is very important for teachers to consider. Teachers must be clear about their instructional objectives. They must also be clear about what behaviors, products, or experiences will constitute evidence that their objectives have been or are being attained. If they do not

[2]Harry D. Berg, "The Objective Test Item," in Harry D. Berg, ed., *Evaluation in the Social Studies*, Thirty-fifth Yearbook of the National Council for the Social Studies (Washington, D.C.: National Council for the Social Studies, 1965), p. 60. Reprinted with the permission of the National Council for the Social Studies and Harry D. Berg.

know what they are looking for, they obviously cannot select or prepare evaluative items to measure whether the objectives have been attained.

An important part of validity is *comprehensiveness*. All the various categories of objectives should be appraised to determine the degree to which they are being attained. Not only knowledge, but also the development of thinking, attitudes, feelings, values, and skills needs to be assessed. To ensure comprehensiveness, two-way grids or charts can be used to classify objectives and to make certain that all categories will be evaluated. Table 7.1 illustrates such a chart. The outline for a unit on the New Deal was presented in Chapter 3. The unit content is listed vertically along the lefthand side of the page. The behaviors desired are listed along the top of the page. Wherever an X appears in a box, this indicates an objective to be attained. Thus one objective, as indicated on the chart, is that students will be able to generalize about the effects of the Depression upon people's lives. Such a two-way chart is an effective device that teachers can use to ensure that all categories of objectives are being evaluated.

A further requirement of a valid test is that it should reflect fairly closely the same proportion of emphasis that different objectives have received. Table 7.2 for example, illustrates the kinds of questions a hypothetical test on the New Deal unit might contain, and the types of questions that will be asked about each topic. Thus there will be ten recall, five explanatory, and 15 analytic questions asked about the Nature of the Depression. The subtotals for each kind of question suggest that the test emphasizes recall questions the most while questions requiring synthesis make up only 10 percent of the total. Such an analysis can point up strengths and weaknesses of a particular test that might otherwise go unnoticed.

RELIABILITY

A second important characteristic that all tests should possess is reliability. A reliable test is *consistent*—that is, if it is repeated, students score roughly the same as they did the first time they took the test. For example, if a student takes a test that asks him to describe what kinds of crops would grow in various climatic zones around the world, a second testing on the same or similar items should place him in the same relative position as he was in after completing the first test.

As Ebel[3] suggests, several factors influence the degree to which a test is reliable. If the items are too easy, too difficult, or unclear, they will

[3]Robert S. Ebel, *Measuring Educational Achievement* (Englewood Cliffs, N.J.: Prentice-Hall, 1965), pp. 310–311.

TABLE 7.1

A TWO-WAY ORGANIZATIONAL CHART FOR OBJECTIVES

COURSE CONTENT (Content aspect of objectives)	Demonstrates understanding of key facts, concepts, and ideas (knowledge)	Demonstrates ability to conceptualize (thinking)	Demonstrates ability to generalize (thinking)	Applies previously learned information (thinking) in a new and different situation	Identifies and locates needed information (academic skill)	Gives oral or written report on results of research (academic skill)	Works effectively with others in small groups (social skill)	Listens to divergent views (attitudes and values)	Encourages variety of ideas (attitudes and values)	Helps others in joint projects (attitudes and values)
I. Nature of the depression A. Problems facing the new administration in 1933	X				X	X				
B. Effects of the depression on people's lives	X	X	X	X	X	X		X		
II. Totalitarian models		X	X	X		X	X	X		
A. Fascist Italy – the idea of the corporate state	X				X					
B. Germany – the program of Adolf Hitler	X				X					
C. The Soviet Union – a planned economy	X				X					
D. Appeals in the U.S.		X	X			X	X	X		
1. Socialists	X			X	X					
2. Townsend Plan	X			X	X					
3. EPIC–Upton Sinclair	X			X	X					
4. Huey Long	X			X	X					
5. Father Coughlin	X			X	X					
III. Dealing with the depression A. Pre-1932 philosophy of government	X	X		X	X	X		X		
B. Legislation		X	X			X		X		
1. Emergency relief	X			X	X					
2. Recovery	X			X	X					
3. Reform	X			X	X					
C. Reactions to FDR's program	X	X	X			X				
IV. Evaluation of the New Deal		X	X	X		X	X	X	X	X
A. Herbert Hoover	X					X				
B. FDR	X					X				
C. Frank Freidel	X					X				
D. Dexter Perkins	X					X				
E. James MacGregor Burns	X					X				
F. Howard Zinn	X					X				

TABLE 7.2

PROPORTION OF DIFFERENT TYPES OF OBJECTIVES
TO BE ASSESSED AT THE END OF A UNIT
OF INSTRUCTION ON THE NEW DEAL

Unit Content	Recall	Explanation	Analysis	Synthesis	T
I. Nature of the Depression	10	5	15		30
II. Totalitarian Models	15	10			25
III. Dealing with the Depression	10	15	5		30
IV. Evaluation of the New Deal			5	10	15
Total	35	30	25	10	100

yield unreliable scores. If the students who take the test vary greatly in personal characteristics (e.g., alertness, drive, emotional stability, etc.), the scores will be less reliable. If the person who scores the test papers does not establish and apply uniform standards to all test papers (rather than momentary considerations), the scores will be unreliable. Furthermore, the test must provide *enough* examples of the behavior we are attempting to assess. If we wish to draw some conclusions about a student's ability to conceptualize, for example, we must give him more than one opportunity to do so. We cannot reliably measure his ability if we only allow him one opportunity to demonstrate that ability. We cannot reliably assess how much a student knows about the Soviet Union if we only ask him one question about Moscow.

Reliability and validity are closely intertwined. If a test has validity it must have reliability. If a test measures what it purports to measure, it also measures consistently. As DeCecco points out, "If a test fails to measure with consistency, then it cannot purport to measure anything at all. A rubber yardstick which changes its length as you apply different amounts of tension to its ends is neither a reliable nor a valid measure of length or distance."[4] The reverse is not true, however. A test can be reliable but not valid. A teacher might teach about certain aspects of African life, for example, and then construct a test which questions students about other aspects that they hadn't studied. All students would probably do quite poorly on successive administrations of the test. The results, though undesirable, would certainly be reliable. The test, however, would certainly not be a valid measure of what the students know about Africa.

[4]John P. DeCecco, *The Psychology of Learning and Instruction: Educational Psychology* (Englewood Cliffs, N.J.: Prentice-Hall, 1968), p. 616.

OBJECTIVITY

A third characteristic that all tests should possess is objectivity. Objectivity refers to the absence of subjective judgments. It is very difficult to attain, and is probably never attained completely. Many teachers assume, for example, that "objective" tests (e.g., true-false, multiple-choice, etc.) are not subjective. While they are more objective than essay tests as far as scoring is concerned, even true-false and multiple-choice tests possess some subjective characteristics. What teacher has not argued (sometimes heatedly!) with a student over the correct response to a multiple-choice question? DeCecco suggests two factors that may reduce the objectivity of objective items: "(1) The question may fail to indicate all the conditions and qualifications necessary to make one and only one response correct; (2) the question may pertain to opinions and theories about which there is little agreement."[5] Submitting objective test items to a panel of judges for review and then throwing out those items upon which the judges cannot agree is one way of improving the objectivity of objective items. The answers to essay tests, unfortunately, are even more open to disagreement, since the judgment of "experts" cannot be previously obtained.

BASIC RULES OF TEST-MAKING

The characteristics of validity, reliability, and objectivity that all tests should possess suggest a number of basic rules for teachers to consider in making up their tests. The Educational Testing Service[6] suggests the following as basic rules of test construction that all teachers should consider:

(1) Be clear as to the purpose of your test. Do you wish to determine how well your students have attained a certain set of objectives? Do you wish to rank your students according to differences in their abilities? Do you wish to diagnose individual strengths and weaknesses, or other characteristics? Check to see that your test assesses all the different kinds of objectives you have been trying to develop.

(2) Plan, *in writing*, the proportion of different kinds of questions you will ask. Use of a two-way grid, as shown in Table 7.2 on page 283, is an excellent device to help you in this regard.

[5]J. P. DeCecco, *The Psychology of Learning and Instruction*, p. 617.
[6]Quentin Stodola *et al., Making the Classroom Test: A Guide for Teachers*, #4, 2nd ed. (Princeton, N.J.: Educational Testing Service, 1961), p. 14.

(3) If your purpose is primarily one of *diagnosing* a basic skill (e.g., ability to interpret maps), prepare at least ten questions—preferably more —on *each skill* you are assessing.

(4) If your purpose is primarily one of diagnosing individual strengths and weaknesses in a particular skill (e.g., ability to write a logical and coherent composition), prepare at least ten questions—preferably more— on *each aspect* of the skill that students must master in order to attain the skill as a whole. For example, a teacher named Miss Barstow was faced with the challenge of helping a group of remedial students to improve their composition writing. The English Department of the school had designated six basic types of errors in composition writing that the teacher was to try and correct. These included:

1. Run-together sentences, or the comma-splice:
   "It is snowing very hard today, the children will probably go sleigh-riding tomorrow."
2. Incomplete sentences:
   "When the boat struck the rock and the water poured in and the sailors climbed up into the rigging."
3. Misspelling of common everyday words:
   "You should recieve an answer tomorrow."
4. Disagreement between subject and verb:
   "When they was told what to do, they did it."
5. Confusion as to the case of pronouns:
   "The man refused to tell either Harry or I where the money was hidden."
6. Use of unacceptable colloquial expressions:
   "He could of won the race if he had tried harder."[7]

The teacher developed a test whose purpose was to find out the extent to which each of her students made each of the preceding errors. Miss Barstow proceeded to construct her test as follows:

> To get an accurate picture for individual diagnosis, Miss Barstow realized that she needed a fairly long test. She wrote 20 items for each of the six kinds of error—a total of 120 items. Then she wrote 30 sentences that had no errors at all. She now had a total of 150 items in the test. She put all these items in random order and left enough space between them for the students to write in the necessary corrections. She told the students that, although 30 of the sentences were correct, each of the others contained a common error in either spelling, usage, or grammar. Then she allowed the students two fifty-minute periods to make whatever changes they thought necessary to correct the sentences.

[7]From *Making the Classroom Test: a Guide for Teachers*, p. 13. Copyright © 1959, 1961, 1969 by Educational Testing Service. Reprinted by permission.

After the students had finished the test, Miss Barstow divided the sentences into the types of error they represented and then scored each group of 20 sentences separately. Thus she had six scores for every student, one for each of the six kinds of error. The 30 correct sentences were not included in the scoring. Their function was to make it a bit more difficult for the students to identify the errors.

Using the test results, Miss Barstow was able to plan remedial work for each student's specific weaknesses.[8]

(5) If your purpose is primarily one of determining how well your class has mastered a particular set of objectives, you should develop a test that parallels work in class.

(6) If your purpose is primarily one of ranking students in the order of their achievement, your questions should focus on the "critical" points of learning—i.e., the knowledge or responses that go beyond the obvious, but that will distinguish those students who know or can do more from those who know or can do less. Questions on these "critical" points will usually involve the higher mental processes such as comprehending, translating, interpreting, applying, analyzing, synthesizing, and judging, rather than just remembering. Examples of items that appraise student ability to use such processes will be presented later in the chapter.

After a teacher has decided on the purpose or purposes for which he is testing, and prepared in writing a plan for the test he wants to develop, he then needs to decide on the form of test that he wants to use. The most common forms that teachers prepare are objective tests and essay tests. When should each be used?

OBJECTIVE TESTS VS. ESSAY TESTS

There are no clear-cut rules for using either essay or objective tests. It is helpful, however, to be aware of the major characteristics of each type so that you can decide which is the more suitable on different occasions for the purpose you have in mind. Ebel[9] describes the following differences and similarities between objective and essay tests.

Differences

Objective tests	Essay tests
1. Requires students to choose among two or more alternatives.	1. Requires the student to plan his own answer and express it in his own words.

[8]From *Making the Classroom Test: a Guide for Teachers*, p. 13. Copyright © 1959, 1961, 1969 by Educational Testing Service. Reprinted by permission.
[9]R. E. Ebel, *Measuring Educational Achievement*, pp. 84–109.

Differences

Objective tests	Essay tests
2. Consists of many rather specific questions requiring only brief answers.	2. Consists of relatively few, more general questions which call for extended answers.
3. Students spend most of their time reading and thinking.	3. Students spend most of their time in thinking and writing.
4. Quality is determined by the skill of the test constructor.	4. Quality is determined largely by skill of the grader reading.
5. Is relatively tedious and difficult to prepare, but easy to score.	5. Is easy to prepare, but relatively tedious and difficult to score.
6. Affords much freedom for test constructor to express his knowledge and values.	6. Affords much freedom for the student to express his knowledge and individuality.
7. States student's tasks and the basis for judgment more clearly.	7. States student's tasks and basis for judgment less clearly.
8. Permits and occasionally encourages guessing.	8. Permits and occasionally encourages bluffing.
9. Distribution of scores is determined by the test.	9. Distribution of scores is controlled largely by the grader-reader.

Similarities

1. Both tests can measure almost any important instructional objective that any written test can measure.
2. Both tests can encourage students to learn concepts, principles, and problem-solving.
3. Both tests involve the use of subjective judgment.
4. Both tests yield scores whose value is dependent on objectivity and reliability.

Ebel goes on to suggest the following conditions as being especially appropriate for the particular use of either objective or essay tests:

Use essay tests under the following five conditions:

1. The group to be tested is small and the test should not be reused.
2. The instructor wishes to do all possible to encourage and reward the development of student skill in written expression.
3. The instructor is more interested in exploring the student's attitudes than in measuring his achievements. (Whether an instructor should be more interested in attitudes than achievements and whether he should expect an honest expression of attitudes in a test he will evaluate seems open to question.)
4. The instructor is more confident of his proficiency as a critical reader than as an imaginative writer of good objective test items.
5. Time available for test preparation is shorter than time available for test grading.

Use objective tests under these conditions:

1. The group to be tested is large or the test may be reused.
2. Highly reliable test scores must be obtained as efficiently as possible.
3. Impartiality of evaluation, absolute fairness, and freedom from halo effects are essential.
4. The instructor is more confident of his ability to express objective test items clearly than of his ability to judge essay test answers correctly.
5. There is more pressure for speedy reporting of scores than for speedy test preparation.

Use either objective or essay tests for the following purposes:

1. Measure almost any important educational achievement which a written test can measure.
2. Test understanding of ability to apply principles.
3. Test ability to think critically.
4. Test ability to solve novel problems.
5. Test ability to select relevant facts and principles, to integrate them toward the solution of complex problems.
6. Encourage students to study for command of knowledge.[10]

THE MEASUREMENT OF UNDERSTANDING

THE IMPROVEMENT OF OBJECTIVE ITEMS

Test items can be classified according to the form they take or the purpose they serve. The most common forms of objective items are true-false, completion, matching, and multiple-choice. Each of these is better adapted for some purposes than others. True-false items are most useful when a teacher wishes to test for popular misconceptions or superstitions, in testing situations where it is impossible to find enough plausible alternatives to make a multiple-choice item, or where there are *only* two possible alternatives. Matching items are helpful when a teacher wishes to economize on space and time in appraising knowledge of descriptive information like names, places, and dates. Completion exercises are useful for measuring comprehension and application. Multiple-choice items lend themselves better than the others to measuring student ability to interpret data. Examples of the four major types of objective items follow below.

[10]R. E. Ebel, *Measuring Educational Achievement*, pp. 109–110.

Multiple-Choice

The Point Four Program and the Alliance for Progress are similar in that both
1. are chiefly recovery rather than development programs.
2. are limited to the Latin American nations.
3. require the gradual outlay of huge sums of money.
4. are intended to assist underdeveloped countries.[11]

At present Presidential electors are chosen at large rather than from single member districts within a state. What would be a likely development if the latter became the case?
1. Only a candidate with a majority of the popular votes could win an election.
2. Campaigns would be concentrated within the most populous states.
3. The two-party system would be strengthened.
4. The electoral votes of a state would be split among rival candidates.[12]

The event which occurred during Washington's term as President which tested the power of the Federal Government to enforce the Constitution was: (choose one)
1. the Whiskey Rebellion
2. the bill to charter a national bank
3. the appointment of the Supreme Court
4. the assumption of a state debt.[13]

Matching

Read the statements below, carefully paying attention to their relation to one another. Then next to each statement mark A, B, C, or D as indicated.
    (A) If the statement contains the *central* idea around which most of the statements can be grouped.

[11]Harry D. Berg, "The Objective Test Item," in H. D. Berg, ed., *Evaluation in the Social Studies,* Thirty-fifth Yearbook of the National Council for the Social Studies (Washington, D.C.: National Council for the Social Studies, 1965), p. 60. Reprinted with the permission of the National Council for the Social Studies and Harry D. Berg.
[12]Harry D. Berg, "The Objective Test Item," in H. D. Berg, ed., *Evaluation in the Social Studies,* Thirty-fifth Yearbook of the National Council for the Social Studies (Washington, D.C.: National Council for the Social Studies, 1965), p. 62. Reprinted with the permission of the National Council for the Social Studies and Harry D. Berg.
[13]Morris R. Lewenstein, *Teaching Social Studies in Junior and Senior High Schools* (Skokie, Ill. Rand McNally, 1963), p. 464.

(B) If the statement contains a main *supporting* idea of the central idea.

(C) If the statement contains an *illustrative* fact or detailed statement related to a main supporting idea.

(D) If the statement contains an idea or ideas which are *irrelevant*.

1. The Roman roads connected all parts of the Empire with Rome.
2. The Roman roads were so well built that some of them remain today.
3. One of the greatest achievements of the Romans was their extensive and durable system of roads.
4. Wealthy travelers in Roman times used horse-drawn coaches.
5. Along Roman roads caravans would bring to Rome luxuries from Alexandria and the East.
6. In present-day Italy some of the roads used are original Roman roads.[14]

Gronlund[15] has identified several examples of column relationships that teachers in various fields identified as being important to consider for matching purposes.

A	B
Men	Achievements
Dates	Historical events
Terms	Definitions
Rules	Examples
Symbols	Concepts
Authors	Titles of Books
Foreign words	English equivalents
Machines	Uses
Plants or animals	Classification
Principles	Illustrations
Objects	Names of objects
Parts	Functions

Completion or Fill-In

In the blank provided, write the word which best completes the sentence.

[14]From *Making the Classroom Test: a Guide for Teachers*, p. 19. Copyright © 1959, 1961, 1969 by Educational Testing Service. Reprinted by permission.
[15]Norman E. Gronlund, *Measurement and Evaluation in Teaching* (New York: Macmillan, 1965), pp. 136–138.

1. If people's eyes were not sensitive to blue light, objects which now appear blue would appear. . . . . .[16]

True-False

In the space at the left mark whether the statement is true or false. Mark plus for true and zero for false.

. . . . 1. If the Cascade Mountains were 500 miles farther east, western Oregon would have an increased rainfall.[17]

A WORD OF CAUTION

The writing of good objective items requires care. Dangers to watch for are extensively treated in the literature on test writing.[18] Some of the most common errors to avoid include failing to make all the possible choices in multiple-choice questions plausible, using "give-away" words like "always" or "never," using overly technical or abstruse language, and using exactly the same wording in the examination question as found in the textbook. Three other obvious pitfalls to watch out for are:

● *Reading Difficulty of the Item.*   Unless you are testing for reading ability, write your items in language that students can easily understand. The Educational Testing Service gives this example:

Poor: If a man makes a business transaction wherein he purchases a motor vehicle for one thousand five hundred and twenty-five dollars and at a later date sells said vehicle in another business transaction for one thousand two hundred and sixty dollars, what is his net loss?

Better: A man buys a car for $1525 and sells it later for $1260. What is the difference between the purchase price and the selling price?[19]

● *Ambiguities.*   Be sure that there can be only one interpretation to your question.

[16]From *Making the Classroom Test: a Guide for Teachers*, p. 19. Copyright © 1959, 1961, 1969 by Educational Testing Service. Reprinted by permission.

[17]From *Making the Classroom Test: a Guide for Teachers*, p. 20. Copyright © 1959, 1961, 1969 by Educational Testing Service. Reprinted by permission.

[18]See H. D. Berg, "The Objective Test Item," in Berg, ed., *Evaluation in Social Studies*; R. S. Ebel, *Measuring Educational Achievement*; and N.E. Gronlund, *Measurement and Evaluation in Teaching*.

[19]From *Making the Classroom Test: a Guide for Teachers*, p. 20. Copyright © 1959, 1961, 1969 by Educational Testing Service. Reprinted by permission.

Poor: Which of the following books can be called humorous?
(A) *A Christmas Carol*
(B) *Tom Sawyer*
(C) *Treasure Island*
(D) *Silas Marner*
(The student might think he is expected to select more than one of the options because several of the books contain humorous incidents.)

Better: Which one of the following books is most humorous?
(A) *A Christmas Carol*
(B) *Tom Sawyer*
(C) *Treasure Island*
(D) *Silas Marner*[20]

- *Mixing the Kinds of Elements to Be Found in the Columns of a Matching Exercise.*

Directions: On the line to the left of each achievement listed in column A, write the letter of the man's name in column B who is noted for that achievement. Each name in column B may be used once, more than once, or not at all.

Poor: Column A

Item: _____ 1. Invented the telephone
       _____ 2. Discovered America
       _____ 3. First United States astronaut to orbit earth
       _____ 4. First President of the United States

Column B

A. Alexander Graham Bell
B. Christopher Columbus
C. John Glenn
D. Abraham Lincoln
E. Ferdinand Magellan
F. George Washington
G. Eli Whitney[21]

Better: Column A

_____ 1. Invented the sewing machine
_____ 2. Invented bifocal lens
_____ 3. Invented the cotton gin
_____ 4. Invented the telephone

Column B

A. Alexander Graham Bell
B. Eli Whitney
C. Benjamin Franklin
D. Thomas A. Edison
E. Elias Howe

THE IMPROVEMENT OF ESSAY TESTS

One very important thing that essay tests can do that objective tests cannot is assess student ability to write clearly and logically on a given topic. If a test is really to be an essay test, students must actually be asked to write an essay, defined by Bragdon as a "literary composition, analytical

[20]From *Making the Classroom Test: a Guide for Teachers*, p. 21. Copyright © 1959, 1961, 1969 by Educational Testing Service. Reprinted by permission.
[21]N. E. Gronlund, *Measurement and Evaluation in Teaching*, p. 136.

or interpretive in nature."[22] All essay tests should involve good English. "Good English" means "at least certain elementary virtues: well-constructed sentences, correct spelling and punctuation, avoidance of slang and abbreviations, attention to accurate expression. Unless these are insisted on all through the school, students will get the notion that they are simply idiosyncrasies of English teachers."[23] Here are a few guidelines for improving essay tests:

● *Identify clearly the purpose for which you are testing.* If you are testing student ability to relate facts to ideas or other events, be sure that your question asks them to do this. For example, here is an essay question that asks students to explain a connection between previously unrelated items:

> Explain the relationship between each of the following pairs:
> 1) "Muckrakers" – : : – Theodore Roosevelt
> 2) National Banks – : : – Federal Reserve Banks
> 3) Russo-Japanese War – : : – Root-Takahira Agreement
> 4) "Dollar Diplomacy" – : : – Woodrow Wilson's speech at Mobile, October, 1913[24]

● *Avoid ambiguity.* Be sure that the task you require of students is clear and unambiguous. Here is an example of an ambiguous essay question, followed by an example of one in which the student's task is clear:

> Poor   Discuss the origins of the Cold War.
> Better Assume that Winston Churchill, Nikita Khrushchev, and Harry Truman were invited to speak to our class on "The Origins of the Cold War."
>
> How would each of these men be likely to present the subject?
>
> What events or ideas might each select as the most significant causal factor?
>
> On which points, if any, would they probably agree?
>
> (Support your statements with facts, data, or other evidence.)[25]

[22]Henry W. Bragdon, "Neglected Resource: The Essay Question," in Richard E. Gross, Walter E. McPhie, and Jack R. Fraenkel, *Teaching the Social Studies: What, Why, and How* (Scranton, Pa.: International Testbook Co., 1969), p. 493.

[23]*Ibid.*, p. 493.

[24]H. W. Bragdon, "Neglected Resource . . . ," in R. E. Gross *et al., Teaching the Social Studies*, p. 495.

[25]Frank F. Gorow, *Better Classroom Testing* (San Francisco: Chandler Publishing Co., 1966), p. 88.

• *State the question in enough detail so that students understand what is expected of them.* If the question is stated in terms that are too general, different students will discuss different aspects of the question and their answers will vary considerably as to length and points emphasized. Here is an example of an essay question that is too general, followed by one that is stated in greater detail.

> Poor   Explain why you think the United Nations has been a success or a failure.
>
> Better   An important function of the United Nations is to help settle disputes between nations. Describe how one dispute was handled successfully, pointing out how the settlement illustrates a general strength of the United Nations. Describe also how one dispute was handled unsuccessfully, pointing out how this illustrates a general weakness of the United Nations. Your essay should be about 300–400 words in length (two or three pages in longhand).[26]

Essay questions do take time to prepare, because so many factors must be taken under consideration—what the students can be expected to know, their ability to make inferences based on their knowledge, the amount of time they have available to write their answers, the clarity of the directions, and the clarity of the question itself.

One of the major but often unrecognized values of good essay questions is their ability to allow students to demonstrate their understanding in imaginative ways. Bragdon cites as an example the question "Assume yourself to be someone living in 1932 and explain how you would vote." Students were encouraged to browse through magazines and other documents of the period in order to prepare for the question. Here are examples of the opening paragraphs of three answers by high school students to the question:

> "Here I am slapping flies on the Capitol steps and sweating with a coupla thousand other guys in the same boat. We came here, us vets, 'cause we didn't know how else to get action. An' we ain't feeling too good about anything right now in the middle of July 19 and 32, and we ain't gonna feel any better if old man Hoover tries to kick us outta town the way they say he's gonna do . . . ."
> . . . .
> "So you ask me how I'm going to vote this year? Well, I'll tell you, but first you ought to know about me, so I can explain my choice better. I used to work in a factory in Detroit up to a year ago. The plant used to produce auto parts, but it closed down. The big auto

---

[26]From *Making the Classroom Test: a Guide for Teachers*, p. 22. Copyright ©
1959, 1961, 1969 by Educational Testing Service. Reprinted by permission.

plants closed down too. Now I barely got a job. I got a wife and two kids to support, too. Now I'm working for that banker's wife, Mrs. Couzens, as a gardener. It's a lousy job, but it pays $15 a week . . . ."

. . . .

18 Beekman Place,
New York City,
October 7, 1932

Dear Nicky,

Don't they teach you history at Groton any more? You asked some very foolish questions in your last letter. Of *course* your mother and I shall vote for Mr. Hoover this November. Mr. Hoover represents the Republican party, the party to which your family has always belonged and which acts in your family's interest. With God's help I think Mr. Hoover is perfectly competent to deliver the nation from its present difficulties.

Franklin Roosevelt *used* to be a gentleman. I graduated when he was in the Fourth Form, and I remember him as a rather handsome boy, quite a good sailor. . . .[27]

A recurring problem for all teachers is the difficulty of scoring objectively student responses to essay questions. A clear and comparatively simple method is suggested by Graham:

(1) The teacher *analyzes the points* that he thinks should be made in the ideal response *and assigns a numerical weight* to each point. Some points may be of greater importance; hence, they would be weighted appropriately. The instructor may wish to allow extra credit for clear organization of thinking. Sometimes he may feel that he cannot develop a "scoring key" until he reads a cross-section of students' papers. Whether derived by teacher-analysis, or by analysis of pupil responses, or by a combination of the two approaches, a systematic method of scoring numerical values or percentages increases objectivity. (2) The test reader *evaluates all the responses to one question* before going on to score the next question. (3) As the teacher reads, he *tosses the papers into five piles* (high to low in quality). This procedure may be unnecessary if the instructor is satisfied with the quantitative appraisal described in (1) above; but if he also wants a qualitative estimate, he may need to recheck his classifications to determine if the papers in each pile are indeed of similar quality. (4) *Anonymity is necessary* for the accurate scoring of essay tests because of the ubiquitous "halo effect." The easiest way to prevent this kind of subjectivity is to ask pupils to write their names *only* on the back of their test papers.[28]

[27]H. W. Bragdon, "Neglected Resource . . . ," in R. E. Gross *et al., Teaching the Social Studies*, p. 497.

[28]Grace Graham, "Teachers Can Construct Better Achievement Tests," *Curriculum Bulletin*, University of Oregon, Vol. XII, No. 170, Dec. 1956. Quoted in Q. Stodola *et al., Making the Classroom Test*, pp. 22–23.

THE MEASUREMENT OF THINKING

As was mentioned in Chapters 1 and 5, Bloom, along with several others, developed a taxonomy of objectives dealing with the acquisition of knowledge and other intellectual skills. They identified six major classes of educational objectives: (1) Knowledge, (2) Comprehension, (3) Application, (4) Analysis, (5) Synthesis, and (6) Evaluation, and grouped them under two major headings—knowledge, and intellectual abilities and skills. Knowledge involves the recall of information, methods, and processes, or patterns, structures, or settings. Intellectual abilities and skills refer to organized modes of operation and generalized techniques for dealing with materials and problems.[29] Category 1 falls under the heading of knowledge, while the other five categories fall within the area of intellectual abilities and skills. Sanders[30] used these categories to develop a "taxonomy of questions," changing and expanding the categories slightly in the process. Sanders' categories include "memory," "translation," "interpretation," "application," "analysis," "synthesis," and "evaluation."

A brief description of each of the preceding seven categories of thinking are as follows:

1. *Memory:* The student recalls or recognizes information.
2. *Translation:* The student changes information into a different symbolic form or language.
3. *Interpretation:* The student discovers relationships among facts, generalizations, definitions, values, and skills.
4. *Application:* The student solves a lifelike problem that requires the identification of the issue and the selection and use of appropriate generalizations and skills.
5. *Analysis:* The student solves a problem in the light of conscious knowledge of the parts and forms of thinking.
6. *Synthesis:* The student solves a problem that requires original, creative thinking.
7. *Evaluation:* The student makes a judgment of good or bad, right or wrong, according to standards he designates.[31]

The value of this list of categories for evaluation purposes is that it not only establishes a definition of thinking that is fairly comprehensive, but also provides a checklist that teachers can use to ensure that they are doing more than just asking their students to remember information. Let us

[29]Benjamin S. Bloom *et al., Taxonomy of Educational Objectives: Handbook I, The Cognitive Domain,* pp. 201–207.
[30]Norris M. Sanders, *Classroom Questions—What Kinds?* (New York: Harper & Row, 1966).
[31]*Ibid.,* p. 3.

now look at examples of questions in each category, along with examples
of related objectives that such questions might in part evaluate.[32]

MEMORY

Instructional Objective: Students can recall or identify certain significant historical events.

Sample Test Items:

The revolt of Pennsylvania farmers who objected to paying excise
taxes during George Washington's administration is known as the
(fill in the correct answer)   (recall)

The revolt of Pennsylvania farmers who objected to paying excise taxes during George Washington's term as President is known
as: (choose one) (a) the Hartford Convention (b) the Embargo
Act (c) the XYZ affair (d) the Whiskey Rebellion (recognition)[33]

Items of this type evaluate a student's ability to remember facts. It is important to test for factual knowledge. Some facts are important to know
in and of themselves, such as one's basic rights under the Constitution.
Other facts are considered important because an educated man is expected
to possess them and conversation is limited without them (though any kind
of complete agreement as to what these facts are is probably impossible).
Most important, facts are important to learn as a basis for use in thinking
about and forming conclusions and relationships. Unfortunately social
studies tests are often overloaded with items that test for factual acquisition almost exclusively simply because they are easy to construct. Sanders
points out that "the greatest problem in this category is not how to write
good test items but rather how to determine the knowledge that is worth
remembering. . . . There appears to be a general overemphasis on trivial
information in the social studies."[34]

TRANSLATION

Asking students to translate information from one form to another is
one way of enabling them to demonstrate their *understanding* of information. A common experience that many of us have had is to memorize
something for an examination without understanding its meaning. This is
often seen when teachers ask a student to explain what a certain word or
idea that they have used means and the student is unable to do so. The
student knows the word, but not its meaning. We make things our own
when we are able to express them in our own words.

[32]Only a few examples in each category will be given here. For further possibilities, see both B. Bloom *et al., Taxonomy of Educational Objectives: Handbook I,*
and N. M. Sanders, *Classroom Questions—What Kinds?* Other examples of exercises designed to assess development in thinking can also be found at the end of
Chapter 8.

[33]M. R. Lewenstein, *Teaching Social Studies,* p. 464.

[34]N. M. Sanders, *Classroom Questions,* p. 20.

Translation items require students to express ideas in a form other than the one in which the idea was originally presented without changing the meaning of the idea in the process. Here are two examples:

> *Instructional Objective:* Students can restate definitions in their own words.
>
> *Sample Test Item:*
>   Restate the first paragraph of the Declaration of Independence in your own words.
>
> *Instructional Objective:* Students can recognize a relationship that exists among various concepts.
>
> *Sample Test Item:*
>   Which of the following graphs best represents the demand schedule of a typical commodity under competitive conditions?[35]

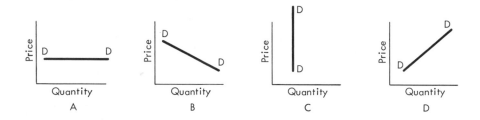

Translation requests can take many forms as shown below. Students can be asked to translate

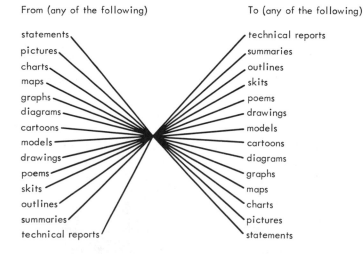

[35]From B. S. Bloom *et al.*, TAXONOMY OF EDUCATIONAL OBJECTIVES: *Handbook I, The Cognitive Domain* (New York: David McKay Company, Inc., 1956), p. 103. Used by permission of David McKay Company, Inc.

INTERPRETATION

When we ask students to interpret, we are asking them to identify a relationship among otherwise unrelated pieces of data. This is another way of enabling them to demonstrate the degree to which they comprehend or understand rather than simply remember information. When we evaluate student ability to interpret data we want to know whether they can derive the most important ideas or thoughts that the data contains. We may ask students to compare and contrast, identify implications that logically follow a given line of reasoning, give examples to support or refute a generalization or form a generalization from a set of data (this is one way of evaluating student ability to generalize, as developed in Chapter 5). Examples of test items that measure student ability to interpret include:

1. *Instructional Objective:* Students can determine whether two ideas are identical, similar, unrelated, or contradictory.

Sample Test Item:
Compare the relations between the English colonies in North America and England from 1750 to 1783 with the relations between the states and federal government in the United States from 1789 to 1865. You may use your textbooks for reference.[36]

2. *Instructional Objective:* Students can identify one or more logical implications that follow from a point of view.

Sample Test Item:
Those who believe that increasing consumer expenditures would be the best way to stimulate the economy would advocate
a. an increase in interest rates
b. an increase in depreciation allowances
c. tax concessions in the lower income brackets
d. a reduction in government expenditures[37]

3. *Instructional Objective:* Students can find evidence in various sources to support or refute a generalization.

Sample Test Item:
Find evidence to support or refute the following statement: "Revolutions in the violent sense do not occur as long as the underprivileged members of a society have some hope that their condition will improve in the near future."

4. *Instructional Objective:* Students can determine whether or not certain generalizations can be made on the basis of data that is present or whether certain additional data are needed.

Sample Test Item:
Directions: Below are some statistics relating to education and occupations. You are to judge what conclusions may be drawn from them.

---

[36]N. M. Sanders, *Classroom Questions*, p. 46.
[37]R. S. Ebel, *Measuring Educational Achievement*, p. 62.

OCCUPATIONS	Current occupational distribution found in a sample of male college graduates*	Distribution of occupations in the population as a whole, 1950
	PERCENTAGES	
Executives, minor officials, partners, proprietors	23.5	9.1
Professional workers	51.3	4.7
Salesmen	6.0	Less than 1%
Skilled workers	7.1	33.8
Clerical workers	8.7	13.4
Unskilled workers	1.7	26.1
Farmers	1.7	13.0
	100.0	100.0

*You may assume that the sample selected is representative of all male college graduates in the United States.

Directions: The following generalizations are sometimes inferred from the foregoing statistics on occupations and education. You are to judge whether or not the generalizations made below can be made on the basis of these data alone or if certain additional data are needed. For the following items, *blacken* answer space

A — if the generalization can be made on the basis of the foregoing statistics, without any additional information.

B — if in addition to or instead of the foregoing statistics you would need to know the percentage of people in each occupation who were unable to attend college.

C — if in addition to or instead of the foregoing statistics you would need to know the percentage of male college graduates in each occupation whose fathers were college graduates and were in the same occupation.

D — if the generalization *cannot* properly be made even if the additional information described in B and C were available.

_____ 1. Unskilled, skilled and clerical workers do not value college education as much as do businessmen.

_____ 2. The low percentage of college graduates in the skilled, clerical, and unskilled worker class reveals a lack of social mobility in America.

_____ 3. Higher education provides a medium in this country whereby some youth improve their status.

_____ 4. Children of business and professional men have a greater opportunity to enter well-paid occupations.

_____ 5. Social mobility in the United States is increasing.[38]

APPLICATION

Application is a higher form of intellectual process than comprehension because we are now asking students to use what they have learned—i.e., to apply previously learned knowledge in a situation new and different. When a student interprets a piece of information, we mean that he understands the meaning behind it and can apply this information *if he is specifically asked to do so.*[39] "The student who has the ability to apply knowledge will by himself recognize the principle involved, select the correct method of solution, and then solve the problem at hand."[40]

Application involves deductive thinking. Students must "search for an explanation of the fact or facts described in the problem situation by means of some *general rule* which asserts a highly probable connection between facts of the kind described in the problem and other facts the student knows to be applicable to similar problems. The question he attempts to answer is: Does the general rule which is suggested by the given facts as an hypothesis for explaining what has happened (or what will happen) actually apply to this specific problem?"[41]

You will recall that one of the strategies for developing student thinking described in Chapter 5 asks students to apply previously learned generalizations in new and different situations. Thus to answer the question "What might happen if a new metal, harder yet more malleable than any yet known, were discovered today?", students would have had to have drawn some conclusions previously about the effect of metal on people's lives. It is this ability to apply ideas that they have previously learned that application test items attempt to measure. Here is an example:

> *Instructional Objective*: Students can apply ideas (generalizations, concepts, principles, laws, etc.) previously learned in situations new and different.

[38]From B. S. Bloom *et al.,* TAXONOMY OF EDUCATIONAL OBJECTIVES: *Handbook I: The Cognitive Domain* (New York: David McKay Company, Inc., 1956), pp. 110–111. Used by permission of David McKay Company, Inc.

[39]*Ibid.,* p. 78.

[40]William D. Hedges, *Evaluation in the Elementary School* (New York: Holt, Rinehart & Winston, 1969), p. 107.

[41]Eugene R. Smith *et al., Appraising and Recording Student Progress* (New York: Harper & Row, 1942), p. 78.

Directions: In the exercise below a problem is given. Below the problem are two lists of statements. The first list contains statements which can be used to answer the problem. Place a check (✔) in the parentheses after the statement or statements which *answer the problem*. The second list contains statements which can be used to explain the right answers. Place a check mark (✔) in the parentheses after the statement or statements which *give reasons for the right answers*. Some of the other statements are true but do not explain the right answers; do not check these.

Problem	In warm weather people who do not have refrigerators sometimes wrap a bottle of milk in a wet towel and place it where there is a good circulation of air. *Would a bottle of milk so treated stay sweet as long as a similar bottle of milk without a wet towel?*	

A bottle wrapped with the wet towel would stay sweet

Conclusions	a. longer than without the wet towel .. ( ) a.	
	b. not as long as without the wet towel ( ) b.	
	c. the same length of time—the wet towel would make no difference ... ( ) c.	

Check the statements below which give the reason or reasons for your explanation above.

(Superstition)	d. Thunderstorms hasten the souring of milk .... ( ) d.
(Right Principle)	e. The souring of milk is the result of the growth and life processes of bacteria .... ( ) e.
(Wrong)	f. Wrapping the bottle prevents bacteria from getting into the milk .... ( ) f.
(Wrong)	g. A wet towel could not interfere with the growth of bacteria in the milk ( ) g.
(Wrong)	h. Wrapping keeps out the air and hinders bacterial growth .... ( ) h.
(Right Principle)	i. Evaporation is accompanied by an absorption of heat .... ( ) i.
(Authority)	j. Milkmen often advise housewives to wrap bottles in wet towels .... ( ) j.
(Unacceptable Analogy)	k. Just as many foods are wrapped in cellophane to keep in moisture, so is milk kept sweet by wrapping a wet towel around the bottle to keep the moisture in .... ( ) k.
(Right Principle)	l. Bacteria do not grow so rapidly when temperatures are kept low .... ( ) l.[42]

[42] E. R. Smith *et al., Appraising and Recording Student Progress*, pp. 89–90.

ANALYSIS

Analysis requires a somewhat more advanced level of intellectual skill than comprehension or application. *Comprehension* involves grasping the meaning of information. *Application* involves remembering and using appropriate ideas or principles on information. *Analysis* emphasizes the breaking down of information into its component parts, and seeing *how* these parts are related and organized. For example, teachers may want to assess student ability to detect fact from opinion, to identify facts which support a conclusion, to distinguish between relevant and irrelevant data, to identify assumptions, or to find evidence to support an argument. Though analysis cannot be made completely distinct from either comprehension (especially interpretation) or evaluation, Bloom and his associates point out that students may comprehend the meaning of a communication without being able to analyze it effectively, while those who are able to analyze a statement effectively may evaluate it badly. They go on to break analysis as an objective into three types or levels: (a) identifying or classifying the *elements* of a communication; (b) making explicit the *relationships* or connections that exist among these elements; (c) recognizing the *organizational principles*, the structure that holds the communication together as a whole.[43] Examples of each follow:

A. *ANALYSIS OF ELEMENTS*

Five specific objectives have been identified under this category:
1. The ability to recognize unstated assumptions
2. Skill in distinguishing facts from hypotheses
3. The ability to distinguish factual from normative statements
4. Skill in identifying motives and in discriminating between mechanisms of behavior with reference to individuals and groups
5. Ability to distinguish a conclusion from statements which support it.[44]

Let us look at a few examples:

Instructional Objective: Students can distinguish fact from hypothesis.
Sample Test Item:

[43]B. S. Bloom *et al., Taxonomy of Educational Objectives: Handbook I*, p. 145.
[44]*Ibid.*, p. 146.

On page 225 of a certain book,[45] the author states: "Many scientists believe that the first cave dwellers lived about 50,000 years ago." Is this statement a fact or a hypothesis? Explain.

Instructional Objective: Students can distinguish a conclusion from statements which support it.

Sample Test Item:

The college committee in charge of social regulations was holding an open hearing on a proposal that the rule on chaperoning coeducational outings (weiner roasts, overnight hikes, campfires, etc.) should be more strictly applied. A student in the audience got the floor and made this speech:

(A) This whole discussion is ridiculous,

(B) for we shouldn't have chaperones at all!

(C) You see, any chaperone you get will either arrange not to see what happens or he will be so badly outnumbered he can't keep track of what is going on.

(D) But chaperones are supposed to guarantee that what goes on is respectable.

(E) So the chaperonage system is utterly ineffective and full of hypocrisy.

(F) Besides, collegians will never develop maturity unless they are given responsibilities to exercise and are really trusted with these responsibilities.

12. There is one statement in the student's argument for which reasons are offered, but which he does not offer as a reason for any other statement. That statement, his main conclusion, is

1. A.
2. B.   4. E.
3. C.   5. F.[46]

B. *ANALYSIS OF RELATIONSHIPS*

The *Taxonomy of Educational Objectives* also identifies a number of objectives that involve analysis of relationships. These include:

- Skill in comprehending the interrelationships among the ideas in a passage.
- Ability to recognize what particulars are relevant to the validation of a judgment.
- Ability to recognize which facts or assumptions are essential to a main thesis or to the argument in support of them.
- Ability to check the consistency of hypotheses with given information and assumptions.

[45]Abraham S. Fischler, Lawrence F. Lowery, and Sam S. Blanc, *Science: A Modern Approach*, Book 4 (New York: Holt, Rinehart & Winston, 1966).

[46]From B. S. Bloom *et al.*, TAXONOMY OF EDUCATIONAL OBJECTIVES: *Handbook I, The Cognitive Domain* (New York: David McKay Company, Inc., 1956), p. 153. Used by permission of David McKay Company, Inc.

- Ability to distinguish cause-and-effect relationships from other sequential relationships.
- Ability to analyze the relations of statements in an argument, to distinguish relevant from irrelevant statements.
- Ability to detect logical fallacies in arguments.
- Ability to recognize the causal relations and the important and unimportant details in an historical account.[47]

Two examples follow:

Instructional Objective: Students can comprehend the interrelationships that exist among the ideas in a passage.
Sample Test Item:
Read the following statement about education in the United States.

Financial support for public education in the United States comes almost entirely from local and state tax revenues. States of low financial ability, with few exceptions, rank at the top in the percentage of their income devoted to schools. Nevertheless, these states rank at the bottom with respect to the quality of schooling provided. It has now become evident that no plan of local or state taxation can be devised and put into operation that will support in every local community a school which meets minimum acceptable standards.

The central thought of the statement above is that
1. the poorer states devote a greater part of their income to education than do the richer states.
2. the richer states have better schools than the poorer states.
3. education will be inadequate in many areas as long as it depends on local or state revenues.
4. no fair system of state or local taxation can be developed.[48]

Instructional Objective: Students can distinguish cause-and-effect relationships from other sequential relationships.
Sample Test Item:
Before each item number, write in the letter designated below to indicate that, in the United States during the period of 1865–1900, an increase in the first tended to be followed by
A. an increase in the second.

[47]B. S. Bloom *et al., Taxonomy of Educational Objectives*, p. 147.
[48]Harry D. Berg, "The Objective Test Item," in H. D. Berg, ed., *Evaluation in the Social Studies*, Thirty-fifth Yearbook of the National Council for the Social Studies (Washington, D.C.: National Council for the Social Studies, 1965), p. 56. Reprinted with the permission of the National Council for the Social Studies and Harry D. Berg.

B. a decrease in the second.

C. no related change in the second.

1. Mechanization of agriculture. Percentage of Americans working on farms.

2. Growth in large-scale enterprise. Acceptance of responsibility for worker's welfare by the owners of business.[49]

C. *ANALYSIS OF ORGANIZATIONAL PRINCIPLES*

A number of specific objectives have also been identified in this category. These include:

- Ability to analyze, in a particular work of art, the relation of materials and means of production to the "elements" and to the organization.
- The ability to recognize form and pattern in literary or artistic works as a means of understanding their meaning.
- The ability to infer the author's purpose, point of view, or traits of thought and feeling as exhibited in his work.
- Ability to infer an author's concept of science, philosophy, history, or of his art as exemplified in his practice.
- Ability to see the techniques used in persuasive materials, such as advertising.
- Ability to recognize the point of view or bias of a writer in an historical account.[50]

Here is an example:

> *Instructional Objective:* Students can recognize an author's point of view or bias as exhibited in his work.
> *Sample Test Item:*
> Here is a short but recent magazine article on civil rights. The author states that he is arguing neither for nor against the position he is writing about, but only describing it. Is this true? Explain.

SYNTHESIS

When students synthesize information, they put together various elements so as to form a whole. They must draw a number of elements together into a pattern or relationship not clearly seen before. The most useful kind of evaluative device for this kind of mental operation is the essay question. One example is as follows:

> *Instructional Objective:* Students can formulate a plausible relationship to explain a hypothesis that may exist among a number of factors.

[49]Hymen M. Chausow, "Evaluation of Critical Thinking in the Social Studies," in H. D. Berg, ed., *Evaluation in the Social Studies,* p. 90.
[50]B. S. Bloom *et al., Taxonomy of Educational Objectives: Handbook I,* p. 148.

Sample Test Item:

Trace the historical development of sectionalism in the United States. Identify the various geographic factors that have affected this development. Write one or more hypotheses that attempt to explain the relationship among the elements of sectionalism, historical development, and geographic factors.[51]

Synthesis can involve the creation of an original communication, such as a poem or essay, a unique plan of action, or perhaps some new and unusual way of organizing data. Synthesis is the area of evaluation of creativity on the part of students. It may involve the writing of original compositions, speaking extemporaneously yet clearly and effectively, illustrating one's ideas through drawing or painting, composing a poem or song, molding clay, writing a short play or mock radio script to be performed in class, planning and leading a class discussion, making a model, or designing a costume. The point to stress is that the evaluation of synthesis often requires that students produce a product of one sort or another, expressing their own individuality in the process.

In the *Taxonomy*, the authors define three kinds of products:

1. Production of a unique communication (e.g., an original essay, a poem, a song, a report, a painting, a model, a skit. etc.).
2. Production of a plan, or proposed set of operations (e.g., a new way to solve a problem).
3. Derivation of a set of abstract relations (e.g., finding a pattern (or patterns) that exists among a set of related data, or deducing a new idea from one or more ideas that he has been presented with).

Examples of synthesis exercises include:

Instructional Objective: Students can propose and defend a number of qualities they believe a question should possess if it is to be considered as important for historical study.

Sample Test Item:

This is an exercise asking eighth-grade students to derive a set of abstract relations in a unit on the Civil War. As an introductory step, the students identify the most important and the least important questions for historical study from the following list:

A. What were the causes of the Civil War?
B. Could the Civil War have been prevented if the leaders had made wiser decisions?
C. Were the slaves of the South better off than factory workers in the North?
D. Was Jefferson Davis a capable leader?
E. Is slavery wrong?

[51]Frederick H. Smith and C. Benjamin Cox, *New Strategies and Curriculum in Social Studies* (Skokie, Ill.: Rand McNally, 1969), pp. 96–97.

F. Which side won the Battle of Gettysburg?

G. What was the population of New Orleans in 1861?

H. If Grant had been in command of the Northern armies from the beginning of the Civil War, would it have been concluded sooner?

I. What were the results of the Civil War?

J. Who was President of the United States during the Civil War?

K. What were the strengths and weaknesses of the North and South as they entered the Civil War?

Next the students are asked: *What are the qualities of a question that make it important for historical study? What are the qualities of a question that make it unimportant for historical study?*[52]

> *Instructional Objective:* Students can form plausible hypotheses to explain a given phenomenon.
>
> *Sample Test Item:*
>
> What hypotheses can you suggest that would explain why nations in the tropics seldom develop a high level of civilization?[53]

EVALUATION

Evaluation, as defined in the *Taxonomy*, involves the use of criteria and standards to determine if, and to what extent, a certain objective has been met. It is ranked highest in the *Taxonomy* because it is assumed that evaluation involves all of the other mental processes exemplified earlier—knowing, translating, interpreting, applying, analyzing, and synthesizing. To be classified as an evaluation item, a question must require a student to make a judgment with certain distinct criteria clearly in mind. Quick decisions that are made without such precise criteria are more properly viewed as *opinions* than evaluations.

The two most common types of evaluation in the sense described above involve internal and external standards of criticism. Internal standards in general relate to the internal accuracy of a particular work—its consistency, its logic, and the absence of internal flaws. External standards generally relate to the purpose or end for which the work was created and the appropriateness of various means to bringing about this end. External criteria that can be used may be the degree to which the end in question is achieved; standards in the field by which such works are generally judged; or a comparison of the work with other works already existing in its field. (That is, a work of history would be judged by criteria appropriate to works of history rather than works of fiction.)

---

[52]Excerpt from pp. 133–4 in CLASSROOM QUESTIONS—WHAT KINDS? by Norris M. Sanders. Copyright © 1966 by Norris M. Sanders. Reprinted by permission of Harper & Row, Publishers, Inc.

[53]*Ibid.*, p. 134.

JUDGMENTS IN TERMS OF
INTERNAL EVIDENCE

Instructional Objective: When given a new document or other work, students can determine the specific ways in which the work is accurate and internally consistent, or the flaws within it that make it internally inconsistent.

Sample Test Item:

Social Security officials sometimes face perplexing problems in studying appeals for unemployment compensation. Some major-league baseball players in Ohio and Missouri decided in January that, because they had not played ball since the end of the season, they had a right to consider themselves unemployed. Although some of them were earning good salaries of $8,000 to $10,000 a year in baseball, they maintained that they were entitled to the benefits of the unemployment section of the Social Security Act.

Team owners urged these players not to apply for unemployment compensation. According to the owners' interpretation, the players were under contract all year around, although they worked and were paid only during the playing season. On the other hand, the state officials in Ohio and Missouri were inclined to agree with the players that they were entitled to benefit payments.

> Directions: Examine the conclusions given below. Assuming that the paragraphs above give a fair statement of the problem, which *one* of the conclusions do you think is justified.

Conclusions

A. The players were entitled to the benefits of the unemployment section of the Social Security Act.

B. The players were *not* entitled to the benefits of the unemployment section of the Social Security Act.

C. More information is needed to decide whether or not the players were entitled to the benefits of the unemployment section of the Social Security Act.

> Mark in   A. Statements which explain why your conclusion is
> column   logical.
>   B. Statements which do not explain why your conclusion is logical.
>   C. Statements about which you are unable to decide.

Statements

1. The state officials are the ones who consider appeals for unemployment compensation, and their opinion carries more weight than the opinions of team owners.

2. The Social Security Act may or may not provide that a man

who works and receives pay during only part of each year is unemployed during the remaining part of the year.

3. The players argued indirectly (if others receive compensation, why shouldn't we?) and forgot that others needed the compensation more than they.

4. A changed definition may lead to a changed conclusion even though the argument from each definition is logical.

5. No one who earns $8,000 a year or more should get unemployment compensation.[54]

JUDGMENTS IN TERMS OF EXTERNAL CRITERIA

Instructional Objective: Students can determine the degree to which a particular act measures up to certain standards.

Sample Test Item:

Mr. X believes that any law should meet these standards: (A) Not increase the power of the federal government at the expense of the state and local governments; (B) Not increase government debt; (C) Not undermine citizens' character by giving them something for nothing; (D) Not restrict the honest operation of business and industry; (E) Not be inflationary.

If Mr. X used only these standards, how would he rate the following laws?

A. Sherman Anti-trust Act, 1890
B. McKinley Tariff, 1890
C. Pure Food and Drug Act, 1906
D. Mann-Elkins Act, 1910
E. Federal Reserve Act, 1913[55]

The Measurement of Affective Objectives

Some of the most important objectives in social studies education include such things as attitudes, interests, feelings, and values. Yet rarely is student growth in any of these appraised. Why is this so?

We have already examined or inferred many reasons for this state of affairs in Chapter 6. A basic tenet of any democratic society is the idea that any individual may like or dislike whom or what he chooses, and that as long as his actions do not violate another's basic rights, his preferences

[54]From B. S. Bloom *et al.*, TAXONOMY OF EDUCATIONAL OBJECTIVES: *Handbook I, The Cognitive Domain* (New York: David McKay Company, Inc., 1956), pp. 196–197. Used by permission of David McKay Company, Inc.
[55]Excerpt from p. 147 in CLASSROOM QUESTIONS—WHAT KINDS? by Norris M. Sanders. Copyright © 1966 by Norris M. Sanders. Reprinted by permission of Harper & Row, Publishers, Inc.

are his own business, not to be interfered with. Furthermore, as we saw in Chapter 1, non-cognitive objectives are very difficult to pin down and specify precisely. What does "to appreciate" or "to like" mean? How do attitudes, feelings, and values differ from each other? Are they related? If so, in what way(s)? The term "value" always produces difficulty. How do we measure the development of attitudes and values? Assessment, however imperfect, must be attempted if we are to determine whether growth is taking place.

One thing is rather generally agreed and that is that all of these traits (attitudes, interests, opinions, feelings, and values) are internal conditions whose existence can only be detected on the basis of inference. On the basis of observed behavior, we infer that a certain attitude, etc. is present. Thus we may infer on the basis of a child's smile (behavior) that he is happy (feeling good). The problem is that the same behavior may indicate a variety of feelings. Thus a smile might represent a positive feeling or attitude toward something for one student but a negative feeling for another.

As Mayhew suggests, assessment always requires the observation of a sample of a particular kind of behavior. This behavior may be some kind of physical action, it may be speaking, writing, drawing, or something else. Once it has been observed as reliably as possible, the significance of the behavior needs to be determined.[56] This poses quite a difficult problem when it comes to non-cognitive behaviors. "An observer may hear much complaining among a student body and infer low morale only to discover that, in the few weeks after Christmas, students complain and that actually the student body has a consistently high morale, or one may judge on the basis of an attitude test that students like the humanities only to discover that they stay away in large numbers from lectures and concerts."[57]

In spite of these problems, the importance of encouraging the evaluation of changes in non-cognitive objectives remains. Many of the devices presented in Chapter 2 (e.g., open-ended titles, multiple-choice endings, unfinished stories, sociograms, interest inventories, anecdotal records) are useful in this regard and should be reviewed at this point. Some further devices that teachers can use have been developed and will be presented. The most important thing is that teachers base the inferences they do make upon as much evidence as possible. As was suggested in Chapter 2, the more assessment data that can be gathered on students, the more reliable any inferences based on such data are likely to be. Inferences based on the results of only a single device, or even several devices administered

[56]Lewis B. Mayhew, "Measurement of Noncognitive Objectives in the Social Studies," in H. D. Berg, ed., *Evaluation in the Social Studies*, p. 118.
[57]*Ibid.*, p. 119.

within a fairly close period of time, may be quite misleading, since student attitudes and the like may change quite rapidly. It is worth repeating once again, therefore, that diagnosis and evaluation should be an ongoing activity. A variety of different kinds of data needs to be frequently collected, analyzed, and checked against personal observation and actual performance, in order to assess accurately changes in student behavior.

The basic assumption under which all attitude-testers operate is that it is possible to discover attitudes (and opinions, interests, feelings, or values) by requiring students to respond to a series of statements of preference. For example, if a student is asked to respond to the statement "Capital punishment should be abolished" and he indicates that he agrees, we may infer that he has a negative attitude toward capital punishment (assuming that he understands the meaning of the statement and is sincere in his response). We shall now look at some of the ways currently available in which such statements can be presented to students.

OPINION POLLS

One of the most common kinds of responses that teachers are interested in is student opinion. What do students believe or think about such topics as crime and punishment, poverty, world government, ecology, drugs, dissent, and foreign involvement? Relatively simple devices, such as a list of statements to respond to, can be prepared, scored, and analyzed by teachers. Mayhew suggests several cautions to keep in mind, however.

1. Understand clearly the object or its attribute about which opinions are to be solicited. Ambiguities first creep into questions when the writer is unclear himself as to the dimensions of the topic. In this connection the more specific attributes of an object or topic are susceptible to more precise opinion measurement. Thus the General Assembly rather than the United Nations and the United Nations rather than international government should be the objects of questions.
2. Be careful in the words used. Many of the words popularly used to determine opinion are too obscure to elicit exact responses. Words selected should point directly to the attribute concerning which response is desired. Thus avoid a question, "What is your opinion about the United Nations?" Rather use a form which allows students to respond "yes," or "no" or "don't know" to statements such as "The United Nations has prevented or limited war," "The United States does not use its veto power," "UNESCO is filled with Communist sympathizers."
3. Do not prepare more questions than can reasonably be used and the responses interpreted. A tendency of people who begin to design a check on opinions is to become overly complicated. Opinions are important and should be checked but the assessment should not be more complicated than the specific opinion warrants. In a unit on the American political party system there are not many opinions which can reasonably be affected by the teacher. These and these only are the ones to study.

4. After preparing questions let them sit for a few days then revise them. Normally ambiguities creep into the initial writing which remain undetected if revision is attempted at once. A few days later they appear quite clearly. After revision it always helps to try the questions out on others. A few students, colleagues or one's family can spot weaknesses which are invisible to the writer.

5. After administering a set of questions to students, tabulate the responses, discuss the results in class and leave the matter. Much of the assessment of opinion has high teaching or learning potential. It should be exploited.[58]

ATTITUDE SCALES

An attitude scale consists of a set of statements to which an individual is asked to respond. The pattern of his responses constitutes evidence from which an inference can be made about his attitude. The subject of attitude scales is treated quite extensively in the literature on test writing.[59] The most feasible for classroom use is the scale developed by Likert.[60] Likert designed this scale to measure the intensity of an attitude. Students are asked to indicate the extent to which they agree or disagree with each of several statements. For example, here are a few examples taken from a Likert scale.[61] The number in parenthesis below each alternative represents the score value of that alternative. On a positively worded item, the scores run from (5) for strongly approve to (1) for strongly disapprove. On negatively worded items, the scores are reversed.

In the interest of permanent peace, we should be willing to arbitrate absolutely all differences with other nations which we cannot settle by diplomacy.

Strongly Approve (5)	Approve (4)	Undecided (3)	Disapprove (2)	Strongly Disapprove (1)

We must strive for loyalty to our country before we can afford to consider world brotherhood.

Strongly Approve (5)	Approve (4)	Undecided (3)	Disapprove (4)	Strongly Disapprove (5)

[58]Lewis B. Mayhew, "Measurement of Noncognitive Objectives in the Social Studies," in H. D. Berg, ed., *Evaluation in the Social Studies*, Thirty-fifth Yearbook of the National Council for the Social Studies (Washington, D.C.: National Council for the Social Studies, 1965), pp. 130–131. Reprinted with the permission of the National Council for the Social Studies and Lewis B. Mayhew.

[59]For example, see David Krech, Richard S. Crutchfield, and Egerton L. Ballachey, *Individual in Society* (New York: McGraw-Hill, 1962), pp. 147–169.

[60]A. Likert, "A Technique for the Measurement of Attitudes," *Archives de Psychologie*, June 1932, No. 140.

[61]*Ibid.*, p. 149.

Likert-type scales are fairly easy to construct. You would prepare a list of statements that you believe reflect an attitude you are interested in measuring, refine them, and administer them to some students. Get a total score of each student paper using the 1-5 scoring scheme described above (be sure to reverse the scoring for negative items). Tally the responses for each item for the upper half of the papers and for the lower half. Throw out those items on which more students in the lower half than in the upper half responded favorably. Use the rest as your final list of statements to be given to the students whose attitude you wish to measure.

PAIRED COMPARISONS AND FORCED RESPONSES

This technique is appropriate when you desire to rank your students in terms of their attitude toward a rather small number of objects. Mayhew describes the technique as follows: "This involves pairing each object with every other object and in each event asking the student to select the one he favors. For example, pair a picture of a Ford, Plymouth and Chevrolet with each other. A stable ranking will result. A more gross ranking can be obtained by asking students to number the rank order of their preferences from a list of objects. An even more gross ranking can be obtained by asking students to select the three, four or five preferred objects from a larger list. Tabulation of the results reveals the pattern of preferences if such exists."[62]

A more complicated device which can be used is the technique of forced responses. Present students with sets of three statements and require that they select the one they like best and the one they like least. Rather extreme statements can be included in this method which still will yield useful information. Thus one might present a series of sets comparable to (1) Communism, (2) Fascism, (3) Anarchy. No one is satisfactory and without the element of force would not receive many takers. Forcing allows the questions to elicit underlying motivations.[63]

DISGUISED TECHNIQUES

Though all attitude measurement is indirect, some methods are more indirect than others. Attitude scales involve an explicit, rather "head-on" approach to the underlying attitude, by requiring students to respond to statements that refer more or less directly with the attitude in question. Other approaches may be more indirect, employing a disguised approach

[62]L. B. Mayhew, "Measurement of Noncognitive Objectives in the Social Studies," in Berg, ed., *Evaluation in the Social Studies*, p. 131.
[63]Lewis B. Mayhew, "Measurement of Noncognitive Objectives in the Social Studies," in H. D. Berg, ed., *Evaluation in the Social Studies*, Thirty-fifth Yearbook

to the attitude. The value of using disguised techniques is twofold: (a) they may reveal attitudes that a direct approach would miss, such as those which violate cultural norms and that an individual would hesitate to reveal publicly and (b) they enable us to get information on the attitude without affecting the attitude itself. The open-ended questions and themes, unfinished stories, and multiple-choice ending devices suggested in Chapter 2 are all examples of disguised techniques that can be used.

ROLE-PLAYING

Role-playing is a rather refined way of observing students in action. Students can be asked to act out the role of someone possibly faced with a crisis or in a conflict situation (as suggested in Chapter 6) without a script. Whites can be assigned to play black roles, blacks the roles of whites, or students the role of teachers and/or administrators. Thus a teacher might assign a number of black students to play a group of white teen-agers hanging around a street corner after curfew. Two white students can be assigned to portray black policemen who come upon the group. What will they do? The teacher must always exercise caution in the type of roles he assigns, however, since role-playing, as a projective device, can bring forth deeply held but previously unrevealed feelings that many students may not yet be ready to face openly.

OTHER WRITTEN DEVICES

Mayhew suggests what he calls a "self-ideal-self" checklist.[64] This device presents students with a number of descriptions of a hypothetical person. The student is asked on one day to check off those characteristics which he would say characterize him. At another time he is asked to indicate which characteristics describe how others see him and on yet another time how he would like to be. Mayhew then suggests other written possibilities:

> A number of adjectives descriptive of a school can be presented and students asked to pick out those most like the school. At another time they are to select how the faculty might see the school and at still another how parents might view it. The object of this exercise is of course to detect variation in how students believe various types of people perceive reality.

---

of the National Council for the Social Studies (Washington, D.C.: National Council for the Social Studies, 1965), p. 131. Reprinted with the permission of the National Council for the Social Studies and Lewis B. Mayhew.

[64]L. B. Mayhew, "Measurement of Noncognitive Objectives . . . ," in Berg, ed., *Evaluation in the Social Studies*, p. 134.

Psychoanalysis has proven the importance of early memories in shaping the attitude of people. Classroom teachers can apply some of the same theory for evaluation purposes. A teacher might ask all students to think back and describe themselves when they were much younger. Or the teacher might ask for an autobiography written as though it were twenty years in the future. In either event students reveal much about their affective selves as they select from the immense range of material available the data with which to construct an earlier or later image of themselves.[65]

VALUE ANALYSIS

Asking students to respond to certain questions after being involved in emotion-laden experiences can provide evidence for making inferences about their values. Several of the value strategies suggested in Chapter 6, for example, are helpful in this regard. Hunt and Metcalf cite as a further example the following questions for use after viewing a movie or recording:

1. Some incidents in the movie are more important than others. Which incidents or scenes seem to you to be the most important? (Do not name more than *three*.)
2. Why do you think these incidents are important? What makes them significant as far as you are concerned?
3. How could each situation be improved so as to contribute to the growth of everyone in the situation?[66]

THE CRITICAL INCIDENT

A final suggestion is the critical incident technique devised originally to select fighter pilots in World War II. It has since been used in judging speaking, teaching, and students' values. "It consists of asking a number of people to tell something they had seen recently which was an effective incident of the behavior being considered and something which was an ineffective example. If a large number of such incidents are collected they will reveal the dimensions of a particular problem. It has been used successfully in studying student values. Students were asked to relate something they had seen recently which was a good act and something they had seen which was a bad act. This study was done of students in elementary school, high school and college and revealed significantly different standards of values at each level of schooling."[67]

---

[65]Lewis B. Mayhew, "Measurement of Noncognitive Objectives in the Social Studies," in H. D. Berg, ed., *Evaluation in the Social Studies*, Thirty-fifth Yearbook of the National Council for the Social Studies (Washington, D.C.: National Council for the Social Studies, 1965), p. 134. Reprinted with the permission of the National Council for the Social Studies and Lewis B. Mayhew.

[66]M. P. Hunt and L. E. Metcalf, *Teaching High School Social Studies*, p. 257.

[67]L. B. Mayhew, "Measurement of Noncognitive Objectives . . . ," in Berg, ed., *Evaluation in the Social Studies*, pp. 134–135.

THE MEASUREMENT OF SOCIAL AND ACADEMIC SKILLS

Skill development in the social studies can be considered as falling within six major categories. These include:

1. Critical-thinking skills
2. Communications skills
3. Skills associated with developing a sense of place
4. Skills associated with developing a sense of time
5. Skills involved in interpreting tables, graphs, and charts
6. Human-relations skills

We have already discussed the evaluation of critical thinking skills earlier in the chapter, and many of the types of items presented are also appropriate for assessing other kinds of skill development. Sample evaluative items or procedures for each of the other categories will thus be presented below.[68] Realize that the evaluation of social studies skills involves test items similar in form to many of the examples already presented. This is especially true for categories 3, 4, and 5 presented above.

COMMUNICATIONS SKILLS

Communications skills involve the ability of students to read and to listen intelligently. These abilities further include such skills as being able to explain what a word or statement means, identifying the main and subordinate ideas being expressed by an author, identifying similar and different points of view, organizing data, and assessing the reasoning of others. Many of the types of questions presented earlier to measure the development of thinking, having to do with the reliability of data and the analysis of ideas or generalizations, therefore would be applicable in this regard. Here are some further suggestions:

> *Instructional Objective:* Students indicate that they understand what a word or statement means in a given context by explaining it in their own words, or otherwise defining it.

[68]Once again, only a few examples will be given for illustrative purposes. For further examples and a more extensive treatment, see Dana G. Kurfman and Robert J. Solomon, "Measurement of Growth in Skills," in Helen McCracken Carpenter, *Skill Development in Social Studies*, Thirty-third Yearbook of the National Council for the Social Studies (Washington, D.C.: National Council for the Social Studies, 1963), pp. 274–295; and Howard R. Anderson, "Evaluation of Basic Skills in the Social Studies," in Berg, ed., *Evaluation in the Social Studies*, pp. 100–114.

Test Items. Any of the following may be useful in evaluating the above objective:

   a. Asking students to explain in their own words what a particular word, statement, or passage means.

   b. Dividing the class into small groups of four or five and having these groups work together to rewrite in their own words an author's idea.

   c. Asking students to write four or five questions that they could use to help other students determine whether they understood the main idea of a passage.

   d. Asking students to summarize in at most two sentences the main idea of a story or passage.

   e. Asking students to suggest synonyms for difficult words which students do not understand.

Instructional Objective: Students are able to organize information into some sort of logical order.

Test Items: The following procedures can be used to evaluate this objective:

   a. Asking questions such as the following concerning any reading material:
      • Is there any single idea on which the rest of the material in the passage appears to depend?
      • Where is this idea located?
      • Is there a better place where the idea might be located? If so, where might this be?
      • Are there some ideas in the passage which are easier to understand once others have been explained?
      • What facts, ideas, or conclusions might make more sense if they are rearranged in a different way?

   b. Asking student to identify and eliminate extraneous material. They can be asked, for example, to rate statements about the context of a passage by marking such statements as follows:
      (+) any statement which is true and logically supported by information in the passage
      (?) any statement which might be true, but which is not logically supported by information in the passage
      (0) any statement which is false as evidenced by information in the passage.

   c. Asking students to place in order, from most to least important, the key ideas contained in a reading assignment.

   d. Asking students to classify information. For example, students can be given a list of familiar objects and asked to classify them as household or non-household objects. Once they understand what simple classification means, they can be asked frequently to classify certain aspects of their reading. (For example, whether certain factors would or would not be considered causes of prejudice and discrimination in the United States today.)

e. Asking students to write one or more appropriate titles for a passage.

f. Asking students to identify the main thrust of an author's thought, or to explain why he emphasizes or omits a particular point.

SKILLS ASSOCIATED WITH DEVELOPING A SENSE OF PLACE

These skills primarily involve developing in students a sense of direction and a sense of distance. Some sample test items follow:

Instructional Objective: Students can read a map correctly.

Test Items:

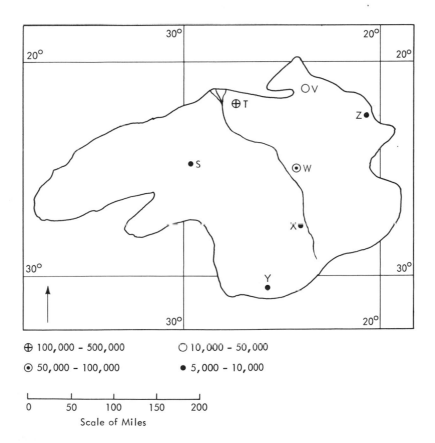

⊕ 100,000 – 500,000   ○ 10,000 – 50,000

◉ 50,000 – 100,000   ● 5,000 – 10,000

```
0      50     100    150    200
```
Scale of Miles

Use the map above to answer the following questions:

The river is flowing generally
    (A) Northwest   (C) Southwest
    (B) Northeast   (D) Southeast
Which city is nearest the mouth of a river?
    (A) T   (C) W
    (B) V   (D) X
In relation to the equator the position of the island pictured above is
    (A) North   (C) East
    (B) South   (D) West
The distance from W to Z is approximately
    (A) 25 miles   (C) 300 miles
    (B) 100 miles   (D) 500 miles[69]

Instructional Objective: Students can identify where certain places are in relation to other places.

Test Item:

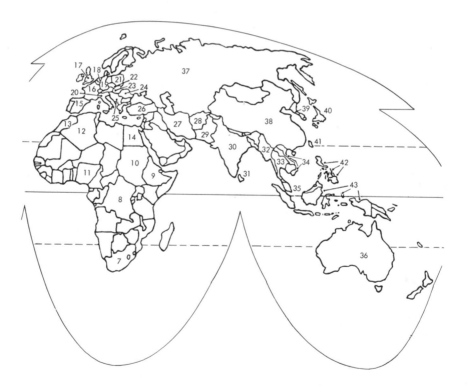

[69]Dana G. Kurfman and Robert J. Solomon, "Measurement of Growth in Skills," in Helen McCracken Carpenter, ed., *Skill Development in Social Studies*, Thirty-third Yearbook of the National Council for the Social Studies (Washington, D.C.: National Council for the Social Studies, 1963), pp. 290, 292. Reprinted with the per-

Which nation is identified by the number ten?
  (a) Burma
  (b) Peru
  (c) The Sudan
  (d) Ethiopia[70]

Instructional Objective: Students can make probability inferences from data shown on a real or hypothetical map.
Test Item:

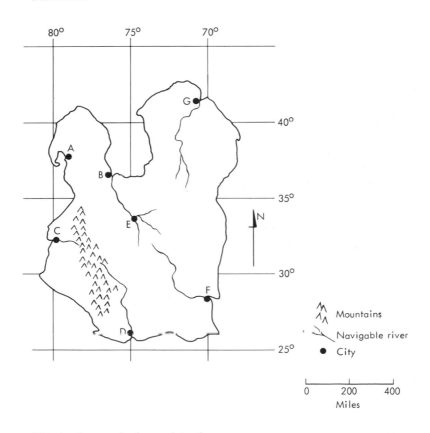

This land must be located in the
  (a) eastern hemisphere south of the equator
  (b) western hemisphere south of the equator

---

mission of the National Council for the Social Studies, Dana G. Kurfman, and Robert J. Solomon.

[70]Dana G. Kurfman, "Evaluating Geographic Learning," in *Focus on Geography: Key Concepts and Teaching Strategies,* Fortieth Yearbook of the National Council for the Social Studies (Washington, D.C.: National Council for the Social Studies, 1970), p. 362. Reprinted with the permission of the National Council for the Social Studies and Dana G. Kurfman.

(c) eastern hemisphere north of the equator

(d) western hemisphere north of the equator

If there were highlands not shown on the map, they would probably be located between

(a) the rivers on which F and G are located

(b) F and G on the coast

(c) A and B

(d) B and E[71]

SKILLS ASSOCIATED WITH DEVELOPING A SENSE OF TIME

The development of a sense of time involves helping students to progress from rather general concepts like "before" and "after" to more precise terms such as day and hour, year, and century. Here is an example of a test item that assesses student understanding of time.

> *Instructional Objective:* Students can indicate whether a given event occurred before or after another event.
>
> *Test Item:* Of the developments listed, which began first?
>
> (A) The Crusades
>
> (B) The industrial revolution
>
> (C) The Islamic religion
>
> (D) The commercial revolution[72]

Other possibilities involve asking students to indicate which of several events took place within five (ten, twenty, etc.) years of another, asking them to rearrange several chronologically out-of-order events into the order in which they occurred, or using a time-line like the following:

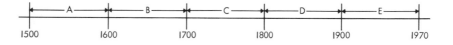

Students can be asked to use the appropriate letter to indicate when a given event or events occurred.

[71]Dana G. Kurfman, "Evaluating Geographic Learning," in *Focus on Geography: Key Concepts and Teaching Strategies*, Fortieth Yearbook of the National Council for the Social Studies (Washington, D.C.: National Council for the Social Studies, 1970), p. 364. Reprinted with the permission of the National Council for the Social Studies and Dana G. Kurfman.

[72]D. G. Kurfman and R. J. Solomon, "Measurement of Growth in Skills," in H. M. Carpenter, ed., *Skill Development in Social Studies*, p. 291.

SKILLS INVOLVING THE INTERPRETATION OF
TABLES, GRAPHS, AND CHARTS

The ability to interpret graphs, tables, and charts relies on certain other skills that students must already possess. They must be able to perform certain arithmetical computations. They must also understand what the graph, table, or chart is describing (e.g., that pie-charts are commonly used to indicate the percentages assigned to various parts of a whole). The teacher must determine therefore, in assessing student ability to interpret data found on a chart, graph, or table whether any difficulty discovered may not be due to lack of development of certain more basic skills.

You have already been presented with one example of a test question designed to assess student ability to draw conclusions from tabular data (see page 300). Here is another example:

> *Instructional Objective:* Students can identify which of several assumptions must be made in order for a given conclusion to be valid.
>
> *Test Item:* Look at the data in the chart below to answer the question below.

U.S. MERCHANDISE EXPORTS AND IMPORTS,
BY CONTINENTS, 1920, 1930, 1940, 1950
(VALUE IN THOUSANDS OF DOLLARS)

Year	Exports			Imports		
	Europe	*Asia*	*Africa*	*Europe*	*Asia*	*Africa*
1920	4,446,091	1,043,184	165,662	1,227,843	1,476,691	150,285
1930	1,838,377	555,707	92,362	908,846	889,286	67,548
1940	1,645,428	713,693	160,609	390,161	1,015,542	131,162
1950	2,893,324	1,638,218	349,354	1,387,445	1,907,597	493,661

52. In the light of what she was buying from us in the way of goods, Europe had less wealth in 1950 than she had in 1920. Which of the following three assumptions would be necessary for this interpretive statement to be valid?

   (A) The richer a continent, the less it can afford to import.

   (B) The larger a continent and its resources, the less it needs to import.

   (C) What Europe buys from us in the way of goods is some indication of how much wealth Europe has.[73]

[73]Dana G. Kurfman and Robert J. Solomon, "Measurement of Growth in Skills," in Helen M. Carpenter, ed., *Skill Development in Social Studies*, Thirty-third Yearbook of the National Council for the Social Studies (Washington, D.C.: National Council for the Social Studies, 1963), p. 293. Reprinted with the permission of the National Council for the Social Studies, Dana G. Kurfman, and Robert J. Solomon.

HUMAN RELATIONS SKILLS

Several devices for assessing human relations skills have already been described in Chapter 2, so only a few additional comments will be made about them here. They are probably the most difficult kind of skill about which to gather reliable data. A major reason, as we have seen, is the difficulty involved in defining what growth in these areas implies. How does a teacher determine if students are becoming more tolerant, empathetic, courteous, responsible, open-ended, etc.? Such terms are notoriously difficult to define. Nevertheless, as was argued in Chapter 1, teachers need to attempt such definitions. For example, as Kurfman and Solomon point out, if the development of group discussion skills is an objective, a list like the following might be used:

1. Asks questions which clarify the issue under discussion.
2. Makes statements relevant to the issue.
3. Speaks audibly and clearly.
4. Contributes to the discussion without monopolizing it.
5. Encourages others to express themselves.
6. Summarizes conclusions.[74]

One or more of the many procedures identified in Chapter 2 (e.g., checklists, attitude scales, role-playing, etc.) can then be used to observe student behavior systematically to see if a greater incidence of these behaviors occurs over time.

ESTABLISHING A MORE ADEQUATE EVALUATION PROGRAM

Table 7.3 outlines a series of basic steps that teachers can follow to increase the adequacy of their evaluation efforts. We shall discuss each briefly.

[74]Dana G. Kurfman and Robert J. Solomon, "Measurement of Growth in Skills," in H. M. Carpenter, ed., *Skill Development in Social Studies*, Thirty-third Yearbook of the National Council for the Social Studies (Washington, D.C.: National Council for the Social Studies, 1963), p. 293. Reprinted with the permission of the National Council for the Social Studies, Dana G. Kurfman, and Robert J. Solomon.

TABLE 7.3

*STEPS IN ESTABLISHING A MORE ADEQUATE
EVALUATION PROGRAM*

Translate Evaluation Findings into Improvement
of Curriculum and Instruction
↑
Select or Develop Appropriate Devices for Getting
Evidence of Changes in Students
↑
Establish Evaluative Criteria
↑
Gather Data on Learners That May Hinder
or Help Attainment of Objectives
↑
Clarify Instructional Objectives

CLARIFYING INSTRUCTIONAL OBJECTIVES

Before evaluation can even be contemplated teachers must decide in what ways they want their students to change. What kinds of knowledge do they wish them to acquire? What kinds of attitudes and values do they want them to display? What kinds of feelings do they want them to have? What kinds of thinking skills do they want them to develop? What other kinds of skills to master? This judgment is essentially an arbitrary one, but responsible teachers will do their best to be comprehensive in their efforts, and to bring about a change not only in what students know, but also in how they think, what they feel, what they value, and what they can do.

It is essential, therefore, that evaluation efforts be consistent with objectives. No matter what teachers stress in class, students will concentrate on those things about which they are examined. If logical thinking is stressed in class, but students are examined only on the amount of information they have acquired, it is the latter rather than the former that is reinforced. Teachers must continually ask themselves: "What kind of change do I want?" and "Am I trying to develop student attitudes, feelings, values, thinking, and skills *as well as* knowledge?"

Teachers must clarify as precisely as possible the kind of behaviors, products, or experiences they want students to develop, produce, or engage in. We have already seen in Chapter 1 that some objectives lend themselves more easily to evaluation than others. It is much more difficult to measure instructional objectives that contain verbs like "to appreciate" or "to have faith in" than it is to measure objectives which contain verbs like "to describe" or "to explain." The latter are more explicit than the former. Whenever possible, therefore, teachers should indicate clearly the kinds of behaviors, products, or experiences they expect students to develop, products they want students to create, or experiences they want students to have.

GATHERING DATA ON LEARNERS
THAT MAY HELP OR HINDER
ATTAINMENT OF OBJECTIVES

Once a teacher is clear about his objectives and has checked to ensure that his objectives are comprehensive, he needs to consider the various factors that may help or hinder attaining these objectives. The socio-economic background of students, peer group attitudes and values, previous learnings, underlying concerns, special abilities and/or interests, resources and materials available, the nature of the school and community— all can affect the attainment of certain objectives and accordingly the kinds of evaluation attempted. Teachers need to collect as much of this kind of data on students as is possible. (Refer again to Chapter 2 for devices that you can use to gather such evidence.) As Taba suggests, "one cannot judge the ability to interpret data of students who have had little opportunity to learn to do so in the same manner as that of students with a long history in training in processes of interpretation. Nor does failure to appreciate literature mean the same thing for students with ample books around them as it does for students who see books only in school."[75] It is at this point also that a teacher's philosophy of education becomes important. He must think carefully about what he considers most important—what kinds of students he wants to help develop, and then design appropriate learning experiences to bring these desires about. If he is not sure in this regard, he may succumb to emphasizing (and evaluating) only those outcomes which are easiest to understand and measure.

ESTABLISHING EVALUATIVE CRITERIA

When the objectives are clear and the nature of the student population has been considered, teachers need to determine what kinds of student behavior will constitute an acceptable performance. Too often teachers base their determination of what is acceptable student performance on intuitive judgment, such as the amount of "creativity" that an essay possesses. Such criteria are highly subjective (unless "creativity" can be defined much more precisely by stating examples of the kind of behaviors or

[75]Hilda Taba, *Curriculum Development: Theory and Practice*, p. 327.

products that would constitute observable evidence of creativity). The student, as a result, faces considerable difficulty in determining how to improve his performance. A more preferable and just procedure is for teachers to define clearly what is and what is not acceptable behavior, and to make clear the levels or degrees of "acceptability." These standards should then be applied consistently.

For example, suppose a teacher desires to develop student ability to remember and understand the factual content of a story or film, and to recognize and use any new words that appear. Bradfield and Moredock[76] suggest a set of evaluative criteria that could be used to evaluate these objectives, as shown in Table 7.4. The "Performance" column indicates the range of possible behaviors that students might display; the "Level" col-

TABLE 7.4

*AN EXAMPLE OF DEFINITIONS OF EVALUATIVE CRITERIA**

Level	Performance
I. Unsatisfactory	Cannot pronounce correctly the new words when seen written. Cannot answer questions about the most obvious facts contained in the story.
II. Fair	Can pronounce the new words correctly when seen written. Can answer questions about the most obvious facts contained in the story when the questions are phrased the same way as the statements in the story.
III. Good	Same as level II, and in addition: Can underline the new words from among other words when the new words are spoken. Also has a rough idea of the meaning of the new words. Can answer more subtle questions about the content of the story when the questions are phrased differently from the sentences in the story. Also can recall the sequence of the story.
IV. Excellent	Same as levels II and III, and in addition: Can correctly use new words in sentences of his own construction drawn from his own experience, and can identify when the new words are improperly used. Can relate the content of the story to his own experience and can give plausible explanations of the events in the story.

*From MEASUREMENT AND EVALUATION IN EDUCATION by J. M. Bradfield and H. S. Moredock. Copyright © 1957 by The Macmillan Company. Reprinted by permission of J. M. Bradfield and H. S. Moredock.

[76]J. M. Bradfield and H. S. Moredock, *Measurement and Evaluation in Education* (New York: Macmillan, 1957).

umn indicates a judgment or evaluation of each of these behaviors. Level of performance is thus linked to level of acceptability.

SELECTING OR DEVELOPING APPROPRIATE DEVICES FOR GETTING EVIDENCE OF CHANGES IN STUDENTS

Students need opportunities to demonstrate desired behavior, produce desired products, or participate in desired experiences. If all four categories of objectives are to be appraised, a variety of evaluative instruments are necessary. Teachers need to select those instruments they feel are most appropriate for obtaining the kinds of evidence they need. The selection of certain devices rather than others depends on the objectives to be appraised, the kinds of students involved, the type of classroom, and the behaviors, products, or experiences to be evaluated. If a teacher wishes evidence, for example, of how well students work together in groups, direct observation of them participating in group activities is necessary. If he desires evidence of their ability to conceptualize, a concept development exercise as presented in Chapter 5 is called for. If he desires insight into their feelings about other people, anecdotal records may be used. The point being stressed here is that teachers must first determine the kind of evidence they need before they can select the evaluative device that is most appropriate for attaining that kind of evidence. Michaelis, for example, lists the following as proposed by one group of teachers for evaluating various outcomes, pointing out that other devices could be added to each category as special needs indicated:

> *Critical Thinking.* Tests, observation, group discussion, checklists, charts.
>
> *Attitudes.* Questionnaires, checklists, scale of beliefs (attitude scales), observation, anecdotal records, recordings, discussion, individual interviews.
>
> *Interests.* Observation, diaries and logs, interest inventories and checklists, questionnaires, records of activities and use of leisure time.
>
> *Concepts and Generalizations.* Observation of use, group discussion, tests, samples of written work.
>
> *Work-Study Skills.* Samples of work, tests, observation of use, checklists, charts, group discussion, interviews.
>
> *Functional Information.* Tests, charts, discussion, observation, samples of work.
>
> *Group Processes.* Observation, group discussion, charts, checklists, sociograms.[77]

[77]John U. Michaelis, *Social Studies for Children in a Democracy*, 4th ed. (Englewood Cliffs, N.J.: Prentice-Hall, 1968), p. 523.

TRANSLATING EVALUATION FINDINGS INTO IMPROVEMENT OF CURRICULUM AND INSTRUCTION

Evaluative data, once obtained, must then be utilized. Unless the results of evaluation are used to improve instructional processes and materials, evaluation itself becomes useless. The results of evaluation should reveal the extent to which students have attained the various categories of objectives. Review, revision, reteaching, or further instruction can then be planned. For such planning to be realistic, however, it must be based on as much empirical evidence as can realistically be obtained. Without such evidence, teachers will have little choice but to rely upon their intuition as their guide in planning where to go next—a foundation for instructional decision-making that seems shaky at best.

SUMMARY

This chapter dealt with the nature of summative evaluation, focusing in particular on the preparation of pencil-and-paper tests. A number of basic characteristics (validity, reliability, objectivity) that all tests should possess were discussed and certain basic rules of test construction suggested. Similarities and differences that exist between objective and essay tests were presented and certain conditions that are appropriate for using each type were identified. Examples of poor and improved objective and essay questions were presented, and common errors to avoid in order to write good questions in each category were discussed. A method for scoring student responses to essay questions was described. Several test items for measuring a variety of intellectual skills and abilities, as well as a number of devices for assessing non-cognitive objectives were presented. Finally, five basic steps for teachers to consider to increase the adequacy of their evaluation efforts were suggested.

EXERCISES*

I. The steps listed below are ordered incorrectly. Indicate the order in which they should be followed if a teacher is to increase (or check on) the adequacy of his evaluation efforts by placing a "1" in front of the step which should be followed first, a "2" in front of the step which should come next, and so on.

a. _____ Gathering data on learners that may help or hinder attainment of desired objectives.

b. _____ Selecting or developing appropriate evaluation devices for getting evidence of behavioral change.

c. _____ Establishing criteria for evaluation.

d. _____ Clarifying instructional objectives.

e. _____ Translating evaluation findings into improvement of instruction.

II. Place the letter of the correct term from Column A in front of its definition in Column B.

A	*B*
Reliability **(R)**	**1.** _____ The idea that a test measures what it says it measures.
Validity **(V)**	
Objectivity **(O)**	**2.** _____ The fact that students score roughly the same on a second administration of a test as they did on the first administration.
	3. _____ A test that actually measures the kinds of behavior identified in an instructional objective.
	4. _____ Synonymous with consistency.
	5. _____ More difficult to attain in essay than objective tests.
	6. _____ The idea that all desired categories of objectives being stressed in the instructional program should be assessed to determine the degree to which they're being attained.

*The author's suggestions are on page 403.

A   B

7. _____ A characteristic of a test item the answer to which many judges agree.

8. _____ Least likely of the three to be completely attained.

III. Place an (E) in front of those situations listed below in which it would be more appropriate to use an essay test than an objective test; an (O) in front of those situations in which it would be more appropriate to use an objective test than an essay test; a (B) if either an essay or objective test would be appropriate.

1. _____ A situation in which you desire students to select from among three alternatives.

2. _____ A situation in which you must test a class of seventy-five students.

3. _____ A situation in which you wish to gain some insight into the ability of students to express themselves clearly.

4. _____ A situation in which the amount of time you have available to prepare a test is quite short.

5. _____ A situation in which you wish to assess student ability to apply what they've learned in one situation to another new and different.

6. _____ A situation in which you wish to obtain test scores that are as reliable as possible.

7. A situation in which you must report the results of testing quickly.

8. _____ A situation in which you wish to assess student ability to analyze relationships.

IV. Place an S in front of those statements that indicate a similarity between essay and objective tests and a D in front of those statements that indicate a difference between them.

1. _____ The use of subjective judgment.

2. _____ The number of questions likely to be included.

3. _____ The measurement of student thinking ability.

4. _____ Ease of preparation.

5. _____ Ease of scoring.

V. Several poor test items are listed below. Place the letter of the reason that indicates the weakness the item possesses in front of the appropriate item.

A. ambiguous   D. contains "give-away" words
B. insufficient detail   E. all choices not plausible
C. hard to read   F. clues given that suggest correct
                                    answer

_____ 1. Place the correct letter of the term in Column A in front of the statement or phrase to which it refers in Column B.

A	B
a. "War Hawks"	_____ Leader of an Indian uprising
b. Lewis and Clark	_____ French minister to United
c. Alexander Hamilton	States
d. Genet	_____ Those who demanded war with
e. Anthony Wayne	England
f. Tecumseh	_____ Negotiated a treaty with Eng-
g. John Jay	land, 1795
	_____ Defeated by Indians in the
	Northwest[78]

_____ 2. Discuss several reasons why the United States became involved in Southeast Asia in the 1960s.

_____ 3. The Supreme Court
  a. always follows its own precedents
  b. never follows its own precedents
  c. overrules its previous decisions only after careful consideration when they seem unsound
  d. does not have precedents

_____ 4. Which one of the following men was the first man to circum-
navigate the globe?
  a. Alan Shephard
  b. John Glenn   **d.** Ferdinand Magellan
  c. Abraham Lincoln   **e.** Dwight Eisenhower

_____ 5. Explain why you think certain kinds of dissent among young people in the U.S. today is on the increase or decrease.

VII. Make a list of some particular objectives (both cognitive and affective) that you believe are worth developing. Try to write one or more test items that would indicate the degree to which students are achieving these objectives. Show your test items to some of your classmates and see if they agree that your items measure student attainment of your objectives.

---

[78] R. W. Tyler, "The Functions of Measurement in Improving Instruction," in E. F. Lindquist, ed., *Educational Measurement*, p. 73.

PLANNING

(PUTTING OBJECTIVES, SUBJECT MATTER,

LEARNING ACTIVITIES, TEACHING STRATEGIES,

AND EVALUATIVE DEVICES TOGETHER)

Objectives, subject matter, learning activities, teaching strategies, diagnostic and other evaluative measures must be organized in some fashion or another to encourage effective instruction. Thus the need for planning.

The first section of the chapter describes the nature and preparation of course outlines, and illustrates how such outlines can help a teacher decide on what subject matter to include in his course of study. Several examples of course outlines are presented.

The second section discusses the importance of teachers having a clearly thought out and logically defensible rationale for the subject matter they do select.

The third section discusses the organization of teaching/learning units, presents an example of an idea-oriented unit, and describes the steps involved in writing such a unit.

The fourth section deals with lessons and lesson plans. The nature of lesson plans is discussed, two examples of imaginative lessons are illustrated, and criteria that teachers can use as guidelines for judging the effectiveness of potential lessons are presented.

When you have finished reading this chapter, therefore, you should be able to:

- *explain* what a course and unit outline is, and *write* your own course and unit outlines;
- *explain* what is meant by the concept "rationale," and *give* at least three reasons why a clearly thought out and logically defensible rationale is important to have when selecting subject-matter;
- *explain* what is meant by an idea-oriented teaching/learning unit, and *write* your own units;
- *distinguish* between lesson and unit planning, *state* (orally or in writing) at least four examples of criteria that you could use in designing a lesson plan, and *write* your own lesson plans using such criteria.

THE ORGANIZATION OF OBJECTIVES,
SUBJECT MATTER, LEARNING ACTIVITIES,
TEACHING STRATEGIES, AND EVALUATION DEVICES

Thus far we have discussed the nature of objectives, diagnostic procedures, subject matter, learning activities, teaching strategies, and evaluative procedures and presented examples of each. We now need to consider how each of these elements can be organized and interrelated in some fashion in order to further effective teaching and encourage student learning. The *order* of instruction has to be determined. Hence the need for planning.

One way to begin is to conceptualize a *course of study*. A course of study represents the subject matter to be learned by students over a particular period of time, usually a semester. What subject matter is to be emphasized at a particular grade level? (For example, what characteristics of various cultures might be analyzed? What groups might be studied? What historical periods might be explored? What geographical areas might be considered?)

One way to go about determining this is to prepare what is frequently referred to as a *course outline*. For example, Table 8.1 illustrates several examples of course outlines—two dealing with World History (one chronologically organized and the other topically organized) for the tenth grade; one dealing with selected concerns of many people around the world (organized by questions) for the eighth grade; and one dealing with selected communities around the world (organized by ideas) geared for the third grade.

Notice that each course outline consists of a list of topics (problems, questions, etc.) to be dealt with in some manner or another during a particular period (semester, year, etc.). Such topics suggest what subject matter is to be focused on within a particular grade. How does a teacher select and order such topics? There is no magic formula for this, no one answer that all teachers will find satisfactory. The order in which a teacher develops such topics (e.g., topically, chronologically, etc.), the sources of information he uses to develop those topics he selects (e.g., textbooks, paperbacks, current newspapers, and magazine articles, etc.), the very nature of the topics themselves (a wide variety of topics is possible within the social studies, e.g., "The American Revolution"; "Families Around the World"; "The Drug Scene—Help or Hangup"; "Black Power"; "A Comparative Study of Athens and Sparta"; etc.) depends on the objectives he has in mind, his own interests, knowledge, and abilities, the materials he has available or can obtain, and the needs and interests of his students. Caution is in order, however. If a teacher selects too many topics for inclusion within a particular course of study, the development of each may be limited and superficial in nature. On the other hand, if too few are selected, the semester's or year's work may be too narrow in scope.

TABLE 8.1

SAMPLE COURSE OUTLINES: WORLD HISTORY
(10th grade, one semester)

1. *Chronological Organization*	2. *Topical Organization*
I. Introduction to the Study of History	I. The Development of Resources for Better Living
II. Prehistoric Man	II. The Development of Economic Life
III. Ancient Egypt	III. The Development of Government
IV. Mesopotamia	
V. Ancient Greece	IV. The Development of Religion
VI. Ancient Rome	V. Western Art
VII. The Middle Ages	

SAMPLE COURSE OUTLINE: UNIVERSAL CONCERNS OF MANKIND
(8th grade, one semester)

3. *Organized by Questions*

Unit   I. What is an American? (To focus on an investigation of the characteristics of the American people both now and in the past.)

II. What makes a people revolt? (To focus on the nature of revolutions —specifically the American, French, Russian, and Cuban.)

III. Are all men created equal? (To focus on the nature of prejudice and discrimination in the United States, with particular attention to the plight of minority groups in the U.S.)

IV. What makes men explore the unknown? (To focus on the nature of exploration—from Columbus to the moon landings.)

V. Why do men fight? (To focus on the nature, reasons for, and costs of, war.)

VI. What lies ahead? The world of the twenty-first century. (To focus on the tremendous social, political, and economic changes occurring in the modern world, and what these may mean for life in the future—with particular reference to Toffler's book *Future Shock.*)

SAMPLE COURSE OUTLINE: THE LOCAL COMMUNITY
(2nd grade, one year)

4. *Organized by Ideas*

I. All communities have certain needs. These needs are met by different groups of people who engage in many different activities.

> II. The people in a community organize themselves in different ways in order to accomplish various tasks.
> III. The nature of a particular community influences the life style of the people living in that community.

Once again, it becomes obvious that teachers must choose. In this instance, they must choose the kind of organization they want. As was mentioned in Chapter 3, honest men will legitimately differ about the optimum way to achieve a particular goal. The important thing is to be sure about what our goals are—about what we want to accomplish, but even more important, to know why we consider these goals important in the first place. As was emphasized in Chapter 3, it is necessary not only to make choices, but also to make *the reasons* for these choices clear. Once a teacher's goals are clearly established and their underlying rationale made explicit, he can design the kind of organization that will most effectively achieve his goals and that is most consistent with his rationale.

THE IMPORTANCE OF A RATIONALE

"A stimulating experience for any teacher is to stop and ask himself why he teaches his subject. What is it for? What difference does he expect to result in his learners from having acquired it? How does it contribute to the learner? Many teachers confronted with this problem will say they teach it because it is good. This leads to the query, 'good for what? for whom? when? and why?' "[1]

Teachers *continually* need to ask themselves "Why should students learn this?" For example, it is not enough for a teacher simply to inform students that "for the next four weeks, we are going to be studying about the American Revolution." Students are entitled to know *why* the teacher feels such a topic is worth learning about in the first place! One thing is for sure. If teachers cannot explain why a particular topic is worth investigating, it is questionable, to say the least, whether students will be very enthusiastic about learning about that topic. When a teacher determines why something is worth learning and teaching about, he clarifies its significance for both himself and his students.

To clarify the point further, let us consider an example. A teacher might choose as a topic for study "A Comparative Study of Communities in Other Cultures," deciding to investigate a range of communities that differ among themselves and from other communities in the United States. He might defend this choice by arguing not only that a wide variety of

---

[1] Earl C. Kelly, *Education for What Is Real* (New York: Harper & Row, 1947), p. 99.

other cultures are intrinsically interesting and worth studying in their own right, but also that students will gain a greater understanding of their own culture and of the concept of "difference" if they contrast their own culture with other cultures.

Let us consider another example. We mentioned in Chapter 3 that a teacher might consider it important for students to learn about the New Deal programs inaugurated under Franklin D. Roosevelt in the 1930s. He could say to his students:

a) For the next four weeks you will have the opportunity to learn about the New Deal in order to analyze the role(s) which the Federal Government plays in the national economy of the United States.

Or he could say, *in addition* to the preceding statement:

b) By understanding the role(s) which the Federal government plays in the national economy of the United States, you hopefully will:
   —see that the state of a country's economy can affect a people's spirit (and perhaps gain some insight into why we feel the way we do sometimes);
   —observe that nations and people react to crises in different ways (and thus understand that others may react in different ways than we do, but that this is not, in and of itself, either good or bad);
   —realize that people attempt to deal with problems in different ways (and thus see that perhaps something is to be gained by listening to other people's ideas).

Which of the two do you think appears most likely to encourage student interest and involvement?

As a final example, here is the rationale which one teacher developed for one of the world history course outlines presented earlier.

Topical Course Outline
One Semester WORLD HISTORY, with Supporting Rationale
   I. *Development of Resources for Better Living:*
      By studying this unit the student should realize:
      —that all groups of people have to deal with certain common problems (e.g., survival needs/adjustment to environment), and thus gain some insight into some of the ways in which men throughout the world are similar.
      —that difficult living conditions in all ages have caused man to invent and discover ways to improve his standard of living; and thus realize *men, if they act,* can change things, and often for the better.
      —that all groups set up standards for themselves—and that the more civilized a group is, the higher is its standard of living; and thus realize perhaps why standards are important to people.

—that the culture and standards of a group influence how far any one individual in the group can advance; and thus realize the extent to which an individual's culture influences his (or her) actions.

—that present-day culture is an outgrowth of the cultures of the past but that the levels and types of cultures achieved by man have varied in the past and also vary today; and thus realize the fact that all men are shaped to a considerable extent by the culture in which they live.

II. *Development of Economic Life:*

By studying this unit the student should realize:

—that most of mankind has always had to work long hours in order to supply basic needs, but that this is not necessarily so today for large numbers of people; and thus gain some insight into why men perform the tasks they do.

—that effective economic systems require cooperation among the individuals within the group (e.g., division of labor) and that living and working cooperatively with others is important to group survival; and thus gain some insight into the value of cooperation as a way of acting.

—that groups benefit by the achievements of other groups—the importance of interchange of ideas and products through trade; and thus realize the importance and value of sharing ideas.

—that geographical location is important to local economy in the development of resources/industry, as well as its importance with regard to international commerce (transportation/trade routes, etc.); and thus gain some insight into the influence of geographic factors on people's lives.

III. *Development of Types of Government:*

By studying this unit the student should realize:

—that human aims and needs have produced a necessity for some form of government (organization, regulation, cooperation) and that human beings play a vital part in the designation of the type of government and the role it will play in any society; and thus gain some insight into the nature of the interactive relationship that exists between human beings and the government under which they live.

—that a body of law is important in the regulation of a society; and thus gain some understanding of the importance of law as a means of social regulation and control.

—that the ideal of "citizenship" or national identity is important to individual development within a society as well as to the development of the society as a whole; and thus realize the importance of ideals for human beings.

—that an understanding of basic principles and practices of leading world governments as these affect international relations can illuminate the strengths and weaknesses of our democratic system; and thus gain some realization of how effectively the democratic system functions, and of how it might be made to work more effectively.

IV. *History and Role of Religion:*

By studying this unit the student should realize:

—the part religion has played and is playing in shaping civilization, and thus gain some insight into the important part which religion plays in the lives of many men.

—that religion is an integral part of all cultures, serving as a unifying factor in promoting cohesiveness; and thus gain some insight into the effect which religious ideas and figures have had in the past upon political states.

—that, as well as differences, all religions have fundamental likenesses; and thus gain some insight into the reasons why many men hold religious beliefs.

—an increased respect for other persons (cultures) and growth in insight into ethical values and principles; and thus gain a greater insight into the nature of his own values.

V. *Western Art:*

By studying this unit the student should realize:

—the importance of artistic contribution, in all aspects, to the study of history as a method of recording information to further the understanding of a given culture (life, customs, beliefs, history); and thus gain some appreciation for the value of art as a source of information.

—that, as in all other aspects of culture, as civilization progresses, so does the level of artistic sophistication; and thus realize why different individuals often perceive and value the same work of art differently.

—that individual self-expression is always influenced by cultural conditions; and thus gain further insight into the influence of an individual's culture upon his actions.

—that art is considered by some to be the universal form of intercultural communication, both as an historical link and among contemporary societies; and thus gain some insight into its power as a means of communication.

Notice that others may not agree with the particular rationale offered in each of the cases given above. This is not especially important. What is important is that a teacher can explain *why* he considers a certain topic, idea, people, period, area, problem, event, relationship (or whatever) worthy of student investigation. When a teacher knows why he believes something to be worth learning and teaching, he is in a strong position both logically and psychologically. He knows not only *what* he wants students to learn, but also *why!* When asked by a student: "Why are we studying this (whatever it may be) anyway?" a teacher can give a more adequate answer than "because it is required"; "it's good for you"; "it's necessary for you to get into college"; or something similar.

THE DEVELOPMENT OF TEACHING/LEARNING UNITS

Once a teacher has selected a number of topics, questions, problems, or ideas for development he then faces the question of selecting and organizing content (i.e., the facts, concepts, and generalizations discussed in

Chapter 3) along with relevant and appropriate learning activities, teaching strategies, and evaluative measures into teaching/learning units for each topic (question, problem, idea, etc.). Units, like courses, can be organized in a number of ways. Once again there is no magic formula that will satisfy all teachers. It is argued here, however, that the building of teaching/learning units around generalizations (ideas) that serve as hypotheses to be investigated is a particularly effective way of organizing content and learning activities for instruction. As was mentioned in Chapter 3 (see p. 123), revisions are simplified since a teacher is not forced to rebuild his units completely every so often in order to stay on top of new developments in the world.

Depending on the idea(s) being investigated, the amount of time spent on certain units can be increased or reduced as needed. Particular ideas can be investigated in a variety of ways, using a variety of different content samples. Current factual data can replace that which is outdated. Different kinds of learning activities can be planned for, allowing teachers to take into consideration differing student needs and interests. Let us consider an example of an idea-oriented unit, in this instance designed for use with seventh graders.

The unit you are about to examine was designed as part of a curriculum developed for teaching social studies in the first through eighth grades.[2] Basic to this curriculum are certain powerful concepts selected from history and the social sciences for their power to organize and synthesize large numbers of relationships, specific facts, and less powerful concepts. As was suggested in Chapter 3, these key concepts are treated again and again throughout the eight grades. Thus, as the student's own experience broadens and his intellectual capacities develop, the curriculum provides him repeated opportunities in a variety of contexts to develop an increasingly sophisticated understanding of these concepts. (See Table 8.2.)

As you examine the unit, notice the following:

• The statements of *Objectives* in the unit reflect the growing emphasis on expressing objectives in behavioral terms. However, too much insistence on

[2]This unit represents one of several which I wrote as part of the Taba Curriculum, Grades 1–8, developed at San Francisco State College. Professor Enoch Sawin of San Francisco State College prepared the objectives, and Professors Norman E. Wallen of San Francisco State and Anthony H. McNaughton of the University of Auckland, New Zealand, along with Sawin, developed the evaluation exercises. See Jack R. Fraenkel, *Western Civilization: Perspectives on Change*, prepared under a grant from the United States Department of Health, Education, and Welfare, Office of Education, Cooperative Research Project OE 6-10-182, San Francisco State College, 1969. Available from Addison-Wesley Publishing Company, Menlo Park, California.

stating objectives strictly in terms of observable and highly specific behaviors may distort the intent of the educator and/or yield lists that are too long to be used effectively.

An attempt was made therefore to reconcile the two points of view so as to have the best of both worlds. Each objective is stated first in terms of observable behavior. Where necessary for full communication of the intent, illustrations of the kinds of specific behaviors desired are included. This procedure was chosen rather than listing all of the possible specific behaviors implied by an objective which would, of course, be almost endless. Following each description of behavior is a summary of the rationale for the objective—why it is important, how it is related to other outcomes, and how it can be conceptualized in terms of certain psychological constructs such as *comprehension, comparison, analysis, attitude, feelings, sensitivity*, or *empathy*. The parallel expression of objectives in terms of both behavior and rationale seemed desirable because it is difficult to express certain objectives in terms of specific behaviors only and others appeared incomplete when expressed in terms of constructs without behavioral component.

It should be emphasized that the list of objectives does not exhaust the possible number of objectives that might be developed in a curriculum. Rather, it indicates those considered of primary importance.

The objectives do not contain precise indications of the *level of proficiency* expected since this will depend in part on the initial level of proficiency or "entering behavior." Thus, the objectives, as stated, are much the same throughout the eight grades, though one would expect increasing levels of "proficiency" if students have studied the curriculum throughout several grades. If, however, the curriculum were introduced for the first time at all grade levels, one would not expect as much difference between, say, first and fourth graders. The evaluation exercises provide some guidelines as to "typical" responses of pupils, but in the last analysis, each teacher must set his own expectations.

- The *Rationale* for each objective indicates *why* that objective is considered important for teachers to develop.

- The *Teaching Plan* outlines in simplified form the order in which the unit is developed, and provides for dividing the class into groups in order to facilitate the comparing and contrasting of data at appropriate points.

- The *Main and Organizing Ideas* for the Unit are listed across the top of all pages in the unit to serve as a reminder to the teacher of the unit's primary focus.

- The *Learning Activities* column identifies the sequence of learning activities in which students will be asked to engage throughout the unit. The *Development* of the sequence represents the body of learning activities in which students engage throughout each unit. These learning activities are organized into a carefully planned and ordered sequence. In addition, explanatory paragraphs, written across the entire pages and intersecting both the "Notes to the Teacher" and the "Learning Activities" columns, appear from time to time to explain the emphasis which a particular sequence of learning activities develops.

- The *Notes to the Teacher* column explains, where necessary, the purpose of certain learning activities; provides, when necessary and appropriate, addi-

TABLE 8.2

CONCEPT THREADS

Causality

Events often can be made meaningful through studying their antecedents. Hence, to some extent, future events can be predicted.

Events rarely have a single cause, but rather result from a number of antecedents impinging on one another in a given segment of time and space.

Conflict

Interaction among individuals or groups frequently results in hostile encounters or struggles.

Conflict is characteristic of the growth and development of individuals and of civilization as a whole.

There are culturally approved and disapproved means for resolving all varieties of conflicts.

Irrational conflict is reduced by recognition of the inevitability of differences and of the difficulty of determining their relative value.

In most situations, some form of compromise is necessary because of the serious consequences of sustained conflict.

Cooperation

The solution of important human problems requires human beings to engage in joint effort.

The more complex the society is, the more cooperation is required.

Cooperation often requires compromise and postponement of immediate satisfactions.

Cultural Change

Cultures never remain static, although the context of the change (economic, political, social, and technological), the speed of the change, and the importance of the change, vary greatly.

Cultural change is accelerated by such factors as increased knowledge, mobility, and communication, operating both within and between cultures.

Differences

The physical, social, and biological worlds (including human beings and their institutions) show extreme variation.

Survival of any species depends on these differences.

Conflicts and inequities often result from assigning value to particular categories of differences, such as white skin or high intelligence.

Interdependence

All persons and groups of persons depend upon other persons and groups for satisfaction of needs.

Behavior of each person and group affects other persons and groups in important ways. These effects on others are often indirect and not apparent.

Modification

As man interacts with his physical and social environment, both he and the environment are changed.

Man has often exploited his physical environment to his own detriment.

Power

Individuals and groups vary as to the amount of influence they can exert in making and carrying out decisions which affect people's lives significantly.

As a strong motivating factor in individual and group action, the desire for power often leads to conflict.

TABLE 8.2 (Cont.)
CONCEPT THREADS (*Cont.*)

Societal Control

All societies influence and attempt to mold the conduct or behaviors of their members. The techniques used include precept, example, and systems of reward and punishment; the specifics of those techniques vary greatly from one society to another.

Marked differences in child-rearing practices often exist among societies.

All societies have some way of punishing adults who do not conform to established ways. The means of punishment include ridicule, shaming, and ostracism, as well as physical punishment and execution.

Written laws are an attempt to clarify the rules by which society operates and to promote an impartial treatment of its members.

Everyone belongs to many groups with overlapping membership, different purposes, and often conflicting demands on members in terms of duties, responsibilities, and rights; each, by exerting social controls, shapes the personality structure and behavior of its members.

Tradition

Societies and the groups and individuals within them tend to retain many traditional values, attitudes, and ways of living and dealing with current problems, whether or not that behavior is appropriate.

Certain institutions in societies, such as the family, religion, and education, tend to change less rapidly than do other elements of societies.

Values

Those objects, behaviors, ideas, or institutions which a society or an individual consider important, and desires constitute values.

Whether or not a person holds a value can be inferred by others only on the basis of an extensive sample of his behavior.

Societies and individuals often differ significantly in the values they hold.

Values develop through both nonrational and rational processes.

The survival of a society is dependent upon agreement on some core of values by a majority of its members.

The greater the variety of values within a society, the greater the likelihood of disagreement and conflict; in some societies such conflict is accepted as necessary to the realization of core values.

---

tional information and ideas for the teacher to consider in involving the class in the various learning activities and suggests points at which evaluation of student progress is appropriate.

- In this unit the *Opener* serves two functions. It provides the teacher with a diagnostic tool to gain some idea of what information the class possesses prior to beginning the unit, and it offers an opportunity to engage students in the cognitive task of developing concepts.
- *The Interactive Use of Learning Activities.* Note that in activities 5 and 6, teachers are alerted to save students' replies to the questions asked in these activities since they will be referred to in later activities.
- *Map Skills.* Activity 6 is one example of an activity bent on developing student skills in map-reading and interpretation.
- *Formulating Hypotheses.* Activity 5 also asks students to hypothesize, and

the note to the teacher points out that these hypotheses will be checked in later activities.

- *Relevance to the World of Today.* Activity 12 asks students to compare and contrast the activities of the ancient Greeks with the activities of men in today's world. Such comparisons are encouraged throughout the unit.
- *Synthesizing Activities.* Activity 36 provides an opportunity for students to draw together the information they have gathered and organized and to make such inferences as are justified by the data.
- The *Evaluation Exercise* measures the extent, at this point, to which students are achieving unit Objectives. Such evaluation exercises appear at appropriate points throughout the unit.

UNIT OBJECTIVES

1. Given access to appropriate materials on the peoples studied in this unit, or other content, the student lists a number of items on the people or on their environment, then groups the items and assigns logically defensible and conceptually powerful (that is, abstract) labels; and when requested, re-forms and re-labels the items in equally defensible ways. Examples of the kinds of items the students will list, group, and label are things students consider important in life, and values held by the ancient Greeks.

    Rationale: Acquiring ability to list, group, and label (concept development) is an important intermediate step in acquisition of other thinking skills and is considered a powerful intellectual skill in its own right, because it facilitates student ability to develop more abstract concepts. Ability to re-group is regarded as an important component of intellectual flexibility.

2. Given two or more different samples of information, the student correctly states differences and similarities. Examples of such comparisons are: Things valued by the ancient Greeks, and living conditions during the days of ancient Greece and today.

    Rationale: Ability to make such comparisons is an important component of the thinking skills to be developed in this unit. It is also essential to development of higher level thinking skills such as the ability to form generalizations, state hypotheses, and make explanations of causes of human behavior.

3. Given a detailed set of facts, the student states valid generalizations that he had not been given previously, and when asked, provides the sources and limitations of the generalizations. Examples of facts and acceptable generalizations based on them that students might state are as follows:

KINDS OF FACTS GIVEN	EXAMPLES OF GENERALIZATIONS
Patterns of family living in various cultures.	All of the people we have studied have some rather definite sets of roles for different members of the family.

KINDS OF FACTS GIVEN

Detailed information on the ways of life of various peoples and many samples of their art.

Information on a number of major social changes and on factors associated with them.

EXAMPLES OF GENERALIZATIONS

You can tell a lot about how people think and how they live by their art work.

Some of the things that help to bring about change are new ideas, inventions, and visits to other countries.

> *Rationale:* Ability to form generalizations is one of the skills that is emphasized in this unit and is important in relation to other thinking skills such as the formation of hypotheses. Making generalizations is also an important aspect of the development of attitudes.

4. Given a set of events (one of which is identified as the event to be explained) occurring in a social setting, the student gives a plausible and logically sound explanation of the chains of cause-and-effect relationships that resulted in the occurrence of the event. Examples of some things to be explained and some explanations by students that would be acceptable are as follows:

THINGS TO BE EXPLAINED

Much can be learned about the values and beliefs of people by observing what they spend money for.

EXAMPLES OF EXPLANATIONS

If a person buys an item, like a phonograph record, something *caused* him to buy it. Usually it is because he likes or wants what he buys—that is, it has value for him. He may sometimes buy things for other reasons, though, so if we want to be more certain about his values, we have to note what he buys on a number of occasions. Beliefs are important, too. For example, a person is not likely to spend money on astrology unless he believes in it. A man won't spend money on exercise equipment unless he believes exercise will be good for his health or body development.

> *Rationale:* Ability to explain cause-and-effect relationships is one of the sub-categories of the general objective of thinking skills. This ability also has important uses in making predictions and forming hypotheses. It is assumed that the student has previously acquired the generalizations needed in making the explanation and that he has not previously studied the explanation he gives.

5. Given relevant facts about a society or a personal situation, the student states logically sound but informally worded hypotheses (that he had not

previously given) about that society or situation today, in the past or in the future. Ability to state hypotheses includes, but is not limited to, ability to predict future events on the basis of present conditions. Examples of given facts and a hypothesis that students might state are:

KINDS OF FACTS GIVEN	EXAMPLE OF HYPOTHESES
Ancient Greece lacked fertile soil to support her people, but had good harbors and shipbuilding skills.	They probably did a lot of trading of things they could make with people who could grow a lot of food.

Rationale: Ability to form hypotheses is part of the general objective of thinking skills, and, of course is essential for anyone who hopes to deal constructively with problems in social studies. One of the most important functions of hypotheses is to provide "focus" for thought processes. That is, they make it possible to narrow down the range of concerns so as to increase the likelihood of successfully coping with the problem being considered. One's thinking is likely to be unproductive if the problem is conceived too broadly or if an attempt is made to analyze too many kinds of facts in too many ways all at the same time.

6. Given a discussion setting or other situation in which students can express their ideas without censure or ridicule, the student makes statements that describe what the teacher judges to be the probable feelings or other thoughts of people studied in this unit. Statements indicative of the desired attitude are:

"I can see how the Greeks felt very proud of their architecture and sculpture."

"People who seem to us to be wrong believe what they believe as much as we believe in what we think is right."

"Some of the people must have felt great uncertainties when they encountered things that undermined their religious beliefs."

Rationale: These kinds of behaviors represent an attitude of empathy. Such an attitude is important because it is a part of the decentering process. That is, it is a step in the direction of overcoming the self-centeredness, which, according to Piaget and others, characterizes much of the behavior of the young child. Unless the child has empathy for the thoughts and feelings of others, he will have difficulty understanding and applying generalizations pertaining to cooperation and to resolution of conflicts among individuals and groups.

7. Given detailed information on activities and patterns of living in various societies, the student makes what the teacher judges to be accurate descriptions (that he has not been previously given) of the probable aspirations of individuals or groups in the society. An example of such a description that a student might give is: "One of the greatest hopes of many Spartan boys must have been to demonstrate their physical courage in combat of some sort."

Rationale: Understanding the aspirations of people in a society is fundamental to understanding the nature of the society and to an analysis of its problems. It also represents another instance of ability to perceive the thoughts and feelings of others as required in the process of decentering. It is, further, an important kind of hypothesizing.

8. Given a situation that encourages free expression, the student makes statements that describe his own values. Some illustrative statements follow:

"I believe in property rights. I like to share my things with people, but I think they should ask me first."

"The idea of the greatest good for the greatest number makes a lot of sense to me."

"Rigid distinctions of class or caste seem wrong to me because they imply that some people are better than others."

"I think minority groups have a right to fight for their rights even when they are outvoted."

Rationale: Ability to conceptualize one's own values is essential in order to identify inconsistencies in one's value system or to analyze relationships of one's own values to those of other people.

9. Given information on the values of people in two or more cultures other than his own, the student describes differences and similarities in the values within and among the cultures and their relationships to his own values. For example, a student might say, "For me I like to be as free as possible from routines and set ways of doing things, but I can see how people in some cultures or sub-cultures get a lot of security out of routines and orderly ways of doing things. It is very important to some people and of little or no importance to others."

Rationale: Ability to relate one's own values to those of others is crucially important in any inquiry directed at clarification or resolution of value conflicts. This objective is an important corollary of objective 2 above on making comparisons.

10. The student indicates comprehension of the meaning of the *Organizing Ideas* and concepts therein in this unit by such behaviors as giving illustrations, explaining meanings, and other actions involving uses. In making the explanations and descriptions, the student correctly uses factual information about the ancient Greeks and himself. In addition, the student indicates comprehension of other ideas not encompassed in the *Organizing Ideas* but related to the key concepts listed in the introductory material. For example, one key concept is *interdependence,* and illustrative student statements that indicate comprehension of the concept are:

"As trade developed, people became more dependent on each other because many of their needs were met by things produced by other people."

"Scholars are greatly interdependent; they make use of, but build upon, ideas of others."

Another key concept is *power*. Statements by students suggesting comprehension of it are as follows:

"The upper classes had a tremendous amount of control over the lower classes. That's power."

"As trade developed, money became a source of influence and power."

Rationale: One of the general objectives of this unit is acquisition of a broad base of knowledge of social studies content. The generalizations around which the units are built are considered to represent powerful ideas having general acceptance in the various disciplines dealing with social studies. This knowledge is considered important so that students can understand the world and themselves more adequately. It is used in this unit in developing thinking skills and attitudes referred to in other objectives.

Generalizations (Ideas) To Be Investigated

MAIN IDEA: THE ACTIONS OF A PEOPLE ARE INFLUENCED BY THE VALUES THEY HOLD.

Organizing Idea: The daily activities of the ancient Greeks reflected their values.

Contributing
  Idea: 1. The activities of individuals and societies reflect what they value.
  Content
  Sample: Ancient Greece—a case study

Contributing
  Idea: 2. Societies, as well as individuals, often differ in their values.

  Content   Athens
  Samples: Sparta

Contributing
  Idea: 3. Societies sometimes punish those who question established values.

  Content   Socrates
  Samples: Loyalty oaths

SUGGESTED ORGANIZATION OF THE CLASS

TEACHING PLAN

The gathering, organizing, and interpreting of information can be accomplished in a variety of ways. Because skill in group process is one of social studies' objectives, the suggested plan on p. 349 provides for dividing the class into groups at the point where contrasting information is sought in greater depth.

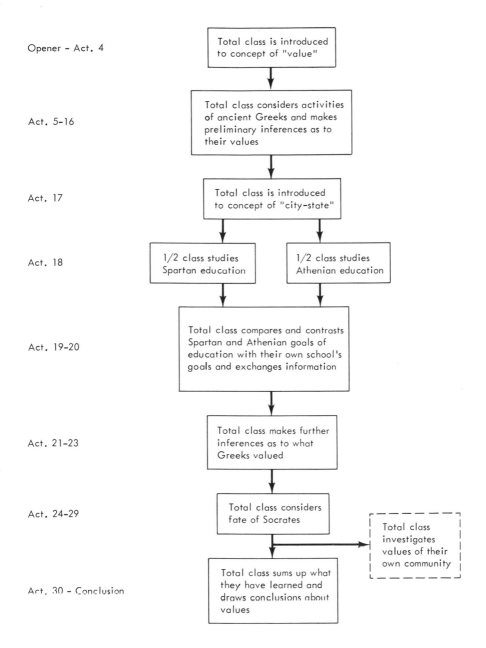

Opener – Act. 4 → Total class is introduced to concept of "value"

Act. 5-16 → Total class considers activities of ancient Greeks and makes preliminary inferences as to their values

Act. 17 → Total class is introduced to concept of "city-state"

Act. 18 → 1/2 class studies Spartan education | 1/2 class studies Athenian education

Act. 19-20 → Total class compares and contrasts Spartan and Athenian goals of education with their own school's goals and exchanges information

Act. 21-23 → Total class makes further inferences as to what Greeks valued

Act. 24-29 → Total class considers fate of Socrates → Total class investigates values of their own community

Act. 30 – Conclusion → Total class sums up what they have learned and draws conclusions about values

DEVELOPMENT OF THE UNIT

MAIN IDEA: THE ACTIONS OF A PEOPLE ARE INFLUENCED BY THE VALUES THEY HOLD.

Organizing Idea: The daily activities of the ancient Greeks reflected their values.

Notes to the Teacher	*Learning Activities*
	Opener
Diagnosis	Have the students write a one-page paper on the topic:
The purpose of the Opener is to introduce the concept of *value* to the students. We will return to these responses later as we begin to develop the concept in greater depth.	What do you think of as really important in life? Why? (Save for later use.) (This could be an oral assignment if you prefer, only be sure to tape-record your discussion so that it can be referred to later.)
Developing Concepts	On the chalkboard, list enough of the responses to practice grouping and categorizing.
Attitudes, Feelings, and Values This discussion should help students *begin* to realize that people differ in terms of what they consider important. Because this unit as a whole is concerned with values, particular learning activities dealing with attitudes, feelings, and values will not be identified hereafter. *Evaluation*—see criteria under *Explaining*, end of unit.	Then discuss with your class: Which of the items on the list are more important to boys? Which of the items on the list are more important to girls? Why? Which of the items on the list would you say are also considered important by parents? Why? Which of the items on the list do you think most of the people in the United States consider important?* What could you offer as evidence that Americans consider these things important?

Activities 1–4 attempt to introduce the concept of *value* and to get students thinking about what they mean when they say, "I value this." These activities also introduce the idea that different people "value" different things.

	Development
	1. Let the students write what they would do if they were given $300 to use in any way they wished. How would they use it? (Avoid the word "spend.") From the writings, select several to show the differences that can be found even within one classroom: Spending Saving Wasting Giving, etc.
Be sure to avoid making any value judgments. Otherwise	Ask:

Notes to the Teacher	Learning Activities
students will tell you what they think you want to hear rather than give their own opinions.	How can you explain the fact that various members of the class would use this money differently?
	2. Ask for volunteers who would be willing to have their essays (written in Activity 1) read to the class. (Do *not* reveal the authors of these essays.)
	Then:
	Read the essays that these people wrote in the Opener (or play a section of the tape recording), by their permission, of course.
	Ask:
	Do you notice any connection between the two papers? Explain. Who or what influences how we use our money? Can we tell anything about a person from the way he uses his money? Explain. Can we tell anything about other people when they tell us how to use our money? Explain.
This would be a likely spot to help students realize the difference between *evidence* (which is usually considered to refer to a tangible object, statement, or sign that tends to prove the existence of something) and an *inference* (which is a conclusion or decision arrived at by reasoning from known facts or evidence). For example: from your *smile* (evidence) *I infer that you are pleased* (inference).	Alternate Activity:
	Read two or three of the ways different individuals would use their money. Then ask:
	What can we tell about people from the way they would use their money? Explain.
	Then read to the class some examples from the newspaper in which people are using money in some way or another. Ask the class what they can tell about the people involved from the way they are using the money.
	3. Duplicate the next page or reproduce it on a transparency and let the students, working in pairs, decide in writing what each of these people value. You might wish to work orally on one or two to help them discover implied values. List on a transparency what values the class suggests. Then ask:
	What conclusion(s) can you draw from the fact that some members of the class saw different values in the same behavior?
The question of how one decides what one values is im-	Then discuss:

Notes to the Teacher	*Learning Activities*
portant and is well worth discussing with your students when the opportunity permits, because it raises the whole question of criteria. You might start your students thinking about various kinds of criteria people use, such as self-interest, "the greatest good for the greatest number," practicality, pleasure, etc. *Evaluation* of the last question —see criteria under *Ethical Concern* at end of unit.	Which of the values discovered in this exercise are important to you? Which of the values discovered in this exercise are important to others? Are some of these values more important than others? *How does one decide? 4. Discuss: What problems might a school have in trying to teach some particular thing which a society values or thinks important for students to learn (for example, honesty)?

List to be Duplicated for Activity 3

After each sentence write what you think these people value that causes them to behave this way.

1. John ran to school because he was late.

2. Henry practiced kicking the football every spare minute he had.

3. Mr. Jones refused to sell his home to anyone who was not white.

4. Parsees expose the dead to be eaten by vultures.

5. Susan and Alice continually teased a new girl in class. Phyllis joined in, but Mary, watching, kept silent.

6. Mrs. Thompson gave $1.00 to a man who asked her for a cup of coffee.

7. Tim Jones burned his draft card.

8. Hopi Indian children never try to win at games.

9. Modest Chinese women wear a high collar to cover the neck.

10. American soldiers who kill their enemies in wartime are given medals; in peacetime they are imprisoned and sometimes executed.

11. Natives in the Gilbert Islands belch loudly when they are finished eating.

12. Moslems pray five times a day.

Notes to the Teacher	*Learning Activities*
	The major thing for students to realize is that in a pluralistic society such as ours, different

Notes to the Teacher	Learning Activities
	groups of people will hold different values, and these values often may conflict. Hence, if the school attempts to teach any one set of values as "the" set, it is bound to alienate and confuse a sizable number of its students. They may not realize this now, but will, hopefully, by the conclusion of the unit. Therefore, list and save their replies for later use.

The activities of individuals and societies reflect what they value. In Activities 5–16, some of the activities of the ancient Greeks are investigated to gain a broader understanding of some of the things people value and to try to determine in what ways the values of others are similar to or different from our own.

Notes to the Teacher	Learning Activities
	5. On a wall map of the Mediterranean area, have a student point out from where the founders of Greece came; the mountainous terrain; the many islands; the coastline; the latitude of Greece. Then ask:
Formulating Hypotheses These hypotheses will be checked in Activity 17. *Evaluation* of responses to either or both of these questions could be made on the basis of criteria of *Variety*, on the numbers of relevant and plausible *Explanations* given, and on the numbers of spontaneous *Comparisons*—see exercises, end of unit.	*What effect might these geographic factors have upon the development of Greece? *What other factors might have contributed to its development? Save the replies for later reference.
Save these maps for future reference.	6. Have students locate, on an outline map, any of the following as they come across them in their work.

Athens   Bay of Salamis   Asia Minor
Sparta   Marathon   Mediterranean
Corinth   Thermopylae   Sea
Mycenae   Hellespont   Aegean Sea
Olympia   Troy   Knossus
Miletus   Thebes   Delphi
Crete   Mt. Olympus   Sardis
    Macedonia

Suggested References:

America's Old World Frontiers, by Thomas D. Clark and Daniel I. Beeby (Chicago: Lyons & Carnahan, 1965), pp. 102, 126.
Exploring the Old World, by Stuart O. Hamer (Chicago: Follett, 1967), p. 101.
Story of Nations, by Lester B. Rogers, Fay Adams,

Notes to the Teacher	Learning Activities
	and Walter Brown (New York: Holt, Rinehart & Winston, 1968). *World Background for American History*, by Harold H. Eibling, James Harlow, and Fred King (River Forest, Ill.: Laidlaw, 1965), p. 82.
*Have students take notes on these questions since they will want to put the information on retrieval charts later on. *Evaluation* of responses could be done on the basis of the criteria *Explaining*—see criteria, end of unit.	7. Have all students read widely about the ancient Greeks to gain a general impression of Greek life. Then give the class specific questions on Greek civilization listed below: *Suggested Study Questions: • Who were the Greeks? • When did they live? • Where did they live? • What things did they leave behind (that is, artifacts, writings, etc.) that tell us something about them? • What kinds of work did they do (i.e., jobs and occupations and kinds of places where these are located)? • What objects or things did they produce or create (i.e., products)? • What did they do for recreation (i.e., how did they entertain or amuse themselves)? • What kinds of family patterns did they develop? Community structure? • How did they govern and control (i.e., type of government)? • What customs and beliefs did they hold (i.e., traditions, religious views, etc.)? • What events, individuals, or ideas are they particularly known for? How did these events, individuals, or ideas affect their lives? • What problems did they have (i.e., conflicts, difficulties, changes, etc.)? • How did they attempt to deal with these problems (i.e., ways they went about trying to ease or eliminate the problem)? Alternate periods of research with the activities which follow. This research is background reading to assist the class in discussion. Point out to the students that they are not necessarily expected to read all these pages. These references indicate mainly where pertinent information can be found when it is needed. Do encourage students to read as much as possible. You will need to help them, however, to learn to read selectively so that they will realize that some books are read in detail; others are only skimmed.

Notes to the Teacher	*Learning Activities*
	America's Old World Frontiers (Clark and Beeby), pp. 112–166. *The Art of Ancient Greece*, by Shirley Glubok (New York: Atheneum, 1963). *The Changing Old World*, by Margaret Cooper (New York: Macmillan, 1965), pp. 86–100. *Classical Greece*, by Maurice Bowra (Morristown, N.J.: Silver-Burdett, 1965), excellent pictures. *Exploring the Old World* (Hamer), pp. 97–119. *The Golden Days of Greece*, by Oliva Coolidge (New York: Crowell, 1968), throughout. *Greece*, by Alexander Eliot (New York: Time, Life World Library Series, 1963), pictures. *Story of Mankind*, by Hendrik Willem Van Loon (New York: Liveright-Tudor, 1968), pp. 49–77. *Story of Nations* (Rogers), pp. 72–104. *They Lived Like This in Ancient Greece*, by Marie Neurath and John Ellis (New York: Franklin Watts, 1968), throughout. *World Background for American History* (Eibling), pp. 79–126.

8. Optional Activity:
   Show one of the following films if available:
   Ancient Greece
   Life in Ancient Greece: Home and Education, film (Chicago: Coronet Films).
   Life in Ancient Greece: Role of the Citizen, film (Chicago: Coronet Films).
   Life in Other Times: Greece: Cradle of Culture, filmstrip (Jamaica, N.Y.: Eye Gate House).
   Life in Other Times: Life in Ancient Greece, filmstrip (Jamaica, N.Y.: Eye Gate House).

   Prepare the class ahead of time by asking them to take notes on the following questions:

   • What is happening in this film?
   • How are things happening?
   • Why do you think they are happening in this way?

   Tell the class to note especially:

   • What things does the film indicate the Greeks valued?
   • What things does the film include that they did not find in their reading?
   • What things does the film omit that were contained in their reading?

Notes to the Teacher	*Learning Activities*
These conclusions will be referred to in Activity 30.	How can they explain any differences they notice? Have the class add to their study questions (begun in Activity 7) any further information they do not have.
Time lines are important in that they help students gain a sense of chronology and a framework within which to put events as they occur.	9. Have the students begin a time line entitled "Significant Dates in Greek History." Have students add to it as the study progresses, placing beneath each date a brief statement of why it is important.
These selections all deal with Greek life. You may wish to look over the readings ahead of time and then identify the particular passages you wish the students to read.	10. Divide the class into three groups, each to read one set of the selections given in Appendix 1. Have each group record all the things it feels that its selection indicates the Greeks valued, and give its supporting evidence.
Developing Concepts	11. Have the class look at some of the pictures listed on one or all of the following pages: Group and label, if you wish. *America's Old World Frontiers* (Clark and Beeby), pp. 124, 133, 134, 136, 137, 141, 148, 150, 152 *Exploring the Old World* (Hamer), pp. 102, 104, 105, 106, 109, 113, 114 *World Background for American History* (Eibling), pp. 88, 90, 92–99, 101, 102, 110–117
Inferring and Generalizing *Evaluation* of Question 3 could be by criteria of *Inclusiveness, Abstractness, Ethnocentrism, Comparison*—see exercises, end of unit.	1. What do these pictures tell you about the Greeks? 2. Which pictures are different? Similar? Explain. *3. What can we say about the Greeks after looking at these pictures?
Exchanging information orally.	12. Have some students give illustrated oral reports on the following aspects of Greek life: • Sculpture • Sports (focus on the Olympic Games) • Architecture • Religion • Drama
Guideline questions for oral reporting are intended to help establish a sense of direction for the reports. They are *not*	Prepare students ahead of time by giving them the following questions to serve as guidelines.

Notes to the Teacher	Learning Activities
intended to indicate certain "right" answers that students will be expected to "come up with."	• Describe what the Greeks meant by each of these terms. • What part did this play in Greek life? (Give evidence or examples.) • How did the Greeks feel about each of these? How do you know? • How do you feel about each of these? *Why do you think you feel this way? • Were any of these important in Greek life? Why or why not? • Are any of these important in your life? Why or why not?
Attitudes, Feelings, and Values *Evaluate the "Why do you think you feel this way?" on the basis of criteria of *Explaining* and *Variety*. See exercises, end of unit. Compare results with previous activities of the same kind.	
	Have the class take notes and add relevant information to the study questions begun in Activity 7.
	Suggested References:
	Basic texts will not be adequate here. Have students consult other books and standard reference works, in addition.
	America's Old World Frontiers (Clark and Beeby), pp. 112–121, 151–152 *Classical Greece* (Bowra), Chaps. 3, 5, 7. Excellent pictures throughout *Greece* (Eliot), pp. 38–45. Pictures *Story of Mankind* (Van Loon), pp. 63–66 *Story of Nations* (Rogers), pp. 86–90; 96–99 *World Background for American History* (Eibling), pp. 84–86, 109–113
These conclusions will be referred to again in Activity 30.	13. Have students bring in pictures from newspapers or magazines showing contemporary statues or buildings. Ask:
Comparing and Contrasting *Apply the criterion of *Explaining* to both of these. Generally the *Similarities* comparison will be the most difficult and should therefore be given more weight for *evaluation* purposes.	*What differences and similarities do you notice between these examples and Greek sculpture and architecture? *How can you explain these differences and similarities?
	Optional Activity:
	Let one student prepare an illustrated report comparing and contrasting the sculpture and architecture of ancient Egypt with that of classical Greece.
	Suggested References:

Notes to the Teacher	Learning Activities
	Ancient Egypt by Lionel Casson (Morristown, N.J.: Silver-Burdett, 1965). *Classical Greece* (Bowra)
Comparing and Contrasting *The last guideline question could be evaluated by an *Ethical Concerns* criterion (Activity 3) and comparisons made with Activity 3 in size and composition of groups. Appropriate changes may then be made in the instructional program. At this point, you might again explore the concept of criteria by which choices are made.	Suggested guideline questions: • What does this sculpture and architecture tell you about the people who created it? Explain. • In what ways are the sculpture and architecture of these two cultures different? • In what ways are they similar? *• Which do you prefer? Why?
	This would be a likely place to have a professor or teacher of art from a nearby junior college or high school visit the class and give his or her opinions on the nature of art. Prepare the class ahead of time, however, by having them ready to ask questions such as: What do we mean by "art"? What does it include? Does "art" differ for different peoples? Explain. Does "art" differ over time? Explain.
Record and save for use in Activity 30.	14. Have the class read "The Gods and Goddesses of Greece" in *America's Old World Frontiers* (Clark and Beeby), pp. 115–121. Then ask: What can you say about the religious beliefs of the Greeks?
Save these charts. They will be referred to again later.	15. Let the class exchange the information gathered in Activity 7–14 by having spokesmen from each of the groups formed in Activity 10 report their findings, with the balance of the class using the chart below to take notes.
This discussion is intended to help students realize that abstract concepts like bravery,	Point out to the class that this is only one kind of bravery (to defend the state).

Findings (Evidence)	Values
Spartan mother's comment to her son (Appendix 1)	Bravery

Notes to the Teacher	Learning Activities
justice, dignity, etc. are not easy to define because there are many different kinds of bravery, etc. and different people will define such concepts in different ways.	What other kinds of bravery can students think of? How are these examples of bravery different? Similar?
This discussion is intended once again to relate the activities of people in the past to the lives of people today. *Evaluation* of ability to support opinions with evidence. See Opener, and compare results.	16. Have the students refer again to the chart in Activity 15. Ask: How many of the things which the Greeks valued do you think Americans value? In what ways did the values of the Greeks influence their behavior? How do the values that Americans hold influence their behavior? *What evidence can you offer to support your viewpoint?

Societies, as well as individuals, often differ in what they value. To deepen an understanding of Greek values, certain aspects of two Greek city-states—Athens and Sparta—will be looked at in depth in Activities 17–22.

You may want to give the class more understanding of the Greek *polis* than is present in the texts. It was more than a political organization. It meant the land and little villages surrounding the city, the community of people to whom one owed allegiance and to whom one could appeal for justice in face-to-face dialogue, the center for cultural activities, with an emphasis on participation by each citizen. The English language does not have a word that correctly translates *polis*. Teacher Reference: *Classical Greece* (Bowra)	17. Have a student report on the growth of the city-states in Greece. Prepare him ahead of time by giving him the following questions to serve as a research outline: • What were the city-states? • How did they develop? • What contributions did they make to Greek life? Suggested References: *America's Old World Frontiers* (Clark and Beeby), pp. 128–130, 138–140 *Exploring the Old World* (Hamer), pp. 103–104 *Story of Nations* (Rogers), pp. 76–83 *World Background for American History* (Eibling), p. 90. Have the class refer to the hypotheses they made in Activity 5. Would they change any of their statements? Why or why not?
Evaluate responses to the last question using *Ethical Con-*	18. Divide the class in half to read about Spartan and Athenian education. Suggested study questions:

Notes to the Teacher	*Learning Activities*
cerns criterion for the first part and *Explaining* for the second. Note changes in class and individual positions and plan to accelerate change in desired directions for both criteria. A further comparison should be made on the basis of *Decentering*. See exercises, end of unit.	• Who was educated? • Who did the teaching? • What did they learn? • What were the goals of education? • What methods were used to encourage striving towards these goals? *• Do you approve of the methods which they used? Why or why not? Point out to the class that the way we view another time is always conditioned by how things are done in our own day. Thus we must continually try to ask ourselves: "How would an individual living *at that time* have felt? Suggested References: *America's Old World Frontiers* (Clark and Beeby), p. 145. *Exploring the Old World* (Hamer), pp. 109–111. *Voices of the Past, Vol. 1, Readings in Ancient History*, by James Hanscom, Leon Hellerman, and Ronald Posner (New York: Macmillan, 1967), pp. 91–95. "The Ephebic Oath" "The Training and Education of Spartan Boys" "Pericles' Funeral Oration" *World Background for American History* (Eibling), pp. 94–99 Optional Activity: Listen to the record: *When Greek Meets Greek* (University of Indiana: Ways of Mankind, Side 7). (This record is difficult to understand without some introduction to it. Accordingly, you should preview it and then generally explain to your class what it is about.) Ask: What does this record describe? What difference in behavior do you notice between the Spartans and the Athenians? What reasons for these differences does the record suggest? What information does the record provide which your texts do not? How would you explain this?

Notes to the Teacher	Learning Activities
	You may wish to have students make a chart similar to the one in Activity 15.

Findings (Evidence)	Values
Sparta	
Athens	

Again, it would be wise for you to point out that these values (for example, honor, courage, etc.) represent a certain kind. There are also other kinds—and a class discussion on the point would help you develop the idea that values differ for different people.

This is another attempt to relate material from the past to the lives of students today.

19. Have students write a two-page essay comparing and contrasting Spartan and Athenian goals of education with those of their own school.

   (This may require students to interview teachers, counselors, and the principal, to check the school constitution, etc. to determine the goals of the school.)

   In what ways are they different?
   In what ways are they similar?

   Alternate activity for less able students:

   Have students first *list* all the Spartan and Athenian goals that they can find and then compare these lists with a similar list of their own school's goals.

   Whose educational system did the best job of preparing children to be citizens? Why?
   (This might be a good place to introduce the idea of absolute vs. relative value through asking questions such as the following):

   Are there some things that are always better than others? Why or why not?

*Do not try to come to any definite conclusion at this point, just start students thinking about the idea. This will be returned to later.

*How do we determine what is best?

20. Divide the class in half. Let students exchange information (from the study questions begun in Activity 7) by taking notes on the information the rest of the class has collected and put it onto an individual or group chart.

Notes to the Teacher	Learning Activities

Basic Study Questions	Ancient Greece
See list in Activity 7	

21. Let the class discuss what they consider to be the most important values of Sparta and Athens as indicated by their education (or other evidence), perhaps organizing it in chart form as follows:

Evidence	Spartan Values	Athenian Values
Educational System	Physical Fitness	Obedience to Law
	Plain Living	Physical Fitness
	Courage	Honor

Evaluation of ability to support opinions with evidence. See Opener and Activity 16 for criteria and compare results.

Push students here to defend their answers. They should begin to determine what their values are, and thinking through the question of "absolute value" (in a new form) can help them to decide whether or not they think something is really important.

From the preceding list, select a characteristic that both Sparta and Athens valued and that some Americans value too (such as physical fitness, courage, etc.).* What evidence can you offer to support your view that Americans hold such values?

How do the three societies differ in the way they teach children to value physical fitness, courage, etc.?
In which society would this value (pick any one that all three share) be strongest? Why?
Should this be an important value of every society? Why or why not?

22. After many years, Socrates, one of the leaders of Greece, came to believe that only the most intelligent people should run the government of Athens. Today in the United States, many people believe that only the most intelligent students should be educated and that the rest should be taught some kind of job skill.

Who might favor this idea? Why?
Who might oppose this idea? Why?
Would you support this idea? Why or why not?

Notes to the Teacher	Learning Activities
	23. Compare the charted information in Activity 21 with the information charted in Activity 15.
Inferring and Generalizing *Evaluate* responses with criteria of *Inclusiveness, Abstractness, Qualification* or *Explanation, Comparison*—see exercises, end of unit.	Ask: *Can you make any statements about what the Greeks valued that would be true of all Greece? Of only part of Greece? What evidence can you give in support of such statements?

Not all values are accepted in any society. To disagree with the values of one's society may be dangerous because societies sometimes punish those who question established values. This idea will be explored in Activities 24–28.

24. Show the motion picture *The Death of Socrates* (New York: McGraw-Hill Text Films).

Prepare the class beforehand by having them take notes on the following questions:

What does this film describe?
What does it emphasize?

Then discuss:

What choices of action did Socrates have?
Why do you think he chose what he did?

Alternate Activity:

If you cannot obtain the film, orally paraphrase for the class the fate of Socrates. Then use the same questions as above. (Or combine Activities 24 and 25.)

Suggested References:

Classical Greece (Bowra), pp. 137–139
Voices of the Past, Vol. 1, Readings in Ancient History (Hanscom), pp. 97–98
World Background for American History (Eibling), pp. 116–117

25. Read to the class an example of the Socratic method of teaching.

Ask:

What does this tell you about Socrates?
How does this method compare with methods which you have experienced?

Notes to the Teacher	Learning Activities
	Suggested References:
	Classical Greece (Bowra), p. 139
	Voices of the Past, Vol. 1, Readings in Ancient History (Hanscom), pp. 98–100
This role-playing activity is intended to increase students' awareness of what it means to hold an "unpopular" belief.	26. Hold a mock trial in which you recreate the trial of Socrates.
	Suggested questions for the members of the "jury" (the class) to ask of Socrates and his accusers:
	What is the charge against Socrates? What evidence exists to support this charge? What is Socrates' response to this charge?
	Then discuss: What would you have done in Socrates' place?
	27. Read California Loyalty Oath (pages 394–396) to the class. Then have a student report orally to the class on the following:
	What were the reasons for the State of California requiring this oath?
	Ask:
Comparing and Contrasting *For *evaluation* of the first question, see criteria under *Theme Comprehension* at the end of unit.	*In what ways is what this reading describes similar to what happened to Socrates? In what ways is it different?
**Evaluation* of the last question will be on similar criteria to Activity 3 and comparisons made with it in order to decide what remedial action might be necessary.	Ask: Who was "right" in each of these cases? *How does one decide?
This is a further attempt to relate incidents that happened in the past to the world of today.	28. Ask the class to see if they know of or can locate other examples of incidents similar to those in Activities 24 and 27.
	29. Have the class interview other friends, teachers, and adults whom they know to obtain answers to the following question:
	Are there any kinds of things that it is better *not* to question? How does one decide?

Notes to the Teacher	Learning Activities
	30. Have the class once again refer to the conclusions they made in Activities 8, 13, 14, 15, and 18. Prepare a summarizing chart of what the Greeks valued, based on evidence of this value from their study questions, begun in Activity 7.

Evidence	Valued
Olympic Games Training in sports Statues of athletes Calendar from first Olympiad	Athletic skill
Athena, goddess of wisdom Admired men who spoke with reason Asked questions about everything Discoveries in medicine, science, mathematics Education to train the mind	Thinking
Hired the best artists to build temples Painted pottery	Beauty
Written laws Courts and jurors	Law and order
Citizens voting Citizens must participate Wrote about it, talked about it	Democracy (Athens)

31. Alternate Activity: (Easier for some classes)

List on the chalkboard things that the Greeks did, anything that the class offers. Then, let them decide what the Greeks valued.

What They Did	What They Valued
Voted for laws, people to run government	Democracy for citizens
Boys learned sports, music, fighting, reading, writing	Trained mind Beautiful body Bravery
Gave prizes for best	Writing ability

Developing Concepts

Notes to the Teacher	Learning Activities

*Criteria for this concept development activity could be applied to individual written responses or to a checklist filled in as class responses are recorded on the blackboard. The criteria are detailed in the Opener to this unit. Changes in size and composition of groups should be noted for instructional purposes.

What They Did	What They Valued
athletes, best plays	Fame, honor
Boys learned Iliad, Odyssey	Poetry Heroes of the past Courage

*Another possibility is to list everything first and ask them to group items and categorize before deciding on values.

This is an attempt to introduce the discrepant event—information that does not "fit" precisely—in order to get students to refine their conception of what the Athenian Greeks valued.

32. Call attention to the list of values charted in Activity 30 and/or 31. Ask the class how, then, could the Athenians:

- Ostracize Themistocles whose brilliant leadership built the Athenian Navy, the walls around Athens, saved them from Persia, etc.
- Put Phidias, their most creative sculptor who supervised the building of the famous Parthenon, into jail, where he died.
- Put to death Socrates, the outstanding thinker of the times. (According to one historian, the only man in 90 years of democracy sentenced to death.)
- Turn against Pericles who led Athens into a (relatively) Golden Age of beauty and prosperity that lasted for 30 years.

*Evaluation of ability to resolve discrepancies. See suggestions for evaluating this at end of unit.

*Ask the class if they can explain why there are inconsistencies between what people do and what they value. Might values change over time?

**Explanations could be written prior to a class discussion and used for evaluation purposes. Criteria for this would be similar to those used in the Opener with the addition of Comparisons (i.e., the extent to which they bring in examples from other cultures).

Discuss:

**Do we determine what a person values by what he says, or by what he does? Explain your reasoning.

33. Tell the class you are going to give them a checklist to let them determine how much they have learned. Ask them to use their books, notes, and any other materials they need, to cite evidence to support or refute the statements about Greece given below. Then share with the class, having students present their evidence.

Notes to the Teacher	Learning Activities
	What evidence can you give to support, refute, or qualify the statements given below? Ask yourself: • What did the Greeks do? How do you know? • Why did they do what they did? *• Are these statements true or false, or only partially so? How do you know?
*The explanations given for each of these statements can be evaluated on the basis of a criterion of *Variety* and abstractions.	1. The geography of Greece influenced its development. 2. The Greeks learned much from other peoples. 3. Greeks were patriotic and loyal to their own city-state. 4. Religion played an important part in the lives of the ancient Greeks. 5. The Greeks believed in the importance of the individual. 6. The Greeks believed that all the people should have a say in the government. 7. The Greeks loved manly beauty and athletic skill. 8. Architecture, literature, and education were not important to the Greeks. 9. Little of the Greek culture was spread through the lands around the Eastern Mediterranean. 10. The modern world is influenced by the ancient Greeks.
This should provide some evidence on how well students can draw together what they have learned in this unit.	34. Have the class write an essay on the question: Do values affect behavior?
Inferring and Generalizing *The two activities (35 and 36) should be evaluated on criteria of *Inclusiveness, Abstractness, Comparisons* (only for Activity 36), *Ethnocentrism*. Note the cumulative record of the class (as in size of top and bottom groups for each criterion) and individuals. Such a procedure will assist in planning to meet individual and group needs in the next	35. Inform the class that they now want to try and draw together what they have learned. Have students refer to their time lines, notes, and maps. *Ask: —What can you say about the Greeks? —In what ways are the Greeks similar to any of the ancient civilizations you studied earlier? In what ways are they different? —What does your investigation indicate that the Greeks valued? —What evidence can you offer as an indication of their values?

Notes to the Teacher	Learning Activities
Unit. Responses to the last question in the *Conclusion* are particularly important for these purposes.	—Do any of their values appear to conflict with one another? Which are consistent and which are not? How would you explain this? —Can you offer any evidence to indicate that their values changed over time? 36. Let each student write a summary paragraph or two entitled: "What the Greeks valued" 37. If time and student inclination permit, have the class as a whole investigate similar aspects of their local community as they did for ancient Greece, researching the study questions listed in Activity 7. The chart begun in Activity 20 can now be expanded, as suggested below, to include this additional information.

Basic Study Questions	Ancient Greece	Local Community
See List in Activity 7		

38. When the now expanded chart suggested in Activity 37 has been completed, ask the class to look at the information opposite the various questions to see if they can discern any similarities and/or differences and to suggest possible cause-and-effect relationships.

Conclusion

Hold a culminating discussion on values. Plan a *question sequence*, for example:

- What things did the Greeks value? How do you know?
- Did any of their values change over time? How do you know?
- What things which the ancient Greeks valued do Americans value? What evidence can you offer in support of your opinion?
- Do values influence behavior? Explain.
- Can values be changed? How?
- What do you think we have been saying about values in this unit?

EVALUATION

I. *Developing Concepts*—(See Opener, Activity 31)

If individual written responses are made to this exercise, they may be evaluated in the following way so that measurements can be made of Objective 1 at the beginning of the unit.

A. *Style.* This can be determined from the reasons students give for placing one item with another and/or by the label they give a group.

The four suggested categories are:

1. *Functional* (or locational)

Items are grouped because of a student's personal experience with them, i.e., he groups them because they are specifically important to him and are so because of personal experience. They are essentially selfish and self-centered, e.g., "Bikes are good because I like them," (no reason given).

2. *Descriptive*

Items are grouped because of some physical similarity, e.g., "Lake and sea swimming because they're both water and water is fun."

3. *Class*

Items are grouped because of some common quality or characteristic which is expressed as an abstraction, e.g., "Reading and skating because they're both leisure."

4. *Mixed*

Items are placed in one group when they really belong in more than one. A student usually adds an item which he links to one above for a different reason than has been given for the others.

B. *Quality*

1. Labels and reasons for grouping may be grouped in order as follows:
   a. The lowest group is *Mixed* because of the confusion involved.
   b. The next highest is *Functional* because of the narrow subjective nature of the response.
   c. The highest would be *Descriptive* and *Class* because of the implied objectivity. *Class* groups may be considered higher because of their greater abstractness.

C. *Flexibility*

Note the number of valid changes that are made to groups and labels by individuals when they are asked to suggest, or write down, *other* ways they might be grouped and/or labeled. Then,
   a. Group (and note the names of students in it) responses that have *three or more* valid changes.

b. Group those with *two* changes.

c. Group all other responses. (This group could be subdivided into "one change" and the rest, if there were, say, ten or more who made one change and, say, five or more who made no changes.)

D. *Abstractness of Labels*

The extent to which the group labels are expressed as qualities rather than as concrete items which can be experienced by the senses, e.g., "Desires" would be abstract and so would "Transportation" and "Communication," whereas a label like "Tools" would be relatively concrete.

1. Group all responses which have *three or more* abstract labels in them.

2. Group all responses which have *two* accurate abstract labels in them.

3. Group all the rest.

A variation of this way of categorizing responses may be necessary, if all labels are abstract and accurate. In this case, group those labels that most effectively sum up the essence of the grouped items below them and put all the rest in another group.

E. *Possible Use of Results*

1. Prepare a list of students' names and column headings of *Flexibility* and *Abstractness* (leaving space for other headings to be added for other exercises) and note the group into which each individual's response fell, e.g., Top, Middle, Bottom or 1, 2, and 3. Where a two-group division is made, you might use *Top* and *Rest*. See Table 8.3.

TABLE 8.3

*EVALUATIVE CHART**

CRITERIA																		
Names	Flexibility						Abstractness						Etc.					
Activity or Unit	1	2	3	4	5	6	1	2	3	4	5	6	1	2	3	4	5	6
John Brown																		
Paul Smith																		
Barry Jones																		
Etc.																		

*Adapted from Hilda Taba, Mary C. Durkin, Jack R. Fraenkel, Anthony H. McNaughton, A TEACHER'S HANDBOOK TO ELEMENTARY SOCIAL STUDIES, 2nd Edition, 1971, Addison-Wesley, Reading, Mass.

2. Comparisons in the composition of top and bottom groups should be made between this exercise and similar ones later in the year.

II. *Explaining*—(See Opener, Activities 5, 7, 23, 32, 35)

The following criteria could be used to evaluate responses in order to gain some indication of the attainment of Objectives 4 and 7 at the beginning of the unit. An increase or decrease in any of these categories over time should be noted.

A. *Use of factual information*   The number of relevant facts used in an explanation.

B. *Use of inferences*   The number of plausible and relevant inferences that are included in explanations.

C. *Logical Coherence*   The extent to which facts and/or inferences and the event to be explained are logically linked.

D. *Tentativeness*   The extent to which students indicate the possibility of fallibility in explanations.

III. *Ethical Concern*—(See Activities 3, 13, 18, 20, 27)

Responses to the question "How does one decide" in Activity 3 could be written by individuals prior to a class discussion. The following category and sub-categories could be used to measure attainment of Objective 6 at the beginning of the unit.

A. *Expedient*   Decisions are made on the basis of "my likes" or some other form of self-centered response, or responses are given for reasons that are based on a "because I think so" principle with no further explanation offered.

B. *Rule-dominated*   Unquestioned, or nearly unquestioned, adherence to rules is given as desirable. This may be implicit in the way the response is given, or stated explicitly. No argument is given beyond an implied, "Everyone knows this is what should be done."

C. *Fairness*   Based on a stated belief that people should be fair to each other or that a person should always be treated fairly.

D. *Concerned*   Based on a thoughtful recourse to a few key values, such as altruism and respect for human dignity. Reference is usually made to these few basic ethics by rational argument rather than as truths deriving from a particular authoritative source.

IV. *Descriptions*—(See Activities 5, 11, 12, 13, 18, 23, 33)

This exercise may be used as evidence on the attainment of Objectives 6 and 7 at the beginning of the unit. The following criteria could be applied to written sentences of individual students or to a checklist for oral responses from the class.

A. *Variety*—Use criteria suggested on page 373.

B. *Abstractness*   The extent to which the responses contain precise, abstract instead of concrete, terms in them.

1. Group together all those responses that have *two or more* precise, abstract (and, of course, accurate) words in them, e.g., conditions, suitable, appropriate, climate, enough. (Note that qualifying adjectives and adverbs can be abstract.)

2. Group together all those responses with *one* precise abstract word in them.

3. Group together the rest. (This group may be subdivided, if it is seen to contain more than one kind of response.)

Note: As a separate analysis arising out of the analysis of *Abstractness*, a record could be made of the number of times feelings and/or attitudes are mentioned. This record would provide evidence on the attainment of Objective 7.

C. *Decentering* The extent to which students consider this problem of change from the viewpoint of the people in the pictures.

1. Group together responses that contain at least one explanation (relevant and plausible) of good effects *and* one explanation of bad effects, both of which show adequate decentering.

2. Group together responses that have *only* one decentered explanation (relevant and plausible).

3. Group together responses that have *one* decentered and one nondecentered explanation.

4. Group together the rest.

D. *Ethnocentrism* The extent to which responses reflect some prejudice or other factor which indicates that the students have judged reasons to be exactly the same as apply to them today. They have, therefore, not decentered, and not recognized that an individual's responses need to be appropriate to the times and the associated circumstances.

a. Group together all those responses that contain *no* evidence of ethnocentrism as well as at least *one* clear indication of the need to decenter and look at this Greek world through the eyes of one who lived in it.

b. Group together all responses with *no* evidence of ethnocentrism but also no qualification as suggested in *a*.

c. Group together the rest.

Further subdivisions of these levels may be found to be appropriate as all responses are inspected.

E. *Inclusiveness*

1. Group those that omit only *one* of the important ideas.

2. Group those that omit *two and up to*, say, *four* of the important ideas. (This may be modified to—*up to three*.)

3. Group the rest. (This group may be subdivided to include *up to four*, and the rest.)

F. *Coherence* That is, the extent to which the essays build up in a coherent and logical way rather than as a series of discrete items presented in the form of a list.

1. Group all those essays that have a high degree of coherence in them.

2. Group together and tally those essays that are coherent at one or more points but do not sustain the quality throughout.

3. Group together and tally the rest.

G. *Comparisons* The number of relevant and valid comparisons that are made between one society and another.

   1. Group those essays that have *two or more* such comparisons.

   2. Group those that have *one* comparison.

   3. Group the rest.

H. *Possible Use of Results*

   1. A note could be made of the size of the top and bottom groups for each criterion and comparisons made, for instructional purposes, with group sizes for comparable exercises.

   2. Individual groupings should be recorded as suggested above.

   3. An overall qualitative grade could be given each essay by first following the preceding procedure and then selecting the essays that fall in all of the top groups for the above criteria and those that fall in all of the bottom groups. Subdivision of the balance of the groups into the best, the worst, and the rest will produce, in all, a five-point grade scale which could be designated A, B, C, D, and E.

   4. Data on *Inclusiveness, Ethnocentrism, Abstractness* can be recorded against students' names, and adjustments made to the instructional program for the whole class or for individuals.

   5. Data on *Explanations* should be examined for immediate use in the instructional program and details of whole-class and individual performance compared with later performances. Instruction on explaining procedures might initially take the form of, "Are there any other reasons that you could give?" and/or "What do you think of this (teacher may give relevant, plausible explanation) as a possible explanation?"

V. *Map Exercise*—(See Activity 5)

   This exercise may be used to measure the extent to which students are achieving Objective 4 at the beginning of the unit. Use the following criterion for this measurement, which will be more satisfactorily done if individuals write their answers prior to any discussion. Responses to 1, 2, and 3 may be evaluated separately or together.

A. *Variety* The extent to which responses contain a suitable range of different and valid reasons or explanations for the areas designated as being heavily or sparsely settled.

   1. Group together all responses that contain *three or more* valid reasons for the degree of density of settlement and for the difference between their map from Activity 4 and this one.

   2. Group together all responses that contain *two* valid reasons.

   3. Group together all other responses. The teacher may wish to subdivide this group into, for example, those that have *incorrect*

responses in them, and those with no incorrect and up to one correct response.

B. *Explanations*—Use criteria suggested on page 371.

C. *Comparisons*—Use criteria suggested on page 373.
Note any gaps in information, misconceptions, and emphases that need to be accounted for in the instructional program.

VI. *Theme Comprehension*—(See Activity 27)

Responses to this question will give evidence concerning Objective 10 at the beginning of the unit. The responses can be judged on the basis of a student's capacity to recognize an underlying theme linking the two situations. The following broad criteria and process are recommended:

A. *Theme-based* The extent to which students recognize an underlying common theme, e.g., commitment to a carefully thought-out position, based on clear principles, in the face of threats or punitive action.

B. *Part theme-based* The extent to which responses include comparisons based on a part of the total theme, e.g., they deal with adherence to principles alone.

C. *Concrete Elements* The extent to which the comparison is based on specific, concrete similarities, e.g., physical assault.

D. *Possible Use of Results*
  1. Note in a column opposite each student's name the group into which his response places him and compare with subsequent exercises of a similar kind.
  2. Note the numbers in each group and take immediate steps to reduce any large numbers in the lowest group.

VII. *Discrepant Events*—(See Activity 32)

In this exercise evidence can be obtained as to the attainment of Objectives 4 and 10 at the beginning of the unit. Responses may be placed in three broad groups:

A. Responses that say in any culture values may conflict and that for any given event in which they do predictions as to how people will behave are difficult to make. To illustrate this they may also draw examples from their own culture.

B. Those responses that explain a particular event (or two of them) in terms of an understandable conflict, but do not put all the events in the same general category.

C. Those that accuse the Greeks of inconsistency and blame them for it. The principles for this grouping are similar to those described in Activity 27. Results should be treated in the same way as recommended there and comparisons made for instructional purposes.

GUIDELINES FOR PREPARING
IDEA-ORIENTED UNITS

Let us now consider how to write idea-oriented units such as the one you have just examined. Listed below are some basic guidelines that you can use.

1. Make an initial list of objectives to be developed. Be sure to consider all four of the basic categories—knowledge; thinking, research, and social skills; attitudes and feelings; and values that need to be developed. (Reconsider the appropriateness of these objectives after steps 4, 7, and 9 below.)

2. Decide on a content area within which to build a unit (e.g., World History) and choose a topic within that area. A topic is a particular theme, period, or subject (e.g., the nature of values) to be studied. It suggests much of the subject matter for the unit.

3. Decide on a generalization or main idea (i.e., a hypothesis that suggests a powerful relationship about the world) around which to structure the unit. A "unit" as defined here consists of a series of *learning activities*, plus organizing and contributing ideas, organized and sequenced around a main idea (a powerful generalization). Remember that the main idea is viewed as a hypothesis to be tested, however, rather than a truth to be confirmed.

4. Prepare an outline of the essential information (i.e., subject matter— events, people, and ideas) that students will need to study to consider and understand to some degree (depending on their individual capabilities) the idea under investigation. An example of one such outline is on pages 120– 121 of Chapter 3.

5. Think up an exciting and interesting activity to introduce the students to the unit, to motivate them to begin investigation, and to help you (the teacher) to gain some idea of what the students already know about the topic (e.g., the nature of values) to be investigated. In many cases, this initial motivating activity may be a concept development task (see pages 190–198 in Chapter 5) or a task which asks students to formulate hypotheses and then check them out later.

6. Research and collect a variety of materials and resources (books, films, records, slides, newspapers, magazines, paperbacks, etc.) that deal with the topic under investigation (i.e., the nature of values) and have them available for students to use (preferably in the classroom; at the very least in the library). It is important that these materials be as varied as possible in order to provide for individual differences.

7. Decide on a *particular* content sample for students to study first (e.g., ancient Greece), and prepare a set of basic study questions for the class as a whole to answer about aspects of this particular sample, such as the

ones from Activity 7 of the unit you examined that are repeated below. Other questions may be necessary, however, depending on the nature of the topic under investigation.

1. Who were the Greeks?
2. When did they live (i.e., time period)?
3. Where did they live (i.e., location)?
4. What things did they leave behind (i.e., artifacts, writings, etc.) that tell us something about them?
5. What kinds of work did they do, and where did they do it (i.e., jobs and occupations and kinds of places where these are located)?
6. What objects or things did they produce or create (i.e., products)?
7. What did they do for recreation (i.e., how did they entertain or amuse themselves)?
8. What kinds of family patterns did they develop? community structure?
9. How did they educate their young (i.e., practices for inculcating the young into the established culture)?
10. How did they govern and control (i.e., type of government)?
11. What customs and beliefs did they hold (i.e., traditions, religious views, etc.)?
12. What events, individuals, or ideas are they particularly known for? How did these events, individuals, or ideas affect their lives?
13. What problems did they have (i.e., conflicts, difficulties, changes, etc.)?
14. How did they attempt to deal with these problems (i.e., ways they went about trying to eliminate or ease the problem)?

Notice that these are all factual questions, and can be answered by obtaining information directly. Once this information is collected, however, we may want to ask a different *kind* of question *about* this information, such as "What do they consider important (i.e., their values)?" This is an inferential question—i.e., the answers are inferred from the factual information earlier obtained. (See Activity 35 in the unit presented earlier.)

8. Let the students, working independently or in small groups of three or four, begin collecting information about each of the study questions. Decide on a way to organize the material obtained by the student, such as an organizing chart like the one shown in Table 8.4 for students to complete in their notebooks.

9. Design a number of additional learning activities (e.g., oral and written reports, map-making, panel discussions, mock "Meet the Press," or "Face the Nation" programs, field trips, interviewing, role-playing, etc.) to help students organize, understand, and use the information they are being exposed to (i.e., through the sources and resources you have collected in step 5 earlier) and intersperse these among the data-collecting activities of answering questions, interviewing, etc. (In other words, to prevent boredom, provide a variety of things for students to do. Day after day of only data collection will fatigue even the most eager and dedicated of students.) At this time begin to think about the order in which you place all of these activities—that is, the *sequence* of the activities. In general, follow intake activities (reading, viewing, and interviewing) with organizing activities (charting, outlining, and note-taking) and demonstrative activities (role-playing, analyzing, and reporting). Then follow demonstrative activities eventu-

TABLE 8.4

AN ORGANIZATIONAL CHART

Basic Study Questions	Ancient Greece
1. Who were the Greeks?	
2. When did they live (i.e., time period)?	
3. Where did they live (i.e., location)?	
4. What things did they leave behind (i.e., artifacts, writings, etc.) that tell us something about them?	
5. What kinds of work did they do, and where did they do it (i.e., jobs and occupations and kinds of places where these were located)?	
6. What objects or things did they produce or create (i.e., products)?	
7. What did they do for recreation (i.e., how did they entertain or amuse themselves)?	
8. What kinds of family patterns did they develop? community structure?	
9. How did they educate their young (i.e., practices for inculcating the young into the established culture)?	
10. How did they govern and control (i.e., type of government)?	
11. What customs and beliefs did they hold (i.e., traditions, religious views, etc.)?	
12. What events, individuals, or ideas are they particularly known for? How did these events, individuals, or ideas affect their lives?	
13. What problems did they have (i.e., conflicts, difficulties, changes, etc.)?	
14. How did they attempt to deal with these problems (i.e., ways they went about trying to eliminate or ease the problem)?	

ally with some kind of creative activity (composing poems or essays, solving problems, predicting). The activities should become gradually more and more abstract, inclusive, complex, and difficult, but never beyond the capabilities of the students with whom you are dealing. Check also to ensure that each of the activities are in one way or another related to one or more of the contributing ideas, and that all are helping students consider or deal with some aspect of the main idea around which the unit as a whole is organized.

10. While the students are collecting their data, have them look from time to time for similarities and differences among aspects of the particular content sample being studied (e.g., ancient Greece) and their own lives and culture, and then ask them to make generalizations about the topic under investigation (e.g., the nature of values).

11. Now select or have the class select at least one other content sample quite different from ancient Greece (e.g., medieval France, contemporary San

Francisco) to study. Again gather a wide variety of materials and resources which students can use to obtain intake (data) about this new content sample as in step 6 above.

12. If more than one other content sample is being studied, divide the class into committees of a few students each (say 4–6), each committee to investigate one of the new content samples.

13. Now have the class (or each committee) investigate the same aspects of its particular content sample (e.g., medieval France, contemporary San Francisco) as they studied in the first content sample. In short, they again research the same study questions that they did in their study of the first content sample (ancient Greece) and enter their information on an organizational chart.

14. Again decide on a way for collecting and organizing this additional data. (See Table 8.5.)

15. Ask the class to look at the questions of the now expanded organizational chart one by one, looking for similarities and differences among the various content samples that have been studied and possible cause-and-effect relationships, and then ask them to generalize once again about the topic under investigation (e.g., the nature of values).

16. Study as many other content samples (other cultures) and their dimensions as time, interest, resources, energy, and the nature of your class permit and deem feasible.

17. Now ask the students to look at the chart as a whole (i.e., *all* the content samples studied) and identify differences and similarities in order to formulate generalizations about the nature of values *in general.*

18. Take any one of the generalizations that the students have formed (see steps 10, 15, and 17), and invent or suggest a new situation that has not yet been studied (e.g., dissent by many young people throughout the world today), and ask students what they think will happen as a result of this? (In essence, we are asking students to make predictions, basing their predictions—we hope—on some of the generalizations and earlier thinking that they have developed in their investigation of values.

19. Design a wrap-up activity to conclude the unit. This activity should help students draw together all that they have learned in the unit and come to some conclusion as to whether or not the main idea that is being investigated, and around which the unit is organized, should be supported or refuted.

Note: Generalizations and other kinds of conclusions formed in one unit should be continually validated and rechecked in subsequent units when and wherever feasible and appropriate.

LESSONS AND LESSON PLANS

I wish to repeat that the preceding unit guidelines suggest an organization of subject matter and learning activities to encourage student investiga-

TABLE 8.5

EXPANDED ORGANIZATIONAL CHART

Basic Study Questions	*Ancient Greece*	*Contemporary San Francisco*	*Etc.*
1. Who were the Greeks?			
2. When did they live (i.e., time period)?			
3. Where did they live (i.e., location)?			
4. What things did they leave behind (i.e., artifacts, writings, etc.) that tell us something about them?			
5. What kinds of work did they do, and where did they do it (i.e., jobs and occupations and kinds of places where these were located)?			
6. What objects or things did they produce or create (i.e., products)?			
7. What did they do for recreation (i.e., how did they entertain or amuse themselves)?			
8. What kinds of family patterns did they develop? community structure?			
9. How did they educate their young (i.e., practices for inculcating the young into the established culture)?			
10. How did they govern and control (i.e., type of government)?			
11. What customs and beliefs did they hold (i.e., traditions, religious views, etc.)?			
12. What events, individuals, or ideas are they particularly known for? How did these events, individuals, or ideas affect their lives?			
13. What problems did they have (i.e., conflicts, difficulties, changes, etc.)?			
14. How did they attempt to deal with these problems (i.e., ways they went about trying to eliminate or ease the problem)?			

(In this example we simply add on to the chart begun in step 8.) Realize that much of the work of the various committees involves collecting the data asked for in step 7 earlier so that the class can eventually compare it. Hence each committee might elect a secretary to summarize the data that her (or his) committee begins to bring in, listing the most important and significant information on the organizational chart from time to time. (In other words, the entire organizational chart does not have to be filled in at one particular time, but data can be added gradually by the secretary as the committee obtains it.)

tion and formulation of relationships (ideas). How many "lessons" or "periods" are necessary to develop and help students investigate the ideas, and to involve them in the learning activities of any particular unit will vary depending on the nature and abilities of the students and teacher involved.

The planning of individual lessons within a unit, like the units themselves, can be done in a variety of ways and using a variety of formats. Once again there is no magic formula for the "successful" or foolproof lesson. I would suggest that there are really only five essentials that teachers need to consider in planning lessons.

1. A clear idea of what they wish to accomplish by the end of the lesson (i.e., a clear purpose or objective). This can range from an objective as specific as being able to give five reasons why the United States went to war with Spain in 1898 to one as general as wishing to learn more about the nature and causes of prejudice and discrimination throughout the world. As was mentioned previously, lesson objectives can come from students as well as teachers.

2. A clear idea of the procedures and activities they will use to help students attain the objectives they have in mind. Will they have students read? write? answer questions? discuss? do research in the library? listen to a guest speaker? go on a field trip? It is important in this regard for teachers to ask themselves whether they have laid the necessary groundwork so that students *will be able* to participate effectively in whatever the teacher has planned. For example, if a teacher intends for students to discuss various conflicting views as to the reasons for dissent by many young people today against government policies, prior exposure (through readings, films, speakers, etc.) to what these policies are and to various reasons for dissent that have been given would be essential.

3. Ensuring that the materials (books, newspapers, magazines, records, tapes, etc.) that students will need to obtain information are available.

4. A clear idea of the *order* in which they will proceed to use the materials and activities. One recommendation here is to reconsider the idea of rotational activity sequences described in Chapter 4 (see pp. 159–164). The important thing is that the teacher knows where he is going and how he plans to get there, using what resources. Much confusion results when students must continually ask: "What do I do next?" Here is one example of a teacher's plan that illustrates a carefully ordered lesson. The teacher's intention is to encourage students to arrive at a working definition of imperialism.

> (1) Tell them that we're going to try to evolve a satisfactory definition of imperialism. Demonstrate that the ones that we have conflict.
> (2) Have them suggest the names of "imperial" powers, and put the names of these on the board. (At least a half dozen.)

(3) Have them describe for each of the powers listed the specific act by which they have identified this power as "imperialistic." Here is the place to insist upon precision and specifics.

(4) Have them distinguish any different *kinds* of imperialism. If there is difficulty suggest that they examine the motives behind the acts.

(5) Once distinguishing between political, economic, and cultural "imperialism," have students produce more examples of each of the three to be sure that the difference between them is anchored.

(6) Have them sort out the elements that are common to all three; and list these elements on the board.

(7) Have them discuss each of the elements in turn to see if there is agreement or disagreement as to (1) whether element *is* common to all three, (2) whether element then is *essential* part of a definition.

(8) Have students at their desks work the remaining elements on the board into a concise written definition.

(9) Single out the best of these and put up on the board for approval. Get two or three and have class tell which they like best and why.[3]

The above is not to imply, however, that a sequence must always be rigidly prescribed and adhered to. No teacher can predict what may come up on any given day in his classroom. A particular event may occur in the community that leaves the class unable to talk about anything else. A resourceful teacher would not hesitate to deviate from his plan for the day to deal with this event. On occasion, a particular aspect of a topic may spark student interest and the class may wish to pursue this aspect in depth. But such occurrences are more the exception than the rule. Most lessons, if well thought out in terms of objectives, materials, procedures, and sequence, can be accomplished as planned.

5. Provision for some means to evaluate whether or not the objective for the lesson was achieved. This *does not* mean that students must be formally "tested" at the end of every lesson. But a teacher needs to continually seek feedback as to how well students are progressing. Evaluation has been discussed quite fully in Chapters 2 and 7, but realize that student questions, looks of puzzlement, replies, performance or lack thereof, protests, and other reactions of a rather informal nature can also provide the teacher with cues as to how well his instructional efforts are proceeding.

In short, any effective and well-planned lesson should be able to answer five questions:

1. What do I want students to learn?
2. Why?
3. How do I expect them to learn this?
4. With what materials and/or resources?
5. Have they learned it?

[3]David F. Kellum, *The Social Studies: Myths and Realities* (New York: Sheed & Ward, 1969), pp. 114–115.

Whether the lesson plan is written down in any one particular form or not is irrelevant.

TWO EXAMPLES OF IMAGINATIVE LESSONS

Cuban[4] argues that all lessons should contain an emphasis on people, concreteness (as opposed to abstractness), conflict, and relevance, an argument with which I would agree. Look for these elements in the lessons which follow:

1. An eleventh grade lesson dealing with the topic of slavery as one cause of the American Civil War:

> The teacher begins the class by handing out a short reading list and then writing four names on the board:
>
> J. G. Randall
> Charles Beard
> Arthur Schlesinger, Jr.
> James Ford Rhodes
>
> "We'll take these names to represent historians' views. You'll remember Beard's thesis—'the clash between the Lords of the Lash and the Lords of the Loom.' There were only 347,000 slave owners in the South, 3,500,000 who didn't own slaves. Now, how many of *you* would say slavery was the cause of the Civil War. Let's divide it three ways here—Beardians, Stampps, and Fanatics. . . ." The class shows five Beardians, thirteen Stampps, and three Fanatics, with nine keeping their hands down.
>
> "I know," the teacher says, "there are some of you who say, 'There's a little bit of each.' That's fine. My opinion is that it was slavery. You've got to remember, though, that the facts don't change—historians' opinions change. You have a glass of water; you can say it's half full or half empty, it's up to you."
>
> A boy contributes, "I've read Olmsted, and I think he's right. It was a clash of nations. It wasn't economic, it was social."
>
> "All right," the teacher says. "Now, I say I could have prevented the Civil War. With Lincoln's idea—what was that?"
>
> A girl says, "Compensated emancipation."
>
> "What does that mean?"
>
> "Buy the slaves from the Southerners and set them free."
>
> "Would it have worked? Would it have prevented the Civil War?"
>
> The class groans, "No."
>
> "Why not?"
>
> A number of ideas are thrown forth—the Northerners didn't want to spend the money, you couldn't have set a price, the whole system

[4]Larry Cuban, *To Make a Difference: Teaching in the Inner City* (New York: Free Press, 1970), p. 184.

was based on slaves. A girl says, "The Southerners wouldn't do it because it would make the Negroes equal to them."

"Let's get back to Beard," the teacher says. "Here. Less than ten percent of the Southerners owned slaves, but they all fought for slavery. How could they persuade the ninety percent to fight? You try it." He addresses two Negro girls and a Negro boy seated at his extreme left. "You're the slave owners. The rest of the class doesn't own slaves. You persuade them to fight for you."

One girl, giggling, tries, "Those Yankees, they want to come down and take everything away from you."

"Oh, no, they don't," the teacher says. "Just from you. I don't have anything they want."

"Our whole economy is based on slaves," says the boy.

"No, sir," says a boy in the non-slaveholding section, falling into the spirit of the situation. "My economy isn't. I got to do my own work."

The debate rages for a while, the teacher grinning over it, objecting where the 90 percent can't find a reply "Come on, now," he says. "Why will these four million fight for four years? If you can't come up with this, class, the whole thing is completely unreal, just something in a textbook."

Finally, in the heat of the argument, one of the Negro girls in the slaveholding section comes up with, "Remember those slave rebellions? Remember what happened on those plantations? The Yankees will come down here and raise up those Negroes to be *your equals*, and there'll be no controlling them." The class roars with laughter at her, and she bends her head.

"Let's give it a name," the teacher says. He writes on the board, "WHITE SUPREMACY." He asks, "Any of you ever hear of U. B. Phillips?"

One boy has read it, and says, "He thinks that's the whole theme of Southern history."

The one white boy in the class, a West Virginia redneck, now makes his contribution: "You can find reasons all you like," he says. "I think they fought because they were told to fight."

The teacher says, "Maybe. Now, when we discuss Reconstruction, we'll find this same argument of White Supremacy used to justify . . . what? . . . anybody know?"

And a Negro boy says, "Segregation."[5]

2. A beginning attempt to get eighth-grade students interested in poetry:

. . . I was looking through my materials when I came across an anthology of Langston Hughes' poetry. I noted a poem entitled "Motto":

[5]From pp. 158–160 in *Where, When, and Why: Social Studies in American Schools* by Martin Mayer. Copyright © 1962, 1963 by Martin Mayer. Reprinted by permission of Harper & Row, Publishers, Inc.

I play it cool.
And dig all jive.
That's the reason I stay alive.
My motto, as I live and learn,
Is: To dig and be dug
In return.[6]

I made about thirty copies and, with the permission of the English teacher, took them into her classroom. The children stared at me, probably wondering what I was up to. Without saying a word, I distributed the copies of the poem so each child had one.

There was a moment or two of silence, while they read the poem. Finally, I heard someone mumble, "Tough!" followed by, "Hey now, this is really tough, man!"

Being familiar with their jargon, I realized they had paid the poem a supreme compliment, although it probably didn't appear that way to the other teacher.

"Hey now . . . this cat's pretty cool. Who wrote it?"

"Langston Hughes," I answered.

"Who's he?"

"He's a very famous Negro author, poet, and playwright." I saw that most of the class hadn't heard of him. "Do you know what this poem is talking about?" I asked them.

"Sure," they said.

"How come?"

"Well, it's written in our talk."

"Oh! Then you understand everything this is saying?"

"Sure," they said.

"That's good. Maybe you can tell me then what the first line means by 'playing it cool.' They had great difficulty in verbalizing the concept of coolness. "Are there any brave souls in here who would try something with me?" A boy's hand shot up. "Good! come up here. Now I'm a teacher standing in the middle of the hallway. You're coming toward me down the hall, but you're walking on the wrong side. I'm going to tell you something, and when I do, I want you to play it cool. Okay?"

"Yeah," he said.

The boy started walking toward me, and I said in a very fierce manner, "Hey you! You're walking on the wrong side of the hallway. Get over where you belong!"

The boy, very calmly and without raising his head, moved with deliberate slowness to the other side of the hall and sauntered on as if I did not exist.

"Is that playing it cool?" I asked.

The class agreed that it was.

"I'll tell you what," I said to my volunteer. "Let's do the same thing, only this time show us what would happen if you didn't play it cool." Our little scene began again. But this time, after I had ordered him to move to the proper side of the hall he stopped angrily and said, "Who you talkin' to?"

"To you," I said.

"I ain't doin' nothin!"

He became very belligerent and a hot verbal battle ensued.

I stopped the scene before it got any hotter, and said to the class, "Well, what's the difference between playing it cool and not playing it cool?"

Finally, one pupil came up with, "When you're cool, you're calm and collected."

"Very good," I said, writing *calm* and *collected* on the board. "Anyone else?"

They were able to supply a few more words. I then gave them a few, such as *indifferent* and *nonchalant*. They were especially intrigued by *nonchalant*, and kept repeating it aloud to themselves.

"Now, how about this word 'jive' in the second line: 'And dig all jive'?"

One pupil said, "It means jazz."

Another told how jive meant "teasing" in the expression "stop jivin' me."

Then, a third boy chimed in with this incident: "I was in another city once, walkin' through a strange neighborhood. These guys were standing on the corner and one of them, he yells to me, 'Hey man, *cut that stroll.*' Now I never heard that before, so I turned and said, 'What?' That's all I had to do. If there wasn't a cop on the corner I might have been messed up good."

"Do you know what *stroll* means now?" I asked.

"Oh yeah. It's when you're walkin' like this." He proceeded to demonstrate. It was a walk with a limping gait or strut that I have seen our children use many times. It seemed to generate a "devil-may-care," or "watch out, it's me," attitude.

"It's like they were tellin' me," the boy continued, "that I was walkin' too big to suit them!"

"How does all this show what the word *jive* means?"

"Well, I just didn't dig their jive and almost got messed up."

"Then what's another word for jive as you have just used it?"

"I guess . . . talk, a kind of talk," he answered. "This here poem is written in jive talk."

"Do you think that 'all jive' in this poem could mean 'all kind of talk'?"

They nodded in agreement.

"What does *dig* mean?" Again we compiled our multiple meanings on the board. To dig someone is to like him; to dig someone later is to see him later; and to dig something is to understand it. When I asked which of the three meanings fit best with "dig all jive," they readily agreed that "to understand" was it.

We continued similarly to the end of the poem. The final interpretation was that "to understand and be understood in return"
was the poet's rule for life.

"How many kinds of jive do you understand?" I asked them.

"Oh, we understand all of it."

"Well, let's see if you can understand my kind of jive. Okay?"

"Go ahead," they said.

I then proceeded to give an elaborate oral essay on the nature of
truth, using some of the most complicated words I could think of.

At the conclusion, I said, "Did you dig my jive?"

They looked at me blankly.

Then I said, "Now let's see if I can dig yours. Would you like to
test me?"

They responded eagerly. Expressions were thrown at me. I was
able to get five out of six, which impressed them greatly.

"According to Langston Hughes, who has a better chance of staying
alive, you or I?"

"You."

"Why?"

"You dig more than one kind of jive."

"All right," I said, "I think I agree with Mr. Hughes, and I feel
very lucky that I do understand many kinds of talk. In certain situations I'm able to use one kind of jive and in others, another kind.
But you sitting in this class, have, up to this point, mastered only
one kind, and one that I think is very beautiful. But it still is
only *one*. You've got to dig the school jive as well as your own, and
also jive that might be needed in other situations. School helps you
dig all jive and helps you stay alive."[7]

Both of the foregoing lessons meet Cuban's four criteria. If you will
refer again to the criteria suggested in Chapter 3 (see pp. 131–138), you
will find that the two lessons meet many of those criteria as well. As a
final suggestion, here is a rather simple checklist that you can use as a
guide for judging how effective your lessons are likely to be:

I. Pre-planning
  A. Are you clear about *what* you want students to learn in this lesson?
  B. Are you clear *why* you want them to learn this?
  C. Have you planned to connect or relate this lesson to what students
    have learned previously?
  D. Will alternative routes to attain these objectives be available?

II. Development
   A. Is everything in the lesson related to a central concept or idea?
   B. Does the order or sequence of the lesson proceed logically from point to point?
III. Summary
   A. Have you provided some way of tying together and emphasizing the main point(s) you've been trying to get across?
   B. Will students have an opportunity to use that which they've learned?
IV. Interest
   A. Can you show the class how the lesson is relevant to their needs and interests (i.e., worthy of their attention and time)?
   B. Is the lesson focused on people?
   C. Does it present conflicting points of view?
   D. Are the materials to be used themselves interesting (e.g., dealing with ideas, anecdotes, real people involved with real problems, vivid illustrations, readable, etc.)?

SUMMARY

This chapter discussed the organization of objectives, subject matter, learning activities, teaching strategies, and evaluation devices—in short, the nature of planning. The nature and preparation of a course outline was discussed and several examples of such outlines were presented. It was argued that a clearly thought out and logically defensible rationale is essential for effective teaching. It was further argued that the building of teaching/learning units around ideas that serve as hypotheses to be tested is a particularly effective way of organizing subject matter and learning activities for instruction. An example of such an idea-oriented teaching/learning unit was then presented and analyzed, together with guidelines for writing such a unit. Lessons and lesson plans were discussed, and two examples of imaginative lessons illustrated. Finally, criteria that teachers can use to help them design effective lesson plans were presented.

EXERCISES*

I. Place an "O" in front of any statements below which represent objectives and an "R" in front of any statements which represent a rationale.

*The author's suggestions are on pages 403–404.

1. _____ Exposed to two or more different samples of information, the student correctly states differences and similarities among those samples.

2. _____ Presented with a detailed set of facts, students can state valid generalizations that they had not been given previously, and when asked, can provide the sources and limitations of the generalizations.

3. _____ Given a set of events (one of which is identified as the event to be explained) occurring in a social setting, the student gives a plausible and logically sound explanation of the chains of cause-and-effect relationships that resulted in the occurrence of the event.

4. _____ Students indicate comprehension of the meaning of a given number of ideas and concepts.

5. _____ Students will occasionally make comments in a discussion session that depart significantly from the rather general agreement of the class as a whole, and which are judged by the teacher to have some likelihood of leading to useful relationships or conclusions.

6. _____ Ability to relate one's own values to those of others is crucially important in any inquiry directed at clarification or resolution of value conflicts.

7. _____ When students can obtain information from maps and globes, they possess a very useful skill for learning about man's activities and environment.

8. _____ Being able to form hypotheses is essential for anyone who hopes to deal constructively with problems in social studies. Hypothesizing provides a focus for thinking about a problem. One's thinking is likely to be unproductive if the problem is conceived too broadly or if an attempt is made to analyze too many kinds of facts in too many ways all at the same time.

9. _____ Understanding the aspirations of people in a society is fundamental to understanding the nature of the society and to an analysis of its problems.

II. Which of the following statements of rationale for having students learn about the American Civil War of 1861–1865 do you think is most justifiable?

A. The Civil War is a vital part of our American Heritage, and as such, is something that every student should learn about.

B. Questions about the Civil War are always asked on College Board Examinations.

C. Some events from the past are important to know about if one is to become an educated man. The Civil War is one of these events.

D. Studying about the Civil War may help students to realize that honest men may legitimately differ in the goals which they consider worth attaining.

The author's answer to the preceding question is given on page 403. Would you agree with his choice? Why or why not?

III. Place the letter of the appropriate term in Column A in the space in front of the term's definition (as used in this chapter) in Column B.

A	B
a. course of study	**1.** _____ an organization of the subject matter to be learned by students over a semester or year.
b. teaching/learning unit	
c. lesson plan	**2.** _____ an organization of subject matter and learning activities designed to attain a specific instructional objective.
d. topic	
e. content sample	
f. concept	**3.** _____ a series of learning activities plus organizing and contributing Ideas, organized and sequenced around a powerful generalization and designed to attain several objectives.
g. instructional objective	
h. generalization or main idea	**4.** _____ a specific event, occurrence, action, individual, or idea selected and studied in detail as an example of an organizing idea.
	5. _____ a hypothesis that suggests a powerful relationship among concepts.
	6. _____ a particular theme, subject, or period to be studied within a given course.

IV. Listed below are a number of terms discussed and defined in this chapter. Place the letter of the term from Column A in the space in front of the definition (as used in this chapter) to which it refers in Column B.

<table>
<tr><td>A</td><td>B</td></tr>
</table>

A

a. Rationale

b. Teaching strategies

c. Instructional objectives

d. Main ideas

e. Evaluation devices

f. Learning activities

g. Key concepts

h. Opener

i. Content sample

B

1. _____ Focus around which a teaching/learning unit might be organized

2. _____ Operations in which students engage.

3. _____ Reasons why a particular objective or set of objectives is considered important.

4. _____ Introductory learning experience that can serve as a diagnostic tool to give the teacher some idea of the information a class possesses prior to beginning a unit.

5. _____ Powerful "threads" or ideas developed and investigated in many units and grades.

6. _____ Operations in which teachers engage.

7. _____ Indicators of degree to which desired objectives have been attained.

8. _____ Desired outcomes of instruction.

9. _____ Factual data.

V. Try to write a unit of the type described in this chapter yourself. What suggestions do you have for improving such units?

VI. Go back and take a look at the model presented in Figure 1.2 on page 43 of Chapter 1. What changes, if any, would you make in the model?

APPENDIX TO SAMPLE UNIT IN CHAPTER VIII

CONTENTS:

Athenian Character

Being poor is no disgrace; the true disgrace is doing nothing to avoid it. We regard a man who takes no interest in public affairs not as a harmless, but as a useless character. The greatest barrier to action is, in our opinion, not discussion, but the lack of knowledge gained by discussing things before one acts. We think before we act. The bravest person is the one who, knowing all the pains and pleasures of life, still does not shrink from danger. We make our friends by conferring rather than receiving favors.[1]

---

[1]Adapted from "The Glory of Athens," in S. Eisen and M. Filler, eds., *The Human Adventure* (New York: Harcourt Brace Jovanovich, 1964), pp. 40–41.

The Hippocratic Oath

I swear by Apollo Physician, by Asclepius, by Health, by Panacea, and by all the gods and goddesses, making them my witnesses, that I will carry out, according to my ability and judgment, this oath. To hold my teacher in this art equal to my own parents; to make him partner in my livelihood; when he is in need of money to share mine with him; to consider his family as my own brothers, and to teach them this art, if they want to learn it, without fee; to impart all instruction to my own sons, the sons of my teacher, and to pupils who have taken the physician's oath, but to nobody else. I will use treatment to help the sick according to my ability and judgment, but never with a view to injury and wrongdoing. Neither will I administer poison to anybody when asked to do so, nor will I suggest such a course. . . But I will keep pure and holy both my life and my art . . . Into whatsoever houses I enter, I will enter to help the sick, and I will abstain from all intentional wrongdoing and harm . . . And whatsoever I shall see or hear in the course of my profession, as well as outside my profession . . . if it be what should not be published abroad, I will never divulge, holding such things to be holy secrets. Now if I carry out this oath and break it not, may I gain forever reputation among all men for my life and for my art; but if I transgress it and forswear myself, may the opposite befall me.

Hector, the Greek

Hector looked at his son and smiled, but said nothing. Andromache (his wife), bursting into tears, went up to him and put her hand in his. "Hector," she said, "you are possessed. This bravery of yours will be your end. You do not think of your little boy or your unhappy wife, whom you will make a widow soon. Someday the Achaeans (uh'kee'unz, Greeks) are bound to kill you in a massed attack. And when I lose you I might as well be dead. There will be no comfort left, when you have met your doom—nothing but grief." . . .

"All that, my dear," said the great Hector of the glittering helmet, "is surely my concern. But if I hid myself like a coward and refused to fight, I could never face the Trojans and the Trojans' ladies. . . . Besides, it would go against the grain, for I have trained myself always, like a good soldier, to take my place in the front line and win glory for my father and myself." . . .

Then . . . (Hector) prayed to Zeus (zoos', greatest of the Greek gods) and the other gods: "Zeus, and you other gods, grant that this boy of mine may be, like me, preeminent in Troy; as strong and brave as I; a mighty king of Ilium (ihl'-ih•um, Troy). May people say, when he comes back from battle, 'Here is a better man than his father.' Let him bring home the bloodstained armor of the enemy he has killed, and make his mother happy."[2]

Greek Sayings

"Know thyself."

---

[2]Homer, *The Iliad*, trans. C. V. Rieu (Harmondsworth, Middlesex, England: Penguin Books, 1950), Book VI, pp. 128–130.

"Nothing in excess."

"Come back with your shield or on it." (Saying of a Spartan Mother to her son about to leave for battle.)

"A slave is he who cannot speak his thought." (Euripides)

Philosophers

Read selections from Plato's "The Philosopher as King."[3]

Courtship

How to Capture a Woman's Love:

"Just play whatever part she'd have you play. . . "
Yield to rebuff; yielding will win the day;
Just play whatever part she'd have you play;
Like what she likes, denounce what she denounces
Say what she says, deny what she denies.
Laugh when she laughs. She weeps? Be sure you weep.
Let her dictate the rules your face must keep . . .
Gladly the footstool at her sofa put,
And bring the slipper for her dainty foot."[4]

Religion

Aeschylus on Religion:

"And, truly, what of good
ever have prophets brought to men?
Craft of many words,
only through
evil your message speaks.
    Seers bring aye
terror, so to keep
    men afraid."

Citizenship

The Athenian Oath of Good Citizenship:

We will never bring disgrace to our city by any dishonest or cowardly act. We will fight for the ideals and sacred things both alone and with our companions. We will revere and obey the laws of the city. We will always try to encourage the sense of civic duty in others. We will strive in every way to pass on the city to our sons greater and better than it was when our fathers passed it on to us.

Stoicism

Never value anything as profitable to thyself which shall compel thee to break thy promise, to lose thy self-respect, to hate any man, to suspect, to curse, to act the hypocrite. . . .

[3]Plato, *The Republic*, trans. H. D. P. Lee (Harmondsworth, Middlesex, England: Penguin Books, 1955), pp. 233–234, 236, 245–247.

[4]L. P. Wilkinson, *Ovid Recalled* (Cambridge, England: Cambridge University Press, 1955), pp. 128–129, 131–133.

In the morning when thou risest unwillingly, let this thought be present— I am rising to the work of a human being. Why then am I dissatisfied if I am going to do the things for which I exist and for which I was brought into the world? Or have I been made for this, to lie in the bedclothes and keep myself warm? But this is more pleasant. Dost thou exist then to take thy pleasure, and not at all for action or exertion? Dost thou not see the little plants, the little birds, the ants, the spiders, the bees working together to put in order their several parts of the universe? And art thou unwilling to do the work of a human being, and dost thou not make haste to do that which is according to thy nature? But it is necessary to take rest also. It is necessary: However, nature has fixed bounds to this, too. She has fixed bounds both to eating and drinking, and yet thou goest beyond these bounds, beyond what is sufficient.[5]

On Greek Women

Girls should "see and hear as little as possible, and ask the fewest questions."

Religious Beliefs

From the Egyptians and Babylonians, the Greeks adopted the belief that one could foretell the future by studying various marks found on the livers and kidneys of animals. Greek priests also studied the sky, the flights of birds, and the movements of horses for telltale signs. Many times they relied on such "signs" to decide whether or not to fight a battle or propose a law.

Reason

Aristotle on Reason:[6]

Since then reason is divine in comparison with man's whole nature, the life according to reason must be divine in comparison with (usual) human life. Nor ought we to pay regard to those who exhort us that as men we ought to think human things and keep our eyes upon mortality: nay, as far as may be, we should endeavor to rise to that which is immortal, and live in conformity with that which is best in us. Now, what is characteristic of any nature is that which is best for it and gives most joy. Such to man is the life according to reason, since it is this that makes him man.

California Loyalty Oath

The State of California requires that teachers, nurses, and other individuals desirous of obtaining any job paid completely or in part by state funds must sign a "loyalty oath."

Who Must Sign Oath—All public employees including permanent, temporary, emergency and exempt employees of any State agency and volunteers in any State civilian defense organization accredited by the California Disaster

[5]*The Thoughts of the Emperor Marcus Aurelius,* trans. George Long (New York: The F. M. Lupton Company), pp. 56, 61–62, 67–68, 80.
[6]Edith Hamilton, *The Greek Way* (New York: Time Books, 1963), p. 30.

Council and Members of the California National Guard and California Defense and Security Corps. All public employees are declared to be "Civil Defense workers."

When Oath Must Be Signed—Before entering upon the duties of their employment. For intermittent, temporary or emergency employments an oath or affirmation may, at the discretion of the employing agency, be effective for all successive periods of employment which commence within one calendar year from the date of the oath.

Where Oaths Are Filed—All oaths for State employees, State Civil Defense Volunteers, members of the California National Guard or California Defense and Security Corps shall be filed with the California State Personnel Board within 30 days of the date the oath is executed.

Failure to Sign Oath—No compensation or reimbursement for expenses incurred shall be paid to any public employee or civil defense worker by any public agency unless such public employee or civil defense worker has taken and subscribed to the oath of affirmation.

Penalties (Government Code)

"3108. Every person who, while taking and subscribing to the oath or affirmation required by this chapter, states as true any material matter which he knows to be false, is guilty of perjury, and is punishable by imprisonment in the state prison not less than one nor more than 14 years."

"3109. Every person having taken and subscribed to the oath or affirmation required by this chapter, who while in the employ of, or service with, the State or any county, city, city and county, State agency, public district, or civilian defense organization advocates or becomes a member of any party or organization, political or otherwise, that advocates the overthrow of the Government of the United States by force or violence or other unlawful means, is guilty of a felony, and is punishable by imprisonment in the state prison not less than one or more than 14 years."

Oath of Allegiance (For persons employed by the State of California)

"I, _____, do solemnly swear (or affirm) that I will support and defend the Constitution of the United States and the Constitution of the State of California against all enemies, foreign and domestic; that I will bear true faith and allegiance to the Constitution of the United States and the Constitution of the State of California; that I take this obligation freely, without any mental reservation or purpose of evasion; and that I will well and faithfully discharge the duties upon which I am about to enter.

And I do further swear (or affirm) that I do not advocate, nor am I a member of any party or organization, political or otherwise, that now advocates the overthrow of the Government of the United States or of the State of California by force or violence or other unlawful means; that within the five years immediately preceding the taking of this oath (or affirmation) I have not been a member of any party or organization, political or otherwise, that advocated the overthrow of the Government of the United States or of the State of California by force or violence or other unlawful means; except as follows:

---

and that during such time as I hold the office of employee of the State of California I will not advocate nor become a member of any party or organization, political or otherwise, that advocates the overthrow of the Government of the United States or of the State of California by force or violence or other unlawful means."

Communism

Since the end of World War II in 1945, there has been a growing belief among the American people that Soviet communism posed a considerable threat to America's interests abroad and to security at home. In the late 1940s President Truman established loyalty boards in all the executive departments of the federal government. Their job was to hold preliminary investigations of any cases involving suspected disloyalty. With the assistance of the FBI and the Civil Service Commission, the government eventually checked the loyalty of all employees in the executive department, as well as investigating all new applicants. Only "nine one thousandths of one per cent of all those checked" were dismissed for disloyalty.

The fear of possible Communist infiltration and control has grown, however. In 1949, a federal court decreed that the purpose of the Communist Party was to overthrow the government of the United States by force and violence. Since then, a number of people have feared the Communists may have won control of many American labor unions and infiltrated their way into many college and university faculties. Thus, increasingly, in a number of states besides California, there has been a tendency to required special loyalty oaths of teachers.

A number of people, however, have resented having to sign such loyalty oaths. In the 1950s, for example, many faculty members at the University of California at Berkeley resigned their positions rather than sign the oath shown above:

Why do you think these faculty members resigned?

EXERCISE KEYS

KEY: EXERCISES

Chapter I: INSTRUCTIONAL OBJECTIVES

I.
a. No	**f.** No
b. No	**g.** No
c. No	**h.** Yes
d. Yes	**i.** Yes
e. Yes	

II.
a. Not clear	evaluate
b. Not clear	develop
c. Clear	indicate
d. Clear	give
e. Clear	responds, challenges
f. Not clear	know
g. Clear	ask

III.
a. No	locate
b. Yes	explain
c. No	describe
d. Yes	ask
e. Yes	tell
f. Yes	judge
g. Yes	choose, tell
h. Yes	hypothesize
i. Yes	compare
j. No	define
k. No	describe
l. No	name
m. No	list

n. Yes   design
o. Yes   plan, implement
p. Yes   apply (suggest)

IV.   **a.** T
       b. T
       c. K
       d. V
       e. K
       f. V
       g. T
       h. A
       i. S
       j. R
       k. T

V.   **a.** Not appropriate
       b. Not appropriate
       c. Appropriate
       d. Not appropriate

KEY: EXERCISES

Chapter II: DIAGNOSTIC EVALUATION

I.

1.	X
2.	X
3.	X
4.	X
5.	X
6.	X
7.	X
8.	X
9.	X
10.	X

II.

1. h, i
2. g
3. j
4. b, c, i, k
5. a
6. a, b, c, i, k
7. d
8. e, f
9. a, b, i, k

KEY: EXERCISES

Chapter III: THE SELECTION AND ORGANIZATION OF SUBJECT MATTER

I.	II.	III.
1. A	**1.** C	**1.** P
2. A	**2.** D	**2.** D
3. B	**3.** C	**3.** P
4. B	**4.** R	**4.** P
5. A	**5.** C	**5.** P
6. B	**6.** D	**6.** P
7. B	**7.** C	**7.** P
8. A	**8.** R	**8.** D
9. A	**9.** R	**9.** D
10. B	**10.** C	**10.** D
11. A		

IV.	V.
1. E	**1.** YES
2. B	**2.** NO
3. A	**3.** YES
4. C	**4.** YES
5. A, C, G	**5.** YES
6. G	**6.** NO
7. B	**7.** YES
	8. NO
	9. NO
	10. YES
	11. NO
	12. YES
	13. YES
	14. YES
	15. YES

KEY: EXERCISES

Chapter IV: SELECTION AND ORGANIZATION
OF LEARNING ACTIVITIES

I.
1. f
2. a
3. c
4. b
5. d
6. e

II.
1. I
2. O
3. I
4. D or C
5. O
6. C
7. I
8. O, D, or C. It depends on the amount of original interpretation required. If the activity is designed primarily to have students draw together and place the main points of two arguments alongside each other, it is essentially organizational in nature.
9. C
10. O, D, or C
11. O or D
12. O
13. C. The emphasis here on interpreting suggests a unique, original effort.
14. I
15. D or C. This also depends on the amount of original interpretation required.
16. O
17. C
18. O
19. O
20. C

III.
1. A
2. A
3. A

4. S
5. A
6. S
7. S
8. A
9. A
10. A
11. S
12. S

KEY: EXERCISES

Chapter V: Teaching Strategies for Developing Thinking

I.
1. Descriptive
2. Synthesizing
3. Recall
4. Judgmental
5. Open-ended
6. Recall
7. Explanatory
8. Explanatory
9. Open-ended
Note: Any of the preceding questions could be recall questions if the student simply repeats various reasons or statements he has memorized from a text or other source.

II.
1. Recall or Recognition
2. Judgmental
3. Explanatory
4. Synthesizing
5. Recall or Recognition

V.
(Developing Concepts)   (Attaining Concepts)

a. 4   **a.** 4
b. 1   **b.** 1
c. 3   **c.** 2
d. 2   **d.** 6
e. 5   **e.** 5
                                     f. 3

VI.

(Hypothesizing)			(Generalizing)
a. 4		a.	2
b. 2		b.	3
c. 7		c.	6
d. 3		d.	5
e. 1		e.	1
f. 6		f.	4
g. 5			

(Using Previously Formed Generalizations
in Situations New and Different)

a. 2
b. 4
c. 1
d. 3

KEY: EXERCISES

Chapter VI: Teaching Strategies for
Developing Valuing

I.
Objectives a, e, f, and g suggest
specific examples of behavior.

II.
a. D
b. VJ
c. F
d. D
e. D
f. VJ
g. D
h. F
i. VJ
j. G

III.

(Identifying Values)		(Exploring Value Conflicts)
a. 2		a. 2
b. 6		b. 3
c. 1		c. 5
d. 3		d. 1

e. 5
f. 4

e. 4
f. 7
g. 6

(Developing Empathy)

a. 3
b. 4
c. 6
d. 2
e. 5
f. 1

V. (Evaluating Policy Decisions)

a. 4
b. 1
c. 5
d. 3
e. 2

KEY: EXERCISES

Chapter VII: SUMMATIVE EVALUATION

I.	II.	III.	IV.	V.
a. 2	1. V	1. O	1. S	1. F
b. 4	2. R	2. O	2. D	2. A
c. 3	3. V	3. E	3. S	3. D
d. 1	4. R	4. E	4. D	4. C
e. 5	5. O	5. B	5. D	5. B
	6. V	6. O		
	7. O	7. O		
	8. O	8. B		

KEY: EXERCISES

Chapter VIII: PLANNING

I.	II.
1. O	D
2. O	

3. O
4. O
5. O
6. R
7. R
8. R
9. R

III.

1. a
2. c
3. b
4. e
5. h
6. d

IV.

1. d
2. f
3. a
4. h
5. g
6. b
7. e
8. c
9. i

SUBJECT INDEX

NAME INDEX

O'Hara, R. P., 62
Oliver, Donald W., 229, 238, 262, 263, 272
Orlandi, Lisanio R., 18
Osgood, Charles, 62

Pavlov, Ivan, 146
Payette, Roland F., 57, 58
Perrucci, Robert, 115
Pertti, Pelto, 124
Plato, 393
Porterfield, John, 132, 133
Posner, Ronald, 360
Pribram, Karl, H., 150
Price, Roy, 124, 230

Quigley, Charles N., 272
Quinley, Harold, 231

Raths, Louis E., 153, 229, 232, 236, 237, 238
Rieu, C. V., 392
Rogers, Lester B., 353, 355, 357, 359
Rogers, Vincent R., 110, 149
Roosevelt, Franklin D., 119
Rose, Caroline B., 124

Sanders, Norris M., 296, 297, 298, 308, 310
Sawin, Enoch I., 11, 15, 21, 47, 66, 78, 79, 82, 83, 86, 193, 214, 221, 235, 244, 248, 340
Schmuck, Richard, 54, 64, 65, 72
Schultz, Mindella, 123
Scriven, Michael, 56, 229, 254, 255, 256, 258, 266
Senesh, Lawrence, 112, 115
Shaftel, Fannie R., 153, 247, 249
Shaftel, George, 153, 247, 249
Shaver, James P., 92, 187, 188, 229, 238, 240, 242, 262
Sheen, Bishop Fulton J., 137
Sigel, Irving, 220
Simon, Sidney B., 229, 232, 236, 237, 238

Skager, Rodney W., 106, 107
Smith, B. Othanel, 97, 98, 99, 199, 204
Smith, Eugene R., 301, 303
Smith, Frederick H., 307
Smith, Philip G., 198
Sokolov, E. N., 151
Solomon, Robert J., 317, 320, 322, 323, 324
Stakes, Robert E., 57
Stark, Rodney, 231
Stevens, W. W., 110
Stodola, Quentin, 284
Suchman, J. R., 185
Suci, G., 62
Sutherland, Edwin H., 75, 137
Sykes, A. J., 258

Taba, Hilda, 5, 15, 37, 61, 65, 77, 81, 83, 84, 88, 128, 130, 131, 133, 150, 151, 164, 188, 202, 217, 218, 245, 326
Tannenbaum, P., 62
Thomson, Robert, 102
Torrance, E. Paul, 182, 183, 184, 186
Truman, Harry, 24
Tyler, Ralph W., 279

Urick, Ronald V., 162

Van Loon, Hendrik W., 355, 357

Wallen, Norman E., 9, 11, 188, 193, 214, 221, 235, 244, 248, 340
Way, Walter L., 135
Webb, E. J., 83, 86
Weinberg, Carl, 106, 107
Weinstein, Gerald, 94, 134, 247, 286
Whitehead, Alfred North, 104
Wilkinson, L. P., 393
Williams, David M., 59
Wilson, John, 95
Wright, Herbert F., 83
Wright, Richard, 24